VD
MA

LUTHERAN QUARTERLY BOOKS

Editor

Paul Rorem, *Princeton Theological Seminary*

Associate Editors

Timothy J. Wengert, *The Lutheran Theological Seminary at Philadelphia*
Steven Paulson, *Luther Seminary, St. Paul*
Mark C. Mattes, *Grand View University, Des Moines, Iowa*

Lutheran Quarterly Books will advance the same aims as *Lutheran Quarterly* itself, aims repeated by Theodore G. Tappert when he was editor fifty years ago and renewed by Oliver K. Olson when he revived the publication in 1987. The original four aims continue to grace the front matter and to guide the contents of every issue, and can now also indicate the goals of *Lutheran Quarterly Books:* "to provide a forum (1) for the discussion of Christian faith and life on the basis of the Lutheran confession; (2) for the application of the principles of the Lutheran church to the changing problems of religion and society; (3) for the fostering of world Lutheranism; and (4) for the promotion of understanding between Lutherans and other Christians."

For further information, see www.lutheranquarterly.com.

The symbol and motto of *Lutheran Quarterly*, VDMA for *Verbum Domini Manet in Aeternum* (1 Peter 1:25), was adopted as a motto by Luther's sovereign, Frederick the Wise, and his successors. The original "Protestant" princes walking out of the imperial Diet of Speyer in 1529, unruly peasants following Thomas Müntzer, and from 1531 to 1547 the coins, medals, flags, and guns of the Smalcaldic League all bore the most famous Reformation slogan, the first Evangelical confession: The Word of the Lord remains forever.

THE BOOKSTORE

Lutheran Quarterly Books

Living by Faith: Justification and Sanctification, by Oswald Bayer (2003).

Harvesting Martin Luther's Reflections on Theology, Ethics, and the Church, essays from *Lutheran Quarterly*, edited by Timothy J. Wengert, with foreword by David C. Steinmetz (2004).

A More Radical Gospel: Essays on Eschatology, Authority, Atonement, and Ecumenism, by Gerhard O. Forde, edited by Mark Mattes and Steven Paulson (2004).

The Role of Justification in Contemporary Theology, by Mark C. Mattes (2004).

The Captivation of the Will: Luther vs. Erasmus on Freedom and Bondage, by Gerhard O. Forde (2005).

Bound Choice, Election, and Wittenberg Theological Method: From Martin Luther to the Formula of Concord, by Robert Kolb (2005).

A Formula for Parish Practice: Using the Formula of Concord in Congregations, by Timothy J. Wengert (2006).

Luther's Liturgical Music: Principles and Implications, by Robin A. Leaver (2006).

The Preached God: Proclamation in Word and Sacrament, by Gerhard O. Forde, edited by Mark C. Mattes and Steven D. Paulson (2007).

Theology the Lutheran Way, by Oswald Bayer (2007).

A Time for Confessing, by Robert W. Bertram (2008).

The Pastoral Luther: Essays on Martin Luther's Practical Theology, edited by Timothy J. Wengert (2009)

The Pastoral Luther

Essays on Martin Luther's Practical Theology

Edited by

Timothy J. Wengert

William B. Eerdmans Publishing Company
Grand Rapids, Michigan / Cambridge, U.K.

Published 2009 by
Wm. B. Eerdmans Publishing Co.
2140 Oak Industrial Drive N.E., Grand Rapids, Michigan 49505 /
P.O. Box 163, Cambridge CB3 9PU U.K.

Printed in the United States of America

14 13 12 11 10 09 7 6 5 4 3 2 1

Library of Congress Cataloging-in-Publication Data

The pastoral Luther : essays on Martin Luther's practical theology /
edited by Timothy J. Wengert.
p. cm. — (Lutheran quarterly books)
Includes bibliographical references.
ISBN 978-0-8028-6351-5 (pbk.: alk. paper)
1. Luther, Martin, 1483-1546. 2. Theology, Practical — History —
16th century. 3. Pastoral theology — Lutheran Church —
History — 16th century. I. Wengert, Timothy J.

BR333.5.P65P37 2009
253.092 — dc22

2008046907

www.eerdmans.com

Contents

V. THE PASTOR IN THE WORLD

Abbreviations

BC	*The Book of Concord.* Edited by Robert Kolb and Timothy J. Wengert. Minneapolis: Augsburg Fortress, 2000.
BSLK	*Die Bekenntnisschriften der evangelisch-lutherischen Kirche.* 12th printing. Göttingen: Vandenhoeck & Ruprecht, 1998.
LC	Large Catechism
LW	*Luther's Works* [American edition]. 55 vols. Philadelphia: Fortress; St. Louis: Concordia, 1955-86.
SC	Small Catechism
WA	*Luthers Werke: Kritische Gesamtausgabe* [*Schriften*]. 65+ vols. Weimar: H. Böhlau, 1883-.
WA Br	*Luthers Werke: Kritische Gesamtausgabe: Briefwechsel.* 18 vols. Weimar: H. Böhlau, 1930-85.
WA DB	*Luthers Werke: Kritische Gesamtausgabe: Bibel.* 12 vols. Weimar: H. Böhlau, 1906-61.
WA TR	*Luthers Werke: Kritische Gesamtausgabe: Tischreden.* 6 vols. Weimar: H. Böhlau, 1912-21.

Contributors

Charles P. Arand holds the Waldemar A. and June Schuette chair as Professor of Systematic Theology at Concordia Seminary, St. Louis. His chapter first appeared as "Luther on the Creed," *Lutheran Quarterly* 20 (2006): 1-25.

James M. Estes is emeritus Professor of History at the University of Toronto, Victoria College. His chapter was published as "Luther on the Role of Secular Authority in the Reformation," *Lutheran Quarterly* 17 (2003): 199-225.

Eric W. Gritsch is emeritus Professor of Church History at the Lutheran Theological Seminary at Gettysburg. His contribution was originally published as "Luther on Humor," *Lutheran Quarterly* 18 (2004): 373-86.

Robert Kolb is the Mission Professor of Systematic Theology and Director of the Institute for Mission Studies at Concordia Seminary, St. Louis. His chapter first appeared as "Luther on the Theology of the Cross," *Lutheran Quarterly* 16 (2002): 443-66.

Beth Kreitzer is Lecturer in History and Theology at Belmont Abbey College (Charlotte, North Carolina). Her chapter was published originally as "Luther regarding the Virgin Mary," *Lutheran Quarterly* 17 (2003): 249-66.

Robin A. Leaver is Professor of Sacred Music at the Westminster Choir College of Rider University (Princeton, New Jersey). His contribution first appeared as "Luther on Music," *Lutheran Quarterly* 20 (2006): 125-45.

Mickey L. Mattox is Associate Professor of Historical Theology at Marquette University (Milwaukee, Wisconsin). His chapter originally appeared as "Luther on Eve, Women and the Church," *Lutheran Quarterly* 17 (2003): 456-74.

Ronald K. Rittgers holds the Erich Markel Chair in German Reformation Studies at Valparaiso University (Valparaiso, Indiana). His chapter, based upon his book on the same subject, first appeared as "Luther on Private Confession," *Lutheran Quarterly* 19 (2005): 312-31.

Robert Rosin is Professor of Historical Theology at Concordia Seminary, St. Louis. He first published this chapter as "Luther on Education," *Lutheran Quarterly* 21 (2007): 197-210.

Reinhard Schwarz is emeritus Professor of Church History at the Ludwig Maximilian University of Munich. He published his chapter as "The Last Supper: The Testament of Jesus," *Lutheran Quarterly* 9 (1995): 391-403.

Jane E. Strohl is Associate Professor of Reformation History and Theology at Pacific Lutheran Theological Seminary (Berkeley, California). Her chapter, based upon her dissertation, first appeared as "Luther's 'Fourteen Consolations,'" *Lutheran Quarterly* 3 (1989): 169-82.

Christoph Weimer is pastor in Obereisenheim (Württembergische Landeskirche, Germany). His chapter first appeared in English as "Luther and Cranach on Justification in Word and Image," *Lutheran Quarterly* 18 (2004): 387-405.

Dorothea Wendebourg is Professor of Church History in the Theology Faculty of the Humboldt University in Berlin, Germany. Her chapter first appeared in English as "Luther on Monasticism," *Lutheran Quarterly* 19 (2005): 125-52.

Timothy J. Wengert is the Ministerium of Pennsylvania Professor of Church History at the Lutheran Theological Seminary at Philadelphia. His contributions were first published as "Luther and the Ten Commandments in the Large Catechism," *Currents in Theology and Mission* 31 (2004): 104-14 (used by permission) and "Luther on Prayer in the Large Catechism," *Lutheran Quarterly* 18 (2004): 249-74. The introduction was written specifically for this book.

Vítor Westhelle is Professor of Systematic Theology at the Lutheran School of Theology at Chicago. His chapter was first published as "Communication and the Transgression of Language in Martin Luther," *Lutheran Quarterly* 17 (2003): 1-27.

H. S. Wilson is the Executive Director of the Foundation for Theological Education in South East Asia. His chapter first appeared as "Luther on Preaching as God Speaking," *Lutheran Quarterly* 19 (2005): 63-76.

Introducing the Pastoral Luther

Timothy J. Wengert

Martin Luther was, more than anything else, pastor and preacher for his Wittenberg flock. This volume will take soundings in that pastoral life from five different perspectives: its theological heart, its proclamation of the living Word, its teaching ministry, its encounter with the people, and its social milieu. However, the broad scope and remarkable depth of Luther's pastoral work make it impossible for a single volume to provide comprehensive coverage of the topic. The current collection of essays will allow readers to consider Luther's life and thought from the perspective of his calling as pastor. Most of the chapters here first appeared in *Lutheran Quarterly* between 2002 and 2007.[1] However, to cover certain areas more fully, several articles have been taken from earlier issues of the journal, and one is reprinted with the permission of *Currents in Theology and Mission.* This book is also the second volume of such collected essays from *Lutheran Quarterly* and, as a result, does not include some articles on pertinent subject matter already included in the first volume.[2] As a consequence, this introductory chapter will not only discuss the new contributions printed

1. For assistance in preparing these articles for publication, the editor is especially grateful to the Reverend Martin Lohrmann, Ph.D. candidate at the Lutheran Theological Seminary at Philadelphia.

2. *Harvesting Martin Luther's Reflections on Theology, Ethics, and the Church,* ed. Timothy J. Wengert (Grand Rapids: Eerdmans, 2004), to be cited as *Harvesting Martin Luther's Reflections.*

here; it will also direct the reader to those essays from the first collection that also adumbrate aspects of Luther's pastoral ministry. Between the two volumes, an outline of the pastoral Luther emerges — useful not only to scholars but also to parish pastors and others in ministry.

Again: Martin Luther was, more than anything else, pastor and preacher for his Wittenberg flock. This simple, almost innocuous commonplace holds one of the most important, yet virtually unexplored, keys to understanding Luther's impact on the history of the Christian church. Just how unexplored this topic is may be demonstrated by a recent, exhaustive handbook on Luther studies, edited by the respected German theologian Albrecht Beutel.[3] Next to chapters on Luther as monk, professor, and reformer, one searches in vain for a single chapter on Luther as *pastor*, despite the fact that, next to his work in the lecture hall, more of Luther's daily life in Wittenberg was taken up with pastoral duties than with anything else.

In a similar fashion, Luther's biographers — from whom one would surely expect to find thorough discussions of this topic and attempts to integrate it fully into his life story — have consistently treated his parish work in Wittenberg as a sidelight, worthy in some cases of a separate chapter, perhaps, but only near the end of the work and as almost an aside. One notable exception to this lack of interest in the subject came with Gerhard Ebeling's last major work on Luther, *Luthers Seelsorge: Theologie in der Vielfalt der Lebenssituationen an seinen Briefen dargestellt (Luther's Pastoral Care: Theology in the Variety of Life Situations, Depicted on the Basis of His Letters).*[4] This, too, however, showed only a small slice of Luther's broader pastoral work, since it focused on Luther's correspondence. Nevertheless, at least it points us in the right direction.

It is not as if Luther's own age did not recognize the importance of this topic. Of all the ways to excerpt Luther's life and thought for the generation that followed him, Conrad Porta (1541-84) chose a pastoral approach in his *Pastorale Lutheri*, first published in 1582 in Eisleben, where he was then the pastor at the church of Sts. Peter and Paul. The full title demonstrates Porta's intent: to aid parish pastors. It reads: *A Pastoral Book of Luther: That Is, Helpful and Necessary Instruction Belonging to the Most Im-*

3. Albrecht Beutel, ed., *Luther Handbuch* (Tübingen: Mohr/Siebeck, 2005). To be sure, it does contain a chapter on Luther's preaching, but, as we shall see, this is only one aspect of his parish ministry.

4. Tübingen: Mohr Siebeck, 1997; paperback, 2001.

portant Parts of the Holy Ministry and Correct Answers to Some Important Questions about Difficult Cases That May Occur in the Aforesaid Office. For Beginning Preachers and Church Ministers Collected from Both Editions of All of His Books Printed in Wittenberg and Jena, and Also from the One in Eisleben and from Other Writings.[5] It was republished in an expanded version in 1586 and 1591, and then six more times, into the nineteenth century.[6] Robert Kolb has shown that Porta offered a somewhat skewed version of Luther's theology. Nevertheless, this volume stands as an important witness to the high regard for Luther's *pastoral* ministry among Lutheran pastors and preachers of the late sixteenth century and beyond, especially given the peculiar neglect in modern Luther studies.[7]

Although the topics in Porta's book may not be all that helpful, especially since it reduces pastoral work to certain *loci communes* (commonplaces) using Philip Melanchthon's famous method of systematizing Lutheran theology, nevertheless this work from the scholar who lived and worked where Luther was born and died does help to raise the central question of definition. What does it mean for us to call Luther a pastor? First and foremost, of course, we are talking about pastoral acts: baptizing, celebrating the Lord's Supper, absolving sin (publicly or privately), visiting and comforting the sick and dying, instructing the young and ignorant, and — above all else — preaching. However, in Luther's view pastoral actions are not effective *ex opere operato* (by mere performance of the rite) but involve delivering real promises to desperate people in need of consolation and faith. Thus, for Luther, the pastorate is by definition always a matter of dis-

5. *Pastorale Lutheri: Das ist, Nützlicher und nötiger Unterricht, von den fürnembsten Stücken zum heiligen Ministerio gehörig, unnd richtige Antwort auff mancherley wichtige Fragen von schweren . . . Casibus so in demselbigen fürfallen mögen. Für anfahende Prediger und Kirchendiener zusammen bracht, vnd auff beyderley Edition aller seiner bücher zu Wittenberg und Jhena gedruckt, auch die Eißleb. vnd andere schrifften gerichtet* (Eisleben: Andreas Petri, 1582).

6. Published in Eisleben by Petri in 1586 and again in Eisleben by Hörnig in 1591. In 1597, 1604, and 1615 it was published in Leipzig by Grosse; in 1729 in Jena by Johann Meyer in an expanded version; in 1842 in Nördlingen by Beck, and in an excerpted version in 1897 in Braunschweig by Reuter.

7. See Robert Kolb, "Luther the Master Pastor: Conrad Porta's *Pastorale Lutheri,* Handbook for Generations," *Concordia Journal* 9 (1983): 179-87, and more recently, Amy Burnett Nelson, "The Evolution of the Lutheran Pastors' Manual in the Sixteenth Century," *Church History* 73 (2004): 536-65, who does not seem to be aware of Kolb's work.

tinguishing law and gospel (that is, terrifying the comfortable and comforting the terrified). Moreover, this distinguishing takes place under the shadow of the cross: the Word itself, the pastor who delivers it, and the ones who receive it are weak and live by grace alone. At the same time, pastoral acts arise for Luther out of God's gracious declaration justifying the ungodly, a Word received by faith alone. Furthermore, this declared righteousness must always stand over against the external righteousness of this world (justice) to which pastors also call their flocks, members who also live on earth as forgiven sinners. Thus, Luther conceived pastoral admonition and care (*Seelsorge;* literally, care of souls) as defining all aspects of pastoral ministry, rather than as a separate specialty of the pastor tied to therapy and personal well-being and separated from Word and sacrament.[8]

Becoming a Pastor

The historical facts are quite simple. Luther was ordained in 1505 to be, using his later derogatory comments, a "Mass priest" or "sacrificer" *(sacrificulus),* since what was required of him after that time more than anything else were regular celebrations of (especially) private masses.[9] This did not make Luther a pastor. However, as he rose to prominence in his monastery, for example being appointed subprior in 1512,[10] he became more and more involved in pastoral care for his fellow monks. (See, for example, his brilliant exposition concerning the joyous exchange of Christ's righteousness for our sin in his letter to Georg Spenlein on 8 April 1516.)[11] At von Staupitz's insistence and over Luther's objections, this care included preaching to his Augustinian brothers.[12] Then, in 1514 he became an assis-

8. This is the point Gerhard Ebeling made when in "Luthers Gebrauch der Wortfamilie 'Seelsorge,'" *Luther-Jahrbuch* 61 (1994): 7-44, he argued that Luther himself invented the verb *seelsorgen* (a grammatical impossibility in the original Latin, *cura animarum*) and that his use of *Seelsorge* matched his evangelical understanding of pastoral ministry.

9. WA TR 2:133 (no. 1558); LW 54:156.

10. WA TR 1:101f. (no. 241).

11. WA Br 1:33-36; LW 48:11-14. See Martin Brecht, *Martin Luther: His Road to Reformation, 1483-1521,* trans. James Schaaf (Philadelphia: Fortress, 1985), 150-61.

12. WA TR 3:187 (no. 3143a), where, according to Cordatus, Luther gave fifteen reasons to von Staupitz why he should not be professor and preacher.

tant to the ailing pastor at St. Mary's, the city church in Wittenberg, where he remained a preacher and pastor until his death in 1546.[13]

This pastoral concern may well be the chief instigation for the reformer's most famous work, the Ninety-five Theses. As Luther fans the world over are already gearing up for the celebration in 2017 of the 500th anniversary of their posting on 31 October 1517, too often the celebrations will probably focus on Luther's break with Rome or his Reformation breakthrough rather than on Luther's own stated reason for the dispute: pastoral care for his flock in Wittenberg. In 1541 in his polemical writing against Duke Heinrich of Braunschweig-Wolfenbüttel, *Wider Hans Worst,* Luther looked back on the dispute from the distance of a quarter-century and specifically highlighted this pastoral motivation.

> When many people from Wittenberg rushed over to Jüterbog and Zerbst for this indulgence and I . . . did not yet understand what indulgences really were (indeed no one knew at that time), I began tentatively to preach that one could probably do better and be more certain than by buying indulgences. I had held such a sermon against indulgences previously in the Castle Church and earned the disfavor of Duke Frederick [the Wise], because he loved his [All Saints'] foundation dearly [established to house relics to which was also attached a large indulgence].[14] . . . In this regard, I was informed about how Tetzel had preached awful, horrendous things. . . .[15]

Indeed, Luther's reminiscence of the pastoral impetus for the Ninety-five Theses (bad preaching and its effects on the people) accurately reflected the events of 1517, clearly expressed in the theses' cover letter that Luther wrote to Archbishop Albrecht of Mainz and dated 31 October. In it

13. For this essay we will use the more general English term "pastor" when describing Luther's work. In the sixteenth century the offices of pastor and preacher were separate callings. Wittenberg's chief pastor from 1523 was Johannes Bugenhagen. He had responsibility for both preaching and presiding at the Lord's Supper, as well as for other pastoral acts. Luther was his assistant. There were also some preaching positions in Wittenberg. For example, starting in the 1540s Georg Major was preacher in the Castle Church in Wittenberg.

14. For a sermon to this effect, see the sermon from 24 February 1517 (WA 1:138-41, especially 141, 22-38; LW 51:26-31, especially 31).

15. WA 51:539.4-13; LW 41:231-32.

Luther called the bishop back to the task of overseeing the indulgence preachers and protecting the people from their exaggerated claims ("The first and only duty of all bishops is that the people learn the gospel and the love of Christ"), and he also expressed his own pastoral concern ("I regret deeply the false understanding [of the indulgence preachers' sermons] among the people").[16] The Ninety-five Theses themselves are similarly filled with pastoral concerns for the laity and the preaching of the gospel.[17]

The Literary Pastor

What if, instead of relegating Luther's pastoral work to an appendix or ignoring it altogether, scholars approached the reformer on the basis of his office as preacher and pastor in Wittenberg and integrated this overarching concern into descriptions of his biography and theology? How might this affect our view of him and of his motivations for the various theological positions he took throughout his life? Even some of his most vituperative writings might now find a more appropriate explanation in a pastor's passion for his flock than simply in the ranting of a young heretic or the complaints of an old curmudgeon.[18] What if, as Gerhard Ebeling rightly suspected in 1997, Luther's theology proceeded out of his regular encounter with God's Word and human need in prayer?[19]

Clearly, some of Luther's most poignant writings (beyond those thousands of remarkable sermons) arose directly out of pastoral concerns, a fact demonstrated in a small selection of titles from throughout his career: *Fourteen Consolations for Those Who Labor and Are Burdened* (1520); *Whether Soldiers, Too, Can Be Saved* (1526); *Whether One May Flee from*

16. WA Br 1:108-15; LW 48:43-49.

17. See WA 1:229-38, especially theses 35, 42-51 ("docendi sunt Christiani"; "Christians are to be taught"), 53, 72, and 80-88; LW 31:25-33.

18. For an example of the former, in his 1518 tract against the papal theologian Sylvester Prierias, Luther attacks his opponent's appeal to uncertainty partly on the basis of the effect on the people (WA 1:665.37–667.2). For the latter, see his attack on the papal definition of church in *Von den Konziliis und Kirchen* of 1539 (WA 50:488-553; LW 41:8-178), in contrast to the weak believers for whom Luther claims to speak.

19. His keynote address at the Ninth International Luther Congress in 1997 was published as "Beten als Wahrnehmen des Menschen, wie Luther es lehrte und lebte," *Luther-Jahrbuch* 66 (1999): 151-66, especially 156-57.

Deadly Pestilence (1527); *A Simple Way to Pray for a Good Friend [Master Peter the Barber]* (1535); *A Comfort for Women with Whom Things Have Gone Awry during Childbirth* (1542).[20] These titles — and many more could be added — show Luther at his pastoral best: dealing with specific spiritual problems and demonstrating how the gospel brings sufferers comfort and strength. In many of these and similar pamphlets, the polemical edge that predominates in other writings dissolved, as Luther concentrated on the immediate needs of the recipients: a soldier, a barber, grieving women, frightened citizens.

Perhaps the most pastoral of all his works were, first, his two catechisms of 1529, which arose out of his pastoral work (catechetical preaching in Johannes Bugenhagen's absence in 1528) and out of his pastoral concern (expressed in the most serious terms after his brief stint as an official parish visitor in 1528).[21] Second, his Church Postil, that running commentary on the texts appointed for Sundays and festivals, of which Luther himself was particularly fond, also demonstrated the pastoral center of his work, as did the many editions of his *Prayer Booklet,* a forerunner to the catechisms.[22]

These two activities, teaching and preaching, defined the pastoral center of Luther's theology and life. To be sure, catechesis, especially understood as instruction in the Ten Commandments, the Apostles' Creed, and the Lord's Prayer (what Luther called the catechism), was hardly Luther's invention. He inherited it from late-medieval interest in Christian education and from the ancient church's insistence that adult catechumens should know what they believed before they were baptized. From this heritage, Luther's interest in publishing explanations to the catechism stretched back at least to the spring of 1518, that is, long before the legal case with Rome had heated up, and began with an exposition of the Ten Commandments.[23] In fact, it matched Luther's original, single-mindedly

20. WA 6:99-134, LW 42:117-66; WA 19:616-62, LW 46:87-137; WA 23:323-86, LW 43:113-38; WA 38:351-75, LW 43:187-211; WA 53:202-8, LW 43:243-50.

21. "Dear God! What misery I beheld," he wrote in the preface to the Small Catechism (SC, preface, par. 2, in BC, 347).

22. WA 10II:331-495, with 515-16, and WA 59:70-78; LW 43:3-45.

23. *Eine kurze Erklärung der zehn Gebote (A Short Explanation of the Ten Commandments),* 1518 (WA 1:247-56). An even earlier demonstration of Luther's catechetical concerns comes from a remnant of an exposition on the Lord's Prayer from 1516. See WA 59:23-24.

pastoral publishing interests from 1517, when he produced a preface to the anonymous German mystical tract, the *Theologia Germanica*, and a translation of the seven penitential psalms. This first attempt at catechetical exposition was clearly connected to penance and Luther's role as confessor, as was his reaction to bad pastoral care in the Ninety-five Theses. Thus, it was followed in the same year by *An Instruction for the Confession of Sin* (the Latin translation of the *Erklärung*),[24] *A Sermon on the Worthy Preparation of the Heart for Receiving the Sacrament of the Eucharist*,[25] *The Ten Commandments Preached to the People of Wittenberg*, which Sebastian Franck immediately translated into German,[26] and the *Exposition and Meaning of the Holy Our Father*.[27] In 1519 Luther produced sermons on baptism, the Lord's Supper, and preparation for death, and in 1520 he combined his comments on the Ten Commandments and the Lord's Prayer with some on the Apostles' Creed, to create his first "catechism."[28] This he expanded in 1522 in his *Prayer Booklet*, which he himself connected to catechesis in the preface to his German liturgy, the *Deutsche Messe*.[29]

Sebastian Münster's preface to his German translation of Luther's sermons on the Ten Commandments hints at just how much he and others appreciated the pastoral thrust of Luther's early writings, that is, their spiritual use for common people.

> Daily many books in both Latin and German are being published that are quite salutary and useful for common people. So one finds everywhere people who are so hungry for and desirous of God's Word that they use every free moment that they have to spare from their obligatory work to invest in such books in order to glean comfort and instruction from them. For them this book, written by the godly, spiritual and highly learned man, Dr. Martin Luther, has been translated into German. He explains and interprets the Ten Commandments in such a spiritual, Christian and evangelical way that one will not find its

24. WA 1:257-65; LW 39:23-47.

25. WA 1:325-34; LW 42:167-77.

26. WA 1:394-521, with WA 9:780.

27. WA 9:122-59 for John Agricola's original edition from 1518 and WA 2:74-130 for Luther's own edition from 1519; LW 42:15-81.

28. WA 7:194-229, with 890.

29. WA 10II:376-407; LW 43:3-45. For the Deutsche Messe, see WA 19:77, 11-12; LW 53:66.

> equal, although many teachers have written about them. In this book spiritual and secular, good and evil, sad and tempted, young and old, ruler and subject, in short, all kinds of persons are [informed as to] the way they should go that leads to eternal life (which is what the Ten Commandments are). Here one finds how each commandment is kept according to the letter and the Spirit, and, in addition, how each commandment has several grades and steps.[30]

Luther's preface to *A Short Form of the Ten Commandments, the Apostles' Creed, and the Lord's Prayer* from 1520 demonstrates a similar pastoral concern for the simple folk.

> It does not happen to be a special ordinance of God that for the common Christian folk, who are unable to read the Scripture, it is established for them to learn by heart and know the Ten Commandments, the Apostles' Creed and the Lord's Prayer. Truly, in these three things is fundamentally and completely comprehended everything that stands in Scripture and may be preached upon, indeed everything that it is essential for a Christian to know. And it is summarized in such a short and easy form that no one can complain or make excuses that it is too much or too hard to remember what is necessary for salvation.[31]

Luther's sermons, too, were instant hits in German bookstalls. Beginning with some early publications of his sermons for Lent and Holy Week, the market for Luther's preaching grew until he responded, first, with a Latin postil on the appointed Sunday texts for Advent in 1521 and then, in 1522, with an even more detailed examination of the Gospel and Epistle readings for Advent and Christmas. These early attempts at producing "sermon helps," which is what such postils really were (and *not* sermons per se), derived from Luther's own work in the pulpit.[32]

For the remaining portions of the Church Postil, Luther's assistants,

30. WA 9:780.

31. WA 7:204-5. He continued the preface by distinguishing and ordering the three basic parts of the catechism: the Ten Commandments show human illness, namely, sin; the creed reveals God's medicine (grace) for dealing with our illness; and in the Lord's Prayer the sick person begs for this medicine.

32. See Timothy J. Wengert, "Recently Discovered Notes on Two Sermons from 1520 by Martin Luther," *Sixteenth Century Journal* 14 (1983): 189-200.

first Stephen Roth, later city clerk in Zwickau, and then Caspar Cruciger, Sr., Luther's student and later colleague on the theology faculty, assembled his sermons for the rest of the church year. Of course, not only has the critical edition of Luther's works published listeners' notes, often by the faithful scribe Georg Rörer, on thousands of sermons delivered by Luther over the course of his career, but a host of sermons were also published separately during his lifetime, especially those he delivered on special occasions or in special locations. Yet some of the most remarkable sermons were simply those proclaimed from Wittenberg's pulpit for the weekly uplifting of Luther's own flock.[33]

Of all of Luther's homiletical work, the set of sermons that had the most lasting impact were not even delivered during the Sunday morning service but arose instead from his preaching on the catechism in 1528. After having preached through the catechism (now expanded to include the Ten Commandments, the Apostles' Creed, the Lord's Prayer, baptism, and the Lord's Supper) three times that year, Luther began in December to rework his sermons into what he called his *Deutsch Katechismus (German Catechism)* but that came to be known as the Large Catechism. Along with the Church Postil, this work has profoundly shaped Lutheran piety and teaching to the present day.

Parson to Person

As Gerhard Ebeling's foray into Luther's letters demonstrates, Luther's correspondence, too, overflows with pastoral advice. Even before his death, many of these letters were copied over and over again, and some were even published to comfort others the way Luther had initially comforted the original recipients. Next to a host of letters of consolation published during the 1520s for towns and principalities,[34] some of the most interesting letters were those sent to members of Luther's own family. Caspar

33. This was especially the case during those times when Johannes Bugenhagen was absent from Wittenberg in his various attempts to reform other churches (for example, in Braunschweig, Lübeck, and Denmark). See *Martin Luther's Sermons from Holy Week and Easter, 1529*, trans. Irving Sandberg (St. Louis: Concordia, 1999).

34. See Timothy J. Wengert, "Martin Luther's Movement toward an Apostolic Self-Awareness as Reflected in His Early Letters," *Luther-Jahrbuch* 61 (1994): 54-69.

Cruciger, Sr., published a collection in 1545 that included letters to both Luther's mother and his father.[35]

The same pastoral care may be found in Luther's table conversations. Johannes Schlaginhaufen, who seemed particularly prone to melancholy, recorded the following direct advice in the early 1530s.

> Then he [Luther] said to me [Schlaginhaufen], "Why are you just sitting there? Cheer up!"
>
> But I responded, "O dear Doctor, I want to be happy but I just cannot, since I am weighed down by so many serious temptations."
>
> He said, "What kind of temptations?"
>
> I answered, "Alas, I cannot put my feelings into words."
>
> Then the Doctor said, "Your temptations and those of all people, including myself, are all summarized in the Creed. You may be tempted in the first article, 'I believe in God the Father.' Do you not believe that the Father is your creator? Second, do you not believe that he is your Father? Third, do you not believe that he is near to us? If he is creator, then he has creatures; if he is Father, then he has sons; if he is omnipotent, then he can draw near to me. The second article is 'I believe in Jesus Christ . . . who suffered.' If I believe Jesus to be the Son of God given for me, who suffered and rose again, what else do I lack? Or the third article is, 'I believe in the Holy Spirit, the holy catholic church, the forgiveness of sins.' That is where I am most deficient and also struggle against myself. So, in which article is your temptation? This last one is where Satan attacks me: 'So you only will be God's sons? Are not many wise, upright, etc.?' That is my temptation," said the Doctor.
>
> And again I [Schlaginhaufen] said, "Every time I think about God

35. *Etliche Trostschrifften und predigten, fur die so in tods und ander not und anfechtung sind* [Some writings of comfort and sermons for those facing death or other crises and are under attack] (Wittenberg: Luft, 1545). Besides the sermons, this work contains Luther's letters to his parents (WA Br 5:238-41 [no. 1529], LW 49:267-72; WA Br 6:103-6 [no. 1820], LW 50:17-21), to Barbara Lißkirchen (WA Br 6:86-88 [no. 1811] and 12:134-36 [no. 4244a]), Jonas von Stockhausen (WA Br 6:386-88 [no. 1974]), one from 1521 to an unknown recipient (WA 7:785-91), and one perhaps to Queen Margaret of Hungary (WA Br 6:194-97 [no. 1866]). For the complete table of contents, see WA Br 14:572-73. For a modern collection of similar letters in English, see Martin Luther, *Letters of Spiritual Counsel,* ed. Theodore G. Tappert (Philadelphia: Westminster, 1955).

> and Christ, then it occurs to me, 'You are a sinner, therefore God is angry with you, and thus your prayers will be useless.'"
>
> The Doctor responded, "If I am not allowed to pray until I become righteous, when will I pray? If, therefore, Satan suggests to you, 'You are a sinner; God does not listen to sinners,' you boldly turn that on its head and say, 'Therefore, because I am a sinner, I pray, and I know that the prayers of the afflicted are efficacious in God's sight.' But we would gladly have a tranquil soul not from grace but from ourselves. Why would God want to be gracious to us if we did not feel and acknowledge our sin? 'But when the right knots are there,' God says, 'then I can help.' Therefore it is acceptable to rejoice and be glad."[36]

Luther's pastoral experience also meant that he baptized, celebrated the Lord's Supper, heard confessions, preached at marriages and funerals, visited the sick, comforted the grieving, and even held the dying in his arms.[37] Thus, for example, his proposals for liturgical renewal arose not merely out of speculation about what constituted "correct evangelical worship" but out of care to see that the gospel was preached and celebrated in Wittenberg and among his dear Germans.[38]

The call to take Luther's pastoral ministry seriously is also a serious plea for placing Luther's life and ministry in context and wresting him and his thought away from the clutches of the doctrinaire. Whatever the contributions of systematic theologians or historians of dogma to our understanding of Luther, they always run the risk of hyper-abstraction. Luther was not simply a theologian of an imaginary cross; he was a theologian who, according to his own testimony, experienced that cross. Thus, in his advice to Schlaginhaufen quoted above, he did not merely talk generally about the nature of the devil's assaults *(Anfechtungen)* and their relation to the creed, he pointedly told his distraught listener how he, too, suffered.[39]

36. WA TR 2:114-15 (no. 1492). The conversation continues on the same theme and the problem of the law.

37. On 19 August 1527 Luther reported to Georg Spalatin, his confidant at the Saxon court, about the extent of the plague in Wittenberg and the efforts of Bugenhagen and him to provide care for the people (WA Br 4:232-33). The wife of the Tilo Dhene, the Saxon judge, died in Luther's arms.

38. Helmar Junghans makes this point in "Martin Luther on the Reform of Worship," in *Harvesting Martin Luther's Reflections,* 207-25.

39. Another example of the grounded nature of Luther's theology comes in his ex-

Our modern (and postmodern) addiction to theories and ideas may make it difficult for us to assess properly Martin Luther's own theology, unless and until we resituate it within his parish experience.[40] To be sure, Luther was also professor at the University of Wittenberg and defender in his case with Rome. These and other factors also played a major role in the contours of his theology and life. But whether he was writing against John Eck, his Roman opponent, or against Ulrich Zwingli, his challenger on the meaning of the Lord's Supper, or against any of a number of other foes, Luther composed these documents in a heated room overlooking Wittenberg's walls and the Elbe River, with its rich fields beyond.[41] He walked Wittenberg's streets, climbed faithfully into the pulpit at St. Mary's, and was very much a part of the civic and religious life of that town. No matter what else Luther was doing, he was always at the same time Wittenberg's pastor.

His language alone gives us a helpful glimpse into his everyday world. He filled sermons and lectures with the adages and allusions not just of classic Greek and Latin sources but also of everyday life. For example, in 1535 as he struggled to find words to clarify (to Philip Melanchthon of all people!) that works are not a cause of faith but necessarily follow it, he made the following (curious) remark. Works are necessary "not because they bring about or achieve salvation but because, with the faith that achieves [salvation], they are present or are there, just as I necessarily will be present for my salvation. 'I'll also be present,' says that fellow."[42] Only because the first publisher of Luther's *Table Talk,* Johannes Aurifaber, who also recorded this written exchange between the two reformers, filled in the missing reference in his German translation, do we know that Luther was alluding to the punch line of some true gallows humor. Upon seeing people running to get a good seat from which to view his own hanging, the criminal happily replies, "I'll also be present," having the best seat in the house, so to speak.[43] Earthy humor and language were not sidelines in Luther's theol-

---

hortation to receive the Lord's Supper, appended to the Large Catechism. "This is my struggle as well," he wrote (LC, "Lord's Supper," par. 55 in BC, 472), referring to how unworthy he felt to receive the Supper.

40. In part, this is what Heiko Oberman achieved in his *Luther: Man between God and the Devil* (New Haven: Yale University Press, 1989).

41. Martin Treu, "Waschhaus — Küche — Priorat: Die neuen archäologischen Funde am Wittenberger Lutherhaus," *Luther* 76 (2005): 132-40.

42. WA Br 12:193.97-99.

43. WA TR 6:152.16-21 (no. 6727).

ogy, a quaint quirk in a brilliant repertoire of theological bon mots, but they belong to the very heart of his pastoral approach. His famous dictum for translating ("Look the people in the mouth") actually defined his whole theological method and demonstrated the pastoral heart of the matter.[44]

Luther the Pastor

This collection of essays examines Luther's pastoral ministry from five different perspectives. To get at the theological heart of the matter, Robert Kolb examines Luther's theology of the cross. Three essays look at different aspects of preaching and Luther's use of language. Six essays investigate Luther's teaching ministry, especially in the light of the catechism. Five analyze different aspects of Luther's appreciation for his flock, their religious needs and patterns of piety. Finally, two probe aspects of Luther's social and political world and how they influenced his pastoral ministry. Seen in the light of Luther's parish ministry, these essays provide flashes of light in the otherwise dark and unexplored landscape of his pastoral life and work.

The Theological Heart of the Pastor

Most important is the theological setting for Luther's pastoral ministry. As already mentioned, Luther did not reduce pastoral ministry to acts effective merely by their performance. Even less could he have relegated such ministry to a certain personal style or attitude. Instead, the pastor's activity arises from the encounter with God's scandalizing, justifying Word of mercy and forgiveness. In the 1530s, at table, Luther, playing on the root meaning of the Latin word *pastor* (shepherd), described the pastoral office this way. "In a pastor, feeding and protecting must go together. Without

44. See WA 30II:637.17-22; LW 35:189: "For a person must not ask the letters in the Latin language about how one should speak German, as these jackasses do, but instead one must ask the mother at home, the children on the street, the commoner in the marketplace and look them in the mouth to see how they talk and only then translate, so that they understand and notice that one is speaking German to them." Similarly, his use of such categories as *adiaphora* (in Luther always in the Latin equivalent: *indifferentia*, undifferentiated matters) and *epieikeia* (balance or fairness) shows how important parish life and peace were for his ethical thinking.

protection the wolves will undoubtedly come and eat both the sheep and their food."[45] At perhaps the same meal Luther added, "The preacher ought to be both warrior and shepherd *(pastor)*. He must have teeth in his mouth. To be a teacher is a difficult art. Like Peter, Paul had to exhort with sound teaching and refute what contradicted it."[46] When Johannes Aurifaber combined these two sayings in the first printed version of the *Table Talk*, he added one line to clarify the connection between the two: "Nehren ist lehren" (to feed is to teach). This connection means that pastors cannot fulfill their office simply by saying nice things or being nice people but must speak the truth that always feeds and protects.

Already in our first volume of essays, *Harvesting Martin Luther's Reflections*, Robert Kolb probed Luther's theology in the light of the twofold righteousness of God.[47] In this volume he looks at perhaps the most paradoxical and yet, at the same time, comforting aspect of Luther's thought, the theology of the cross. This approach is particularly fitting for unlocking Luther's pastoral theology because, as Kolb writes, it "is precisely a framework that is designed to embrace all of biblical teaching and guide the use of all its parts."[48] The theology of the cross also shows itself to be the proper underpinning for the life of the pastor precisely because it does not simply "address the fleeting problems and miseries of one age. It refines the Christian's focus on God and on what it means to be human."[49] Through its contrast to theologies and theologians of glory, the theology of the cross functions not just to feed but also to protect. Further, it demonstrates Luther's peculiar theory of language that "calls a thing what it is" and thereby destroys the self-justifying person with all those claims of glorious rationality or performance, leaving us with faith in the God who comes in dust alone.

After using the term "theology of the cross" and ringing the changes on this theological paradox, it might seem at first glance that after 1525 and his refutation of Erasmus Luther abandoned this approach to theology altogether. Indeed, Luther did tend to talk more "baby talk" and less paradox in his later sermons and in other writings intended for his flock. However, the

45. WA TR 1:305 (no. 648).

46. WA TR 2:236 (no. 1843).

47. Robert Kolb, "Luther on the Two Kinds of Righteousness," in *Harvesting Martin Luther's Reflections*, 38-55.

48. See below, 34.

49. See below, 35.

concept itself — God revealed in the last place one would reasonably look *(revelatio Dei sub contrario specie)* — runs throughout his career. For example, nearly every time Luther preached on the entry of Jesus into Jerusalem on a donkey (the appointed text for the first Sunday in Advent), he noted the weakness of his coming. Apart from Luther's earliest preaching, we read in Stephen Roth's edition of Luther's Church Postil, published in 1528:

> Thus, when you are smitten by the preaching of the law and end up overwhelmed with doubt, you may think that you are on Mt. Sinai. But when you are comforted by the gospel and are once again made alive, you may think how the Lord Christ comes riding on a donkey, in a gentle and friendly fashion and how you now will have him. Then say to yourself, "See, your King comes to you gently and rides on a donkey and on the colt of a beast of burden." It is as if he wants to say, "See, you daughter Zion, you believing soul, you have heard previously and seen the entry onto Mt. Sinai, which you cannot bear to hear. See, now I am coming to you in such a friendly, sweet and gentle manner that you would now like to run after me."[50]

In 1530 he reminded his listeners, "Christ is a pauper, a poor donkey rider, seated on a borrowed animal," whose appearance scandalized those looking for an imperious king.[51] Six years later he would draw out the same paradox in this way.

> "Look, you have a king who comes to you in misery and righteousness. And as proof of this you will see him riding on a donkey. This must be preached to the daughter Zion." So Christ must be depicted as merciful and righteous. This is the grace by which he justifies us through himself, so that we believe that our sins are taken upon him and thrown into hell and he clothes those who believe with his righteousness. So Christ takes away my sin and yours and casts it into hell and lifts up his righteousness into heaven.[52]

When in 1544 Veit Dietrich, the preacher in Nuremberg, published Luther's *House Postil,* a collection of sermons delivered in Luther's house in 1533-34

50. WA 21:11.25-36.
51. WA 32:207.36.
52. WA 41:731.1-7.

and written down by Dietrich (who lived with the family), the later readers received the same message, this time associated with the sacrament of holy baptism.

> This is now our king: the dear Lord Jesus Christ, and this is his realm and office. He does not walk around in robes with great castles and worldly pomp. No, indeed! Instead, when we have to die and can no longer hold onto life, then this is his office and work: both that we know through his suffering and death where we should remain and that we can say, "I am made holy through my King Jesus Christ, who came in such a miserable manner and allowed himself to be nailed to the cross, because he wanted to make me holy and drown in me my sin and death." All who thus believe what they hear preached in the Gospel, they have that very thing. For this reason holy Baptism has been instituted, so that he can clothe you in his righteousness, so that his holiness and innocence may be yours. For we are all poor sinners, yet in baptism Christ comforts us and says, "Give me your sin and take my righteousness and holiness. Let your death be drawn away from you and put on my life." This is in reality Christ's government. For his entire office and work consists in this: that he daily takes off our sin and death and puts on his holiness and life.[53]

Preaching the Living Word

The pastor preaches! In fact, although the sixteenth century in many instances distinguished the pastoral and preaching offices from each other, Luther often mixed them together, so central for his understanding of pastor was preaching. The theology of the cross forms the heart of Luther's message. In a sermon on John 3:17, he once remarked, "When I preach, I make antitheses as Christ does here."[54] This linguistic and rhetorical observation was also profoundly theological; it meant preaching law and gospel under the cross, that is, in such a way as to destroy unbelief and create faith or, as we read in his *House Postil,* to take off the old clothes of sin and put on the new clothes of Christ's righteousness.

53. WA 52:13.20-35.
54. WA 36:183.20-21.

To spell out this aspect of Luther's pastoral ministry we have assembled three articles: one on Luther's language, one on the preaching act itself, and one on the specific, and unique, aspect of Luther's humor. For Luther, words matter! Indeed, Luther's use of language demands an entire study of its own.[55] Vítor Westhelle has recently published two essays on the subject, one of which we include here.[56] He argues that "there was an incisive linguistic gesture in Luther's theology that intensively focused on the language of the people, offering the people a way of finding their relationship to God, to everyday life, and to themselves."[57] This subversive use of language is linked in Luther's thought to his theology of the cross, a theology that declares the weak powerful and thus always implies a certain revolutionary way to communicate God's word.

Another way Luther transgressed language was through his remarkable use of humor. For Luther, God laughs, Eric Gritsch reminds us, and thereby brings the eschaton (the end of the serious matters of sin, death, and the devil). This also allowed Luther to "play the fool" over against his contemporaries. In addition to the marvelous examples Gritsch provides, one thinks, on the ethical plane, of Luther's outrageous letter to Elector Frederick the Wise regarding the case of Christophel Pfaffenbeck, whose unspecified crime had resulted in a punishment that would doubtless have brought him to complete ruin. The poor man turned to Luther for support; in addition to several letters to Spalatin,[58] Luther wrote an appeal to the elector himself, including these words:

> Your Electoral Grace may be certain that I will not let this fellow become [a beggar]. I would myself sooner beg for him, and if that doesn't help, also rob and steal, especially what I find nearest at hand, most of

55. See Dennis Bielfeld, "Luther on Language," *Lutheran Quarterly* 16 (2002): 195-220; Birgit Stolt, *Martin Luthers Rhetorik des Herzens* (Tübingen: Mohr/Siebeck, 2000); Gerhard Ebeling, "The Beginnings of Luther's Hermeneutics, Part I (II, III)," *Lutheran Quarterly* 7 (1993): 129-58, 315-38, 451-68.

56. The other, "Luther on the Authority of Scripture," *Lutheran Quarterly* 19 (2005): 373-91, not only investigates the centrality of the notion of *sola Scriptura* understood under the scandal of the cross but also investigates the meaning of law and gospel in this connection.

57. See below, 64.

58. See the introduction to letter 453 in WA Br 2:445, LW 48:382, and WA Br 2:485-86 (no. 467); 492-93 (no. 472); 525-26 (no. 489); and 3:24-25 (no. 578).

> all from the Elector of Saxony. For Your Electoral Grace is duty bound to provide him sustenance. Therefore I beseech Your Electoral Grace also graciously to hear me for my sake, that it will not be necessary for me now to begin to steal and grab. For I want above all to remain unhanged by Your Electoral Grace, if I, in such a necessity, were to rob a jewel from the All Saints' [Church's collection of reliquaries]. My completely impudent or foolish writing I ask obediently that Your Electoral Grace will not accept ungraciously. My heart is in God, as much as I feel I am his. May the Almighty God keep Your Electoral Grace in health and salvation, according to his mercy! Amen.[59]

Scandal and humor, however, did not become for Luther ends in themselves but always served God's Word, whether delivered to an unjust prince or, more especially, delivered by the preacher from the pulpit in the Christian assembly. Here the work of H. S. Wilson, a part of his original doctoral dissertation on the subject, uncovers the heart of such preaching: *Deus loquens* (God speaking). But it is, at the same time, God speaking through Luther the pastor to his simple hearers. At table in 1540, Luther contrasted other evangelical preachers and their erudite styles to his own.[60]

> Concerning this matter [of sermon style] I talked with [Martin] Bucer in Gotha that he and [Andreas] Osiander abstain from [such] erudition [in their sermons]. Philip [Melanchthon] does not need to be taught, nor do I teach or speak for his sake. We teach publicly for the sake of the simple folk. Christ also could easily have taught in such a high manner, but he wanted to explain his teachings very simply, so that the commoners could understand. Good God! Girls of sixteen come into the church, and women, old folks and peasants. They do not understand such sublime things. . . . Therefore whoever is able to teach with greatest simplicity and in a childlike and popular way is the best preacher. I want to make everything short and to the point. But when it comes to disputing, come to me in the lecture hall. I will make it sharp enough and answer such a person no matter how clever the

59. WA Br 2:486-87 (no. 468).

60. See both WA TR 4:476 (no. 4763) and 634-35 (no. 5047), translated here (LW 54:382-84).

> question. One of these days I'm going to have to write a book against these smart preachers.[61]

Eight years earlier Luther talked about his own method of preaching in this way. "In my preaching, I try hard to take a single comment [from Scripture] and stick with it and explain it to the people, so that they can say, 'This was the sermon.'"[62] Of course, he was realistic about the results (or lack thereof), saying at another time that preaching was like singing in the woods, where all one hears is an echo — preaching to God's glory never guaranteed results.[63] As to the content, Luther opined in 1532: "We preach Christ, the cross and suffering. Those who preach a political righteousness come and say, 'You teach incorrectly, and you are not right in what you do.' You can judge for yourselves! It is going to turn out just as Christ says [John 5:43], 'I come in my Father's name, and you do not receive me.'"[64] As to the preacher, "A preacher is a smithy, and his tool is the Word of God. However, because the subjects on which he works vary, he cannot always pursue the same course of teaching but for the variety of subjects sometimes he must console, terrify, reprove, or calm."[65]

The Teaching Ministry

For Luther the pastoral office centered in teaching. Indeed, he assumed that preaching itself was often a form of teaching, especially teaching the catechism to the ignorant. "The Catechism is the most perfect teaching and thus must be taught continuously. I want it to be preached daily and also read from a book. Our preachers and hearers already know everything perfectly, and thus are embarrassed about such an insignificant teaching, and become bored with it. They say, 'Our pastor always plays the same chord, always preaches the same thing.'"[66] This catechetical single-mindedness marks Luther's approach to education in the parish.

61. WA TR 4:635.

62. WA TR 2:163 (no. 1650); LW 54:160. He goes on to compare this approach to Jesus' own.

63. WA TR 2:417 (no. 2320a).

64. WA TR 2:143 (no. 1586), dated 1532.

65. WA TR 1:98-99 (no. 234), from 1532, LW 54:31.

66. WA TR 1:504 (no. 1002), from 1530.

This section of the present volume contains analyses of various parts of the catechism (Ten Commandments, Apostles' Creed, Lord's Prayer, the Lord's Supper, and confession).[67] To place these narrower works in context, however, Robert Rosin has provided an article on Luther's approach to education in general, since it makes little sense to ignore either the influence of the foremost educational movement of the time, humanism, or Luther's other vocation as university professor.

Luther wrote two essays, published in 1524 and 1530, in which he urged his fellow citizens to establish schools and send their children to them. In the latter, *A Sermon on Keeping Children in School* (1530), he even revealed a nonutilitarian reason for schooling, which may have reflected his own passion: learning for its own sake. "I will say nothing about how fine a feeling it is that a man is educated — even if he were never to hold any kind of [secular or ecclesial] office — that he can sit at home by himself and read all kinds of things, converse and associate with educated people, and travel and trade in foreign countries. For such a feeling motivates at best only a few people."[68] This love of learning, combined with his pastoral desire to deliver the gospel, infects all of Luther's involvement in Christian education for the parish.

As for the catechism itself, Luther could not say enough about its importance in the home, school, and parish life. In 1539 he even listed catechesis as one of the seven marks of the church.[69] In the 1540s Luther summarized the catechism in this way:

> The Catechism is the Lay Bible, in which is comprehended the entire content of Christian teaching that every Christian needs to know for salvation. As Solomon's Song of Songs is called a song above all other songs, so the Ten Commandments is the Teaching of Teachings, a teaching above all teachings from which God's will is recognized: what God demands and what is lacking in us. The Apostles' Creed, the confession of our holy Christian faith, is a History of Histories, a history above all histories, the absolute highest history, in which is recounted the immeasurable wonders of the divine majesty from the beginning

67. Already in *Harvesting Martin Luther's Reflections*, 23-37, Mark Tranvik provided a helpful introduction to Luther's understanding of baptism.

68. WA 30II:565.22-26; LW 46:243.

69. WA 50:628.29–644.11, in *Von den Konziliis und Kirchen*, 1539; LW 41:143-78.

> of the world unto eternity: how we and all creatures were created; how we were redeemed through the Son of God by means of his incarnation, suffering, death and resurrection; how also through the Holy Spirit we are made holy and new creatures, are assembled into God's people, have forgiveness of sins and will be eternally blessed. The Lord's Prayer, the Our Father, is the Prayer of Prayers, a prayer above all prayers, the absolute highest prayer, which the most high Master taught and in which all spiritual and bodily needs and the most excellent comfort in all attacks, sorrows and at the last hour are comprehended. The sacraments are the Ceremonies of Ceremonies, the highest ceremonies, which God himself bestowed and instituted and in which he insured for us his grace.
>
> Therefore, we should cherish and honor the catechism and instruct children in it with diligence. For in it are drawn together the right, true, old and pure divine teaching of the holy Christian church. Moreover, it will protect us from everything that stands against it — be they novelties or false, misguided and irreligious teachings, no matter how long they have been around.[70]

Each of the five essays on the parts of the catechism clarifies Luther's pithy summary. Indeed, the essay "Martin Luther and the Ten Commandments in the Large Catechism" shows the diversity of approaches that Luther employs to interpret the Decalogue to his people: narrowing or broadening the commandments' meanings in accord with the needs of his people and his dynamic understanding of the law written on human hearts. In "Luther on the Creed," Charles Arand focuses on Luther's own creedal question ("What kind of God do you have?") to reveal the triune giving of God, a giving that does not simply reveal God's work with human beings (what is traditionally labeled the economic Trinity) but far more the very depth of God's own heart (Luther's peculiar approach to the immanent Trinity). In "Luther on Prayer in the Large Catechism," we discover how closely Luther's own life of prayer, illustrated with three separate examples, elucidates his catechesis in the introduction to prayer from the Large Catechism. Luther lives in prayer where God's command to pray and promise to answer reveal Luther's deepest needs.

Mark Tranvik wrote a chapter on baptism in *Harvesting Martin Lu-*

70. WA TR 5:581-82 (no. 6288).

ther's Reflections, and this volume examines two other aspects of the sacraments. In an article from 1995 by the eminent Luther scholar Reinhard Schwarz (translated by Gerhard Forde), we come to appreciate that Luther viewed the Last Supper chiefly as Jesus making a testament and thereby defining such activity as a sacrament. This unique approach to the Supper quickly spread into the writings of other evangelical preachers of the 1520s and the woodcuts that illustrated their tracts. Ronald Rittgers provides a helpful look at the "third" sacrament of Lutherans, private confession and absolution, which is at once an extension of holy baptism and a nearly forgotten rite in today's churches.[71] Not only does he show how thoroughly re-formed the sacrament became in Luther's hands, but he also investigates a later dispute over private absolution in Nuremberg involving Andreas Osiander on the one side and Luther and Melanchthon on the other. When Osiander tried to use Luther's own words to support his cause (against his local opponents and an official opinion written by Wittenberg's theological faculty), Luther continued to insist on the integrity of an evangelical pastorate, in which there could be no return to the late-medieval confessional — where the priest insisted on complete confession of all sins (public and private) and where his absolution was effective *ex opere operato* (by the mere performance of the rite).

The Pastor and the People's Piety

"Denn weil wir kindern predigen, muessen wir auch mit yhn lallen" [When we preach to children, we have to talk baby talk to them].[72] With these onomatopoetic words from the Large Catechism (*lallen* means to say "la, la"), Luther expresses one of the most important features of pastoral ministry: accommodation to one's flock. Speaking baby talk to children, using down-to-earth images for adults, populating one's sermons with farmhands, maids, and even beer barrels — all point to Luther's uncanny knack for adapting his message to his people. At the same time, however, Luther also could judge the very cultural milieu that he was addressing, so that he could

71. See, more extensively, his *The Reformation of the Keys: Confession, Conscience, and Authority in Sixteenth-Century Germany* (Cambridge: Harvard University Press, 2004).

72. WA 30I:143.9-10, LC, Ten Commandments, par. 77, in BC, 396.

be critical of religious customs (for example, comparing monastic praying to "howling and growling" [*heulen und murren*]) and economic practices (for example, criticizing "armchair bandits" [*Stulräuber*]).[73]

Such accommodation and criticism of his people's social and religious practice had so many sides that it is impossible to cover them completely. Already *Harvesting Martin Luther's Reflections* examined Luther's understanding of spirituality (Scott Hendrix), his approach to poverty and greed (Lindberg and Rieth), his view of marriage (Hendrix), and his proposals for reforming the liturgy (Junghans).[74] The current collection provides glimpses of other aspects of religious life in early modern Germany. In "Luther regarding the Virgin Mary," Beth Kreitzer sets Luther's view of Mary in the context of late-medieval piety, where the cult of Mary and her family had come to dominate religiosity.[75] Luther did not merely criticize the attempts by Gabriel Biel and others to make Mary into the co-redemptrix and mediatrix of human salvation, he also continued to show enormous respect for her in preaching and teaching. As also found in the *Table Talk,* Luther could, on the one hand, criticize the late-medieval cult of Mary using himself as his best worst example. Having inadvertently stabbed himself as a student, while his friends ran for a surgeon, he cried, "O Mary, help me!" To his listeners in 1531 he added, "There I would have died in Mary's name."[76] Yet, in comments at table on translating a portion of the Magnificat ("He has regarded the low estate of his handmaiden"), his devotion for Mary shows through, shaped profoundly by his theology of the cross: God is revealed in the last place one would reasonably look.

> How will you translate this into German? I know no better German than when I say, "That miserable maid." For she was a miserable young

73. Both examples are from the Large Catechism in WA 30I:196.23-24 and 165.11 (LC, Lord's Prayer, par. 25 and Ten Commandments, par. 229, in BC, 443 and 417), respectively, where, in the second instance, out of ignorance, Luther mistook a Middle Low German word for usury *(stohl)* as the High German word for chair *(stuhl).*

74. Scott Hendrix, "Martin Luther's Reformation of Spirituality"; Carter Lindberg, "Luther on Poverty"; Ricardo Willy Rieth, "Luther on Greed"; Scott Hendrix, "Luther on Marriage"; Helmar Junghans, "Luther on the Reform of Liturgy," all in *Harvesting Martin Luther's Reflections,* 240-60, 134-51, 152-68, 169-84, and 207-25, respectively.

75. Saint Anne, to whom Luther cried during that famous thunderstorm in 1505, was not only the patron saint of miners but also Mary's mother.

76. WA TR 1:46 (119); LW 54:14-15.

> girl. The royal line was completely wiped out by Herod, so that no one was left except the two of them [Elizabeth and Mary], so that the good maid took as husband a poor carpenter's assistant. That is why she says, "Ach! I am such a poor maiden. How did I come to this honor, that I should become the mother of our Lord God?" And in the prophets [Isa. 11:1] it is called the "root of Jesse." This is not a green root but one that is completely spoiled and rotten. And it is from this that a green branch is to grow.[77]

Distantly related to the importance of Mary for Luther's flock is Luther's view of women themselves as refracted through Luther's lectures on Genesis. As Mickey Mattox demonstrates, Luther showed himself to be both stubbornly traditional and curiously open regarding the place of women in matters of faith and life. Using Luther's early and later understandings of Eve, the author traces shifts in Luther's thoughts to the importance of his doctrine of the three estates *(Dreiständelehre).* Eve becomes for Luther a heroine and a saint; women ought to lead households and (perhaps) even bear the gospel in public. His wavering opinion about the role of women in the public sphere also shows itself in Luther's comments at table. An interesting pastoral combination of both traditionalism and openness arose in 1538, when Luther discussed a rebuke issued by the Roman bishop of Meissen to Duchess Elizabeth of Rochlitz, when this widowed daughter-in-law of Duke George of Saxony began to introduce the Reformation into her tiny fiefdom of Rochlitz. The bishop warned her that women are to keep silent in church. She responded that Paul's words in 1 Corinthians 14 were addressed to bishops, "but because they did not want to be vigilant in their offices and were plainly mute, she was compelled by the welfare of her subjects." Luther concluded, "But I wrote to her the psalm, '[My heart] overflows [with a good word; I speak my words to the king. . . .].' and concluded the letter with these words, 'If they do not listen to men, then they must listen to women and let children speak.'"[78]

Two articles provide insight into Luther's use of the arts among his people. On the one hand, Robin Leaver provides a summary of Luther's view of music — a small excerpt from his own book in the Lutheran Quar-

77. WA TR 5:414 (no. 5977; cf. no. 5699).

78. WA TR 3:633-34 (no. 3813). Luther was interpreting Ps. 45 as being spoken by a woman.

terly Books series.[79] "After theology," Luther opined, "I give to music the pride of place and the highest honor."[80] More than that, Luther insisted that God used music itself to spread the gospel.[81] A second contribution, "Luther and Cranach on Justification in Word and Image," by Christoph Weimer, allows a glimpse into the collaboration between artist and pastor. Luther, who often turned to Cranach and his workshop for visual support of his ideas, found especially in Cranach's depictions of "law and gospel" a powerful tool for explaining and proclaiming the gospel. Luther's delight in the sensual — pictures and music — contrasted sharply with the attitude of such reformers as Ulrich Zwingli, who banned organs from worship and stripped Zürich's churches of all images. This delight had its origins in Luther's amazement at the incarnation itself and allowed him to serve the very humanity of his flock rather than force them to deny it. In fact, quite in line with his theology of the cross, it was precisely human attempts to escape their own fleshliness that constituted the core of every theology of glory.

Luther's radical approach to pastoral care demands a book of its own. It is intimately connected to pamphlets like the ones listed above and includes countless letters and comments recorded in the *Table Talk*. Thus this section concludes with another example of Luther's pastoral approach to his people, where, early in his career, he used a medieval literary genre of "fourteen consolations" to comfort sufferers. Jane Strohl's splendid article from 1989, the distillation of her dissertation on the same subject, grants a glimpse into Luther's pastoral heart, as it were. By using a single example, she uncovers how the theology of the cross functions in expressing care for sufferers and how that theology transforms medieval piety (one that continued at least into the nineteenth century and Engelbert Humperdinck's famous prayer to the fourteen angels in his opera, *Hansel und Gretel*). In 1530 Luther could summarize his view this way: "Human comfort consists in external, visible help that a person can touch, see and feel. God's com-

79. Robin Leaver, *Luther's Liturgical Music: Principles and Implications* (Grand Rapids: Eerdmans, 2007).

80. WA TR 6:348 (no. 7034).

81. WA TR 2:11-12 (no. 1258); LW 54:129-30: "What is law remains fixed in place; what is gospel goes freely from one place to another. That is why God has preached the gospel even through music, like that of Josquin [de Prez, one of Luther's favorite composers], whose compositions flow freely, willingly, and sweetly with nothing forced or repressed with rules like the finch's song."

fort consists only in the Word and the promise, and thus it is impossible to see, hear or feel [such comfort]."[82] At this point, several manuscripts of the *Table Talk* also include these words: "A baptized believer must be very dear to our Lord Christ."[83]

The Pastor in the World

The final section of this book gives two sidelong glances at Luther's pastorate — examinations of the social and political milieu in which Luther lived and worked. Several important essays in *Harvesting Martin Luther's Reflections* enhanced this somewhat limited appraisal. In that volume Karlfried Froehlich provided a handy introduction to Luther's understanding of vocation, even using the vocation of the pastor as a test case. Gregory Miller investigated Luther's understanding of the Turkish Empire and Islam, an international power that cast a long shadow over much of sixteenth-century political and parish life.[84] The aforementioned articles on marriage, poverty, and greed also contain important aspects of Luther's pastoral life in the world, as does Robert Kolb's on the two kinds of righteousness. In the current volume, Dorothea Wendebourg's "Luther on Monasticism" contrasts Luther's harshest judgments with his own "monastic" view of the Reformation. Written in 2005 to mark the 500th anniversary of Luther's entry into the monastery, Wendebourg's essay shows how Luther could be rabidly opposed to monasticism while still borrowing heavily from its theological and practical insights, for example, in his simple proposals in the Small Catechism for household worship.[85]

In the final essay, James Estes analyzes Luther's relation to secular authority, a neuralgic issue in his theology and in the development of evan-

82. WA TR 2:254 (no. 1893).

83. WA TR 2:254 (no. 1892; cf. no. 1893, note 7).

84. See Karlfried Froehlich, "Luther on Vocation," and Gregory J. Miller, "Luther on the Turks and Islam," in *Harvesting Martin Luther's Reflections,* 121-33 and 185-203, respectively.

85. For another essay, written independently but coming to many of the same conclusions, see Timothy J. Wengert, "'Per mutuum colloquium et consolationem fratrum': Monastische Züge in Luthers ökumenischer Theologie," in *Luther und das monastische Erbe,* ed. Christoph Bultmann (Tübingen: Mohr/Siebeck, 2007), 243-68.

gelical churches and, we would add, of the evangelical pastorate.[86] It was precisely in 1527, with the onset of the Electoral Saxon Visitation of the parishes in its realm, that Luther's pastoral motivation (bringing the gospel to his dear Saxons) encountered the political realities of using the good graces (and authority!) of the Saxon elector. This slow and painful development of the notion of the *cura religionis* (care over religion) by evangelical princes, whatever its weaknesses and failures, also must be viewed in light of Luther's pastoral motivation. The *Table Talk* reveals that Luther had no illusions about princes. Indeed, they often come in for some hefty criticism.[87] However, he could also realize the difficulty of their office and their positive role in protecting pastors and the gospel. In 1532 he could make this observation: "God takes care of the Word in his church, otherwise who would want to teach the gospel or preach Christ? By the same token, if all princes were enemies of the Word, the church could not exist for a single day. But God has even among the princes some who worship him and provide hospitality for ministers of the Word. Moreover, in the courts of ungodly princes, kings and bishops, God has some who worship him and impede many plans of the ungodly against the church."[88]

In his commentary on Psalm 84, which Luther constructed as a mirror for princes and which Estes analyzes in his essay, Luther discussed three virtues of such Christian princes, the first of which was supporting and protecting a good pastor. This resulted in one of Luther's most lyrical descriptions of the pastoral office and its effect and well serves as the proper peroration for this introduction.

> The first [virtue of princes] is that they can make God-fearing people and restrain the godless. . . . Many kings and princes have founded great, glorious churches and built temples . . . but how would all of these large, glorious things compare to a right, honest, God-fearing pastor or preacher? Such a one can help thousands of souls both for eternal life and in this life. For he can bring them to God through the Word and make them into productive, capable people, who serve and

86. This article sketches out some of the most important conclusions in his book on the subject: *Peace, Order, and the Glory of God: Secular Authority and the Church in the Thought of Luther and Melanchthon, 1518-1559* (Leiden: Brill, 2005).

87. See, for example, WA TR, nos. 1762, 1810, 1930, and 3903.

88. WA TR 2:243-44 (no. 1872).

honor God and, at the same time, are beneficial and useful in the world. . . . But [compared with glittering church buildings] who is a pastor? And who has eyes to see such a virtue in a lord or prince? Supporting or protecting a poor, honest pastor or preacher does not shine or sparkle; it is really nothing at all to look at. . . . But to build a marble church or give golden jewels, to serve dead stone and wood, now that sparkles, that shines, that is called a royal, princely virtue! Well, let it shine and let it sparkle, while my dingy pastor practices the virtue that increases God's realm, fills heaven with saints, plunders hell, robs the devil, protects from death, restrains sin and, moreover, instructs and comforts the world — each in his or her own walk of life — supports peace and unity, trains fine young people and plants all kinds of virtues in the people. In short, he creates a new world and builds not a temporary, pitiable house but an eternal, beautiful paradise, in which God himself wants to dwell.[89]

89. WA 31I:199-200; LW 13:52-53.

PART I

The Theological Heart of the Pastor

CHAPTER 1

Luther on the Theology of the Cross

Robert Kolb

In John 14:8, where Philip spoke according to the theology of glory, "Show us the Father," Christ straightaway set aside his flighty thought about seeing God elsewhere and led him to himself, saying, "Philip, he who has seen me has seen the Father" (John 14:9). For this reason true theology and recognition of God are in the crucified Christ.[1]

Of all the places to search for God, the last place most people would think to look is the gallows. Martin Luther confessed that there, in the shadows cast by death, God does indeed meet his straying, rebellious human creatures. There God reveals who he is; there he reveals who they are. Not in flight beyond the clouds, but in the dust of the grave God has come to tell it like it is about himself and about humanity.

In late April 1518 Luther's monastic superiors summoned him to Heidelberg to explain himself, at an assembly of the German Augustinians. He did not comment on the issues that had gotten him into trouble with the church, his critique of indulgences or his defiance of ecclesiastical authorities. He cut to the quick and talked about the nature of God and the nature

1. "Heidelberg Disputation, 1518," WA 1:362.15-19; LW 31:53.

This essay appeared in substantially the same form under the title "Deus revelatus — Homo revelatus, Luthers theologia crucis für das 21. Jahrhundert," in Robert Kolb and Christian Neddens, *Gottes Wort vom Kreuz, Luthers Theologie als Kritische Theologie, Oberurseler Hefte* 40 (Oberursel: Lutherische Theologische Hochschule, 2001), 13-34.

of the human creature trapped in sin. His assertions on these topics constituted a paradigm shift within Western Christian thought in the understanding of God's revelation of himself, God's way of dealing with evil, and what it means to be human. His Heidelberg theses floated before his monastic brothers a new constellation of perspectives on the biblical description of God and of human reality. Luther called this series of biblically based observations a "theology of the cross," and he later called this theology of the cross "our theology."[2] "The cross of Christ is the only instruction in the Word of God there is, the purest theology."[3]

What he offered his fellow monks in Heidelberg was not a treatment of a specific biblical teaching or two. He presented a new conceptual framework for thinking about God and the human creature. He provided a new basis or set of presuppositions for proclaiming the biblical message. Luther stepped to the podium in Heidelberg with an approach to Christian teaching that came at the task from an angle significantly different from the theological method of his scholastic predecessors. They may have disagreed among themselves on a range of issues, but they all practiced a theology of glory, according to the Wittenberg professor. Luther called for a different way of thinking about — and practicing — the proclamation of the gospel of Jesus Christ. Indeed, more than a proposal for a codification of biblical teaching, a theology of the cross, Luther called for the practice of this theology in the proclamation and life of theologians of the cross.

However, Luther's followers in the sixteenth century very seldom talked about their theology as a theology of the cross, and they preserved this new orientation for addressing theological topics only partially. They had no intellectual equipment for the analysis of presuppositions and conceptual frameworks. Melanchthon had taught them to think in terms of organizing ideas by topic *(loci communes)*, and they presumed that all rational people would share their orientation to the material. They took for granted that the inner logical and theological structure of their thinking would be obvious to all. Luther's "theology of the cross," however, is precisely a framework that is designed to embrace all of biblical teaching and guide the use of all its parts. It employs the cross of Christ as the focal point and fulcrum for understanding and presenting a wide range of specific topics within the biblical message. In Melanchthon's *Loci communes theologici* and

2. "In XV Psalmos graduum, 1532/33" (1540), WA 40III:193.6-7 and 19-20.

3. "Operationes in Psalms, 1519-1521," here on Ps. 6:11: WA 5:217.2-3.

similar works written by his and Luther's students, the dogmatic topic "cross" treated human suffering,[4] not God's suffering on the cross. Thus, the cross served a very different, and less all-encompassing, purpose than providing the point of view from which to assess God's revelation of himself, humanity-defining trust in that revelation, the atonement accomplished through Christ's death and resurrection, or the Christian life. In subsequent Lutheran dogmatic textbooks, this topic consistently treated only one aspect of the Christian life, persecution and afflictions of other kinds.

If already in the sixteenth century Lutherans did not find Luther's theology of the cross particularly helpful, is it possible that Luther's use of Christ's cross as the focal point for determining the dimensions of biblical proclamation is even more out of date and distant today than it was four hundred years ago? For North Americans or western Europeans today the problem is not that we do not have what God wants or expects of human beings (Luther's problem). We define the fundamental human problem differently than Luther did: I do not have and receive what I want and expect — and I want to know the reason why! Luther viewed God as the divine power that was altogether too present in his life, as an angry, demanding parent. We view God as a modern parent — neglectful, absent, too little concerned about us to be of much use. Luther's theology of the cross evolved from a concern that human creatures do not have — they cannot produce! — what God in his justice demands from them. Modern people complain because God does not produce what they demand as their rights from him.

Some might therefore argue that the gap is so great that Luther's paradigm for the practice of theology as theologians, thinkers, under the cross has itself become outmoded. In fact, Luther's theology of the cross reproduces for every age the biblical message regarding who God is and what he does — and regarding the characteristics his human creatures have — beneath the superficial fluctuations of history and culture. The theology of the cross does more than address the fleeting problems and miseries of one age. It refines the Christian's focus on God and on what it means to be human.

4. *Corpus Reformatorum: Opera quae supersunt omnia,* ed. C. G. Bretschneider and H. E. Bindseil (Halle and Braunschweig: Schwetschke, 1834-60), 21:528-36 (2nd ed.) and 934-55 (3rd ed.).

Theology of Glory, Theology of the Cross

Luther's theology of the cross developed in his Heidelberg Theses and in his great work of 1525, *On the Bondage of Human Choice.* Summarizing this framework for the practice of all theology must begin by distinguishing it from a theology of suffering and from a theology of glory.[5]

First, the theology of the cross is not a theology that simply supplies good tips on how to cope with tribulations and tragedies. Luther knew a lot about human suffering, but he never became fixated on suffering, nor on blessing. His faith fixed his attention on God. Luther knew how to give thanks to the Lord, not only for his grace and goodness but also for all the necessities and nourishment of the body, for family and good government, for good weather, good friends, peace, health, for music and a finely crafted poem. He knew how to enjoy God's creation, also with a song on his lyre. But Luther also knew that there are times in the course of human events when guitar music is not appropriate. Physical, emotional, spiritual suffering all fell to him as lot in life with some frequency, and so he was very realistic about the evil of suffering — as the deaths of two of his children overwhelmed him, as he felt betrayed by a beloved student, Johann Agricola, as he coped with the pains of his own body, as his anger and discouragement over the failure of Wittenberg citizens to live under the power of his proclamation drove him out of the

5. Luther's theology of the cross has been analyzed in different ways, with different accents, by scholars. The new discussion of this topic began with Walther von Loewenich's *Luther's Theology of the Cross,* trans. Herbert J. A. Bouman (Minneapolis: Augsburg, 1976), first published in German in 1929; it focuses particularly upon its implications for Luther's concept of faith and the Christian life. Philip S. Watson, *Let God Be God! An Interpretation of the Theology of Martin Luther* (Philadelphia: Muhlenberg, 1947), combines an analysis of the theology of the cross in relation to Luther's understanding of revelation and of the atonement with his doctrine of God's Word. Further important contributions to the topic include Hans Joachim Iwand's essay "Theologia crucis," in his *Nachgelassene Werke II* (Munich: Kaiser, 1966), 381-98; Jürgen Moltmann, *Der gekreuzigte Gott, das Kreuz Christi als Grund und Kritik christlicher Theologie* (Munich: Kaiser, 1972); Dennis Ngien, *The Suffering of God according to Martin Luther's "Theologia Crucis"* (New York: Peter Lang, 1995); Gerhard O. Forde, *On Being a Theologian of the Cross: Reflections on Luther's Heidelberg Disputation, 1518* (Grand Rapids: Eerdmans, 1997); and Klaus Schwarzwäller, *Kreuz und Auferstehung: Ein theologisches Traktat* (Göttingen: Vandenhoeck & Ruprecht, 2000). The topic is also treated in other standard assessments of Luther's theology.

town. But human suffering in itself was not the focus or function of the theology of the cross.

What then is this theology of the cross? Luther says that it is the opposite of a theology of glory. Theologies of glory presume something about God's glory, and something about the glory of being human. First, medieval systems of theology all sought to present a God whose glory consisted in fulfilling what in fact are fallen human standards for divine success: a God who could make his might known, could knock heads and straighten people out when they got out of line, even, perhaps especially, at human expense. These scholastic theologians sought to fashion — with biblical citations, to be sure — a God worthy of the name, according to the standards of the emperors and kings, whose glory and power defined how glory and power were supposed to look. Medieval theologians and preachers wanted a tough, no-nonsense kind of God to demand that they come up to their own standards for themselves and to judge their enemies. They did not grasp that "lording it over" others was the Gentile way of exercising power, not God's.[6]

Second, out of his experience as a student of theology at the University of Erfurt Luther suggested that these medieval systems of biblical exposition taught a human glory, the glory of human success: first, the success of human reason that can capture who and what God is, for human purposes. Gerhard Forde observes that this glory claims the mastery of the human mind in its investigations regarding both earthly matters and God's revelation of himself. "Theologians of glory operate on the assumption that creation and history are transparent to the human intellect, that one can see through what is made and what happens so as to peer into the 'invisible things of God.'" For they attempt to construct their picture of God on the basis of human judgments, abstractions that make universal some selected bits and pieces of the human experience and put human epistemologies in charge of divine revelation.[7]

Alongside this glory of human reason, Luther found in medieval theological systems an emphasis on the glory of human performance, of works that can capture God's favor by sheer human effort, plus some help from divine grace. Religions of glory have as their first and foremost goal the encouragement of good human performance. The theology of the

6. Mark 10:42-45.

7. Forde, *On Being a Theologian*, 72-73.

cross aims at bestowing a new identity upon sinners, setting aside the old identity, by killing it, so that good human performance can flow out of this new identity that is comprehended in trust toward God. Therefore "the theology of the cross is an offensive theology . . . [because] it attacks what we usually consider the best in our religion,"[8] human performance of pious deeds. A theology of glory lets human words set the tone for God's Word, forces his Word into human logic. A theology of glory lets human deeds determine God's deeds, for his demonstration of mercy is determined by the actions of human beings.

Although another element of Luther's presuppositional framework, his distinction between two kinds of righteousness, was not an integral part of his Heidelberg presentation, it was developing about this time, and apart from this presupposition Luther's theology of the cross will not come clearly into focus. Luther revised the theological paradigm of discussing humanity when he posited two ways of being righteous — two ways of being human — that must be distinguished to understand the biblical definition of humanity. Human creatures are righteous in God's sight with a "passive" righteousness; we are human in the vertical sphere of our lives only because of his mercy, favor, and love, because he created us and re-creates us in Christ. At Heidelberg Luther stated simply, "The love of God does not first discover what is pleasing to it but rather creates what is pleasing to it."[9]

Human creatures are righteous in relationship to each other and to the rest of creation, however, with an "active" righteousness; it consists in carrying out God's commands to care for the world around us. That means that human decision and human performance of all kinds are designed for the horizontal sphere of life, where God has given us stewardship for his creatures. When we attempt to use our decisions and performance to please God — or some created substitute we have made into an idol — we are taking them out of their proper sphere and laying upon them responsibility for making us God-pleasing. They break under the weight of this falsely placed responsibility.

A religion dependent on human willing and human works is on the prowl for the hidden God and will inevitably reshape God in our own im-

8. Forde, *On Being a Theologian*, 2.

9. WA 1:254.35, 36; LW 31:41, Thesis 28, following the translation of Forde, *On Being a Theologian*, 112.

age. This kind of religion has nothing to do with the true God. For it misunderstands the purpose and function of God's law. It attributes to the law the power to bestow life. In fact, the law only evaluates life, Luther claimed. God gives and restores life. Thus, in the midst of human life gone astray, the law — as God's plan for what human life really is to be and accomplish — "brings the wrath of God, kills, reviles, accuses, judges, and condemns everything that is not in Christ,"[10] including the noblest of human sinners, according to Thesis 23 of the Heidelberg Disputation. Forde comments, "Thesis 23 announces flatly that in spite of all the glorious hot air, God is not ultimately interested in the law. The real consequence of such wisdom is laid bare: The law does not work the love of God, it works wrath; it does not give life (recall Thesis 1!),[11] it kills; it does not bless, it curses; it does not comfort, it accuses; it does not grant mercy, it judges." "In sum, it condemns everything not in Christ. It seems an outrageous and highly offensive list. As Luther's proof quickly demonstrates, however, it comes right out of Paul in Galatians and Romans."[12] Luther insists in the next thesis that the wisdom of the law in itself is good. It is simply not to be used as a means of winning God's favor. Theologians of glory misuse the law in that way.[13]

Luther found these theologies of glory inadequate and insufficient, ineffective and impotent. For such a theology of glory reaches out for a manipulable God, a God who provides support for a human creature who seeks to master life on his or her own, with just a touch of divine help. That matched neither Luther's understanding of God nor his perception of his own humanity. Theologians of glory create a god in their own image and a picture of the human creature after their own longings. Neither corresponds to reality, Luther claimed.

10. WA 1:354.25-26; LW 31:41.

11. Thesis 1 stated, "The law of God, the most salutary doctrine of life, cannot advance a person on the way to righteousness but is rather a hindrance." WA 1:353.15-16; LW 31:39.

12. Forde, *On Being a Theologian,* 95-96. See also Gal. 3:13, 10; Rom. 4:15; 7:10; 2:12.

13. Forde, *On Being a Theologian,* 97-98.

Calling the Thing What It Is

"A theology of the cross calls the thing what it actually is," he asserted.[14] The cross is the place where God talks our language: it is quite clear what is happening as Christ cries out, "My God, my God, why have you forsaken me?" and dies. At the cross God meets his human creatures where they are, in the shadow of death. For the cross is not an instrument of torture but of death. On it people die. From it Christ made his way back to life. That is where human beings can see what God's experience, God's disposition — even God's essence — really are and what humanity really is, claimed Luther.

The theology of the cross involves not only the cross itself, as the locus of the event that has determined human history. It involves also the Word that conveys that event and its benefits to God's people. The word of the cross is folly to the perishing; this word is God's power for those whom he saves through it.[15] Luther believed that when God speaks, reality results. The cross and the Word that delivers it have created a new reality within God's fallen creation: a new reality for Satan (since God nailed the law's accusations to the cross and rendered them illegible by soaking them in Christ's blood); a new reality for death (since it was laid to eternal rest in Christ's grave); a new reality for sinners (since they were buried, too, in Christ's tomb and raised to new life through the death and resurrection of the Crucified One).

To force Luther's observations from the foot of the cross into four convenient categories for easier consideration, it can be said that he saw from the vantage point of the cross (1) who God really is, (2) what the human reaction to God must be, (3) what the human condition apart from God is and how God has acted to alter that condition, and (4) what kind of life trust in Christ brings to his disciples.

1. *God Hidden, God Revealed.* Luther distinguished the "revealed God" *(Deus revelatus)* from the "hidden God" *(Deus absconditus)*, by which he meant, in different contexts, either God as he actually exists beyond the grasp of human conceptualization — particularly when the human mind is darkened by sin — or God as sinners fashion him in their own image, to their own likings. In addition, it must be noted that the re-

14. WA 1:354.21-22; LW 31:45, Thesis 21.

15. 1 Cor. 1:18.

vealed God hides himself in order to show himself to his human creatures. Luther observed that God is to be found precisely where theologians of glory are horrified to find him: as a kid in a crib, as a criminal on a cross, as a corpse in a crypt. God reveals himself by hiding himself right in the middle of human existence as it has been bent out of shape by the human fall. Thus, Luther's theology of the cross is a departure from the fuzziness of human attempts to focus on God apart from God's pointing out where he is to be found and who he really is.

In the Heidelberg Disputation, and in his expansion of its insights, for instance in his *Bondage of the Will,* Luther focused first on the blank wall created by the impossibility of human and sinful conceptualizing of God; with fallen eyes no one can see God. With fallen human ears no one can return to the Edenic hearing of his Word. Then Luther focused very sharply on God in his revelation of himself:[16] no one has seen God, but Jesus of Nazareth, God in the flesh, has made him known: a God with holes in his hands, feet, and side; the God who has come near to us, into the midst of our twisted and ruined existence. This God on the cross reveals the fullness of God's love as well as the inadequacy of all human efforts to patch up life to please him.

2. *Humanity Defined by Faith.* Human attempts to claim God's attention and approval always draft a plan that tries to place God under the control of human logic, or testing through signs of some sort or another.[17] People draw up job descriptions for God and become angry or disappointed with him when he does not prove himself equal to their tasks. Neither rational nor empirical proofs that would place God under human domination can lead to God. God reveals himself through his still, small voice,[18] through the seemingly foolish and impotent Word from the cross,[19] in the Word made flesh, come to dwell among his people.[20] Luther's theology of the cross is a theology of the Word of the cross, a Word that conveys life itself on the power of its promise. Luther insisted that trust alone — total dependence and reliance on God and what he promises in his incarnation and in Scripture — is the center of life, the living source

16. John 1:18.
17. 1 Cor. 1:22-25.
18. 1 Kings 19:12.
19. 1 Cor. 1:18-25.
20. John 1:14.

of genuine human living. To recognize trust as the core of our humanity is to perceive the true form of being human as God created his human creature. That means that at the core of human life our own performance, accomplishment, behavior, has no place. For "a human work, no matter how good, is deadly sin because it in actual fact entices us away from 'naked trust in the mercy of God' to a trust in self."[21] Not trust in self, nor trust in one's own logical or empirical judgment, can constitute human life. God has designed life to center upon trust in him. Heidelberg Thesis 25: "He is not righteous who does much, but he who, without work, believes much in Christ."[22]

3. *Handed Over for Our Sins, Raised for Our Justification.* By showing how God solves "the human problem," the cross gives humankind its best view of the nature of God, for it reveals his modus operandi, his way of dealing with evil and reclaiming humanity for himself. Luther taught that God's true righteousness — his true nature, his essence — is revealed in the cross, and it turns out that he is love and mercy.[23] For God sent his Son into this world to take sin and death into himself and to bury sinners in his tomb.[24] Apart from his sacrifice of his own life as the substitute for his people under the law's condemnation, there is no life.[25] Exactly how and why it is so is never explained in Scripture. Forde warns against attempts to draft atonement theories that try to elucidate the eternal truth behind the cross. "If we can see through the cross to what is supposed to be behind it, we don't have to look at it!"[26] God's Word simply presents us the cross. The fury of God's wrath appears there in all its horror. God's anger reveals the horror of sin and how it has ruined the human creature whom he loves. But that very presentation of God's wrath appears at that place, Golgotha, where God has poured himself out in order to bury our sinful identity and give us new life. Greater love has no one.[27] Because of our sin God's mercy seat has taken the shape of the cross.

Sin is the problem. It is the original problem, the root of the problem, the motor that drives the enmity between Creator and rebellious hu-

21. Forde, *On Being a Theologian*, 35.

22. WA 1:354.29-30; LW 31:41.

23. 1 John 4:8.

24. Rom. 6:4; Col. 2:12.

25. Rom. 6:23b, 4-18; Col. 2:12-15; 3:1.

26. Forde, *On Being a Theologian*, 76.

27. Rom. 5:6-8.

man creature. Sin means the rejection of God and his standards for being human. Rejection of God is the core kind of sinfulness. Rejection of all the expectations that flow from his gift of identity as his creature and child is the second kind of sinfulness. It can be analyzed, or at least experienced, apart from acknowledgment of the Creator. Death is a symptom of the problem. Disgust at one's own failures, discouragement because of the antipathy or apathy of others, deterioration of health or memory or reputation are all symptoms of the problem. Yet each of these symptoms can be the point at which the cross begins to emerge out of the darkness and come into focus. Any dissatisfaction with life and identity can form the basis of conversation that leads to Calvary and to the heart of the human dilemma. Even in a "guiltless" society the theology of the cross provides the firm undergirding for discussion of topics that seem distant at first, the topics of redemption or atonement.

For even sinners conscious of guilt cannot comprehend the overwhelming extent to which sin has determined human existence after the fall. No one can grasp the enormity of the love of God that overcomes the problem of sin and guilt. Luther rejected any cheap atonement in which Christ bought off the enemies of his people with a pittance of suffering, like a bit of gold or silver.[28] He suffered unto the death of the cross[29] and thus met the law's demand that sinners die.[30] But Luther not only depicted Christ's saving act as a "joyous exchange" of the sinner's sin and death for his own innocence and life.[31] Luther also confessed that Christ had won the battle against Satan in a "magnificent duel," in which he inflicted fatal wounds on Satan, sin, and death.[32] God at his most glorious, in his display of the extent of his mercy and love for his human creatures, appears, Luther believed, in the depth of the shame of the cross. There he is to be seen as he really is, in his true righteousness, which is mercy and love. There human beings are to be seen as those who deserve to die eternally but who now through baptismal death have the life Christ gives through his resurrection,

28. See the explanation of the second article of the creed in the Small Catechism. BSLK, 511; BC, 355; *The Book of Concord: The Confessions of the Evangelical Lutheran Church,* ed. and trans. Theodore G. Tappert (Philadelphia: Fortress, 1959), 345; hereafter cited as BC-T.

29. Phil. 2:8.

30. Rom. 6:23a.

31. E.g., in his Galatians commentary of 1535, WA 40I:432-38; LW 26:276-80.

32. E.g., in his Galatians commentary, WA 40I:228-29; LW 26:163-64.

forever. For it is not true that Luther's theology of the cross excludes the resurrection. "A theology of the cross is impossible without resurrection. It is impossible to plumb the depths of the crucifixion without the resurrection."[33] He died for only one reason: that his people might have human life in its fullest.[34] Only at the foot of the cross can true human identity be discovered. There, realizing whose I am, I realize who I am.

4. *Take Up Your Cross and Follow.* Finally, Luther understood that the Christian life is not necessarily marked by earthly definitions of success or suffering, by neither bane nor blessing, but instead is shaped by Christ and his cross.[35] Christ's cross demonstrates that his people have nothing to fear from any of their enemies, not even death itself. Therefore, they are freed to risk all to love those whom God has placed within the reach of their love. Having come to understand at the foot of the cross what is really wrong with human life — not just its crimes of magnificent proportions but the banality of our evils and the wretchedness of doubt and denial of God — believers also recognize from the vantage point of the cross what joy and peace come from living the genuine human way in self-sacrificial love and giving.

Indeed, the theology of the cross is a paradigm for every human season, also and perhaps especially, the beginning of the twenty-first century, because it presumes and reasserts the biblical assessment of human life. Christian Neddens calls it "relevant and explosive" in its application in twentieth-century theology because it is, according to the appraisal of Udo Kern, a fundamental norm for theological knowledge and practice and therefore a "fundamentally critical theory." Neddens describes the critical function of the theology of the cross in engaging objections to the Christian faith on the basis of modern science and learning, and in regard to human autonomy and human suffering. This theology serves as critical analysis for the misuse of theology and a natural tendency toward theologies of glory.[36]

The theology of the cross functions as both a hermeneutical framework and an orientation for theological criticism. It can aid in sharpening

33. Forde, *On Being a Theologian,* 1.

34. John 10:10.

35. Matt. 16:24-26.

36. Neddens, "Kreuzestheologie als kritische Theologie, Aspekte und Positionen der Kreuzestheologie im 20. Jahrhundert," in *Gottes Wort vom Kreuz,* 35-66, here 35-41. Neddens analyzes the work of von Loewenich, Iwand, Moltmann, Forde, and Schwarzwäller mentioned in n. 5 above.

the formulation of a host of questions, but this essay focuses on its usefulness in discussions of "theodicy" and in defining what it means to be human.

The theology of the cross clears the focus on human life, both as it is misapprehended by those who try to think about humanity apart from God, and as God reveals it through his own incarnation and his death for fallen human creatures on the cross. In Luther's theology of the cross we encounter not only *Deus absconditus* — God beyond our grasp, God as he can only be reimaged by fallen human imagination — and *Deus revelatus* — the only true God revealed in Jesus Christ, who speaks to his human creatures from the pages of Scripture. We also meet — though Luther never said it this way — ourselves, first as *homo absconditus* — the human creature hidden from our own eyes and assessment, in both our sinfulness and in the unexperienced potential of humanity that sinners cannot grasp — and *homo revelatus* — God's perception, the only accurate perception and definition, of what it means to be human.

What it means to be human is a question that interests Western people of this age. Why life does not turn out better than it does, or why God has disappeared, is another such question. If Luther's theology of the cross can aid contemporary searchers for haven and help to understand the gap between their sense of what they could be and their experience of what they are, it might be a message for moderns. And if it could help explain why God, if he really does exist, falls so far short of our expectations — if it can help us justify his treatment or his neglect of us — then it might indeed be a theology for the twenty-first century. These two aspects of the theology of the cross do not exhaust its significance and usefulness for guiding biblical proclamation in this time, as Neddens shows, but this essay focuses on them as examples of its contemporary significance and usefulness.

Deus Absconditus and the Cry of "Why?" *Deus Revelatus* and the Response "Christ"

Luther's theology of the cross developed out of his struggle with the anger of God. But now the tables are turned: God is in the hands of apathetic sinners. At the beginning of the twenty-first century people struggle with the indifference of God, but in this case turnabout seems like fair play, for sometimes those who struggle most with the apparent absence or indifference of God in their lives are those who have not given thanks for a good bottle of Chateauneuf du Pape or a sterling performance on the playing field, to say nothing of their very existence. The burning question Luther posed in the sixteenth century regarding his standing before his Creator has turned into a resentful complaint about God's distance from anything important — that is, anything that escapes our control — in our lives. People who have believed in a Creator have thrown Job's complaints back at the Lord from time immemorial, but only since the Enlightenment have self-confident human beings tried to engage in the attempt to justify God's indifference, impotence, inactivity in behalf of human creatures. Three hundred years ago the German philosopher Gottfried Wilhelm Leibniz devised the term "theodicy" to describe the human attempt to justify God by explaining evil. Theodicy is the attempt to deal with a God from whom we expect all good things when he does not deliver the good we expect. Although Luther was not addressing the question of "how God could do such awful things to us" as he formulated his theology of the cross in 1518, it speaks to the felt needs of the twenty-first-century people around us, at least in the West, to explain evil — in hopes of mastering it.

1. *God Has Come Near in the Blood of Christ.* The theology of the cross focuses our attention on the God who has come near to us in the midst of our afflictions, not just with sympathy but with the solution for the evils that afflict us. In the cross God has rendered his verdict upon sin: it is evil, and it must be destroyed. And on the cross Christ destroyed our sin as the factor that determines our identity. Luther did not fashion a justification for God's permitting evil or his failure to cope with it adequately. Bound to Scripture, he found no more of an answer to the "why" of evil than that given to Job. He simply let God be God. He trusted that the God who had come to engage evil at its ugliest on the cross would triumph finally over every evil. Therefore, he did not feel himself compelled to veil any part of the truth about God or about evil. Theologians of the cross "are not driven to simplistic theodicies because with Saint Paul they believe that God justifies himself precisely in the cross and resurrection of Jesus. They know that, dying to the old, the believer lives in Christ and looks forward to being raised with him."[37] For God has "justified" himself by delivering and restoring us to the fullness of humanity through Christ's self-sacrifice on the cross.

37. Forde, *On Being a Theologian,* 13.

Luther's *On the Bondage of Human Choice* sought above all to confess that God is Lord of all. In that work he did not shy away from those passages in Scripture in which God seems to be responsible for evil. The reformer can be accused of trying to explain too much in this work, and when that is true, he explains God in the way of the Old Testament prophets who saw God at work in good and evil.[38] But Luther did insist that human creatures dare not pry into the secret will of God as he treated Matthew 23:37, Christ's lamentation over Jerusalem,[39] and as he lectured on Genesis a decade after the appearance of *The Bondage of Human Choice,* he did provide a corrective to misimpressions he might have caused in his response to Erasmus. In addressing the question of why some are saved and not others, Luther there interpreted his earlier writing:

> a distinction must be made when one deals with the knowledge, or rather with the subject of the divinity. For one must debate either about the hidden God or about the revealed God. With regard to God insofar as he has not been revealed, there is no faith, no knowledge, and no understanding. And here one must hold to the statement that what is above us is none of our concern. . . . Such inquisitiveness is original sin itself, by which we are impelled to strive for a way to God through natural speculation. . . . God has most sternly forbidden this investigation of the divinity.[40]

Luther then places in God's mouth the following words:

> From an unrevealed God I will become a revealed God. Nevertheless, I will remain the same God. I will be made flesh, or send My Son. He shall die for your sins and shall rise again from the dead. And in this way I will fulfill your desire, in order that you may be able to know whether you are predestined or not. Behold, this is my Son; listen to him (cf. Matt. 17:5). Look at him as he lies in the manger and on the lap of his mother, as he hangs on the cross. Observe what he does and what he says. There you will surely take hold of me. For "he who sees me," says Christ, "also sees the Father himself" (cf. John 14:9). If you

38. Exod. 4:11; Isa. 45:7; Amos 3:6.
39. WA 18:686-90; LW 33:144-47.
40. WA 43:458.35–459.15; LW 5:43-44.

> listen to him, are baptized in his name, and love his Word, then you are certainly predestined and are certain of your salvation.[41]

Luther here goes further. He rejects any discordance between hidden God and revealed God even though the hidden God goes far beyond human grasp.

> If you believe in the revealed God and accept his Word, he will gradually also reveal the hidden God, for "he who sees me also sees the Father," as John 14:9 says. He who rejects the Son also loses the unrevealed God along with the revealed God. But if you cling to the revealed God with a firm faith, so that your heart is so minded that you will not lose Christ even if you are deprived of everything, then you are most assuredly predestined, and you will understand the hidden God. Indeed, you understand him even now if you acknowledge the Son and his will, namely, that he wants to reveal himself to you, that he wants to be your Lord and your Savior. Therefore you are sure that God is also your Lord and Father.[42]

The search for answers ends where the search for God ends: at the cross, where God reveals his power and his wisdom in his own broken body and spilled blood.[43]

2. *Faith Clings to the Crucified One.* Thus, Luther's theology of the cross focuses our attention on trust in the God who loves us and promises his presence in the midst of afflictions. A doctoral student of mine and his wife lost a baby shortly before birth a few years ago. He related that a member of his congregation, trying to offer comfort, had said, "Well, Pastor, at a time like this, all that theology you're learning does not do much good." "In fact," Mark observed, "true comfort comes precisely from knowing the theology of Martin Luther; it gives assurance that God is only that God who shows love and mercy toward us. If we had to wonder what the God behind the clouds really intends and why he is delivering this evil upon us, doubt and distress rather than comfort would be our lot. We cannot know why God took our child, but we do not have to question how God regards

41. WA 43:459.24-32; LW 5:45.
42. WA 43:460.26-35; LW 5:46.
43. 1 Cor. 1:18–2:16.

us. He has shown us that decisively in the cross." The theology of the cross redirects our gaze from probing the darkness further and directs those who hurt and ache to cling to Christ, whose love is certain and whose faithfulness is beyond all doubt.

3. *Evil Identified, Nailed to the Cross, Drowned in Christ's Blood.* The theology of the cross reminds those caught in evil that evil is truly evil, the opposite of what God wants for his human creature. It reminds fallen human creatures that God has come to lift them once again to true human life through his own death and resurrection. Instead of justifying God's failure to end evil today, or justifying human actions that are truly evil, it justifies sinners so that they may enjoy true life, life with God, forever. The problem with "theodicies" is that they have to tell less than the truth, they have to avoid some part of the problem, at one point or another. Whether they are working at justifying God or justifying themselves, they always end up calling what is truly evil good and what is good evil. In the final analysis, sinners in the hands of an almighty God always find it difficult to cope with what is not true, good, and beautiful. Instead of relying on the person of the rescuer, the restorer of human life, they rely on the explanations they have fashioned for mastering their problems.

The realism of Luther's theology of the cross is able to confront the horrors and the banalities of evil in all their perversity because it enables us to avoid feeling obligated either to seek the good in evil or to justify God.

> Whereas the theologian of glory tries to see through the needy, the poor, the lowly, and the "non-existent," the theologian of the cross knows that the love of God creates precisely out of nothing. Therefore the sinner must be reduced to nothing in order to be saved. The presupposition of the Disputation . . . is the hope of the resurrection. God brings life out of death. He calls into being that which is from that which is not. In order that there be a resurrection, the sinner must die. All presumption must be ended. The truth must be seen. Only the "friends of the cross" who have been reduced to nothing are properly prepared to receive the justifying grace poured out by the creative love of God. All other roads are closed.[44]

44. Forde, *On Being a Theologian*, 114-15.

Waiting on God in the midst of the shadows creates the patience that endures and fosters hope when believers can listen to his voice through the darkness. For they know their Master's voice and they have confidence in both his love and his power.

For God does not reveal the past of evil by explaining where and why it arose, but he does tell us something of its present and everything about its future. He comes to us as a God who has experienced loss, suffering, and death, but he does not give answers as to the origins of evil. The alternatives for solving that riddle seem to be two: we are at fault, or he is at fault. The former justifies God, and we are dead. The latter is an even more horrible solution: God gets pleasure from our suffering. Instead of answers about evil's origin, God gives us his presence through the presence of his people and the proclamation of his Word. He gives us the promise of the certain, final, everlasting liberation from evil that he effected through Christ's resurrection.

4. *Cruciform Humanity.* The theology of the cross enables God's children to understand the shape of life as God has planned it for them, following Christ under the cross. It provides the hope and confidence that enable them to conquer evil in the lives of others, as they follow the model Christ gives them. His atoning suffering, death, and resurrection have conquered evil in their lives, and they recognize their call to carry love into the lives of others — in some instances through their own suffering and the bearing of burdens.

True "theodicy" is lived out in the lives, in the love, of his people as they deliver it to neighbors caught in the grip of evil. That theodicic action demands that children of the cross recognize the familial dimension of their new life in Christ. Some evils may be combated by individuals, but most of the perversions of God's plan for human living have roots deep enough and facets numerous enough to demand more than any one Christian can do to bring God's presence to the suffering. Not only the suffering but also the believers need the support that comes from the larger company of Christ's people.

In regard to their own struggles with evil, believers find in the cross the reminder that they pose a false question when they demand to know why the Creator does not treat them better. Finally, the expectations of the human creature cannot demand more of the Creator than he has promised. Indeed, his ultimate promise will bring the end of all evil, but in the interim he has promised his presence in the midst of evil, not its exclusion from our lives. Nor dare our expectations of ourselves be less than God's expectations of us. God's promise of life and of his steadfast love suffices. The promise in fact gives hope and joy and peace. It fosters a defiance of evil and the assurance that the people of God can move through life on the solid ground of the love Christ revealed on the cross.

Homo Absconditus and *Homo Revelatus*: What It Means to Be Fallen and What It Means to Be Human

Luther's *Deus absconditus* and *Deus revelatus* also reveal a great deal about his understanding of what it means to be human. It might be said that his anthropology taught both a *homo absconditus* and a *homo revelatus.*

1. *"Human" Means Trusting God above All Else.* Being fully human is first of all to recognize that God is the fundamental point of orientation for humanity. Not to know him as Creator and Father imposes bondage upon those who are created to trust in him. It enchains them to their false gods, tyrants all. Sin springs from doubt that denies God's place in our lives and defies his lordship. Luther believed that our sinful turning the center of our attention to ourselves hides from our own view the depth of our own sinfulness, indeed the nature of our own sinfulness. In the Smalcald Articles he wrote, "This inherited sin has caused such a deep, evil corruption of nature that reason does not comprehend it; rather it must be believed on the basis of the revelation in the Scriptures."[45] The heart of the human failure to be all that we can be, according to Luther, consists of our failure to fear, love, and trust in God above all things. Both sinners whose behavior openly defies God and the "wise, holy, learned, and religious" who want to secure their lives with their own works refuse "to let God rule and to be God."[46] This failure to trust in God led to the defiance of God's other commands, according to Luther's interpretation of the Decalogue in the Small Catechism.[47]

45. BSLK, 434; BC, 311; BC-T, 303.

46. Philip S. Watson made this expression the central point of his summary of Luther's theology in *Let God Be God!,* especially p. 64. The unclear reference in Watson's footnote at this point is to Luther's *Kirchenpostille,* WA 10I/1:24.4-11; *Luther's Epistle Sermons, Advent and Christmas Season,* trans. John N. Lenker, I (Luther's Complete Works VII) (Minneapolis: Luther Press, 1908), 117.

47. BSLK, 507-10; BC, 351-54; BC-T, 342-44. The words "We are to fear and love

Therefore, until sinners recognize their failure to trust in the true God, revealed in Jesus Christ, they are blind to the depth and the root cause of their troubles in this world. The law crushes sinful pretensions to lordship over life in many ways, but only by driving people to the cross can it focus their understanding clearly enough to see that the original, root, fundamental sin that perverts and corrupts life lies in this lack of trust. When his human creatures do apprehend who God is, in the fullness of his love, they then see themselves as his beloved children. This perception of ourselves as the heirs of Christ and members of the Father's family liberates us from the bondage of caring for ourselves and presiding over our own destinies. We are freed by Christ's cross to be fully human again because our Lord has made us children of God through death to sin and resurrection to new life in him. The success of this identity cannot be measured; the certainty of this identity cannot be shaken. From the foot of the cross we see a grandeur in our humanity so delightful that reason cannot comprehend it.

2. *Bound Not to Trust, Liberated to Trust.* But the fallen human nature cannot fear, love, and trust in God above all things. A vital part of Luther's theology of the cross is his recognition of the impossibility of turning ourselves back to God, of the boundness of human choice. He did not deny that sinners have an active will, as is sometimes suggested by scholars who have not read his *De servo arbitrio* carefully. He did deny that the sinful will is free to choose God as long as it remains caught and trapped by its need to supply an identity for its person since it does not recognize God as creator and giver of our identity. "Free will, after the fall, has the power to do good only in a passive capacity, but it can always do evil in an active capacity,"[48] Luther explained to the Augustinians in Heidelberg. Like water, which can be heated but cannot heat itself, the will is driven by Satan or by God, as it acts in the vertical sphere of life. Instead of trusting the Word of the Lord, we turn to the lie of the Deceptor,[49] and doubt binds our wills as it deafens our ears. Freedom comes only through the new identity given through Christ's death, that becomes our death to captivity and deception.

Under the illusion that God will provide grace enough to supple-

God" that introduce explanations to commandments two through ten echo and stand on the basis of the first commandment, which Luther interprets, "We are to fear, love, and trust God above all things."

48. WA 1:354.7-8; LW 31:40, Thesis 14.

49. Gen. 3:1-5.

ment the efforts of our own strivings — up to 99.9 percent if necessary — those who claim that they can freely exercise enough of their damaged will, at least to accept what God offers, are never able to understand what Jesus meant when he said that we must be born anew to enter the kingdom of God.[50] Indeed, striving for the standards people set for themselves can convince them that they are not able to reach their goals, but apart from the perspective at the foot of the cross they will not understand that the solution lies not in trying harder but in dying to their sinful identity. At the foot of the cross sinners finally lose the presumption that they simply must stretch a bit higher. They fall to the earth to die to their sinful identity. Forde labels the claim that some human contribution, how minimal a mite it might be, can secure human life "effrontery." He compares the vanity of such impertinence to what has to happen to the addict: "a 'bottoming out' or an 'intervention.' . . . there is no cure for the addict on his own. In theological terms, we must come to confess that we are addicted to sin, addicted to self, whatever form that may take, pious or impious."[51]

Thus, the theology of the cross reveals that it is hopeless to hope that human performance of any kind can contribute to improving our status in God's sight. Recognizing that we are no more and no less than creatures frees us from the need to assume the impossible burden of being the God who orders and frees our lives. Luther's "let God be God" lets us be us, creatures who can be all that he made us to be.

3. *Born Anew.* For God has made us anew. He is the Re-Creator as well as the Creator, and his work of re-creation has taken place on the cross and in Christ's resurrection. From this throne of the cross God does our sinful identity to death and gives us new birth as his children. God is in charge. He is Lord. He determines who his human creatures are.

From the foot of the cross, Luther confessed, the bent and broken shape of humanity in flight from, in revolt against, God can be seen for what it is. The fundamental fact of human existence after the fall is that sin pays its wage,[52] and sinners receive what they have earned through their doubt of God's Word and defiance of his lordship — death. Reflecting on Jesus' conversation with Nicodemus,[53] Forde writes, "No repairs, no im-

50. John 3:3.
51. Forde, *On Being a Theologian,* 17; cf. 64, 94-95.
52. Rom. 6:23a.
53. John 3:7.

provements, no optimistic encouragements are possible. Just straight talk: 'You must be born anew.'"[54] Sinners must die, eternally or baptismally. The children of God become his children not by recovering from serious illness but by being born anew, and that new birth presumes death to the old, sinful, identity. For God confronted both kinds of human sinfulness on the cross — the symptoms and the root sin of doubt, denial, and defiance of himself. His declaration of war against them seized the victory in the battle at Calvary, and he delivers the fruits of the victory in baptism[55] and in the return to baptism in daily repentance.

"When Christ calls a person, he bids him come and die," Dietrich Bonhoeffer observed. "Every command of Jesus is a call to die, with all our affections and lusts. But we do not want to die, and therefore Jesus Christ and his call are necessarily our death as well as our life. The call to discipleship, the Baptism in the name of Jesus Christ, means both death and life."[56] By incorporating fallen human creatures into the death and resurrection of Jesus Christ through baptism, the Creator has repeated his modus operandi of the first week, at the beginning. He brings forth a new creature through the creative power of his Word.

Adam and Eve were not given a probationary period in which to demonstrate that they were worthy of their humanity. It could not be earned. It was a gift. Human performance — proper human behavior — flows from the gift of identity, the gift of life. Human identity as child of God cannot be earned. It must be passively received. For those addicted to sin, as for the alcoholic, "Thou shalt quit!" is a salutary command, "but it does not realize its aims but only makes matters worse. It deceives the alcoholic by arousing pride and so becomes a defense mechanism against the truth, the actuality of addiction."[57] Law-ism, behavior-ism, tells the sinner the same kind of lie. The theology of the cross labels as a lie the idea that human performance can establish human identity as a child of God and a true human being.

Beyond this denial of the nature of the evil that captivates us, in our rejection of the love of our Creator, sin also prevents us from perceiving clearly the height of our own possibilities as people freed from sin, law,

54. Forde, *On Being a Theologian*, 97.

55. Rom. 6:3-11; Col. 2:11-15.

56. Dietrich Bonhoeffer, *The Cost of Discipleship* (New York: Macmillan, 1959), 79.

57. Forde, *On Being a Theologian*, 25.

death, and the devil. We have been liberated from slavery to all that focuses life on our works and ourselves. We have been freed to love our neighbor in a way that brings the good to him or her and pleasure to us, which is the fulfillment of our humanity. The light of the cross does liberate sinners from the darkness of the fears that have driven them in upon themselves so that they can appreciate the wonder of the creature God has made them to be. The light of the cross generates the power to fulfill God's plan for human living — in a sinful world, even under the cross — and to acknowledge and appreciate the joys of life as God's child.

4. *Living as a New Creature.* That means that the cross reveals our true humanity to us. The cross reminds us that "'we live on borrowed time' — time lent us by the Creator. Yet we also see in the death of Jesus on the cross our rebellion against that life, and we note that there is absolutely no way out now except one. God vindicated the crucified Jesus by raising him from the dead. So the question and the hope come to us. 'If we die with him, shall we not also live with him?'"[58] In the cross we recognize not only the awful truth but also the wonderful truth about ourselves.

In Christ we recognize ourselves through the Word of the Holy Spirit. We are the forgiven children of God, with identities no longer determined by sin but rather by the forgiving, life-giving Word of the Lord. We are children of God, with great potential, even in the midst of a world plagued by evil, for bringing love, peace, and joy to those God has placed around us. The cross also makes it clear that it is not good for human beings to be alone, according to God's plan for humanity.[59] Gathered into God's family by the cross, those who have been given new life there are inevitably drawn as members of the family, with other members of the family, into that world to demonstrate God's love and to call others to the cross and thus into the family.

Thus, we demonstrate this truth that we are children of God in our actions, and we use God's truth that we are his own as a weapon against temptation. When Satan suggests that, while we indeed have a ticket to heaven, our sinful identity determines who we are on earth, until death, so that we can only live life on his terms, we can tell him to go home. We can assert the promise of God in the cross and smother the smoldering sparks of our inclinations to live life on our own terms rather than God's.

58. Forde, *On Being a Theologian,* 9. Cf. Rom. 6.

59. Gen. 2:18.

For the word from the cross is a weapon in the battle within us as well as outside us.

The theology of the cross cannot be taught and confessed without its implications for the whole human community becoming clear. The cruciform nature of the individual believer's life also stretches out the arms of the body of Christ, the church, in the direction of those around it, within its reach. For the cross was designed to restore the whole family of God as a family.

The cross also invades our lives in the midst of the struggles against those desires that would lead us back to idolatrous living. The Holy Spirit leads us constantly back to the cross to crucify our flesh, our desires to live apart from his love and his plan for daily life. Every believer knows well the struggle that Paul confesses in Romans 7 and 8. All believers recognize that there can be no compromise with the law of sin. We sinners must be put to death. We have been put to death once and for all in our baptisms, but in the mystery of the continuing force of evil in our lives, the rhythm of daily repentance leads us again and again to the cross, to die and to be raised up.

Conclusion

Luther believed that the best view of all reality was to be had from the foot of the cross on Calvary. The death and resurrection of Christ parted the clouds, and he could see God and himself clearly. His theology, the theology of the cross, performs the same function at the beginning of the twenty-first century. In Christ it reveals God's God-ness and our humanity. In an age of profound doubt about God's existence and his love, the cross of Jesus Christ focuses human attention on how God reveals himself to us as a person who loves and shows mercy, in the midst of the evils that beset us. In Christ it shows fallen human creatures who God really is. In an age of profound doubt about what human life is and is worth, the theology of the cross defines human life from the basis of God's presence in human life and his love for human creatures. It shows human beings who they are. Luther's theology of the cross is indeed a theology for such a time as this.

PART II

Preaching the Living Word

CHAPTER 2

Communication and the Transgression of Language in Martin Luther

Vítor Westhelle

During the turbulent years of the beginning of the sixteenth century, when the Reformation movement reached its climax, a struggle on three fronts ensued. With different theological emphases, each one pointed to fundamental anthropological and sociological dimensions of human existence. Each one revealed a facet of the scope of oppression of human existence in the world and has remained as such into our days. In one way or another they all entered the programmatic agenda of the Reformation and lent to this movement its three most basic and defining social and anthropological features. Each one had a significant impact on the theology of the Reformation and its ecclesial and sociopolitical significance. They represented, in the unfolding of the Reformation, Luther's practical concern with the three basic institutions or "orders" of creation *(politia, oeconomia,* and *ecclesia).* However, in the practical articulation of the challenges they represented, Luther's adoption of the medieval doctrine of the "three orders" *(Dreiständelehre)* showed their interconnectedness, and dynamic overlapping features. Each one, therefore, provides an entrance to the others and cannot be discretely isolated from them. The first two will only be mentioned. My concern is with the third front, in which the Word finds itself expressed in words, in language.

The political front can be represented by the fierce debate and tragic outcome of the Peasants' Revolt and its subsequent suppression. The struggle led by enthusiast leaders had several aspects. An important one, the dispute over hermeneutics, has been discussed at length in

Protestant research focusing mainly on the theology of Thomas Müntzer and Karlstadt. But from the peasants' standpoint, if we take it from the "Twelve Articles," what is by far more decisive is the access to land for hunting, fishing, and collecting wood, and the demands for fair taxes and rents, and for the abolition of the "death clause" (by which a widow would lose her husband's right to the land upon his death). It was a cry for a vital space in a late feudal society. Luther, who was first called upon by the peasants themselves as a witness of their cause, later supported the repression launched against them. And the reason, in the Reformer's view, is that competencies were being violated. The Word of God was recruited to legislate over "matters for the lawyers to discuss."[1] Implicitly recognizing the justice of the peasants' claims, Luther even counseled them to suffer martyrdom. The miner's son would not recognize in the peasants' protest the struggle, indeed also a religious one, to preserve and conquer the basic means of life and work. It was a protest against the world and its injustices for the right of labor and the vital space that ensured it.[2] The peasants' demands were not a "class struggle": their revolt was against the world as it stood. Luther's insistence on keeping competencies apart has led both to some of the sharpest criticisms he has ever received[3] and to praise for an austere modern realism that could have prevented the bloodshed.[4]

A second front of the Reformation movement was connected with the emergence of financial capitalism and the practice of usury. Here the Reformation took some ambiguous positions in relation to the official stance of the late-medieval Roman Catholic Church. If Calvin condoned usury within certain interest restrictions, the Roman theologians had a legalistic interpretation of Aristotle's notion of the sterility of money, but creatively reinterpreted it to justify interest on the basis of the risk of the

1. WA 18:337.13-4; LW 46:39.

2. Commenting on the characteristics of peasants' revolts as a protest, not against a class, but against the whole "world," Octavio Ianni, *Dialética e Capitalismo* (Petrópolis: Vozes, 1988), 110, says: "the struggle for land is always also a struggle for the preservation, conquest . . . of a mode of living and working." See also Octavio Paz, *Posdata* (Mexico: Siglo XXI, 1970), 87-92.

3. See Ernst Bloch, *Thomas Münzer als Theologe der Revolution* (Berlin: Aufbau, 1960).

4. Eduardo Hoornaert, "Matim Lutero: Um Teólogo que Pensa a Partir do Povo," in *Reflexões em Torno de Lutero*, ed. Martin N. Dreher (São Leopoldo: Sinodal, 1984), 9-17.

lender and for the maintenance of banking institutions.[5] But Luther, even if not thoroughly consistent, would argue theologically against the exploitation of the poor that usury caused. Accused of revealing only a profound frustration[6] or producing "occasional explosions of a capricious volcano,"[7] the Reformer has indeed revealed a theological concern and rage against the oppression caused by usurers.[8] Usurers are robbers of the means for the sustenance of life, for honoring labor and family. Here Luther's voice in defense of the created goodness of this order is emphatically affirmed.

These two fronts are complemented by a third one, in which the Reformation was most successful and in which Luther had a particularly important role to play. He was foremost the reformer of the church in its earthly (!) task of being an instrument of the Word of God. If the first front represented a cry for a vital space and the second a cry for just social and economic relations for the sustenance of life, the third opened space in the search for a viable realm of communication between the Word of God and the language(s) of the people to whom, in whom, and through whom the Word communes. In what follows I am concerned to explore the main characteristics of this third front.

A Theological Frame

The Reformation movement and particularly Luther were concerned with the re-creation of a language capable of giving voice to the voiceless, of turning unarticulated utterances into meaning, of constituting knowledge for empowerment, because the Word communicates in the medium of language(s). Between the divine utterance of the addressed Word of God and the language of the people we find the cultural equivalent of the dis-

5. See Ronald Preston, *Religion and the Ambiguities of Capitalism* (London: SCM, 1991), 138-39. The classic treatment of this issue is still Benjamin Nelson, *The Idea of Usury* (Princeton: Princeton University Press, 1949).

6. Nelson, *The Idea of Usury,* 46.

7. The expression is R. H. Tawney's, cited in Preston, *Religion,* 141.

8. I have argued elsewhere that there is a consistent theological argument in the apparent illogical outbursts in Luther's relation to usury. "Luther and Liberation," *Dialog* 25 (1986): 51-58; and "Die neue Haut der unsichtbaren Schlange: Die theologische Grundlage ökonomischer Abhängigkeit," *Weltmission heute* 12 (1992): 9-28.

tinctively Lutheran christological doctrine of *communicatio idiomatum* (the "communication of attributes") in all its three classical genres *(idiomaticum, apotelesmaticum,* and *majestaticum).*[9] What the *communicatio idiomatum* means for Christology parallels the relationship between the Word and language: the semantics of the Word are meaningful in the vernacular *(genus idiomaticum);* the effective deeds of the Word are performed in language *(genus apotelesmaticum),* and the defiled character of human language and communication is capable of the sublime Word *(genus majestaticum).*

Luther's understanding of language puts into practice his doctrine of the person of Christ, including the disputes over the Lord's Supper. This is the practice of the *ecclesia,* this earthly order of creation that is the space for a "marvelous exchange" to take place. This celebrated christological axiom[10] finds its linguistic equivalent in his argumentation during an academic disputation in 1537: "All words are made new when they are transferred from their own to another [semantic] context."[11] The new language *(nova lingua)* is the result of this transference; it is not an epiphany. And where this happens, there is the church *(ubi verbum, ibi ecclesia).* This is what grounds Luther's understanding of the church as the creature of the Word.[12] For Luther, the Word cannot exist without the people of God, and neither can the people of God exist without the Word of God.[13] To give it a sharp focus: the question of language in Luther is ultimately about the communication of the Word, and therefore also with the body of the communicative language hosting it. Therefore, to separate the Word of God from the vernacular, or to have a theology of the Word apart from human communication, is a form of linguistic Nestorianism.

9. On the *communicatio idiomatum* in general, see BC, 622 n. 268. The analogous relationship between Luther's Christology and his understanding of language has been well presented by Johann Anselm Steiger, "The *Communicatio Idiomatum* as the Axle and Motor of Luther's Theology," *Lutheran Quarterly* 14 (2000): 144-48. A similar argument in connection with the sacramental dispute with Zwingli is presented by Thomas Wabel, *Sprache als Grenze in Luthers theologischer Hermeneutik und Wittgensteins Sprachphilosophie* (Berlin: De Gruyter, 1998), 257-73.

10. *Mirabilis mutacio.* WA 39I:435.11.

11. *Omnia vocabula fiunt nova, quando e suo foro in alienum transferuntur.* WA 39I:231.1-3.

12. WA 2:430.6-7: *Ecclesia enim creatura est Evangelii.*

13. See WA 50:657-61.

The analogy can be carried further. The limits of one's language are not an impediment to the revelation of the Word, just as the corruption of the flesh does not prevent it from receiving the infinite. However, the attempt to make the flesh worthy before it can host the divine is comparable to the cleansing of language from its vernacular "transgressions" in order to make it worthy of the Word. It is no wonder that Luther would find in the contempt shown toward the base vernacular (including his own!) the same attitude as he found in his own monastic experience of trying to become worthy of divine righteousness. It is therefore in language and its limits that we will find also Luther's appreciation of the glory dwelling in the frailty of the flesh.

Conversely, it is in the inability to use one's language or the active suppression of its validity as a vehicle of the Word that Luther would find a correlation to clericalism's purported ontological difference between those specially called *(vocati)* and the laity. The result is Luther's "engaged literature,"[14] which is in itself a practice of fighting for language in the very midst of itself: ". . . (so it follows) in the midst of common language we have been battling," as Luther wrote in a letter to Spalatin early in 1519.[15] And the effects of this struggle reverberate in Luther's own text, producing rippling effects that he is quite aware of. In comparing his own language to Melanchthon's, he praises the latter's style, logic, and clarity, which he felt exceeded his own. But then he concludes: "I have been born to take up an open fight with the mob and devils, therefore my books are much more tempestuous and belligerent [than Melanchthon's]."[16] It is in the midst of the freedom of language that Luther fights against the oppression of language, against its subjection.

In the axis between language and oppression some of the most significant contributions of Luther for the Reformation movement can be located. And this finally encompasses all his theology. I will suggest in what follows that for Luther language is the medium between the constitution of the self *(coram meipso)* and the relation to the Other *(coram Deo),* both individually and collectively. Language is what allows one to be placed outside of oneself *(extra se),* to use the image of Luther's eccentric anthropol-

14. Birgit Stolt, *Studien zu Luthers Freihitstraktat* (Stockholm: Almqvist & Wiksell, 1969), 139.

15. . . . *mixtim (ut fit) vernacula lingua digladiabamur.* WA Br 1:301.16-17.

16. WA 30II:68-69.

ogy.[17] For Luther, the "genius of languages" *(die Art der Sprachen)*[18] is authenticated in its very use by the "common person."[19]

In the following paragraphs I will argue that there was an incisive linguistic gesture in Luther's theology that intensively focused on the language of the people, offering the people a way of finding their relationship to God, to everyday life, and to themselves. Such a gesture corresponded to his own anticlericalism and is not to be seen as an idiosyncratic peculiarity. This linguistic gesture brought about the liberation from institutional mediations that controlled the access to the sacred, to life and to the people. In Luther's case, such liberation happened through the relativizing of institutional orders encoded in linguistic systems and their regimes of truth controlled by the academia and its philosophy, by the courtroom and its jurisprudence, by politics and its legislations, by the market and its economy, and by the church and its "spirituality."

On Language and Oppression

In Luther's linguistic move we find a compelling illustration of the liberating aspects of the way the Reformation situated our relationship to the world and to God, as well as its impact in distinct semantic realms entailing different rules. Such insight allowed Luther to recognize that to be heard anew the Word also needed to move not only vertically on the relation between God and the world, but also horizontally through different semantic fields of everyday life, from philosophy to the market, from the pulpit to politics, from the kitchen to the court, from the carnival to the children's playground.[20] To transgress these linguistic realms and the limits of their distinct uniqueness and relative legitimacy — to themselves as well as to the Word — destabilized the grip of power held by the regimes of

17. Using Luther's terms, the other two foci of the Reformation movement could be subsumed accordingly under his understanding of the relations *coram mundo* and *coram hominibus.* See Gerhard Ebeling, *Luther: An Introduction to His Thought,* trans. R. A. Wilson (Philadelphia: Fortress, 1970), 198-200.

18. WA 18:155.4-5; LW 40:165.

19. WA 18:154.20-21; LW 40:164.

20. The prefiguring of Wittgenstein's theory of language games is well explored in Wabel, *Sprache als Grenze in Luthers theologischer Hermeneutik und Wittgensteins Sprachphilosophie.*

truth of the day and the disciplinary confines in which each of them was secluded.

Anders Nygren has argued that to understand the uniqueness of Luther one needs to recognize "different motif contexts" that operate in his discourse, changing meaning when a word moves from one context to another.[21] This "semantic shift"[22] is now well recognized when it pertains to the relationship between theology and philosophy. My argument here is that such semantic displacements do not pertain only to the relation between the spiritual and the earthly regimes, but apply as well to "lateral" semantic shifts in which words from diverse everyday-life realms break in and create unexpected meaning. And such lateral semantic moves free a given context of meaning to entertain newness. And in this liberation offered by the unexpected meaning that breaks in, Luther also saw the space for the incursion of the Word of God. It is in the disruption caused by these semantic displacements that space is opened for the formation of what Luther called a "new language" *(nova lingua)* shaped by the grammar of the Spirit.

The surprise of another word, different than those legislated by the regimes of truth that norm the church, the state, the economy, and the household, breaking into these domains, is for Luther an eschatological event. Within the limits of one's regime there is the promise of novelty. Thus the text of "A Mighty Fortress Is Our God": "Let this world's tyrant rage; In battle we'll engage! His might is doomed to fail; God's judgment must prevail! One little word subdues him."[23] For Luther this battle with the world is also the strife of words *(pugna verborum)* for the sake of communication, for the sake of allowing the Word to be uttered. Where this does not happen, there does "this world's tyrant rage," the tyrant who imposes his language and thus sets limits to the world, framing it and keeping the Word at bay in well-regulated and disciplined domains. How does this

21. Anders Nygren, *Meaning and Method* (Philadelphia: Fortress, 1972), 368. Nygren built his case on Wittgenstein's "language games" metaphor, which he renders as "context for meaning" (243-64). A pertinent analysis of the construction of meaning within a semantic domain is offered by Dennis Bielfeldt, "Luther on Language," *Lutheran Quarterly* 16 (2002): 195-220.

22. The expression is found in Dennis Bielfeldt, "Luther, Metaphor, and Theological Language," *Modern Theology* 6, no. 2 (1990): 123.

23. *Lutheran Book of Worship,* hymn 269, trans. Catherine Winkworth.

happen? The following digression with the help of some illustrations will etch the contours of the interface between language and oppression.

In a study of popular culture in Brazil, José de Souza Martins pointed to a regular phenomenon that affects subaltern groups in society, alienating them from official language. "Metaphor, occultation, dissimulation, silence, remain as the language that documents the persistence of the same violence that caused its origin . . . in the language of the oppressor."[24] The encoded or canonical official language of hegemonic institutions is not only an instrument for the communication of power, but it is itself the exercise of power that works by depriving other voices of legitimacy. That is the end of communication, the end of conversation, and the transformation of language into a tool of power and control. The end of a conversation always implies the silencing of the other voice. Domination and oppression are, therefore, always constituted in and by the language of the one who dominates. In this sense the imposition of a linguistic system indicates the very demise of the actuality of language, the suppression of the language of a group, the silencing and dissembling of the knowledge of the other. This is why resistance is manifested in the reverse side of language: in occultation, in jest, in silence, in curse, in whispering, or in cries. These are the limiting fields in which language is at the same time suppressed but in its nonactuality, in silence and dissimulation, the emergent other voice, heteroglossy, is documented first by the very fact of its absence. But it is an exclamatory silence!

In Shakespeare's dialogue between Prospero, the conqueror, and Caliban, the native, in *The Tempest,* Caliban says:

> You taught me language; and my profit on't
> Is, I know how to curse; the red plague rid you,
> For learning me your language![25]

Between official language — the language that imposes power and defines knowledge — and the dissimulated languages of those who survive and resist in dissemblance and silence, there is a cleft that the institutions ignore, or will suppress. Mary Douglas's oft-quoted remark that "every society is

24. José de Souza Martins, *Caminhada no Chão da Noite* (São Paulo: Huicitec, 1989), 116-17.

25. *The Tempest,* 1.2.

fragile in its margin" is right on target in showing that the margin is not the fragile side of a society, but is where the fragility of any society manifests itself. This is why any instituted society needs to hide its margin, to prevent it from becoming visible. And it becomes visible by establishing its own word, by naming its world. The other voice has to be suppressed because it implies the emergence of a new world.

In the prologue to the *Gramática Castellana* of Antonio Nebrija, published in 1492 (the year of the Spanish conquest of the New World when the boy Martin Luther was attending school in Mansfeld) and dedicated to the Spanish queen Isabella, we read the following: "Language has always accompanied domination . . . and since Your Majesty has imposed your yoke to a number of barbarian peoples and nations of different languages, in consequence of their defeat, they would be obliged to receive the laws that the winner imposes to the defeated, and then, the latter could gain the knowledge of them [the laws] through my grammar."[26] Language, in its formal sense, has not always accompanied domination, but when it did — and here Nebrija is right — the consequence of domination was the destruction of the very soul of a people, of the possibility of naming the world.

Throughout history the demand for a language has been intrinsically linked to the human search for self-determination and open communication. The silencing of language is a demonic phenomenon.[27] It deprives the subject from emerging and leaves her or him under the control of alien forces. Antonio Vieira, Jesuit missionary in Brazil and one of the most acclaimed preachers of the seventeenth century, gave us a poignant description of the relationship between language and oppression.

The incapability of expressing itself was the situation of Brazil and the main cause of its ills. This is the reason why nothing was more difficult for Christ than to heal a possessed dumb. The worst crisis faced by Brazil during its illness was the silencing of its speech.[28] Even when not mentioning the exegetical grounds for his remark (probably Mark 9:17-29), Vieira

26. In Ruggiero Romano, *Os Mecanismos da Conquista Colonial* (São Paulo: Perspectiva, 1973), 79. Nebrija's *Gramática* is regarded as the first modern grammar produced in the Western world.

27. See my article "Idols and Demons: On Discerning the Spirits," *Dialog* 41 (2002): 9-15.

28. See "Apresentação," *Estudos Teológicos* 31, no. 2 (1991): 119-20.

was right on the meaning of Jesus' exorcisms. In almost all cases, demonic possession in the New Testament is associated with the incapability of a person to utter an authentic word; either the demon speaks through the person, or the person stutters, or the possessed person is dumb. As much as language provides the limits of one's world (Wittgenstein)[29] or, conversely, provides a home for being (Heidegger),[30] its silencing or suppression is a cipher that allows for the possibility of recognizing the limits of one's world. The silencing of a speech documents and reveals (indeed, *sub contraria specie*) the powers of domination. But it is at this very limit that the experience of heteroglossy, the insurrection of another language that attests to another world, announces itself.

The Insurrection of the Vernacular

There is no great historical event that is not associated with language. The Reformation movement owes its historical impact to the way in which it was able to incorporate the language of the people into its political, religious, and cultural program, expanding it, giving it a dynamic formation and a public character.

It has frequently been stressed that the Reformation's effectiveness cannot be dissociated from the Renaissance's renewal of the classic humanist values. Marked by a return to the classical values of the Western world, the Renaissance represented an elitist move toward the rebirth of classicism within a medieval and feudal world entangled by institutional constraints administered by the church and the empire, and by the emergent powerful financial institutions. There is hardly anything popular about all this. But in an ironic way the Renaissance also contributed to the insurgence of the "common folk"[31] onto the stage that the Reformation movement also helped to shape, and endowed it with a variegated choreography.

29. Ludwig Wittgenstein, *Tractatus Logico-Philosophicus* (London: Routledge, 1981), 148 (5.6: *Die Grenzen meiner Sprache bedeuten die Grenzen meiner Welt*).

30. Martin Heidegger, *Existence and Being* (Chicago: Gateway, 1949), 276: ". . . it is only language that affords the very possibility of standing in the openness of the existent. Only where there is language, is there world."

31. For the role of popular imagery in the theology of the Reformation, see R. W. Scribner, *For the Sake of Simple Folk* (Cambridge: Cambridge University Press, 1981).

As Mikhail Bakhtin demonstrated well in his study of Rabelais,[32] the Middle Ages at the dawn of the Renaissance was divided by the split between popular, national languages and medieval Latin — in his terms, between popular and official language. Medieval Latin attempted to adjust as much as it could to the regional linguistic variations, resulting in a feeble cosmetic attempt at "official contextualization" (certainly a contradiction in terms). The Renaissance's renewal brought back a classic, Ciceronian Latin that had the merit of exposing the syncretistic efforts of corrupt medieval Latin by manifesting its very limits and its deformed face; it had failed to give voice to the people, to allow for heteroglossy, for different voices to enter the conversation. In the words of Bakhtin, "the very desire that the Renaissance had of reestablishing Latin in its antique and classic purity turned it into a dead language." At the same time, it also unmasked the ideological trick of Latin alchemists eager to transform it into a workable everyday language. "The Latin of Cicero" — Bakhtin continues — "illuminated the true character of medieval Latin, its true face, that people saw practically for the first time: until then they had their language (the medieval Latin), without perceiving its deformed and limited face."[33]

The Renaissance opened and revealed the cleft between the two cultures, the popular and the official, a cleft somehow disguised by medieval Latin. Thus from the end of the fifteenth century to the beginning of the sixteenth was marked by this twofold phenomenon: the emergence of classic humanism alongside the dissemination of popular vernacular literature and folk legends. "Humanism," observed Franz Lau, "was the discoverer not only of the antique languages, but also of the language of the people."[34] If the first was an appeal to the past and the recovery of classic human values for the construction of the present, the second was an invocation of the present and the affirmation of nationhood for the reconstruction of the past. In this way, as A. G. Dickens pointed out, they both acted as "mid-wives of the Lutheran Reformation."[35]

The twofold process is never so simultaneous and interconnected as

32. Mikhail Bakhtin, *A Cultura Popular na Idade Média e no Renascimento: O Contexto de François Rabelais* (São Paulo: Huicitec, 1987).

33. Bakhtin, *Cultura Popular,* 411.

34. Franz Lau, *Luther* (Berlin: De Gruyter, 1959), 90.

35. A. G. Dickens, *The German Nation and Martin Luther* (Glasgow: Fontana, 1976), 21-22.

in the humanist emphasis on the biblical languages together with the reemergence of popular myths and folk legends. The recovery of particular myths to sustain the national identity was even read into the biblical text, as with the story of Tuisco (Teutsch), a legendary postdiluvial offspring of Noah, conceived to be the founding hero of Germany.[36] In another myth that linked the popular with the biblical past, we have the story that before "tongues became diversified at the tower of Babel, the human race had spoken German."[37]

If every nation, as Octavio Paz often remarked, is based upon a myth, it was the reconstruction of the German mythology that gave voice and identity to the people, that gave them a language. "Through the myths," observes Paz, "each man and woman of the group felt part of the totality of a natural and supernatural time, for all the dead were also members of the tribe."[38]

Opposing Germany to France (where people and culture would presumably have an original identity), Nietzsche regarded the Reformation as the moment in which a primordial power inhabiting an abyss beneath cultural life came forth and surfaced. Identity became for a moment visible. Luther embodied this affirmation and was its emblematic figure. He was for Nietzsche the one "to whom we shall be indebted for the rebirth of the German myth."[39] And this was for Nietzsche the myth of the people and not of the empire.

In this context the Reformation movement began to build its own program. Far from being unified, it was nonetheless able to give expression (even if for a short period before it became itself institutionalized) to the imagination of a people, long suppressed by the very limits imposed by the prevailing institutions that through language established the limits of the world (among them, the church). Concealed in an array of dialects, the dissimulated languages have their power and knowledge submersed in the strict limits of contexts of meaning closed to otherness.

The most revealing face of the emergence of the vernacular along with myths and folk legends that it brought to light was the remarkable development of the publication of leaflets and pamphlets *(Flugschriften)*.

36. Dickens, *The German Nation,* 23-24.

37. Dickens, *The German Nation,* 16.

38. Octavio Paz, *La otra voz* (Barcelona: Seix Barral, 1990), 72.

39. Friedrich Nietzsche, *The Birth of Tragedy and the Case of Wagner* (New York: Vintage, 1967), 136-37.

The publication of leaflets and pamphlets was known before the Reformation. It was the literature of the masses, breaking with the pattern of aristocratic book production, and was greatly facilitated by the printing press.[40] Yet the early years of the Reformation in particular were marked by an astonishing increase in the production of pamphlets. Between 1518 and 1525 the number of pamphlets published in Germany increased sixfold.[41] Latin continued to be used as a language also for the larger public, but the radically new phenomenon was the massive output of German texts.[42] These were the years of pamphleteering. But not only was this literature aimed at the larger public; Martin Arnold has pointed to a new phenomenon, not to be found in the years before 1523: people belonging to the working class, including women, could be counted as authors in a business previously dominated by the clergy.[43]

In this context Luther made a major contribution, being quite conscious of his own intentions even when his pamphleteering practice led him to be discredited and held with suspicion, as we can read in the opening paragraphs of the *Treatise on Good Works:* "And although I know full well and hear every day that many people think little of me and say that I only write little pamphlets and sermons in German for the uneducated laity, I do not let that stop me. . . . I believe that if I were of a mind to write big books of their kind, I could perhaps, with God's help, do it more readily than they could write my kind of little discourse."[44] But for Luther the pamphleteering does not mean simply the selection of the public to whom the text is addressed. Against Karlstadt he argued that knowledge should not be limited to the confinement of a dissimulated language of a group unable to articulate itself efficaciously against the hegemonic powers.[45] In his introduction to the German Mass he laments what has happened to the Bohemian Waldensians who ended up "hiding their faith in their own language to such a degree of not being able any longer to speak to anyone in a clear way."[46] In his defense of public education the emphasis

40. Dickens, *The German Nation,* 105. See also Martin Arnold, *Handwerker als theologische Schriftsteller* (Göttingen: Vandenhoeck & Ruprecht, 1990), 43.

41. Arnold, *Handwerker,* 38-41; Dickens, *The German Nation,* 106.

42. Dickens, *The German Nation,* 46.

43. Arnold, *Handwerker,* 43-44, 327.

44. WA 6:203.5-14; LW 44:22.

45. Dickens, *The German Nation,* 33.

46. WA 19:74.13-16; LW 53:63.

on the instruction of biblical languages was not intended as moving away from Latin (which he did regard a great poetic language), but as an enhancement of knowledge for the benefit of the youth among whom he (following in this Erasmus) included women, who were traditionally marginalized from formal education (with the exception of those who through religious orders could pursue intellectual endeavors).[47]

Language as Communication

The importance of Luther for the normative nature of the German language is widely recognized and celebrated. However, even for those who assess Luther's view of language as an external expression of an existential language-event (as in Gerhard Ebeling) or for those who follow a cultural-linguistic interpretation (as in George Lindbeck), little attention has been given to the importance of language as the articulation of popular aspirations and desires in the semantically dynamic historical context of late-medieval Europe. These two assessments of Luther's use of language, exemplified by Ebeling and Lindbeck, have a history in linguistic theory that reaches back a few centuries but finds its origin in the late-medieval opposition between realism and nominalism. While medieval realism regarded language as the formal principle that constituted reality as such, nominalism approached it as a functional expression of the world as such. In modern linguistic theory, we find it for example in the distinction that Wilhelm von Humboldt suggested between seeing language either as *ergon* (a work) or as *energeia* (an activity). Humboldt favored a view that language is "the continual intellectual effort to make the articulated sound capable of expressing thought."[48] Thus, for him, *energeia* (and not *ergon*) was the true expression of the nature and craft of language. Language in this case is the outer hardened crust of an inner vitality. The locus of truth that ought to

47. Else Marie Wiberg Pedersen, "Can God Speak the Vernacular? On Beatrice of Nazareth's Flemish Exposition of the Love for God," in *The Vernacular Spirit: Essays on Medieval Religious Literature,* ed. Renate Blumenfeld-Kosinski, Duncan Robertson, and Nancy Warren (New York: Palgrave, 2002), 185-208, notes the remarkable use of the vernacular as a theological language in the writing of religious women three centuries before the Reformation, suggesting it as a gesture that prefigures the Reformation itself.

48. Quoted in Richard Morse, *New World Soundings* (Baltimore: Johns Hopkins University Press, 1989), 12.

be sought is the inner experience out of which the external expression ensues.

This existentialist and expressivist interpretation of language is a position that in the contemporary research on theological language has been associated with the name of Gerhard Ebeling and has had a significant impact on all those who followed his lead in Luther research. For Ebeling, "the authority to use the language of faith is a matter of experience. Language arises only from experience."[49] Conversely what can be regarded as meaningful at the semantic level must be traced back and reconstituted as a subjective experience. Experience is what alone authenticates language.

The opposite view was inspired in modern times by the structural approach to language as presented in Ferdinand Saussure's distinction between *langue* and *parole,* analogous to Humboldt's *ergon* and *energeia.* For Saussure *langue* represented a structurally stable and formative set of rules that was rather the cause and not the effect of experience, while *parole* was regarded as particular, even idiosyncratic, deviations from the norm. Here the external has priority over the internal. George Lindbeck, working with the distinction between a linguistic-cultural model (language as *ergon*) and an experiential-expressive model (language as *energeia*), says "that the former reverses the relation of the inner and the outer. Instead of deriving external features of religious language from inner experience, it is inner experiences which are viewed as derivative."[50] Grammar conditions and controls semantics; meaning presupposes assent to abiding rules.[51]

Are we bound to these two options for our reading of Luther's own view of language? *Tertium non datur* on this alternative? In relation to the contextual situation of Luther's time and the problems issuing from the

49. Gerhard Ebeling, *Introduction to a Theological Theory of Language* (Philadelphia: Fortress, 1973), 206. See also his distinction between "potentiality" and "act" (90): "even the most perfect distillation of a language into vocabulary and grammar must ultimately concede victory . . . to the living and concrete use of language."

50. George Lindbeck, *The Nature of Doctrine* (Philadelphia: Westminster, 1984), 34.

51. Lindbeck, *The Nature of Doctrine,* 17-18. This dual option has certainly a significant genealogy of analogical binarisms in Christian theology, which can be traced back to Paul's distinction between "letter" and "spirit," the medieval opposition between "love" (as *exemplum*) and "work" (as *sacramentum*), and in the Protestant debate between the orthodox defense of the *fides quae* and the Pietist case for the *fides qua,* and other distinctions more vaguely related. What characterizes the present debate is that it is applied to religious language and doctrine as such.

confrontation between official languages and their regimes of truth, on the one hand, and the popular insurgence of heteroglossic "transgression," on the other, either of the options fails to help. The experiential approach is incapable of accounting for the power relation in the confrontation among languages, especially between popular and official usages. It will have to regard some of the boorish expressions in Luther's parlance as idiosyncratic oddities. The cultural structural approach, in its turn, detects well the process of restoration of doctrine as a foundational grammar buried in cultural misrepresentations, official or popular, but is unable to recognize the dynamic nature of language and the displacements of meaning it produces by moving through different semantic fields.

I would like to suggest an alternative approach, following an insight of Mikhail Bakhtin in his reactions against both the subjectivist experiential position that views language as the objective expression of a subjective drive or experience *(energeia)* and the cultural-linguistic analysis that focuses on the codified norms of linguistic systems *(ergon)*. Criticizing the opposition between spontaneous and formal language that is presupposed in both schools respectively, Bakhtin suggested that what is at stake is communication, not language as such. And in communication one needs to focus on the emergence of utterances under the contextual conditions within which they appear. An utterance "will have a meaning different than it would have under any other conditions; all utterances are heteroglot, in that they are functions of a matrix of forces practically impossible to recoup, and therefore impossible to resolve."[52]

What Bakhtin is looking for in language is neither its systemic, grammatical character nor the experiential well out of which it springs, but precisely the emergence of voices that are other than the system (yet do appear at the surface of language). These voices, these appearances, disturb and institute meaning *in loco*. However, this meaning is created because of the shock issuing from the clash among different semantic fields and not as a new spontaneous creation. This is what his understanding of heteroglossy amounts to: "Heteroglossia is as close a conceptualization as is possible of that locus where centripetal and centrifugal forces collide; as such it is that which a systematic linguistics must always suppress."[53] Bakhtin's concern

52. Mikhail M. Bakhtin, *The Dialogic Imagination* (Austin: University of Texas Press, 1982), 428.

53. Bakhtin, *The Dialogic Imagination*, 428.

is with the insurrection of language. Language is not the formal principle of reality or an outer manifestation of inner experience; it neither structures reality nor is it a husk of its inner being. Language is always a function of communication; it is the attempt to keep in tension the relation between the heteronomy of linguistic rules and norms that want to institute reality (Bakhtin's "centripetal forces") and the autonomous drive toward "reinventing" it ("centrifugal forces"). Communication emerges neither when the linguistic forms break down nor when we just pour our hearts out. If language is about communication, then language fulfills its purpose when there is a transgression of a restricted semantic domain, a "collision . . . of senses."[54] In the words of Bakhtin: "Thus at any given moment of its historical existence, language is heteroglot from top to bottom: it represents the co-existence of socio-ideological contradictions between the present and the past, between differing epochs of the past, between different socio-ideological groups in the present, between tendencies, schools, circles and so forth."[55]

In other words, communication happens in and through language not because people are united under an Esperanto or share the same experiences; it happens unexpectedly at the moment when one listens to another's language and wonders: "How is it that we understand it?" (Acts 2:7-8). Communication is always a linguistic surprise. What makes sense is first something unheard of. As an event of communication, "language . . . lies on the borderline between oneself and the other. The word in language is half between oneself and the other. The word in language is half someone else's. . . . it exists in other people's mouths, in other people's contexts, serving other people's intentions: it is from there that one must take the word and make it one's own."[56]

Apart from the reference to the people's mouth, which is also Luther's way of portraying language, it is important to realize that communication implies a transgression of confined semantic domains, a moving of utterances from one realm to another. This lies at the very core of Luther's above-mentioned comment: "All words are made new when they are transferred from their own to another [semantic] context."[57] Different

54. Bielfeldt, "Luther, Metaphor," 127.

55. Bielfeldt, "Luther, Metaphor," 291.

56. Bielfeldt, "Luther, Metaphor," 293-94.

57. *Omnia vocabula fiunt nova, quando e suo foro in alienum transferuntur.* WA

from "poetry," from the creation of language (which is still precommunicative),[58] linguistic communication happens not in creation of language but in this transgressive movement across semantic domains.[59]

Why Luther? "Laughing at the Devil"

Nietzsche defined the Reformation movement as the stupendous moment of the stirring of primordial powers underneath a cultural shell.[60] Although this was not the work of Luther alone, he became its emblematic figure. This emblematic character of Luther — who, however, claimed he did not want to be a master[61] — has all to do with this mixture of humanist sophistication, erudition, and piety blended together with grotesque profanity in style. In a certain way, he represented and unified the very contradictions of the cultural context of the time. And with this he was able to bridge the cleft that separated the heart of the people from the sterile official culture, creating what Bakhtin called the locus of collision. In the words of Agnes Heller: "Luther essentially differed from all previous

---

39I:231.1-3 (A.I). The context of the discussion is the meaning of "works" when used *coram Deo* or *coram mundo.*

58. This is why poetry, strictly speaking, cannot be translated. It is precommunicative but not anticommunicative. It is to communication what bricks are to a building. See Bakhtin, *The Dialogic Imagination,* 296-98.

59. The difficulty of maintaining the dialectical relationship and a steady focus on the locus of collision (Bakhtin) between linguistic system and language event will reveal also the same conservative trends in Luther's understanding of institutions. While the Reformer recognized the relative character of institutions, he was not yet able to regard them as transient. This ambiguity in the relation to institutions is the same that will show itself in the doctrine of the inspiration of the Scriptures where the oscillation between inerrancy and hermeneutics remains unresolved. See Miikka Ruokanen, *Doctrina Divinitus Inspirata: Martin Luther's Position in the Ecumenical Problem of Biblical Inspiration* (Helsinki: Vammala, 1985). For an appraisal of Luther's disregard for institutions, see Sheldon S. Wolin, *Politics and Vision* (Boston: Little, Brown, 1960), 162-64. But the ambiguity of Luther's early "modern" attitude yet still caught in a medieval world is classically presented by Ernst Troeltsch, *Protestantism and Progress* (Boston: Beacon Press, 1958). See also my article "'The Third Bank of the River': Thoughts on Justification and Justice," in *Justification and Justice,* ed. Viggo Mortensen (Geneva: LWF, 1992).

60. Nietzsche, *The Birth of Tragedy,* 136.

61. WA 8:685.14; LW 45:71.

renewers of religion, not because he was oriented toward the world (many others had been as well), but because the notion of election had no part in his ideology and practice . . . he was a man un-shamed of his particularity, unlike St Augustine; on the contrary, he accepted it."[62]

Luther could be content in calling the German people fools or himself a barbarian or a sack of worms or a prideful idiot, and so forth. Some of these expressions could be taken as typical of medieval penitential utterances and practices if it were not for the obvious ironic sense embedded in them. The point is not so much humility (false or not) as it is a carnival-like attitude toward everything.[63] He showed the fearlessness of a fool, but in everyday life and not in the midst of a feast when jest and satire were tolerated and even expected. With his language, Luther brought the carnival to academia, to the pulpit, to the square, breaking down the disciplined frontiers in which these utterances were allowed. He could as much laugh at Melanchthon's dedication to astrology (still a respected discipline, not clearly distinguished from astronomy), saying that he would profit more sitting by a keg of beer, as he could show his rage against his enemies, calling them apostles of the devil or simple asses. In fact, he regarded himself to be even more foolish in believing he could teach them anything.

Such remarks can be multiplied.[64] The point, however, is not to show idiosyncrasies in Luther's personality, but to indicate that his burlesque attitude is to be taken as a central characteristic of his own theological practice and not an occasional deviation. A world divided between the official pomp of the instituted language of the church and the grotesque humor of the lower strata of society that provided the motifs for the carnivals was combined by Luther's jests and theological subtleties. Boorish and burlesque motifs invaded the controlled realm of theological discourse. If we take even the most serious and somber of Luther's texts (those in Latin, and particularly the commentaries), although the form does not reveal his

62. Agnes Heller, *Renaissance Man* (New York: Schocken, 1978), 203. Heller's comments about election and vocation not playing a role in Luther seem to be off the mark, considering the role that both had in Luther's theology. What I read Heller saying is that by leveling all callings and no longer accepting a special vocation that separated clergy from laity, he was in fact including himself among those who did not have any calling that essentially distinguished him from anyone else.

63. On Luther's scatological language see Heiko Oberman, *Luther: Man between God and the Devil* (New York: Image, 1992), 106-10.

64. Plenty of such illustrations are provided by Oberman, *Luther.*

attitudes of mockery and jest, the motifs do. The classical remarks in Luther's theology of creation about the mask or wrapping *(larva* or *involocrum)* of God[65] represent theologically a rupture with the representational attitude that prevailed in theology. The metaphor of the mask is not simply a new way of speaking about God. It broke with the medieval realism, going simultaneously beyond the parsimonious and skeptical stance of the nominalists. It touched the people's imagery in which the mask had a very concrete and popular significance, and it was not the *prosopon* of the Greek theater. To elucidate the images evoked by the mask trope in a context not distant from Luther's own, Bakhtin offers the following commentary:

> The motif of the mask . . . is full of meaning within popular culture. Masks translate the gayness of alteration and reincarnation, the happy relativity, the happy negation of identity and singleness of meaning, the negation of the stupid coincidence with oneself; the mask is the expression of transference, of the metamorphoses, of the violation of the natural frontiers. . . . the mask incarnated the principle of the life-game; it is based on a peculiar interrelation of reality and image, characteristic of the most ancient rites and performances. The complex symbolism of the mask is copious.[66]

"In every line that Luther wrote," commented Karl Holl, "it is apparent what unusual compulsion toward imagery possessed him."[67] And certainly here the word "possess" has a rather strict meaning. Luther's possession by imagery had the very character of possession, of being occupied by the imagery of popular culture, to the point of breaking linguistically with the dichotomous views of society, between the official and the popular. The burlesque in Luther's theology is what allowed the people's imagery to break into and out of the official language of ecclesial and political institutions.

65. See WA 40I:173-74; LW 26:95-96.

66. Bakhtin, *Cultura Popular,* 35. On the motif of the mask see also my article "Cross, Creation, and Ecology: The Meeting Point between the Theology of the Cross and Creation Theology in Luther," in *Concern for Creation,* by Elizabeth Bettenhausen et al. (Uppsala: Tro & Tanke, 1995), 159-68.

67. Karl Holl, *The Cultural Significance of the Reformation* (New York: Meridian, 1959), 147.

There is a technique of reversals applied ingeniously by Luther that links him with the popular burlesque of the carnivals, not however in the feast of fools, where it would be routine, but rather in the interdicted space of the pulpit, of academia, and of publications. Expressions like "God cannot be God without being first the devil" present a reversal that corresponds to this other reversal: "the devil will not be the devil before being God."[68] Such reversals are typical of the transvaluation of popular culture in the realm of the festivals, in breaking with established dominant conceptions: the fool is king; the king is fool.[69] The enraged monk said to have thrown a pot of ink at the devil would later in a libel against the duke of Braunschweig say that he is "laughing at the devils."[70]

The burlesque character of Luther's language has amused a number of commentators, and he is here and there quoted on behalf of courageous defiance. But would this not be a way of shifting the focus away from the deeper core of his burlesque, turning it into a mere idiosyncratic jest? Or else, is Luther not all too frequently submitted to a Romantic transformation of the burlesque into satire, with its negative and lugubrious humor surrendering the open laughter of the text?[71] In Luther the ambivalence of the polarities in his humorous reversals is not a reified antithesis. This brings him rather close to the grotesque with its regenerating comic attitude toward the subject matter. Bakhtin defines the grotesque as the style in which "the corporeal and material principle is perceived as universal and popular, opposed to all separation of the corporeal and material roots of the world from . . . all that has an ideal and abstract character, from all that has pretension of meaning detached and independent from earth and the body."[72]

And such is the character of Luther's remarks when he talks about (scholastic) reason, calling it a whore, or when he says that the church is the great whore *(magna peccatrix)*. To take the latter as an analytic remark on the nature of the church, as it is often done with the former on the matter of reason, makes it evident how the point is missed completely.

68. WA 31I:250.24-25; LW 14:32.

69. For examples of these reversals in popular culture, see Scribner, *Sake of Simple Folk*, 59-94.

70. WA 51:469.23; LW 41:185.

71. About the distinction between the burlesque character of the medieval popular language and its satirical reappropriation in modern Romanticism, see Bakhtin, *Cultura Popular*, 35.

72. Bakhtin, *Cultura Popular*, 17.

In the same spirit he ridicules those who separate heaven and earth as distinct sites.[73] The burlesque and even the grotesque in Luther brings forth his sensitivity toward the mentality of the people that can in life and language live with the *complexio oppositorum*, can turn the noble into the most despised and make of manure a pleasant sight. In the following quotation from the attack on the duke Henry of Braunschweig/Wolfenbüttel, entitled *Against Hanswurst*, Luther uses a German carnival figure (Hanswurst) who in the festivals carried a long leather-made sausage around his neck, wearing a colorful clownlike costume in typical farcical vulgar burlesque. And there he writes: "You should not write a book before you have heard an old sow fart; and you should then open your jaws with awe saying, 'Thank you, lovely nightingale, that is just the text for me!'"[74]

This is what I mean by the popular grotesque in Luther's language and style. While much has been said about the importance of Luther for the German language, his theological burlesque has been regarded more as an attitude of jest or contempt than as a carnival-like subversion of institutionalized values, in order to open space for the dissimulated language of the people to emerge and even to authorize it. The quote from Klopstock is frequently cited: "No one who knows what a language is can come face to face with Luther without venerating him."[75] But particularly the Romantic appraisal of Luther's language has been notorious in failing to recognize his appeal to the popular grotesque as constitutive not only of style and form but also of the very theological practice he was engaged in.

When Luther argues that "Christian theology does not start at the top, in the highest altitudes, . . . but there at the bottom, in the deepest profundity,"[76] he refers to the very core of the language he uses, to the utterly vulgar and pamphleteering character of his writings. In a style marked by the popular boor, Luther intentionally wanted his pamphlets to provide for a transgressive language through which the people could articulate their feelings and longings. It can only be understood in this locus of collision (Bakhtin) in which communication takes place.

73. WA 26:421-22; LW 37:280-81; cf. WA 49:224.30: "Quando dico: Celum celi domini, non intelligo celum situ et loco distincto terra, sed ich meine das regiment mit."

74. WA 51:561.25-28; LW 41:250.

75. Ebeling, *Luther*, 28. For the classical Romantic appraisals of Luther in the literature, see Heinrich Bornkamm, *Luther im Spiegel der deutschen Geistesgeschichte* (Heidelberg: Quelle & Meyer, 1955).

76. WA 40I:79.25-26; LW 26:30.

However, in all this, he was not only a practitioner of communication breaking through semantic domains to elicit new meanings. He was also a poet engaged in unearthing what Bakhtin called precommunicative utterances to which his hymns attest. Poetry, said Heidegger, is what "first makes language possible."[77] And this concern comes explicitly to the fore when Luther laments not having read more poetry: "How I regret now that I did not read more poets and historians, and that no one taught me them! Instead, I was obliged to read at great cost, toil, and detriment to myself, that devil's dung, the philosophers and the sophists, from which I have all to purge myself."[78]

"Look Them in the Mouth to See How They Speak"

The importance of Luther's linguistic subversion is correctly associated with his translation of the Bible. Luther was not the first to translate the Bible into German, but he was certainly the first one to make vernacular German into the normative principle for the whole translation of the Scriptures. "I don't know of any other ground," he said in reference to the validity of norms for uttering theological statements, "than the one offered by the genius of languages as God has created them."[79]

What was important in the translation of the Bible was not the effort of making the message of the Scriptures understandable, but rather of articulating the people's imagery in biblical language. Nowhere is this more clearly expressed than in his essay *On Translation.*[80] There he reacts against the attack he received for his German rendering of Romans 3:28 with the expression "only by faith." In the original Greek, the adverb "only" is not present. In beautiful examples drawn from vernacular expressions, he justifies his introduction of the adverb as necessary for the translation to be in true German and not in deceptive Latin. Accusing the papists of knowing German less than an ass, he summons all who want to judge his Bible

77. Martin Heidegger, *Existence and Being* (Chicago: Henry Regnery, 1949), 283.

78. WA 15:46.18-21; LW 45:370. Luther's poetics is a theme of itself that cannot be dealt with here. It suffices to mention that it is to communication what metaphors are to language, the disclosing of new semantic associations. See Martin Brecht, *Luther als Schriftsteller: Zeugnisse seines dichterischen Gestaltens* (Stuttgart: Calwer, 1990).

79. WA 18:155.4-5; LW 40:165.

80. WA 30II:632-46; LW 35:181-202.

translation to learn the language of the people: "We must not, like these asses, ask the Latin letters how we are to speak German; but we must ask the mother in the home, the children in the street, the common man in the market place about this, and look them in the mouth to see how to speak, and afterwards do our translation."[81]

Hegel recognized the magnitude of this effort well when he said: "for the Christians in Germany to have the book of their faith translated into their mother tongue is the greatest revolution that could happen. . . . Only when uttered in the mother tongue is something my property."[82] Even if Luther did not know the Italian play of words — *traduttore/tradittore* — that makes a translator a traitor, he certainly knew the Greek verb *epididomi,* which can mean both handing over in an act of treason or passing on the tradition (cf. Mark 14:10 and 1 Cor. 11:23, in which the same verb is used for Judas's treason and Paul's conveyance of the words that Jesus spoke at the Last Supper).

And it goes unavoidably in both ways: the translator becomes a traitor and the traitor becomes a translator. Luther claimed the latter in his defense of translating Romans 3:28.

Language is the "mirror of the heart," said Luther, quoting a popular expression.[83] But it is more and less than that. It is more because it opens a possibility for an encounter with otherness in the transference of semantic realms, as we have seen. However, it is also less, because it is also the heart's prison, the limit of one's world. There is no justification through language alone. Language only spans the space that the heart inhabits and in which it gains a profile and a mask, that joyfully reveals and answers its secrets and longings and simultaneously conceals and hides mystery. Language is

81. WA 30II:638; LW 35:190. In defense of the use of the neutral in referring to the bread as the body of Christ, Luther was not concerned in showing the literal accuracy of the neutral Greek, but pointed to the fact that this was the way a German would speak: "Nu wyr wöllen ursach sagen, Warumb Christus 'Tuto' odder 'Das' und nicht 'Der' vom Brot saget. Ynn Deutscher zungen gibts die art der sprache, das, wenn wyr auff eyn ding deuten, das fur uns ist, so nennen und deutten wyrs eyn Das, es sey sonst an yhm selbst eyn Der odder Die, alls wenn ich spreche: Das ist der man, davon ich rede, Das ist die Jungfraw, die ich meyne . . . Hier beruffe ich mich auff alle Deutscher, ob ich auch deutsch rede. Es is ye die rechte mutter sprache, und so redet der gemeyne man ynn Deutschen landen." WA 18:154.12-21; LW 40:164.

82. Georg Wilhelm Friedrich Hegel, *Werke* 20 (Frankfurt: Suhrkamp, 1971), 16-17.

83. WA 11:408-16; LW 29:305-14.

the earthly stuff with which the ecclesial regime conveys and conceals the presence of the Word in a similar way as equity *(Billigkeit)* does for the economy, and reason for the political regime. These three — reason in *politia*, equity in *oeconomia*, and language in *ecclesia* — are the vortexes in and through which God's justification can be both revealed and hidden in the midst of the stations of life we journey through. As such they form the matrix in which Christ's parousia, the eschatological moment, announces itself.

Luther's criticism of medieval realism (language as the formal principle of reality) brought him closer to nominalism, language as the arbitrary signifying accident of reality itself. However, he would not stay attached to nominalism either. He went beyond, envisioning language and particularly the vernacular as the score for the inscription of the Spirit's melody. Luther said it well: "The Holy Spirit has its own grammar; people who grammatically speak falsely, may, regarding the sense of it, speak the truth."[84] That means: new meanings and realities are not only given shape, but also brought about through language in its heteroglossic dynamic movement.

Such a stance in Luther's theology has been called a mixture of philosophical nominalism and theological realism.[85] Through it, Luther contributed to the liberation of the desires and aspirations of the people hidden by the instituted linguistic regimes and kept away from the public sphere. By looking people in the mouth, Luther brought the vernacular, the language of the people, out of the confinement of privacy into the public and allowed its grotesque character to invade the official realm. The carnival was brought to the pulpit and to academia. All of this was entirely consistent with his theological program of letting God be God. Although Luther's poetic search for language is inextricably linked to his theology, his main accomplishment was to free language from the confines of its disciplined domains. And in this lateral move of displacing words among and across its semantic (and heteroglossic) domains, new meanings were produced. What was kept silent and hidden could then find an utterance.

In its indebtedness to the nominalist's suprastructural view of language, the existential-expressivist school of contemporary Luther-reading

84. WA 39II:104.

85. Reijo Työrinoja, "Nova vocabula et nova lingua," in *Thesaurus Lutheri*, ed. Tuomo Mannermaa, Anja Ghiselli, and Simo Peura (Helsinki: Vammala, 1987), 221-36.

misses the point in its attempt to trace the Reformation's insight to some grounding experience; it misses that which cannot be reduced to inner experience but appears as coming from other semantic domains. Much of the Reformers' insights came not from subjective experiences surfacing at the level of language, but from transgressing semantic fields and bringing words along — and in this displacement evincing unexpected new meanings (as the example of the mask illustrates). And, in their indebtedness to medieval realism's formation of reality out of the rules and grammar of language, the cultural linguists' reading of Luther misses the fact that language and communication are heteroglot through and through, as Bakhtin insisted. For Luther, the grammar of faith is always a transgression of its own domains. Whatever is secured in language, as in the writing of a book, is simultaneously also concealed by it: "That one must write books is already a great transgression and an infirmity of the spirit."[86]

The consequence of these remarks for the study of Luther seems to be self-evident. The point is not primarily to know how the dogmatic content of Luther's theology can restore a doctrinal nucleus or to find in it a new expression of faith experience, but how the principle by which Luther articulated his theological thought offered space for the people to articulate the language concerning their relationship to themselves, to the world, and to God, beyond the confines of the regimes that controlled and regulated the proper use of language, creatively transgressing and crossing them.

While many regret the fact that Luther's theology was not more systematic, I am suggesting that the "unsystematic" nature of his writings cannot be dissociated from his theological program of "looking people in the mouth" and giving back to them, like one who lifts a mirror, authentic words, stories that raised them out of silence and dissimulation, constantly transgressing disciplinary domains. As Luther said in the presentation of his treatise *To the Christian Nobility,* "the time of silencing is over, the time to speak has come."[87]

86. WA 10I/1:627.1-2.

87. WA 6:404.11-12; LW 44:123.

CHAPTER 3

Luther on Humor

Eric W. Gritsch

Luther's humor was an integral part of his thought and life. One could say — on the basis of the literal meaning of the Latin word *humor* (derived from *umor*, "fluid" like wine) — that Luther spiked his massive production of words by mouth and pen with an abiding sense of eschatological humor. For Luther, such humor was an expression of the limitation of all human communication by the Word of God in Christ, whose first and second advent define human existence as an interim: a time anticipating final solutions but deprived of them in earthly life. Thus the Bible describes Christians as people on "the Way" (Acts 24:14) to a future "where righteousness is at home" (2 Pet. 3:13); they are "strangers and foreigners on earth" (Heb. 11:13) on the way to the eternal "city of God" (Heb. 11:16).

Nathan Söderblom (1866-1931) is the only Luther scholar who focused his work on Luther's humor, combined with melancholy.[1] He described Luther's humor as "above all the resting-point and safety valve of a tremendously tense soul" that rejected any human fashioning of "the holy." While humor created relief from anxiety, melancholy helped Luther "to dig deep into a depth where he could recognize his own nothingness and collect the light to see the helping grace; so he was strengthened to console others and become a true 'doctor consolator.'" In this sense, humor and

1. Söderblom, *Humor och Melankoh och andrà Lutherstudier* (Uppsala, 1919). German summary by Peter Katz, "Humor und Melancholie und andere Lutherstudien von Nathan Söderblom," *Luther* 5 (1923): 63-65.

melancholy became the components of a religious frame centered in an evangelical trust in God that ended "what had slumbered before in every human breast — the fear of pride *(hybris)* and its punishment. That is why humor and melancholy are peculiar, fortifying additions to the enduring, common needs of the heart." Söderblom shows how the dialectic of humor and melancholy strengthened Luther's faith and enabled him to survive such crises as the condemnation at Worms (1521), the peasant rebellion, and the encounter with Erasmus (1525).

Söderblom offers a psychohistorical review of Luther's religious disposition, linking it to mysticism and to the "history of religion" *(Religionsgeschichte)*.[2] My continuing work tries to show how Luther's eschatological humor shapes his entire thought and action.[3]

Humor in the Mean Meantime

> Wittenberg is hated by its neighbors, but the Lord [will see to it] that his time will come; then he will laugh at them, if only we have trusted in him.[4]

> Perhaps I owe my God and the world another work of folly. I intend to pay my debt honestly. And if I succeed, I shall for the time being become a court jester. And if I fail, I still have one advantage — no one need buy me a cap or put scissors to my head. It is a question of who will put the bells on whom. I must fulfill the proverb, "Whatever the world does, a monk must be in the picture, even if he has to be painted in." More than once a fool has spoken wisely, and wise men have often been arrant fools. Paul says, "He who wishes to be wise must become a

2. Söderblom did a study on the relationship between Luther's trust in God and mysticism. See "Die Ausmundung der Mystik in Luthers Gottvertrauen," in Katz, "Humor und Melancholie," 64. The title also reflects Söderblom's principal interest in the history of religion as disclosed in his major work, *The Living God* (Edinburgh: T. & T. Clark, 1933).

3. Luther's humor as a pastor has been sketched by Fritz Blanke, *Luthers Humor: Scherz und Schalk in Luthers Seelsorge* (Hamburg: Furche Verlag, 1957). See also my essay, "Der Humor bei Luther," *Luther-Jahrbuch* 63 (1996): 19-38. Another recent work is by Athina Lexutt, "Humor und Theologie bei Erasmus und Luther," *Luther* 71 (2000): 4-21.

4. WA Br 2:336; LW 48:221 (letter to John Agricola, 12 May 1521).

> fool" [1 Cor. 3:18]. Moreover, since I am not only a fool, but also a sworn doctor of Holy Scripture, I am glad for the opportunity to fulfill my doctor's oath, even in the guise of a fool.[5]

"If you want to tell people the truth, make them laugh, otherwise they will kill you" (George Bernard Shaw).

Luther expected the end of the world in his lifetime. He even consulted his own chronology, following the traditional medieval scheme of viewing world history as a succession of millennia analogous to the seven days of creation. He envisioned the six ages preceding the end-time as Adam, Noah, Abraham, David, Christ, and the pope.[6] According to Luther, his time was the meanest part of the mean meantime, marked by the struggle between Christ and the Antichrist who leads the anti-evangelical forces ranging from "enthusiasts" *(Schwärmer)* to the pope.[7] Luther exhibited a gallows humor that laughs about the final "comedy" of the Antichrist as the pious embodiment of the pope. He knew such laughter was based on bitter experiences of surviving temptations *(Anfechtungen)*, doubts, diseases, indeed rejection by one's own church. But one must look forward to the full liberation from earthly misery when Christ will return to establish his eternal kingdom. In the light of the end, one laughs.

Luther found God laughing at all the blasphemies on earth when he touched on Psalm 2:4 ("He who sits in heaven laughs") in his lengthy interpretation of the book of Genesis. "We should not think that our Father in heaven does not know these things, or that they are hidden from His eyes. He sees, but is not so swiftly moved to anger as we. He hides His wrath. He laughs a while, not only because He sees that such attempts are vain but because He grants time for forgiveness."[8] God creates an interim,

5. *To the Christian Nobility of the German Nation concerning the Reform of the Christian Estate,* 1520. WA 6:404-5; LW 44:123-24; I have used Luther's self-image as a "court jester" for a study of his life, work, and legacy. See Eric W. Gritsch, *Martin — God's Court Jester: Luther in Retrospect,* 2nd ed. (Ramsey, N.J.: Sigler Press, 1991).

6. *Computation of the Ages of the World (Supputatio Annorum Mundi),* 1541, WA 53:10-15. Details in Gritsch, *Martin,* 100.

7. This struggle is the focus of the Luther interpretation of Heiko A. Oberman, *Luther: Man between God and the Devil* (New Haven and London: Yale University Press, 1989). But his revisionist method is too one-sided. See my review in *Church History* 60 (1991): 383-85.

8. WA 40II:219; LW 12:23.

a mean time that can be quite mean; but knowing that God remains in charge and reveals his love through Christ, Christians can move on with confidence toward Christ's visible kingdom.

> We should, then, become accustomed to these storms in which a Christian must live and continuously dwell, and we should withdraw to the shadows and lay hold of the invisible. Then it will come about that we shall laugh at the fury of the Turk, the popes, tyrants, sects, heretics, and of all the adversaries of Christ's kingdom, as a comical spectacle. He who is able to do this everywhere and always is a true doctor of theology. But neither Peter nor Paul or the other Apostles could always do this. Therefore we must confess that we also are only students and not doctors in this art; although we do not even deserve the name of students since when God laughs, we are either angry or vexed.[9]

Human reason without faith, Luther discovered, is angry with a God who laughs because such a God does not seem to care for people in need; God may even enjoy punishing people in this manner. Luther also knew that human minds are annoyed about a God who laughs at enemies instead of destroying them. Human logic prefers an "either-or," something in "black and white," "visible or invisible." Only truly faithful Christians know why God derides enemies: divine laughing introduces a reprieve, a time for human repentance and forgiveness. Luther felt sad, mad, and satirically glad about his enemies because they were victims of their own desire to be like God — the enduring temptation of human beings (Gen. 3:5: "you will be like God"). At the same time, he could face personal suffering and the calamities in the world with a spiritual nonchalance, with deadpan humor, with satirical polemics, and even with foul language. Without God in Christ, Luther felt, one must admit that "all is vanity" (Eccles. 1:2). With God, one laughs.

Luther liked to describe life in the interim between the first and second advents of Christ as a carnival play that exhibits the struggle between the good Christ and the bad devil. The devil inhabits powerful people like Pope Leo X, Emperor Charles V, and other mighty princes. They are tools for the devil's vexation, and we should only laugh at them as figures in God's carnival play.[10] If Christians are called to do special work for God,

9. WA 40II:226; LW 12:28.

10. A basic theme in the interpretation of Ps. 2 from 1532. WA 40II:187-312.

such as leading a reform movement before the end-time, they should never take their role in the carnival play of the mean meantime too seriously.

> I ask that people make no reference to my name; let them call themselves Christians, not Lutherans. What is Luther? After all, the teaching is not mine, neither was I crucified for anyone. St. Paul would not allow Christians to call themselves Pauline or Petrine, but Christian. How then should I — poor stinking maggot-fodder that I am — come to have people call the children of Christ by my wretched name? Not so, my dear friends; abolish all party names and call yourselves Christians, after him whose teaching we hold. . . . I neither am nor want to be anyone's master. I hold, together with the universal church, the one teaching of Christ who is our only master (Matt. 23:8).[11]

> I have often said: I am like a ripe stool and the world's like a gigantic anus, and we're about to let go of each other. I thank you, dear God, that you allow me to stay in your little flock that suffers persecution for the sake of your Word. It's certainly not on account of harlotry or usury that I am persecuted; of this I am sure.[12]

Telling Samples

Luther's eschatological humor in the mean meantime shows up throughout his works. The following selections demonstrate the breadth of his humor: both the various situations in which he used it and also the various types of humor, from crude jokes to biting irony.

1. Luther was always aware of the danger for theologians in trying to

11. *A Sincere Admonition by Martin Luther to All Christians to Guard against Insurrection and Rebellion.* WA 8:685; LW 45:70-71. For a differing view, see James Kittelson, "Luther on Being Lutheran," *Lutheran Quarterly* 17 (2003): 99-110.

12. WA TR 5:222; LW 54:448, no. 5537. One of the most popular humorous eschatological sayings of Luther cannot be found in his writings: "If I knew that the world would end tomorrow I would still plant a little apple tree today." The saying appeared in Germany after World War II and was attributed to Luther — it sounded just like him! See Martin Schloemann, *Luthers Apfelbaumchen. Bemerkungen zu Optimismus und Pessimismus im christlichen Selbstverstandnis,* Wuppertaler Hochschulreden 7 (Wuppertal: Peter Hammer Verlag, 1975).

explain everything, and he sometimes used a dramatic flourish to make his point. For example, Ulrich Zwingli denied the "real presence" of Christ in the Lord's Supper. When Jesus said, "This *is* (*estin* in Greek) my body," he meant "This *signifies*" (*significat* in Latin), argued Zwingli. The colloquy in Marburg in 1529 yielded no reconciliation. Luther knew that it would not. Before the meeting of the two dialogue teams he wrote with chalk on the table "hoc est meum corpus" ("this is my body") and covered the words with a tablecloth. At the height of the debate he lifted the tablecloth and said, "It is written . . ." The two teams departed in a shallow peace![13]

Luther once tried to write a serious, academic Latin treatise on justification *(De iustificatione)*. Very soon he gave up and just wrote in large letters *Rhapsodia* ("Rhapsody," from the Greek *rapto ode*, "to put a song together").[14] One should sing the doctrine rather than attempt a cold-blooded intellectual understanding. Luther had already published a hymn on justification in 1523, depicting a dialogue between God the Father and God the Son on how to save the world from sin, "Dear Christians, Let Us Now Rejoice."[15]

2. Luther's satirical wit was always directed against the papacy as the most abusive institution of his time. While he was working on his final blast against the papacy in 1545,[16] he conceived a series of ten caricatures about the papacy, produced by the artist Lukas Cranach in woodcuts with Latin titles and German commentaries by Luther. The first tablet shows the origin of the papacy by a she-devil whose anus gives birth to the pope and cardinals; three Furies care for the newborn "Antichrist." The second and third (double) tablet depicts a papal council in Germany: one shows the pope riding a pig and holding filth in his hand, which the pig is sniffing (Germany must eat the filth offered by the pope). The other tablet depicts a donkey playing a bagpipe (the pope as incompetent theologian and interpreter of Holy Scripture). The fourth one shows the execution of a noble man through the pope, disclosing the gratitude of the popes toward emperors. The fifth tablet shows the pope with his foot on the neck of Em-

13. Details in Martin Brecht, *Martin Luther*, trans. James L. Schaaf, 3 vols. (Minneapolis: Fortress, 1990-93), 2:325-34.

14. *Rhapsodia seu concepta in librum de loco iustificationis*, 1530. WA 30II:357-676.

15. WA 35:493-95; LW 53:217-18; *Lutheran Book of Worship* (Minneapolis: Augsburg, 1978), no. 299: "Dear Christians, One and All."

16. *Against the Roman Papacy, an Institution of the Devil*, 1545. WA 54:206-99; LW 41:259-376.

peror Fredrick I, known as "Barbarossa" ("red beard" — 1152-90), to illustrate papal tyranny. The sixth tablet shows the hanging of the pope and cardinals, with their tongues nailed to the gallows because of their slander; devils receive their souls. The seventh and most popular image shows the papal throne in the jaws of hell and the pope as Antichrist (also on the title page of Luther's treatise). Finally, there are tablets with the pope being ridiculed by peasants who expose their hind ends to him; or the pope being an earthly idol used by peasants as a commode.[17]

3. Luther also used irony and exaggeration in contrasting the power of God in the weak Word to the weakness of human grabs for power. This was particularly the case in his dramatic sermons delivered in March of 1522 during the first week of his public return to his Wittenberg pulpit.

> The Word created heaven and earth and all things; the Word must do this thing [Reformation], and not we poor sinners. . . . Take myself as an example. I opposed indulgences and all the papists, but never with force. I simply taught, preached and wrote God's Word, otherwise I did nothing. And while I slept, or drank Wittenberg beer with my friends Philip [Melanchthon] and Amsdorf [Nicholas of], the Word so greatly weakened the papacy that no prince or emperor ever inflicted such losses upon it. I did nothing; the Word did everything. Had I desired to foment trouble, I could have brought great bloodshed over Germany; indeed, I could have started such a game that even the emperor would not have been safe. But what would it have been? Mere fool's play. I did nothing, I let the Word do its work.[18]

4. Luther often just let his mind wander, speculating about anything except the hidden God who can only be known in the revelation of Jesus Christ. The playfulness was especially demonstrated throughout his remarks at table. The scholastics even disputed over where God was before the creation of the world. The doctor (Martin Luther) said, "Yes, Augustine mentioned this. But once, when he was asked, he said, 'God was making hell for those who are inquisitive.' Then he added, 'Where is God now after the creation?'"[19]

17. Many of the illustrations can be found throughout Brecht, *Martin Luther.*

18. "Eight Wittenberg Sermons," 1522. WA 10III:18-19; LW 51:77-78.

19. WA TR 4:611; LW 54:377, no. 5010.

When Luther lectured on the creation of whales ("great sea monsters" — Gen. 1:21), he turned his attention to small animals like mice, flies, and birds.

> Aristotle states that certain animals are produced by their like, others by their unlike. Thus mice belong to the kind produced by their unlike, because mice originate not from mice alone but also from decay, which is used up and gradually turns into a mouse. If you should ask by what power such a generation takes place, Aristotle has the answer that the decayed moisture is kept warm by the heat of the sun and that in this way a living being is produced, just as we see dung beetles being brought into existence from horse manure. I doubt that this is a satisfactory explanation. The sun warms, but it would bring nothing into being unless God said by His divine power: "Let a mouse come out of the decay." Therefore the mouse, too, is a divine creature and, in my judgment, of a watery nature and, as it were, a land bird; otherwise it would have the form of a monster, and its kind would not be preserved. But for its kind it has a beautiful form — such pretty feet and such delicate hair that it is clear that it was created by the Word of God with a definite plan in view. Therefore, here, too, we admire God's creation and workmanship.[20]

5. Luther was clear about the single condition for Christian unity as the leader of a reform movement within the Roman Catholic Church, namely, the gospel. His statement is witty yet also dead serious and shows how Luther used humor to demonstrate paradoxically how serious he was. "All we aim for is that the glory of God be preserved and that the righteousness of faith remain pure and sound. Once this has been established, namely, that God alone justifies us solely by His grace through Christ, we are willing not only to bear the pope aloft on our hands but also to kiss his feet."[21]

6. Luther wrestled all his life with the interpretation of Scripture. Sometimes the commentaries he employed seemed overwhelming in their ponderous attempts to interpret single passages. Exegetes, philosophers, and theologians were especially full of suggestions about the meaning of Genesis 1:6 where God created a "dome" in the midst of waters to separate

20. WA 42:39; LW 1:52.
21. WA 40I:181; LW 26:99.

them. "There, in general, are the teachings of the philosophers. The more recent theologians are in agreement with them. . . . But the Greeks have treated these subjects far more cleverly and intelligently than our scholars have treated them. Ambrose and Augustine have rather childish ideas. *Therefore I recommend Jerome who maintains complete silence on these topics.*"[22] Here Luther recommends the silence of an honored church father as the best exegetical advice and admits that he does not know the real meaning of a part of Holy Scripture — an interesting way of fusing self-criticism, common sense, and irony.

7. Luther's pastoral care and advice exhibit the freedom of living in eschatological time when nothing is absolutely sure and true except the Word of God in Christ. Liturgy is always a sensitive matter involving symbols, emotions, and rites. When Elector Joachim II of Brandenburg introduced a new liturgy in 1539, his young Lutheran pastor George Buchholzer thought that it was very "un-evangelical." He wrote to Luther that the elector ordered the use of Roman vestments and a procession with the eucharistic elements around the church (as was done in the medieval church at the Feast of Corpus Christi). Luther responded in two letters, one to the elector and the other to the pastor. He criticized the elector for introducing devilish customs such as the carrying around of eucharistic elements.[23] He advised Buchholzer to concentrate on Word and sacrament; but he could also use various liturgical ornamentations as long as the consciences of the parishioners are not burdened.

> Why don't you, for heaven's sake, march around wearing a silver or gold cross, as well as a skull cap and a chasuble made of velvet, silk or cotton? If your superior, the Elector, thinks that one cap or one chasuble is not enough, then put on two or three, like Aaron, the high priest, who wore three coats, one on top of the other, and they all looked wonderful [Lev. 8:7]. . . . If your Electoral Excellency thinks one procession is not enough, marching around with singing and with bells, then do it seven times, just as Joshua did in Jericho with the children of Israel. They shouted and blew their trumpets [Josh. 6:4-7]. Perhaps

22. WA 42:22; LW 1:28, emphasis mine.

23. WA Br 8:622.29–623.37 (letter dated 4 December 1539). See also Eric Gritsch, "Luther's Humor as a Tool for Interpreting Scripture," *Lutheran Quarterly* 5 (1991): 199-210.

> your Electoral Excellency might even jump around and dance in front of all the people with harps, drums, cymbals and bells, just as David did before the ark of the covenant on its way to Jerusalem. I completely approve of such things, so long as they are not viewed as necessary for salvation, or as binding on consciences.[24]

Luther closed the letter with the remark that the way of human worship "is a free thing and not a divine mandate."

8. Luther also employed humor in his most intimate personal life. Thus, he treated his wife Katie in a humorous fashion, giving waggish pastoral advice when she became too worried about his stay at Eisleben where he spent his final days.

> I thank you very much for your great worry, which robs you of sleep. Since the date you [started to] worry about me, the fire in my quarters, right outside the door of my room, tried to devour me, and yesterday, no doubt because of the strength of your worries, a stone almost fell on my head and nearly squashed me as in a mouse trap. For in our secret chamber [the toilet] mortar has been falling down for about two days; we called in some people who [merely] touched the stone with two fingers and it fell down. The stone was as big as a long pillow and as wide as a large hand; it intended to repay you for your holy worries, had the dear angels not protected me. [Now] I worry that if you do not stop worrying, the earth will finally swallow us up and all the elements will chase us. Is this the way you learned the *Catechism* and the faith? Pray, and let God worry. You have certainly not been commanded to worry about me or about yourself. Cast your burdens on the Lord, and he will sustain you.[25]

In any event, Luther did not refer to the devil when he told Katie that he was almost killed on the toilet by her worries.

9. Even death allowed Luther to employ delightful, sarcastic humor in one instance. When there were rumors from Italy about his death in 1537, Luther wrote a waggish response that referred to a meeting at Smalcald during the same year where he almost died.

24. WA Br 8:625.11–626.36.

25. WA Br 11:291; LW 50:305-6 (letter to Katherine Luther, 10 February 1546).

> I, Dr. Martin Luther, testify herewith in my own hand that I am of one mind with the devil, the pope and all my enemies, for they wish to rejoice over my death. I begrudge them their joy from the bottom of my heart and would willingly have died in Smalcald, but God was not yet ready to sanction such joy. He will do this, however, sooner than they think, and it will be their misfortune, for they will then say, "Would that Luther were still alive." This is a transcript in German, Greek, Latin, and Hebrew from my grave.[26]

10. Luther liked to surprise serious people with humorous behavior as well as words. That is, he literally "played the fool" about which he had written in 1520. When the papal nuncio Vergerio traveled in 1535 to Germany to seek support for a general council of bishops with the pope regarding the question of reform, he requested a meeting with the famous heretic in Wittenberg. The Saxon court arranged it for 7 November. Luther wanted to appear much younger than he was. He got shaved and wore youthful clothes: a dark double doublet with satin sleeves over which he wore a short, fur-lined coat made of serge, a light woolen material. In addition, he wore a heavy gold chain and several rings. This outfit gave the impression that he was much younger than fifty-two. Vergerio spoke later of Luther's lively black eyes, which suggested that he might have been possessed by demons. Luther bragged about his marriage to a nun who bore him five children, hinting that the oldest son might continue the work of reform.

Luther had his pastor Johannes Bugenhagen with him. When they were driven to the electoral castle for the meeting, Luther joked: "Here they go, the German pope and Cardinal Pomeranus [derived from Pomerania, Bugenhagen's native territory], the tools of God." Luther played the role of a crude German and asked Vergerio whether they knew him in Italy only as a drunkard. When they discussed the council, Luther assured Vergerio that he would be there if invited. Vergerio left convinced that Luther's cause had been overestimated and that the reformer was just a mentally unstable, crude German.[27]

11. Luther's preaching challenged the Wittenbergers in a direct, hu-

26. WA TR 3:440-44; LW 54:238-39, no. 3595.

27. The visit of Vergerio is recorded in various sources, summarized by Brecht, *Martin Luther*, 3:174-76.

morous way to become better Christians. Roland H. Bainton performed excerpts from Luther's Christmas sermons for years at Yale Divinity School where larger and larger audiences could hardly stop laughing. Focusing on the poor conditions under which the baby Jesus was born, he told his listeners:

> There are many of you in this congregation who think to yourselves: "If only I had been there! How quick I would have been to help the baby! I would have washed his linen. How happy I would have been to go with the shepherds to see the Lord lying in the manger!" Yes, you would! You say that because you know how great Christ is, but if you had been there at that time you would have done no better than the people of Bethlehem. Childish and silly thoughts are these! Why don't you do it now? You have Christ in your neighbor. You ought to serve him, for what you do to your neighbor in need you do to the Lord Christ himself. The birth was still more pitiable. No one took her [Mary's] condition to heart. . . . There she was without preparation: no light, no fire, in the dead of night. No one came to give her customary assistance. The guests swarming in the inn were carousing, and no one attended to the woman. I think myself if Joseph and Mary had realized that her time was so close she might perhaps have been left in Nazareth. And now think what she could use for swaddling clothes — some garment she could spare, perhaps her veil — certainly not Joseph's breeches, which are now on exhibition at Aachen.[28]

12. Luther used his satirical humor especially against Archbishop Albrecht of Mainz, who had provoked Luther to debate the question of indulgences. When the archbishop exhibited his large collection of relics in 1542, offering indulgences on the basis of solemnly viewing them, Luther composed a pamphlet and published it without identifying its author, *New Newspaper from the Rhine.*[29] The pamphlet noted that part of the money collected at the exhibition would be used to provide new wrappings for the old relics so that they would not have to freeze in their old ones. In addi-

28. Quoted from Roland H. Bainton, *The Martin Luther Christmas Book* (Philadelphia: Fortress, 1958), 38. Original texts selected from sermons in WA 22.

29. *Neue Zeitung vom Rhein,* 1542. WA 53:404-5. See also Scott H. Hendrix, "Martin Luther and Albrecht of Mainz," *Lutherjahrbuch* 49 (1982): 96-114.

tion, newly discovered relics would be exhibited, with a special indulgence offered by Pope Paul III. The new relics included: a nice section from Moses' left horn (Exod. 34:29, Vulgate: "His face was horned from the conversation with the Lord"); three flames from the burning bush on Mount Sinai (Exod. 3:3); two feathers and an egg from the Holy Spirit; a remnant of the flag with which Christ opened hell; a large lock of Beelzebub's beard, stuck on the same flag; one-half of the archangel Gabriel's wing; a whole pound of the wind that roared by Elijah in the cave on Mount Horeb (1 Kings 19:11); two ells (about ninety inches) of sound from the trumpets on Mount Sinai (Exod. 19:16); thirty blasts from the trumpets on Mount Sinai; a large heavy piece of the shout with which the children of Israel tumbled the walls of Jericho (Josh. 6:20); five nice shiny strings from the harp of David; three beautiful locks of Absalom's hair, which got caught in the oak and left him hanging (2 Sam. 18:9).

The author concluded by sharing a tip he had received from a friend in high places: Archbishop Albrecht had willed a trifle of his pious, loyal heart and a whole section of his truthful tongue to the existing collection; and whoever paid one guilder at the exhibition would receive a papal indulgence remitting all sins committed up to the time of payment and for ten more years, thus giving the people of the Rhineland a unique opportunity to obtain a special state of grace. Luther revealed himself as author after the pamphlet had been widely circulated.

13. Luther also used his wit to distance himself from his own physical problems. In addition to the pressures of leading a reform movement, being condemned by church and state, writing virtually day and night, Luther suffered from kidney stones and gallstones, stomach disorders, frequent headaches, and increasing heart problems (he died of angina pectoris at age sixty-three). But he got energized by his witty polemics; he joked about the useless medieval practices; and he improved his physical and emotional condition through worship (including praying and frequent private confessions), eating, drinking, sleeping with Katie, playing with his children, having a dog as a friend (named *Tölpel,* "boor"), enjoying music, bowling, and using the monastic spiritual discipline of "praying and working" *(ora et labora).* Luther liked to summarize his difficulties with the image of Satan riding through his head, looking for a spa. "I resist the devil, and often it is with a fart that I chase him away."[30]

30. WA TR 1:48; LW 54:16 (30 November 1531), no. 122.

Conclusion

Humor was for Luther the guard to prevent him from crossing the frontier to speculation about God and human life beyond its earthly existence. The revealed God in Christ tempts believers, especially philosophers and theologians, to try to discover the hidden God. Thus Luther told Erasmus in the famous controversy about "free will": "To the extent, therefore, that God hides himself and wills to be unknown to us, it is no business of ours. For here the saying truly applies, 'Things above us are no business of ours.'"[31]

Robert W. Jenson contended in a rare lecture about evil that the devil is not really a true "person" because he cannot give himself over to someone else, to become an object, as it were, and to have himself defined by another being. God is a person in Jesus Christ and "gives himself among us. . . . The devil is personal only on the passion of his refusal to be a person. The devil's jokes are never on himself because he has no self for them to be on."[32] Thus the devil has no real sense of humor but only a *Schadenfreude* ("malicious glee") about the misfortune of others.

Luther learned from the critical study of Scripture and tradition that God's human creatures are at their best when they are not "egocentric," but "excentric," as it were: only "depend on that which is outside ourselves . . . that is, on the promise and truth of God, which cannot deceive."[33] The triune God, who justifies the ungodly through grace and faith in the Son alone, gives the Holy Spirit through the gospel in the Word and the sacraments, effecting "faith where and when it pleases God to those who hear the gospel."[34] The human mind must turn to the problems of the world, to the love of neighbor, and, like the Good Samaritan, find concrete ways for faith being active in love. Here Luther gives good advice to a post-Freudian world where there is often so much analysis that it leads to paralysis.[35]

31. *The Bondage of the Will.* WA 18:685; LW 33:139.

32. Robert W. Jenson, "Evil as Person," in *Encounters with Luther: Lectures, Discussions, and Sermons at the Martin Luther Colloquia,* ed. Eric Gritsch, 4 vols. (Gettysburg, Pa.: Institute for Luther Studies, 1970-89), 4:185-86.

33. Lectures on Galatians, 1535 in WA 40I:589; LW 26:387.

34. Augsburg Confession V, 2-3, in BC, 41; BSLK, 58.

35. Using Luther's satirical humor, the parable of the Good Samaritan (Luke 10:25-37) could be perverted by having the "bad" Samaritan say to the victim, "Whoever did this to you needs a lot of help."

Life in the mean meantime before the Last Day offers a peculiar freedom to be more doxological than logical, indeed to live a joyful life with a humorous distance from evil, sin, and death — grounded in the proclamation of God's glowing love for sinful human creatures. What Luther said about music could also be said about humor: if music deserves the highest praise next to the Word of God,[36] then humor should rank second in the hierarchy of praise. Humor, like music, also casts out Satan — the "sour Spirit" that wants to be the master of the human heart — and makes true Christians laugh in anticipation of a time without sin, death, and the devil. "Then our mouth will be filled with laughter, and our tongue with shouts of joy" (Ps. 126:2).

36. Preface to Georg Rhau's *Symphoniae Iucundae*, 1538. WA 50:370; LW 53:323. See below, Robin A. Leaver, "Luther as Musician."

CHAPTER 4

Luther on Preaching as God Speaking

H. S. Wilson

> The word is meant to be spoken. The majesty of the Word of God is infinite and unspeakable, for which we can never give enough thanks to God. . . . Listen, brother: God, the creator of heaven and earth, speaks with you through his preachers. . . . Those words of God are not of Plato or Aristotle but God himself is speaking.[1]

What is the most important event in Sunday morning worship? Preaching, of course. Then the question is: How is preaching understood by preacher and laity? If the people come with a notion that they are going to hear an expert say something about religion or the Bible, something they can accept or reject, then the purpose of preaching is lost. If the preacher has prepared a "safe sermon" so that he or she will not offend the congregation, the purpose of preaching is likewise lost. "Preaching has been weakened by

1. WA TR 4:531, no. 4812: "Verbum vocale. Infinita et ineffabilis verbi Dei maiestas est, pro qua numquam satis gratias agere Deo possumus. . . . Audi, frater: Deus, creator coeli et terrae, tecum loquitur per praedicatores suos; . . . Illa Dei verba non sunt Platonis, Aristotelis, sed Deus ipse loquitur."

This essay is based upon the author's dissertation, published as *The Speaking God: Luther's Theology of Preaching* (Madras: United Evangelical Lutheran Churches in India, 1982), 128-42.

a frantic effort on the part of the pulpit to deliver a message that is popular. By 'popular' we do not mean the sermons with 'a catchy topic' or the presence of 'the glamour boy' in the pulpit, but rather the message that says to the people what they want to hear and that keeps them coming back for this reason only."[2]

Preaching is then reduced to nothing more than rhetoric: a human being talking to human beings. It is a lecture by an expert to seekers of knowledge. Thus, the whole biblical perspective of preaching as God communicating with people through people is lost. Luther's greatest service to preaching is the recovery of the biblical understanding of preaching — God speaking *(Deus loquens)*. Preaching is not mere human talk, but it is God himself speaking to individuals through preachers.

Chester Pennington pointed out in the 1970s what is even truer today: that many clergy seriously doubt the importance of preaching.[3] One of the problems they face is a "Professional Identity Crisis."[4] "They feel that they are given little support in our society. Their theology lacks clarity and assurance. Consequently, many clergy wonder who they are and what they are supposed to be doing."[5] When a preacher loses confidence in his or her preaching, it will certainly be reflected in the sermon. Instead of speaking God's authoritative yet loving Word, the preacher will communicate doubt and lead people into confusion.

We are not suggesting that there is no place for doubt and, in particular, "self-searching" on the part of the preacher. But it is equally important that preachers be certain about what they are called to do, so that they might have a sense of identity to rely on in these critical times. Luther has pointed out that the "call" to the office of preaching, which comes from God through the people, is a significant assistance to the preacher.[6] Luther said that when he was confronted with the problem of uncertainty and crisis, his comfort came from his (divine and human) calling to the office of preaching. "God has opened my mouth and bidden me speak, and he supports me mightily. . . . Therefore, I will speak and . . . not keep silent as long

2. Donald Macleod, *Word and Sacrament: A Preface to Preaching and Worship* (Englewood Cliffs, N.J.: Prentice-Hall, 1960), 9.

3. Chester Pennington, *God Has a Communication Problem* (New York: Hawthorn, 1976), 2.

4. Pennington, *Communication Problem,* 23.

5. Pennington, *Communication Problem,* 23.

6. See H. S. Wilson, *The Speaking God,* 112.

as I live, until Christ's righteousness goes forth as brightness, and his saving grace be lighted as a lamp. . . . For no matter what I may be personally, still I can boast before God with a good conscience that in this matter I am not seeking my own advantage."[7] One could not comfort a minister more profoundly then or now, than by pointing to the call that ultimately comes from God. When one ignores this call and becomes self-reliant, he or she surely must suffer a pastoral identity crisis.

It is most important for both the preacher and the congregation to be aware that in communicating with people, God uses human beings as coworkers. God has sought the cooperation[8] of human beings in carrying on the work of salvation completed through Jesus Christ. By cooperation we do not mean that people contribute something toward their own salvation.[9] Rather, we mean that God has chosen to use people for the task of spreading the gospel to the whole world. The preacher is the agent of God's message to the people. In his "Sermon on the Gospel of St. John" (28 August 1540) Luther said, "To be sure, I do hear the sermon; however, I am wont to ask: 'Who is speaking?' The pastor? By no means! You do not hear the pastor. Of course, the voice is his, but the words he employs are really spoken by my God."[10] While it is true that Luther considered preaching the minister's activity, it is also true that it is God's activity. God encounters human beings through the preacher's activity. Karl Barth expressed this quite plainly: ". . . preaching has a dual aspect; the word of God and human speech."[11]

The most difficult part of Luther's theology of preaching is his assertion that preaching is God's own speech to people. It is too easy to see preaching as mere speech *about* God.[12] If this latter concept is the under-

7. WA 15:27f.; LW 45:347-48.

8. For Luther's idea of cooperation, see Gustaf Wingren, *The Christian Calling: Luther on Vocation*, trans. Carl C. Rasmussen (London: Oliver and Boyd, 1958), 123-43.

9. Wingren, *The Christian Calling*, 124. "The fact is that the idea of co-operation grows up directly and simultaneously out of Luther's belief in the bondage of the will before God. . . . Cooperation takes place in vocation, which belongs on earth, not in heaven; it is pointed toward one's neighbor, not toward God."

10. WA 47:229; LW 22:528; text: John 4:7.

11. Karl Barth, *The Preaching of the Gospel*, trans. B. E. Hooke (Philadelphia: Westminster, 1963), 9.

12. Gustaf Wingren, *The Living Word: A Theological Study of Preaching and the Church* (Philadelphia: Muhlenberg, 1960), 19.

standing held by the church, preaching is reduced to a rehashing of the old stories and it becomes a memorial speech. Gustaf Wingren explained this as follows: "The Lutheran assertion that . . . preaching, in so far as it is Biblical preaching, is God's own speech to men [*sic*], is very difficult to maintain in practice. Instead it is very easy to slip into the idea that preaching is only speech *about* God. Such a slip, once made, gradually alters the picture of God, so that he becomes the far-off deistic God who is remote from the preached word and is only spoken about as we speak about someone who is absent."[13]

Luther's struggle was against *Deus taciturnus* (a nonspeaking God), the silent God. If God is thought of as silent, then the Bible is reduced to a mere chronicle and one could read it only to gather information. Luther wanted to break through this barrier in order to point out that when one reads the Bible and hears the sermon in faith, it is God himself speaking to that person.[14]

The static God projected by philosophers and scholastic theologians is of no avail for Luther. Through the Scripture he knew that the God who reveals himself speaks and acts continuously.[15] When the preacher preaches and the congregation hears the sermon (in faith), it is God himself speaking and God himself who is heard. Luther believed that God speaks through *persons* to *persons.* It is here that the certainty of the preachers lies,[16] that when they are preaching, it is God himself who is speaking, and the congregation, by accepting or rejecting, accepts or rejects God's message itself.

The core of Luther's understanding of God's dealing with human be-

13. Wingren, *The Living Word,* 19.

14. Gerhard Ebeling said that one could not turn to Luther's works without questioning one's own way of speaking about God. "There is something challenging about the way Luther speaks of God." *Luther: An Introduction to His Thought,* trans. R. A. Wilson (Philadelphia: Fortress, 1964), 242. Jaroslav Pelikan, *Luther the Expositor: Introduction to the Reformer's Exegetical Writings* (St. Louis: Concordia, 1959), 50: "The 'Word of God' was the speech of God, and 'the God who speaks' would be an appropriate way to summarize Luther's picture of God."

15. Warren A. Quanbeck, "The Hermeneutical Principles of Luther's Early Exegesis" (Ph.D. diss., Princeton Theological Seminary, 1948), 74.

16. Ebeling, *Luther,* 248. "For Luther certainty is the essence of God's being with man and therefore of man's being with God. In the presence of God, and there alone, there is no uncertainty. But uncertainty is man's sin, and certainty is salvation."

ings is that "faith and God belong together."[17] Luther has discussed this in the explanation of the first commandment in his Large Catechism. "To have a god is nothing else than to trust and believe him with our whole heart. As I have often said, the trust and faith of the heart alone make both God and an idol. . . . For these two belong together, faith and God."[18] Of course, it is not any kind of faith. For Luther it is the "right kind of faith," "if your faith and trust are right, then your God is the true God. On the other hand, if your trust is false and wrong, then you have not the true God."[19] The important thing is that this right faith is the one that comes through hearing the Word. Only this faith will be able to teach one about God's action and will toward oneself and the whole human race. In other words, God's will toward us is known only through the proclaimed Word. Since people cannot reach up to God, it becomes necessary for God to take the initiative. God must lower himself to reach us; he must speak in a manner people can understand. Luther expressed this in his *Lectures on Genesis* as follows:

> It is for this reason that God lowers himself to the level of our weak comprehension and presents himself to us in images, in coverings, as it were, in simplicity adapted to a child, that in some measure it may be possible for him to be known by us. . . . Therefore he puts before us an image of himself, because he shows himself to us in such a manner that we can grasp him. In the New Testament we have Baptism, the Lord's Supper, absolution, and the ministry of the Word. . . . These are the divine images and "the will of the sign." Through them God deals with us within the range of our comprehension. Therefore these alone must engage our attention.[20]

Because of the human condition, God deals with people through coverings and masks. It is through these masks *(larvae)* that God opens the

17. Ebeling, *Luther,* 250ff., cautioned that one should understand Luther's statement in the light of his whole theology. Otherwise one might conclude that Luther is suggesting that God is a product of human imagination, as Ludwig Feuerbach posited, an anthropocentric way of seeing God.

18. WA 30I:132; BC, 386. The right faith even "consummates the Deity; and, if I [Luther] may put it this way, it is the creator of the Deity, not in the substance of God but in us" (WA 40:36; LW 26:227).

19. WA 30I:132; BC, 386.3.

20. WA 42:294-95; LW 2:45-47.

dialogue with people at their level. "He takes us as we are, as one of us, often a bit awkward at times, so that perhaps we will listen."[21]

But God does not become one with these masks, his creations.[22] They are simply his masks. He is hidden behind them. Only a person of faith is given the understanding that God himself is active behind the masks. "We need the wisdom that distinguishes God from his mask. The world does not have this wisdom. Therefore it cannot distinguish God from his mask. When a greedy man, who worships his belly, hears that 'man does not live by bread alone, but by every Word that proceeds from the mouth of God' (Matt. 4:4), he eats the bread but fails to see God in the bread; for he sees, admires, and adores only the mask."[23] Again the wisdom to distinguish God from his masks comes from God. A person who is given this kind of wisdom will give attention to God's will and put trust in nothing but God himself, who is operating behind these masks. "[I]f someone knows that the power and wisdom of God are of such a sort, he trusts wholly, not in the mask of God but in the Word behind the mask; and he can and does perform wonders, yes, everything, in the Lord."[24] God will continue to confront human beings through masks, but wants people to pay attention to the will and Word hidden behind the mask and not the mask itself.

One of the most direct ways in which God communicates is through the proclaimed Word of the church, that is, the words of the preacher! When one believes in the promise of God communicated through the verbal pronouncement of the preacher, he or she receives God's favor.

Luther's view that God continues to communicate with us through the Word proclaimed by the preacher as found in the Scripture reflects his high regard for the preacher's role in the church. However, this means that a preacher both has and does not have something new to say. T. H. L. Parker failed to do real justice to Luther's understanding of the preacher's role when he suggested that "in binding the Word of Spirit so rigidly to the

21. Edmund A. Steimle, *From Death to Birth* (Philadelphia: Fortress, 1973), 71.

22. Sandra Anderson, "Words and Word in Theological Perspective: Martin Luther's Views on Literature and Figurative Speech" (Ph.D. diss., Northwestern University, 1975), 232 and 530 n. 14, cautioned and drew attention to the danger of pantheism, found in both Nietzsche and Erasmus's *Praise of Folly*, as a result of identifying God with his masks.

23. WA 40I:173-74; LW 26:95.

24. WA 14:578; LW 9:41.

human word of preaching . . . [Luther] was perilously near making the preacher a passive oracle of God."[25] One does not find this view of a preacher in Luther. When the minister preaches, he or she does not just recite the biblical message.[26] Of course, reading of the Scripture precedes the sermon. When a preacher preaches, he or she stands in the long tradition of personal witness to God's saving act. But this witness is carried on by the preacher, keeping in mind the need and situation of the congregation. "Only the *intention* to communicate and to resort to imagination can save preaching from cliché."[27] That means there is ample room in which the individuality of the minister with all his or her personal gifts and faculties can be exercised. In fact, the whole personality of the preacher has to be thrown into the sermon.[28] Charles Rice has further explained the human role in preaching when he said, "the particular vehicle of the Word is a man [*sic*] whose humanity is the medium of the message . . . Christian theology suggests that it is a witnessing man among men who can communicate the gospel."[29]

According to Luther, the preacher has nothing *new* to say other than what is already spoken and written by the apostles. "It is impossible to derive the Word of God from reason; it must be given from above. Verily, we do not preach the human wisdom of philosophers, jurists, medics, or of any other profession. . . . The apostles transmitted it to us, and thus it will continue until the end of the World."[30] Even though a preacher continues to preach the apostles' message, it is his or her responsibility to make the

25. T. H. L. Parker, *The Oracles of God: An Introduction to the Preaching of John Calvin* (London: Lutterworth, 1947), 48.

26. David C. Steinmetz said just the opposite when he quoted Bishop Hagen of Norway in his sermon: "'Our sole task was to deliver messages composed by others. We were not asked to be original or imaginative. We were only asked to be faithful.'" To Bishop Hagen's words Steinmetz added that "The Church has been commissioned, not to be original but to witness to him [Christ]." See his "Woe to Me If I Do Not Preach the Gospel!" *Duke Divinity School Review,* Spring 1975, 9. Even though it is true to say that the church's message is not meant to be original, it is certainly not Luther's position on preaching to say that the preacher is not to be imaginative.

27. Charles L. Rice, *Interpretation and Imagination* (Philadelphia: Fortress, 1970), 77.

28. Adolph Spaeth, "Homiletics," in *The Lutheran Cyclopedia,* ed. Henry E. Jacobs and John A. W. Haas (New York: Scribner, 1905), 226.

29. Rice, *Interpretation and Imagination,* 76.

30. WA 47:187-88; LW 22:477-78.

same message as simple and clear as possible to the people there and then so that everybody can benefit from it. In his *Table Talk* Luther mentioned that this was the pattern of his preaching: "Cursed be every preacher who aims at lofty topics in the church, looking for his own glory and selfishly desiring to please one individual or another. When I preach here [in Wittenberg] I adapt myself to the circumstances of the common people. I don't look at doctors and masters, of whom scarcely forty are present, but at the hundred or the thousand young people and children. It's to them that I preach. . . . If the others don't want to listen, they can leave."[31]

In the task of preaching Luther has a place for human imagination and talent as long as everything is done in subjection to the Word of God and as long as the preacher is aware that with all the talent used in preaching he or she is only giving voice to the Word that is not his or her own. For the sermon is not only meant to speak to the understanding but also to the *heart*.[32]

Given this kind of understanding of preaching, the preacher should proceed to make preaching simple but clear, using examples and illustrations if needed. "For ordinary people are caught more easily by analogies and illustrations than by difficult and subtle discussions. . . . For teaching it is useful to be able to produce many analogies and illustrations; not only Paul but also the prophets and Christ used them."[33] The purpose of all this is to make God's message clear to people. Therefore, a preacher, besides being a faithful servant of the Word, should be gifted with certain qualities and virtues so that the task of preaching can be carried on for the greater glory of God. In his *Table Talk* Luther listed the following ten virtues a good preacher should have:

> A good preacher should have these properties and virtues: first, to teach systematically; secondly, he should have a ready wit; thirdly, he should be eloquent; fourthly, he should have a good voice; fifthly, a good memory; sixthly, he should know when to make an end; seventhly, he should be sure of his doctrine; eighthly, he should ven-

31. WA TR 3:419-20; LW 54:235-36, no. 3573.

32. Paul Scherer, *For We Have This Treasure*, Yale Lectures on Preaching, 1943 (New York: Harper and Brothers, 1944), 67.

33. WA 40I:548; LW 26:359. For other principles of Luther's rhetoric, see Birgit Stolt, *Martin Luthers Rhetorik des Herzens* (Tübingen: Mohr, 2000).

> ture and engage body and blood, wealth and honor, in the word; ninthly, he should suffer himself to be mocked and jeered of everyone. (Finally, he should patiently bear the fact nothing is seen more easily and quickly in those preachers than their faults.)[34]

While looking for qualities and talents in preachers, Luther also pointed out the danger of pride to which particularly a gifted and talented preacher falls victim.

As the disheartened and new preachers get their consolation and courage by looking at their "call" and by seeing preaching as ultimately God's way of communicating with people, so also the danger of overconfidence and pride can be avoided by reminding oneself that all the talents are gifts received and are subject to the faithful teaching of the Word.

The greatness of preaching lies in the fact that it is God himself who is active in preaching and speaks to the people through the preached Word. God is active in preaching insofar as the preacher remains obedient to the Word and seeks nothing but for the people to hear the Word of God. Only then the faithful hearers will be able to say, "Pay attention, we are hearing God's speech."

For right preachers should diligently and faithfully teach only the Word of God and must seek only his honor and praise. Likewise the hearers should also say: I do not believe in my pastor, but he tells me of another Lord, whose name is Christ; him he shows to me; I will listen to him, insofar as he leads me to the true Teacher and Master, God's Son. Then things would be right in the church and it will be well governed, and there would be harmony all around.[35] The preacher's task is clear: to give voice to the Word of God. A preacher is not expected to add anything to the Word, but to express it clearly. Thus "the church has no other teacher but God, and therefore it has no other obedience."[36]

The preacher's task is to tell the "story of God coming into the middle of life, of our lives, opening dialogue with us."[37] This dialogue between

34. WA TR 2:531, no. 2580; LW 54:182, no. 400. "These are the three things, so to speak, which every good preacher should do: first, he takes his place; second, he opens his mouth and says something; third, he knows when to stop" (WA 32:302; LW 21:7).

35. WA 51:191; LW 51:388; "The Last Sermon, Preached in Eisleben," 15 February 1546, on Matt. 11:25-30.

36. WA 46:21; LW 6:30.

37. Steimle, *From Death to Birth*, 70.

God and human beings will go on until the end of time. The initiative is taken by God. In Dietrich Ritschl's words, "It is in the weakness of the human word that God confronts us with himself, and we would miss the point completely if we were to understand this as an unfortunate and special burden for our faith. The very contrary is true: it is because of God's infinite mercy and wisdom that He has chosen our human words to make Himself known to us. If He had decided to speak otherwise, we would not be about to understand Him and to respond to His claim and offer."[38] And people will continue to hear God speaking as long as God provides preachers through the community of believers here on earth. "The Word of God is the Word behind the words"[39] of the preachers provided by God.

Thus for Luther preaching is *Deus loquens* — God speaking — but through *persons,* to *persons.* Even contemporary preaching cannot overlook this view of Luther for proper preaching. Otherwise preaching is reduced to reporting what had happened two thousand years ago. Such a report cannot be called good news as it was called by the people of Christ's time. Luther pointed out that if preaching has to be continually considered as proclamation of the good news that God acted for our salvation, then God's activity in preaching must be recognized. Only human pride can claim anything more as the preacher's task than faithfully proclaiming the Word as it is recorded in the Bible.

The Bible has been written in common human language and words, and so preaching must be. It is how God has decided to communicate and make himself known — in everyday human language. But it is hard to accept that we hear God in that way. It is God the Holy Spirit who convinces the heart of the message of God coming through human words and thereby enables people to recognize God's speech. That is why Luther said, "We have the *jus verbi* (right to speak) but not the *executio* (power to accomplish). We should preach the Word, but the results must be left solely to God's good pleasure."[40]

God's activity and speaking belong together and cannot be separated from each other.[41] In the beginning God spoke; this act resulted in the cre-

38. Dietrich Ritschl, *Die homiletische Funktion der Gemeinde: zur dogmatischen Grundlegung der Predigtlehre* (Zollikon: Evangelischer Verlag, 1959), 75.

39. Roland E. Sleeth, *Proclaiming the Word* (Nashville: Abingdon, 1964), 35.

40. WA 10III:15; LW 51:76.

41. Ritschl, *Die homiletische Funktion,* 25.

ation of the world. In Jesus Christ God spoke again and acted for our salvation. Thereafter, as well as now, God speaks through the preachers. That is how he is active in each individual's life. When God speaks through human beings, it does not reduce the significance of his message or Word. In fact, it is the proper way by which one can hear God. Human beings cannot hear God directly from Mount Sinai through angels, for the mountain was wrapped in smoke and it quaked.[42] However, God is gracious enough to continue to communicate on a human level through human beings using human words. Any person who does not care to hear God in this way will bring about his or her own destruction. On the other hand, every believing person will be saved through his message.

All preaching for Luther had one supreme aim: justification of sinners through faith in what God has done in Christ. That is why, for Luther, the purpose of preaching was not *primarily* to raise consciousness about world issues nor to promote morality in society. These, however, tend to be the only aims of much contemporary preaching. It may include all of this, but first and foremost preaching is God's activity of redemption in history. It is the *viva vox Evangelii,* the living Word of the gospel.

Conclusion

The Reformation was a period of the revival of Christian preaching.[43] Christian preaching goes back to Jesus Christ himself. God spoke to us through him. Jesus not only proclaimed our deliverance and salvation but also brought it about through his life, death, and resurrection. The church from the beginning conveyed this good news of what God has done for us through Jesus Christ through its life and preaching. Although preaching was carried on through all ages, now with more, now with less authenticity, the Reformers gave it new vigor.

More than anything else, "the Reformation was a crisis about the Word of God; it was also a crisis of communication."[44] The Reformers

42. WA 47:228; LW 22:527.

43. However, there were precursors in late-medieval religious life. See Jane Dempsey Douglas, *Justification in Late-Medieval Preaching: A Study of John Geiler of Keisersberg* (Leiden: Brill, 1966).

44. Gordon Rupp, *The Old Reformation and the New* (Philadelphia: Fortress, 1967), 24.

strongly advocated that God primarily deals with and communicates with human beings through the Word. The Word comes in a form alive to every generation through the preaching of the church. That is why Luther upheld preaching as a very important task of the church. It is a God-given responsibility and, as such, *the important mark* of the church.[45] When preaching is neglected, spiritual damage results.

Luther spoke strongly for preaching because he was convinced that God himself is heard in preaching. God's Word is a living and a personal Word. Besides the preacher, God himself is also active in preaching, communicating and seeking personal responses from the hearer. Therefore, the key phrase to explain Luther's understanding of preaching is *Deus loquens,* God speaking, through persons, to persons.

While Luther's understanding of preaching as *Deus loquens* seems a difficult concept to accept, the alternate understanding available to us reduces preaching to a talk *about* God. Preaching about God reduces God to *Deus taciturnus,* the silent God. If God is silent, how can the gospel, which is beyond human reason, be heard and give benefit? This communication problem Luther solved by pointing to God's living Word, heard anew every time the preacher gives it voice.

Since God's message is personal, the proper way to communicate it to people is through the spoken form. "For Luther's whole point is that the Word is not dead wisdom but is finally a personal Word, which must be personally preached and personally heard. Instead of thinking about causal connections, we should think instead about the *mystery of preaching,* in which man [*sic*] the preacher and man the audience and God the speaker and God the enabler (namely, the Holy Spirit) all work to make this miraculous event happen."[46] Preaching for Luther meant declaring anew through the human voice the judgment and the forgiveness of God. When a minister preaches so, in obedience to the Scripture (the written

45. See WA 50:240, Smalcald Articles III.4, in BC, 319, and Luther's treatise on the church, *Von den Konziliis und Kirchen,* WA 50:628-30; LW 41:148-51.

46. Bard Thompson, "Lectures on Luther," mimeographed notes for the exclusive use of graduate students and theological students of Drew University, Madison, N.J. See also Eric W. Gritsch, "The Ministry in Luther's Theological Perspective," *Bulletin* 54 (February 1974): 18. For the Roman Catholic point of view of the mystery of preaching, see the essay by Lambert Claussen, "The Mystery of Preaching: *Christus Praedicat Christum,*" in *The Word,* collection of essays by Karl Rahner et al., compiled at the Canisianum, Innsbruck (New York: P. J. Kenedy and Sons, 1964), 186-95.

Word), God's Word is heard simultaneously with the human word. How this happens is the mystery of preaching. Luther explained: "Thus, the spoken word is indeed a human voice — but instituted by divine authority for salvation."[47]

A Select Bibliography of Recent Studies on Luther and Preaching in English

Asendorf, Ulrich. "Luther's Sermons on Advent as a Summary of His Theology." In *A Lively Legacy: Essays in Honor of Robert Preus,* edited by K. Marquart et al. Fort Wayne, Ind.: Concordia Lutheran Seminary, 1985.

Baue, Frederic W. "Luther on Preaching as Explanation and Exclamation." *Lutheran Quarterly* 9 (1995): 405-18.

Bishop, John. "Martin Luther: Preacher of the Word." *Preaching* 9 (September/October 1993): 59-60.

Campbell, Charles L. "Living Faith: Luther, Preaching, and Ethics." *Word and World* 10 (1990): 374-79.

Ferry, Patrick. "Martin Luther on Preaching: Promises and Problems of the Sermon as a Source of Reformation and as an Instrument of the Reformation." *Concordia Theological Quarterly* 54 (1990): 265-80.

Forde, Gerhard O. "Law and Gospel in Luther's Hermeneutic." *Interpretation* 37 (1983): 240-52.

Grimm, Harold J. "The Human Element in Luther's Sermons." *Archiv für Reformationsgeschichte* 49 (1958): 50-60.

Grope, L. B. "Luther and the Christ-Child." *Lutheran Theological Journal* 17 (1983): 62-66.

Haemig, Mary Jane. "The Other John in John: Luther and Eck on John the Baptist (John 1:19-28)." *Word and World* 21 (2001): 377-84.

Karant-Nunn, Susan C. "What Was Preached in German Cities in the Early Years of the Reformation? Wildwuchs versus Lutheran Unity." In *The Process of Change in Early Modern Europe,* edited by P. Bebb. Athens: Ohio University Press, 1988.

Kolb, Robert. "'What Benefit Does the Soul Receive from a Handful of Water?': Luther's Preaching on Baptism." *Concordia Journal* 25 (October 1999): 346-63.

Laskey, Dennis A. "The Concern for Communio in Luther's Preaching and Liturgical Writing: 1524-1530." *Concordia Journal* 12 (1986): 44-54.

———. "Luther's Preaching on the Lord's Supper: A Comparison with Preaching in the Late Middle Ages." *Concordia Journal* 12 (1986): 167-71.

47. WA 43:71. "Sic verbum vocale est quidem vox hominis, sed authoritate divina instituta ad salutem."

Lischer, Richard. "Luther and Contemporary Preaching: Narrative and Anthropology." *Scottish Journal of Theology* 36 (1983): 487-504.

Lose, David E. "Luther and Calvin on Preaching the Human Condition." *Lutheran Quarterly* 10 (1996): 281-318.

Marty, Martin. "Preaching on the Holy Spirit: A Study of Luther's Sermons on the Evangelical Pericopes." *Concordia Theological Monthly* 26 (1955): 423-41.

Matheson, Peter. *The Rhetoric of the Reformation.* Edinburgh: T. & T. Clark, 1998.

McCue, James F. "Luther and the Problem of Popular Preaching." *Sixteenth Century Journal* 16 (1985): 33-43.

Meuser, Frederick. *Luther the Preacher.* Minneapolis: Augsburg, 1983.

Mosig, Jorg M. Gereon. "Luther's Eight Sermons at Wittenberg: The Credo of a Gentle Reformer." *Heythrop Journal* 40 (1999): 340-49.

Nestingen, James Arne. "Preaching the Catechism." *Word and World* 10 (1990): 33-42.

Oberman, Heiko A. "Teufelsdreck: Eschatology and Scatology in the Old Luther." *Sixteenth Century Journal* 19 (1988): 435-50.

O'Malley, John W. "Luther the Preacher." In *The Martin Luther Quincentennial,* edited by Gerhard Dünnhaupt. Detroit: Wayne State University Press, 1985.

Pfitzner, Victor C. "Luther as Interpreter of John's Gospel: With Special Reference to His Sermons on the Gospel of St. John." *Lutheran Theological Journal* 18 (1984): 65-73.

Pless, John T. "Martin Luther: Preacher of the Cross." *Concordia Theological Quarterly* 51 (1987): 83-101.

Raabe, Paul R. "Children's Sermons and Luther's Small Catechism." *Concordia Journal* 15 (1989): 100-102.

Riegert, Eduard R. "To Impart to Everyone a Little of What God Has Given Me: An Aspect of Luther as Preacher." *Consensus: A Canadian Lutheran Journal of Theology* 9 (October 1983): 3-9.

Robinson, Paul W. "Luther's Explanation of Daily Bread in Light of Medieval Preaching." *Lutheran Quarterly* 13 (1999): 435-47.

Schaibley, Robert. "Lutheran Preaching: Proclamation, Not Communication." *Concordia Journal* 18, no. 1 (1992): 6-27.

Schneider, Stanley D. "Luther, Preaching, and the Reformation: Still Sharing the Gospel." In *Interpreting Luther's Legacy,* edited by F. W. Meuser. Minneapolis: Augsburg, 1969.

Siggins, Ian. "Luther and the Catholic Preachers of His Youth." In *Luther: Theologian for Catholics and Protestants,* edited by George Yule. Edinburgh: T. & T. Clark, 1985.

Stuempfle, Herman G. "How Preachers Should Regard Moses." In *Encounters with Luther,* vol. 1, edited by Eric Gritsch. Gettysburg, Pa.: Lutheran Theological Seminary, 1980.

Vercruysse, Joseph E. "Luther as Reformer within Christendom." *Studia Missionalia* 34 (1985): 351-71.

Whitelaw, David P. "An Examination of Two Early Sermons of Martin Luther: The *Sermo de Duplici Iustitia* and the *Sermo de Triplici Iustitia*." *Theologia Evangelica* 17 (1984): 24-35.
Wood, Arthur S. "Luther as a Preacher." *Evangelical Quarterly* 21 (1949): 109-21.

PART III

The Teaching Ministry

CHAPTER 5

Luther on Education

Robert Rosin

To appreciate fully Martin Luther's contributions to education, we must place him in the broadest historical context possible. Although centuries have passed, Martin Luther continues to capture public interest and make an impact on daily life. In 2003 a poll done by ZDF, the "Second German Television Network," ranked Luther second only to Konrad Adenauer among the most influential Germans of all time. Luther's place is all the more striking given that Karl Marx stood third, still high in memory not long after the *Wende* linking the East and the West.[1] But Luther's strong showing is not confined to German culture. Scan the shelves of any decent liberal arts research library and there are likely to be found more books written about Luther than about any other figure in human history with the exception of Jesus Christ.[2] Luther certainly would not mind finishing second on that list.

Luther cast a shadow across the years with, above all, his focus on the personal assurance of salvation by faith alone due to God's grace alone, his central message rooted ultimately in Scripture alone. But given that the sacred and secular were so intertwined in his era, and given that Luther

1. http://german.about.com/cs/culture/a/bestger.htm is the easiest place to track the story.

2. The observation is from John Todd, a Roman Catholic historian who added to the list with his biography *Luther: A Life* (New York: Crossroad, 1982), xvi. I am willing to take his word for it until someone actually supplies the statistics.

struck hard at both the message and the authority of the institutional church embedded in that mix, he was bound also to affect a broad range of social issues during his lifetime. That influence has held over the years even as Luther sparked a variety of interpretations about both his reform movement and his wider connections in society.

Impassioned debate has long swirled around the Reformer. Already in his lifetime he was consigned to the depths of hell, and a few years later he was made nearly to walk on water — or fly through the heavens as the angel in Revelation 14 bearing the everlasting gospel.[3] In another angle (not angel) more down to earth, Luther's take on natural law and his support for order and stability in society served a seventeenth century keen on building a legal foundation for developing nations.[4] While his understanding of reason was highly nuanced, Luther's dramatic stand at Worms was hardly a seven-league stride toward rationalism. Yet the Enlightenment found the episode too good to let pass unused — misused! — in its effort to trump revelation with the human intellect.[5] In fact, *ratio evidens,* the "clear reason" that Luther invoked before Emperor Charles at Worms, was explained in Luther's lines that followed: his was a conscience captive (that is, a mind shaped) by the Word of God. This was no double standard but rather a mind that "filled in the blanks" of daily life where Scripture did not speak. This mind was the product of a certain kind of education!

In the nineteenth century, some took Luther's law-gospel dialectic as a religious parallel to the Renaissance, soft-pedaling his theological ele-

3. The reports of his death, to steal from Mark Twain, were greatly exaggerated, not to mention premature. With both amusement and disdain, Luther reported on his opponents' wishful thinking in "An Italian Lie concerning the Death of Dr. Martin Luther," in WA 54:192-94 and LW 34:365-66. On the upside, an early effort at biography was the collection of near hagiographical sermons of Johannes Mathesius. An anniversary reprint is *Dr. Martin Luthers Leben* (St. Louis: Concordia, 1883). Other judgments from Luther's lifetime and in the early generations after his death are collected in Robert Kolb, *Martin Luther as Prophet, Teacher, and Hero: Images of the Reformer, 1520-1620* (Grand Rapids: Baker, 1999).

4. Leonard Krieger, "History and Law in the Seventeenth Century," *Journal of the History of Ideas* 21 (1960): 198-210.

5. Walther von Loewenich, *Luther und der Neuprotestantismus* (Witten: Luther Verlag, 1963), 1-24, for example, notes the Enlightenment shift with such figures as Lessing and Kant. See also Heinrich Bornkamm, *Luther im Spiegel der deutschen Geistesgeschichte mit ausgewählten Texten von Lessing bis zur Gegenwart,* 2nd ed. (Göttingen: Vandenhoeck & Ruprecht, 1970).

ments while accenting the existential in tracking toward the modern age. For others, Luther's reform was a drag anchor, for in throwing off one kind of smothering authority — institutional church and pope — Luther opened the door for a different tyranny of dogma resting on the reading — his reading — of texts.[6] Another interpretation did not concern itself with Luther's theology per se but objected to the fact that theology of any sort was taken at face value. So Luther was right for turning religion inward on the self, but he still treated God as a real entity. It would be left to later generations to expose religion for what it really was, namely, self-alienated psychology.[7] Still others would try to seat those alienated ideas in a society that Luther allegedly betrayed, turning on the common people, though he still served a purpose in their march toward power.[8]

A Luther Renaissance in the twentieth century revisited the Reformation as fundamentally a theological movement, though it did not ignore the wider cultural influence.[9] Whether focusing on dialectical ele-

6. Wilhelm Dilthey looked forward, while Ernst Troeltsch gravitated to the social teachings or activities of the dissidents, rejecting a kingdom-as-practical-action approach of some of nineteenth-century Protestantism found in Albrecht Ritschl. Excerpts that lay out these contrasting positions are in Lewis W. Spitz, *The Reformation: Basic Interpretations* (Lexington, Mass.: Heath, 1970), 11-24 and 25-43.

7. Ludwig Feuerbach thought Luther nearly got it right in saying Christ was our brother. Because of the incarnation we see God not across a wide gap but as a family member standing by us. But no wonder there was a family resemblance: we are really looking in a mirror, so looking at God is looking at us. So Luther got close, as close as one might expect for the sixteenth century. For taking the final step and finishing off the reconciliation, Feuerbach could immodestly say, "Ich bin Luther zwei." Ludwig Feuerbach, *The Essence of Faith according to Luther*, trans. Melvin Cherno (New York: Harper and Row, 1967).

8. Friederich Engels, *The German Revolutions: The Peasant War in Germany*, trans. Leonard Krieger (Chicago: University of Chicago Press, 1967); Abraham Friesen, *Reformation and Utopia: The Marxist Interpretation of the Reformation and Its Antecedents*, Veröffentlichungen des Instituts für Europäische Geschichte Mainz, vol. 71 (Wiesbaden: Steiner Verlag, 1974); Brent O. Peterson, "'Workers of the World Unite — for God's Sake!': Recent Luther Scholarship in the German Democratic Republic," in *Luther and the Modern State in Germany*, ed. James D. Tracy, Sixteenth Century Essays and Studies, vol. 7 (Kirksville, Mo.: Sixteenth Century Journal, 1986), 77-99.

9. Though one could debate his decision to settle on a theocentric rather than a christocentric Luther, for example, Karl Holl nevertheless epitomizes the renewed interest in theology, though he did not neglect other cultural influences. Holl, *What Did Luther Understand by Religion?* ed. James Luther Adams and Walter F. Bense, trans.

ments or on confessional accents or making the case for some tack said to have been overlooked — *theosis* — a balanced take on Luther's thought had to appreciate its broad impact in a complex world.[10]

One might wonder what these wide-ranging interpretations have to do with Luther and education. In fact, whether they are on the mark or not, on another level they illustrate the sort of educated engagement with Luther's world of thought that Luther himself might approve. Rather than throttle investigation, Luther saw the gift of the intellect as one of the striking features of humankind as God's special creation.[11] In a long view of Luther's impact on education, these varied interpretations were the product of educational forces Luther himself encouraged. In Luther's day, not only how people saw their relationship with God, but also how they understood their daily-life roles in God's creation all rested firmly on what they came to learn and believe. No wonder Luther had a keen interest in education. It was learning for life to come and for life now.

Luther was a great promoter of education. He was not a tactician or a detail man, leaving others to work on the nuts and bolts. But because of his outsized presence, when he spoke, people listened.[12] He provided an im-

---

Fred W. Meuser and Walter R. Wietzke (Philadelphia: Fortress, 1977); Holl, *The Cultural Significance of the Reformation*, trans. Karl Hertz, Barbara Hertz, and John Lichtblau (New York: Meridian Books, 1959). Erich Vogelsang and Emmanuel Hirsch are other major names in the movement.

10. Karl Barth and Friederich Gogarten emphasized the dialectical understanding, while Paul Althaus and Werner Elert accented the confessional element. See James Stayer, *Martin Luther, German Saviour: German Evangelical Theological Factions and the Interpretations of Luther, 1917-1933* (Montreal: McGill-Queen's University Press, 2000). On the Finnish-sparked interest in *theosis*, see Simo Peura and Antti Raunio, eds., *Luther und Theosis. Vergöttlichung als Thema der abendländischen Theologie. Referate der Fachtagung der Luther-Akademie Ratzeburg in Helsinki,* Schriften der Luther-Agricola-Gesellschaft, A 25 (Helsinki and Erlangen: Veröffentlichungen der Luther-Akademie Ratzeburg, 1990).

11. In contrast to Luther's oft-cited reference to reason as "Frau Hulda" or "the great whore" stands his "Disputation concerning Man" from 1536 with a much more nuanced, appreciative view. WA 39I:44-62; LW 34:105-32. Gerhard Ebeling, *Lutherstudien; Disputatio de homine,* vol. 2, part 1: *Text und Traditionshintergrund;* vol. 2, part 2: *Die philosophische Definition des Menschen. Kommentar zu Thesen 1-19;* vol. 2, part 3: *Die theologische Definition des Menschen. Kommentar zu Thesen 20-40* (Tübingen: J. C. B. Mohr [Paul Siebeck], 1977, 1982, 1989).

12. On the various roles Luther filled when it came to education, see Marilyn J. Harran, *Luther and Learning: The Wittenberg University Luther Symposium* (Selinsgrove,

mense service by arguing simply for the need for more than a cursory education, thinking through the purpose and goal as this all related not only to the Reformation cause but also to life in general. Along the way he tried to persuade and cajole those who took short views and shortchanged education. His was not a selfish concern, simply wanting better-prepared students for the university (though he probably would not have complained). Rather, Luther's interest had theological as well as practical roots. His Reformation grew out of what was going on in education in his day, and his Reformation's expansion and continued success would depend on a strong educational foundation. As time passed, the Reformation realized the debt it owed and continued to incorporate larger educational trends and tools in its curricula. That all is worth a closer look.

Luther had not planned a career in academia. It was really thrust upon him. His climb up the educational ladder — Mansfeld, Magdeburg, Eisenach, Erfurt — was intended to prepare for a legal career that would benefit his family. When law studies gave way to the monastery, Luther convinced himself he could do his family even more good with his devotions and prayers. He would have preferred to learn simply to be a good monk and in serving God also to help save his soul. But others in authority saw potential, so he was soon back in the university, but now in theology, a student first but later appointed to Wittenberg's faculty. Professors were supposed to contribute to the development of theological thought. They could not simply repeat the old arguments but were expected to add to the theological corpus in some way. The pressure was on. Newly minted instructors today can relate: the well is not yet deep enough, everything is all too new, and there are students waiting for something they can etch in stone when the ink on the lecture notes is not yet even dry. So Luther scrambled to help students even while helping himself. He used the best tools available to him from the scholarly world, reaching beyond the standard fare to glean insights from scholars known as humanists, an interesting bunch that paid more attention to the grammar and sense of the texts than the logic of how things might be.

As evangelical biblical theology came clear in Luther's own mind, he

---

Pa.: Susquehanna University Press, 1985). While there is a specific chapter by James M. Kittelson, "Luther the Educational Reformer," 95-114, others dealing with topics such as Luther as professor or Luther as an opponent of scholasticism also are useful for his ideas on education.

took those insights into the classroom, not simply because they filled the lecture hour, but moved by a personal, pastoral connection, Luther realized his students could also be searching for peace just like their professor. When higher-ups in the church condemned him for the Reformation uproar, Luther would have none of it. His superiors had made him a doctor of theology when he only wanted the monk's cowl, not the doctor's cap. He was only doing what was expected of a professor in making the results of his research — thrilling results as it turned out — known to his students and to the larger church. In a sense, then, the Reformation could be seen as the product of an education revolution — the revival of the liberal arts that fueled a theological revolution that would center on Wittenberg. (We will take up below how that change at Wittenberg came about.)

Luther did not come to Wittenberg intending to get involved in educational reform. But he found himself thrown into a university still in formation. Together with key allies — humanist Georg Spalatin, the chancellor/adviser who had the ear of Elector Frederick, who paid the bills — Luther helped transform this fledgling "academic Siberia" into arguably the most influential school of its time. Luther did not do this as a professional pedagogue. He was first a preacher, holding forth with the message he uncovered in the Scriptures. But he understood that even while preachers want to raise up the level of their hearers, so educators also make a difference as they teach the Word. As Luther said, "If I were to or had to give up the preaching office and what goes with it, I would rather have no other office than that of schoolmaster or a teacher of boys, for I know that next to preaching, this is the best and most necessary position."[13] It is a shrewd observation. Preaching is more than exhortation. A sermon also ought to teach people about the faith in some way or from some angle. Conversely, curriculum not only teaches but also preaches a larger message on how that academic community views its task. A curriculum marked by the old approach of logic and dialectic with Aristotle's influence that had dominated now for several centuries shaped minds one way. As Luther discovered the gospel and did so not only without Aristotle but despite Aristotle, he urged that his unofficial approach be taken into the formal curriculum.

The correspondence and documents surrounding Wittenberg's early years show a Luther who is increasingly insistent that the old ways have to

13. WA 30II:569. The comment is from Luther's 1530 *Sermon on Keeping Children in School.*

go. At the same time, he argued for the introduction of new methods, new subjects, new thinking — all a threat to the old guard. But his persistence was rewarded. Renaissance humanism was a cultural and educational movement that had been well under way since the latter half of the fourteenth century, starting in Italy but soon spreading north of the Alps. While the liberal arts had never been entirely forgotten, they had been eclipsed for a variety of reasons, not the least being the use made of Aristotle and his logic since the High Middle Ages. Renaissance humanism argued that man does not live by syllogisms alone. A steady diet of logic was responsible for what Petrarch, the father of humanism, called "the dark ages."[14]

Humanists wanted a place also for grammar, poetry, and rhetoric as a way to shape and educate people. And rather than exist in some logical isolation, real living appreciated the lessons of history that in turn prepared people to deal with the ragged edges of daily life through moral philosophy. Along the way a by-product of studying the past was a revived interest in classical languages — Ciceronian Latin, Greek, and even Hebrew.[15] Humanists such as Faber Stapulensis also offered comments on biblical texts, comments Luther found helpful in working through the grammar and realizing, for example, that "righteousness" was not some quantity to be acquired through a logical quid pro quo approach, but rather it was a quality bestowed only by God's grace, a gift received only in faith. The gates of paradise that were flung wide open bore a resemblance to the schoolhouse door — at least the door into this new learning. So Luther worked hard to show Aristotle the door out and to welcome in this fresh approach. New courses, new faculty and programs — Philip Melanchthon as the Greek teacher for the new *paedagogium* officially embraced by the university — all brought Wittenberg a lot of attention. That

14. Theodore Mommsen, "Petrarch's Conception of the Dark Ages," *Speculum* 17 (1942): 226-42.

15. Basic studies of the Renaissance and humanism are legion. The five-part curriculum core was the focus of Paul Oskar Kristeller, *Renaissance Thought: The Classic, Scholastic, and Humanist Strains* (New York: Harper and Row, 1961); Kristeller, *Medieval Aspects of Renaissance Learning: Three Essays* (Durham, N.C.: Duke University Press, 1974); Charles G. Nauert, *Humanism and the Culture of Renaissance Europe* (Cambridge: Cambridge University Press, 1995); Hannah Holborn Gray, "The Pursuit of Eloquence," *Journal of the History of Ideas* 25 (1963): 497-514; Lewis W. Spitz, "Humanismus/Humanismusforschung," in *Theologische Realenzyklopädie* 15 (1986), 639-61.

meant new students, and the elector was pleased. For Luther, it meant a fresh look at the Word.[16] And the humanist interest in history renewed attention to the church fathers where Luther found others who also struggled and often found answers in the Word as well, though no one seemed to get Saint Paul quite like Luther.[17]

Luther's own education had been very late medieval, steeped in the use of logic and dialectic with a nominalist philosophical take when it came to questions of ontology and epistemology. Luther learned his lessons well — too well perhaps. He once quipped, "If ever a monk could have gained heaven by monkery, it should have been I." The line tends to focus on the cloister, but it also depends on a theology learned with logic. If God is perfect and righteous and makes no mistakes in what he does, and if God gives us the law and commands that we keep it, then there must

16. The university documents and letters are in Walter Friedensburg, ed., *Urkundenbuch der Universität Wittenberg,* Geschichtsquellen der Provinz Sachsen und des Freistaates Anhalt, new series, vol. 3 (Magdeburg: Selbstverlag der Historischen Kommission der Provinz Sachsen und Anhalt Magdeburg, 1926); Friedensburg, *Geschichte der Universität Wittenberg* (Halle: Max Niemeyer, 1917). See also Max Steinmetz, "Die Universität Wittenberg und der Humanismus (1502-1521)," in *450 Jahre Martin-Luther-Universität Halle-Wittenberg,* vol. 1, *Wittenberg, 1502-1817,* ed. Leo Stern et al. (Halle: Selbstverlag der Martin-Luther-Universität Halle-Wittenberg, 1952), 103-39, especially 108-12; Karl Bauer, *Die Wittenberger Universitätstheologie und die Anfänge der Deutschen Reformation* (Tübingen: J. C. B. Siebeck [Paul Mohr], 1928); Maria Grossmann, *Humanism in Wittenberg, 1485-1517* (Nieuwkoop: DeGraaf, 1975); Helmar Junghans, *Der junge Luther und die Humanisten* (Göttingen: Vandenhoeck & Ruprecht, 1985). One recounting of Luther's efforts at curriculum change is Robert Rosin, "The Reformation, Humanism, and Education: The Wittenberg Model for Reform," *Concordia Journal* 16 (1990): 301-18. Even more recently, see the work of Jens-Martin Kruse, *Universitätstheologie und Kirchenreform: Die Anfänge der Reformation in Wittenberg (1516-1522)* (Mainz: von Zabern, 2002).

17. On the larger reception of the fathers, see the two volumes from Leif Grane, Alfred Schindler, and Markus Wriedt, eds., *Auctoritas Patrum: Contributions on the Reception of the Church Fathers in the Fifteenth and Sixteenth Century* (Mainz: von Zabern, 1993), and *Auctoritas Patrum: New Contributions on the Reception of the Church Fathers in the Fifteenth and Sixteenth Century* (Mainz: von Zabern, 1998). In volume 1, note Scott Hendrix, "Deparentifying the Fathers: The Reformers and Patristic Authority," 55-68, on the Reformation's respect for history and those early theologians even as it learned not to live in the shadow. On Luther as part of the larger Renaissance rethinking, see Lewis W. Spitz, *The Religious Renaissance of the German Humanists* (Cambridge: Harvard University Press, 1963).

be some way to do that. To deny that is to say God does not know his business. Sin may not allow us to act simply on our own as if we had the power in and of ourselves to keep the law. (That was Pelagianism, condemned by the church already.) But that still does not deny God's mandate. It means only that there must be some other way — and that happens through the assistance of God's grace that enables us to follow the Law and attain the merit, the righteousness, needed to be saved. After all, does the Law not demand and then offer reward? It is all perfectly logical. It was all very much Aristotle, and Luther learned his lessons well. Unfortunately, all the teachers never had an answer for the question "How much is enough?" As a result, Luther drove himself to distraction trying to find a gracious, accepting God.

In contrast, the message of forgiveness by God's saving grace grasped through faith alone is straightforward and simple — but illogical. God demands righteousness. We cannot meet the demand. Nevertheless — a wonderful Lutheran word! — nevertheless God for Christ's sake forgives us all our sin. Luther learned that God's grace operates not by ergo or therefore but by *dennoch* or nevertheless. The chief parts of the Small Catechism lay out that good word in short order in just a few dozen paragraphs. Yet the biblical theology Luther championed was hardly simplistic. It rested on a huge educational shift in how theology was studied, that is, on a change in method. It no longer revolved around what syllogisms might dictate, but rather centered on what the texts actually say despite what one might logically conclude. Those using the catechism in their homes might not have realized this change immediately, but the results of Luther's change are certainly there. For example, "I believe that I cannot by my own reason or strength believe in Jesus Christ, my Lord, or come to him. But — not therefore but nevertheless — the Holy Ghost has called me by the Gospel. . . ." Simple words that spring from a monumental shift. While most people then and now knew Luther first for his Ninety-five Theses, another set of propositions, his "Disputation against Scholastic Theology," also from 1517, was perhaps a greater challenge to the church with Luther's call to study theology differently, to change methods. "It is an error to say one becomes a theologian without Aristotle. This is opposite the common opinion. Indeed, no one becomes a theologian unless he does it without Aristotle. . . . In short, all of Aristotle is to theology as darkness is to light."[18]

18. Theses 43, 44, and 50. WA 1:224-28; LW 31:3-16.

Luther's own education underwent a radical shift due to the cultural and educational contributions of Renaissance humanism. "No humanism, no Reformation," wrote Bernd Moeller. And it was true in Luther's case, though we might refine the line as "No Renaissance education, no Reformation." Luther's own theological breakthrough benefited from a larger cultural and educational upheaval of the Renaissance that was well under way by his lifetime. The *studia humanitatis*, the study of man or the liberal arts, had enjoyed a revival starting after the mid–fourteenth century. It was part of the Renaissance, an educational and cultural movement that hearkened back to the ideas and interests of antiquity even while it sought to imitate the classical era's lively interest in the world around. Luther could resonate to that because his own theological breakthrough put the world in a new light. No longer something to be endured and survived, though sin and Satan still raged, life in this world could be embraced. After all, God made all things and still preserved them not by reaching down from heaven but through means — not means of saving grace but human means, people who were *larvae Dei*, "masks of God," by which he got things done. If people were to do their tasks well, they needed an education to serve well in whatever vocation God laid upon them. A theological take on life was certainly important, but so were other basic life skills for all, along with a higher education for some.

As mentioned above, Luther was not a professional pedagogue, and for the most part he left the details and implementation to others. He had had his one great experience in that first decade on the Wittenberg faculty when he helped push through change at the university. After that, when it came to advising on education, Luther largely left the heavy lifting to others, being content instead simply to promote the cause in general. So Luther's specific writings on education, while significant, are not numerous. Two famous treatises immediately spring to mind: *To the Councilmen of All the Cities in Germany That They Should Establish and Maintain Christian Schools* from 1524 and Luther's 1530 *Sermon on Keeping Children in School.*[19] His catechisms, small and large, also certainly qualify as core writings, though they have a different focus, written not to defend the purpose and place of schools but rather to serve as basic textbooks for different audiences. After the catechisms the list trails off quickly. Luther's writ-

19. The first treatise along with introductory material is in WA 15:27-53; LW 45:339-78. The second is in WA 39II:517-88; LW 45:207-58.

ings on the *Deutsche Messe* were to educate people about the liturgy, teaching them to look at the service in a different light — the Mass no longer as sacrifice, for example.

Reaching wider, it could be argued that Luther's sermons and postils also bolstered education because he sought to teach how to understand the biblical message and grasp and internalize the Christian faith. Seeing sermons as teaching texts is not far-fetched when we remember that Luther himself drew a strong connection between preaching and teaching and saw himself as educating people in the Christian faith. Education stands behind the scenes of *Freedom of a Christian.* With the Christian liberated and given the opportunity for a life of service, it is incumbent first to explain just what that meant. That is crucial given the theological tenor of the age, an approach that had once plagued Luther's conscience. Once that first famous sentence is made clear — "The Christian is the perfectly free lord of all, subject to none" — then it is important to educate for life in that second sentence — "The Christian is the perfectly dutiful servant of all, subject to all." How that second sentence relates to the first, and how new people of faith then apply their talents in life's opportunities, requires education. The topic of vocation is there in *Freedom of a Christian,* but it is hardly the last word.[20] Efforts to lead and guide believers, to help them understand what new life in Christ means, are included in the catechism explanations for the commandments. The Decalogue was given to an Israel already redeemed, brought through the Red Sea and made God's covenant people. It was given not to prescribe how they might become God's chosen but rather to describe how they were in this new relationship, though it also mirrored the depravity that still plagued and could drag them down. The same might be said of the commandments in the catechism. Luther shuffled the order of the three traditional core parts. By moving the commandments first, Luther makes sure we learn the lesson that we do not measure up, and then he moves on to show (in the creed) what God has done for us in all things, creation and redemption. But in a second pass, the commandment explanations also show how God's people live. We fear and love God that we may not . . . but rather we live this way. . . . That's teaching basics about the Christian life. It is just (!) shuffling the order, but

20. Gustaf Wingren, *Luther on Vocation* (Philadelphia: Muhlenberg, 1957), and George Forell, *Faith Active in Love: An Investigation of Principles Underlying Luther's Social Ethics* (New York: American Press, 1954).

it affected how people came to learn the basics of the faith and how they thought through theology. Luther doubtless made the move for theological reasons and may well have given the pedagogical angle behind the scenes little (or no) thought. Still, looking at Luther's catechism from an educational perspective, there is no doubt the shift affects the learning.

Luther certainly was aware that pedagogy could be both complicated and detailed. In his treatise *To the Christian Nobility of the German Nation concerning the Reform of the Christian Estate,* done in 1520,[21] Luther called for a revamping of schools and universities. In 1527 when Saxon church visitation articles were being prepared, he again urged that attention be paid to schools. But such urgings are not the same thing as rolling up one's sleeves and plunging into the actual details. He knew from his own context that educational reform was time-consuming and could be tedious. Others would become better known for that. Philip Melanchthon, Luther's coworker, would come to be called the *Praeceptor Germaniae,* the teacher of Germany, known for detailed advice on curriculum and method offered to so many schools.[22] Another pedagogical giant was Johannes Sturm, who practiced what he preached at his school in Straßburg. Those who read Sturm could never accuse him of speaking only in generalities. Instead he laid out not only what to teach but also how and why, doing so in great detail.[23] Luther had no quarrel with the focus of Melanchthon or Sturm. He simply left the day-to-day matters for others to sort out.

Education was important for Luther's reform efforts. Faith was trust — *fiducia* — but people must trust in something. Belief has content,

21. WA 6:404-69; LW 35:115-217.

22. Sachiko Kusukawa and Christine F. Salazar, eds., *Melanchthon: Orations on Philosophy and Education,* Cambridge Texts in the History of Philosophy (Cambridge: Cambridge University Press, 1999); Sachiko Kusukawa, *Transformation of Natural Philosophy: The Case of Philip Melanchthon* (Cambridge: Cambridge University Press, 2003). On Melanchthon's contribution to the topic of method as part of the larger Renaissance discussion, see Neal W. Gilbert, *Renaissance Concepts of Method* (New York: Columbia University Press, 1960); John R. Schneider, "Melanchthon's Rhetoric as a Concept for Understanding His Theology," in *Melanchthon in Europe: His Work and Influence beyond Wittenberg,* ed. Karin Maag (Grand Rapids: Baker, 1999), 141-59.

23. Lewis W. Spitz and Barbara Sher Tinsley, *Johann Sturm on Education: The Reformation and Humanist Learning* (St. Louis: Concordia, 1999). The volume begins with an overview of Sturm and then a chapter on his method. Translations of his educational texts follow.

something to lay hold of. The Holy Spirit does not convert and keep in the faith without means, without the message proclaimed and tied to sacraments. That message of the Word has to be learned. Clearly Luther saw a relationship between faith (as both activity and content) and education, between theology and pedagogy.[24] After his 1520 treatises, as Luther emphasized the priesthood of all believers, education became extremely important. That's why Luther paid attention to what was going on in that regard when it came to making parish visitations and providing tools for teaching the faith in homes — parents using the catechism as educators in the Christian faith.

Whether in schools or homes, Luther was not so naive as to think (as some social historians have characterized his work) that education would cleanse the world, moving toward some kind of paradise.[25] That might have been the hope of some holiness groups, but Luther understood that with *simul iustus et peccator,* education was never finished and would never reach perfection. Growth in the Christian faith and life was complicated by the larger struggle between God and Satan in this life, so success in teaching the faith could not be measured in simple quantitative terms like measuring success in learning multiplication tables. When it came to learning theology and especially to what difference theology would make in how people lived, success for teachers, be they professionals or parents, came not in creating a perfect child but in communicating the faith and in teaching the Bible through which the Spirit works, bringing perfect righteousness of Christ.

24. Ivar Asheim, *Glaube und Erziehung bei Luther: Ein Beitrag zur Geschichte des Verhältnisses von Theologie und Pädagogik* (Heidelberg: Quelle und Meyer, 1961). Asheim shows how even with Luther's anthropology, education could make strides helping believers act responsibly in this world, which remains fallen and troublesome until Christ comes again.

25. Gerald Strauss, *Luther's House of Learning: Indoctrination of the Young in the German Reformation* (Baltimore: Johns Hopkins University Press, 1978), is an example of missing the point of Luther's approach and expecting something more akin to the radicals' expectations. Teachers often pitch objectives high. Today's universities trumpet lofty goals and even print them in their catalogues, yet everyone knows those are always out of reach. The sixteenth century understood that as well — with a theological rationale to settle the issue. See also the criticisms by Lewis Spitz, "Further Lines of Inquiry for the Study of 'Reformation and Pedagogy,'" in *Pursuit of Holiness,* ed. C. Trinkaus (Leiden: Brill, 1974), 294-306, and Scott Hendrix, "Luther's Impact on the 16th Century," *Sixteenth Century Journal* 16 (1985): 3-14.

Luther had a hard time understanding why people often supported schools reluctantly. They balked at underwriting school operations and at paying teachers, yet they would spend on barns and cattle or on their businesses.[26] Even those outside the faith understood that children were the future. At the same time, Luther was also realistic. He knew he had to settle for a short school day because children were needed in the fields. But even the little that might be accomplished would pay off in the long run. And the same held for the time and money spent to educate girls. Education made it possible to carry out one's vocation more effectively, and that meant in a more God-pleasing manner. Whether thinking of the world to come or the world in the here and now, education for Luther was not child's play. It was learning for life.[27]

26. An old but still interesting little look at teachers and schools in Luther's day is Charles L. Robbins, *Teachers in Germany in the Sixteenth Century: Conditions in Protestant Elementary and Secondary Schools* (New York: AMS, 1912).

27. For a basic introduction that reaches well beyond this article, see Marilyn J. Harran, *Martin Luther: Learning for Life* (St. Louis: Concordia, 1997).

CHAPTER 6

Martin Luther and the Ten Commandments in the Large Catechism

Timothy J. Wengert

In the coming months and years, there is bound to be plenty of discussion about Martin Luther's understanding of the sixth commandment, especially as it pertains to modern questions about homosexual relations. On the one hand, it is very simple. Luther said little or next to nothing about such behavior, except to condemn it in the most general terms. Like others of his age, he was extremely reticent to talk about any sexual sins, even while he seemed to delight in scatological expressions that leave modern folks longing for censorship. On the other hand, if one inquires after Luther's approach to the Ten Commandments in more general terms, the answer suddenly becomes more complicated and far more interesting for historians and theologians.

This essay will examine one small piece of Luther's wide-ranging commentary on the Ten Commandments within his catechisms in the hopes of gaining more clarity on Luther's interpretation of the commandments and the role they played in his overall theology.[1] These particular documents, standing between expositions in the *Personal Prayer Book* of

1. The most helpful study is Albrecht Peters, *Kommentar zu Luthers Katechismen,* vol. 1, *Die Zehn Gebote,* ed. Gottfried Seebass (Göttingen: Vandenhoeck & Ruprecht, 1990).

This essay first appeared as "Luther and the Ten Commandments in the Large Catechism," *Currents in Theology and Mission* 31 (2004): 104-14 (used by permission).

1522 and *A Simple Way to Pray* of 1536, have the additional advantage of having been included in *The Book of Concord* of 1580. Thus, they provide an important confessional voice for the current deliberations.

The Heart of the Matter Is the Heart

Luther views all of God's commandments in the light of the first commandment. It is "to illuminate and impart its splendor to all the others. In order that this may be constantly repeated and never forgotten, you must let these concluding words run through all the commandments, like the clasp or hoop of a wreath that binds the end to the beginning and holds everything together."[2] The recurring "we are to fear and love God" of the Small Catechism sounds the same theme.

However, to say that this commandment is the heart of the matter is not to have said everything, unless one makes clear what this commandment means. In this case, Luther's explanation is one of the most famous in all of his theology. "It is the trust and faith of the heart alone that make both God and idol."[3] Faith, then, is the heart of the matter for all the commandments. Fearing God's wrath and loving God's mercy are simply more traditional expressions that Luther uses to make the same point. To paraphrase an American political campaign slogan, "It's about faith, stupid," that is, it is about trusting God above all things!

Luther so concentrates on this aspect of all the commandments, that he never misses an opportunity to make the same point over and over again. Faith drives us to call upon God, to listen to God's Word, to obey God's representatives, to love and care for our neighbor — whether in the person of our children, our parents, our spouse, or the poor. In this regard, Luther — who was only too happy to obey any command of God, no matter how stupid ("If Christ commanded me to eat dung, I would do it," he once said to Ulrich Zwingli) — always ties the Ten Commandments to God's purpose and goal for humanity. The Ten Commandments were not given for the same purpose my second-grade teacher handed out mimeographed "seat work": to keep us busy! Instead they serve God and the neighbor always by serving faith.

2. LC, Ten Commandments, 326, in BC, 430.

3. LC, Ten Commandments, 2 (BC, 386).

In this regard, one remarkable thing about statements in the Bible regarding homosexual behavior is that many of them, too, have as their main concern not behavior per se but behavior in the light of faith and unbelief. Most reputable modern scholars, no matter what their specific opinion of the passages in Romans 1 and Leviticus 18, are nearly unanimous in their agreement that the real issue in both places is faith in God. Indeed, when Luther arrives at the sixth commandment in the Small Catechism, he simply assumes that faith alone is the fulfillment of the commandments. "We are to fear and love God so that we live chaste and decent lives. . . ."[4] For Luther, then, the fulfillment of this commandment, like the others, is not simply a matter of external obedience to the letter of the law. Instead, it arises only out of a faith that refuses to worship pleasure or power (in sexual relations or anywhere else) but only worships the God who gives all good things and protects from all evil. Wherever else the present discussion about sexuality may lead us, it dare not lead us away from faith in the triune God, who creates, redeems, and makes holy.

The Inapplicable Ten Commandments

Luther's creative, open approach to the Ten Commandments has always managed to amaze his heirs. Imagine, if you will, Henry Eyster Jacobs's surprise when he discovered Luther did not believe Christians had to keep the Sabbath the way late-nineteenth-century American Protestants were insisting. Jacobs, a professor first at Gettysburg College and later at the seminary in Philadelphia and a translator and editor of *The Book of Concord,* had been asked to assemble Luther's comments on the third commandment by his church, the Pennsylvania Ministerium, and by the General Council to which it belonged. The expectation had been that German Lutherans could once again prove how American they had become. The result was the one document for which Jacobs (much to his chagrin) was most well known.[5] Luther did not much care for the fanatical Sabbath-keeping that so preoccupied nineteenth-century American Protestants.

4. For the phrase "fear and love," see Timothy J. Wengert, "'Fear and Love' in the Ten Commandments," *Concordia Journal* 21 (1995): 14-27.

5. See his summary of the dispute in "Sunday, Luth. View of," in *The Lutheran Cyclopedia,* ed. Henry Eyster Jacobs and John A. W. Haas (New York: Scribner, 1899), 466-67.

The fact remains: Luther was no biblicist and no fundamentalist. He insisted that Moses' rendition of the Ten Commandments was simply his meditation on the natural law of God written on all human hearts. Those parts that belonged to the specific situation of the Israelites, such as the prologue ("I am the Lord your God who brought you out of the land of Egypt"), had nothing to do directly with Christians. Just because the Bible says it, does not mean it applies willy-nilly to us!

There are two striking examples of this refreshing attitude toward the commandments in the Large Catechism.[6] The third commandment is the most obvious case. This commandment, Luther wrote, does not apply to Christians literally. We do not keep the Sabbath holy. In Luther's day, everyone worked on Saturday, which is literally the Sabbath. Moreover, Luther did not think much of the notion that Christians had simply transferred Saturday observances to Sunday. Not only did he have Jesus' own behavior to back him up, but he also introduced here the concept of an "external matter" (related to the term *adiaphora*). The important thing for Luther was the fact that this law did not apply to Christians in a literal sense at all![7] God's Word makes every day of the week holy for a Christian, Luther stated, so what is all the fuss about Saturday or Sunday?[8]

Of course, this does not mean to say that for Luther this commandment had no use at all. He had far too much respect for Scripture as God's Word to say that! What he notes in his explanation, however, should give all obsessive-compulsive legalists pause. First, he underscores just how important it is to give people a day off, especially laborers, a piece of good news for workers in every generation.[9] Second, he insists that the way to apply this commandment to the Christian is to concentrate on its original purpose — not only to provide real rest for tired bodies but also to give people an opportunity to rest in God's Word.[10]

6. A third example, the prohibition of graven images, can only be an argument from silence. Nevertheless, one of the reasons Luther did not renumber the Ten Commandments (as did Ulrich Zwingli and other Reformed theologians) is because he understood the prohibition of graven images as simply one way Moses applied the first commandment to his own people.

7. LC, Ten Commandments, 82 (BC, 397) and n. 64, which refers to *Against the Heavenly Prophets,* 1525 (LW 40:97-98).

8. LC, Ten Commandments, 87-88, 91 (BC, 398-99).

9. LC, Ten Commandments, 83 (BC, 397).

10. LC, Ten Commandments, 84 (BC, 397).

On this second point, his treatise *On Good Works* from 1520 is particularly insightful.[11] Faith itself frees a person from works and provides the proper way to keep the Sabbath not only externally but also in the heart. Thus, God wants people to come together precisely to hear this word that frees us from work. Of course, this means that the biggest Sabbath-breakers, in the view of the Large Catechism, may be found not simply among those who lie dead drunk in taverns on Sunday morning (or not so drunk at sporting events, in fishing boats, or God knows where else) but precisely among those preachers whose sermons are paeans to the law and legalism and among those hearers who listen to a year's worth of good sermons with no appreciable effect![12]

The other place where Luther (cavalierly!) dismisses one of the Ten Commandments comes with the ninth and tenth and applies more directly to the current discussion of sexuality. Luther notes at the outset that these two commandments, which forbid coveting, were given by God to Moses precisely because otherwise the Israelites would have conceived of the commandments as applying only to externals and not to the heart, that is, to faith.[13] Christians have this advantage that they understand this from sermons on the commandments delivered by Jesus (in the Sermon on the Mount) and by Paul (in Romans 7).

However, there is another reason the tenth commandment in particular does not apply directly to Luther and his readers: Germany had no slaves and did not treat women like chattel — both things this commandment clearly assumes by lumping wives and servants in with the cattle.[14] What a remarkable turn of a text! Here Luther, who more than anyone focuses theology on the Word alone, dismisses a clear Word of God as inapplicable for social reasons! We have no slaves, and women are not property! Now, unlike some of the Bible's modern readers, who read everything in the light of their own desires and dreams, Luther does not gloat at this point. "So many lands, so many customs," as he happily proclaims in his preface to the Marriage Booklet, citing an adage familiar to his readers.[15] When it comes to questions of social behavior, Luther glorifies neither the

11. LW 44:54-80, especially 72.

12. LC, Ten Commandments, 90 and 96 (BC, 398-99).

13. LC, Ten Commandments, 293 (BC, 425).

14. LC, Ten Commandments, 294-95 (BC, 425).

15. SC, A Marriage Booklet, 1, trans. Timothy J. Wengert, in BC, 367.

social relations of the Bible nor those of his own time. Instead, he takes both into consideration, as he attempts to find his way as a Christian preacher in this world. We are still not to covet, but we dare not mistake the social situation reflected in the commandment for our own and thereby glorify one or the other.

The Expanding Commandments

If Luther is capable of showing how commandments do not apply literally to his situation, he is equally willing to expand the commandments far beyond their original scope so that they do apply to his own age. This is not the work of a literalist or a legalist but of a believer, who assumes that the clearest statement of God's law written on each human heart came in the Ten Commandments.

This approach of expanding the commandments, to some extent already present in the exegetical tradition,[16] began as a reaction to what Luther viewed as a particularly pernicious way to interpret the biblical text — one that infected the late-medieval church. Already church fathers had distinguished between commandments of God, which were required of all people, and counsels, which a Christian could freely follow. In Thomas Aquinas's *Summa,* the three chief counsels became poverty, chastity, and obedience, and they were best followed by bishops or those under a vow — monks and friars. Such people, by virtue of their vows, were in a status of perfection and, by fulfilling the counsels, their "works of supererogation" produced more merit than those who simply followed the Ten Commandments.[17]

When Luther challenges this myth in the 1520 *Treatise on Good Works,* he delights in repeating for each commandment that there are enough works in each to keep a person busy for a lifetime.[18] There is no need to look for better things to do; the Christian believer simply does not have the time.[19] This same theme runs throughout the Large Catechism as

16. Which looked at how one violated a commandment in "thought, word, and deed" and at the work of the "Devil, the world, and our sinful flesh."

17. *Summa Theologica* II/II, q. 184, a. 1-8 and q. 186, a. 1-10. (See also I/II, q. 108, a. 4.)

18. LW 41:61, for example.

19. He makes some of the same points the following year in his *Judgment of Martin Luther on Monastic Vows* (for example, LW 44:256-61).

well. The first commandment reveals all kinds of idols — not simply graven images but common "gods," like money or fame, and more complicated ones, like works righteousness. In the latter case, he even warns the readers (simple parish pastors) that this may be too complicated for the children to understand.[20] The second commandment, which Luther rightly assumes was meant for the law court, also includes every other case where God's name is used for nothing.[21] The third commandment includes not simply taking a day off or refraining from work on Saturday but also respecting God's Word and preaching — something that many congregations in conflict (and sometimes their pastors) fail to do. The fourth commandment includes not only parents but also all their helpers (schoolteachers, pastors, employers, and the government).[22]

Explanations of the other commandments show a similar generosity. Following Jesus' lead in the Sermon on the Mount, Luther is quick to point out all the other ways we have invented for killing people that do not involve physical death. The sixth commandment includes decency and love and forbids lust. The seventh includes not just pickpockets but bigwigs (accounting firms?) and other "arm-chair robbers."[23] The eighth again goes far beyond Moses' concern for the law courts and includes simple lying, gossip, and a host of other sins especially, but not exclusively, found in parish life today, too. As we will examine below, Luther also includes the positive aspects of these commandments: caring for the neighbor, the spouse, the neighbor's property, and the neighbor's reputation.

"But Instead"

One always must make remarkably important decisions when translating from one language to another. Most translations of the Small Catechism

20. It is also remarkable how many pastors and theologians have remained ignorant of this idol over the years.

21. One of the complaints about the author's translation of the Small Catechism was that it included magic — something that modern folk have grown out of. Of course, its inclusion arose not only from a desire to reflect more carefully Luther's actual text but also from personal pastoral experience.

22. More on these two positive commandments is found in the next section.

23. Luther's clever (but inaccurate) rendering of the low German dialect, *Stohl,* which actually means interest, not stool.

take Luther's little word *sondern,* which occurs in eight of the explanations to the Ten Commandments, to mean "but." Thus, the explanation to the second commandment that I had to memorize as a child ran like this: "We are to fear and love God, so that we do not curse, swear, use witchcraft, lie, or deceive by his name, *but* call upon him in every trouble, pray, praise, and give thanks." However, the word *sondern* is a much more powerful word in Luther's thought, nearly the German equivalent of *immo,* one of Luther's favorite Latin adversatives.[24] It is etymologically related to the English "sunder" (as in: "What God has joined together let no man put asunder"), and it still has that meaning as a verb in German. Thus, the current translation renders this powerful word "but instead."

In fact, the *sondern* in Luther's explanations points to a second important way in which he expands the commandments: by including both "shalt not's" and "shalt's." Every Word of God — whether a command or a promise — always implies for Luther its opposite. In the case of the commandments, every prohibition ("Do not use my name in vain!") implies that God wants us to put that name to good use ("in every need" we are to call on God in prayer, praise, and thanksgiving). Commandments are not busywork; they reveal the best God intends for humanity.

At the same time, every positive command implies that there is something God does not want us to do. Thus, the third and the fourth commandments (which are positive: "Keep the Sabbath" and "Honor your parents") also imply negatives ("Do not despise the Word or preaching" and "Do not despise parents or superiors"). We often forget what Luther did not: that failure to honor God's Word or other people in their God-given offices is not neutral; it always implies despising.

Moses' Good Order

Most people read the Ten Commandments like a phone book, where each entry has equal value. Luther does not. Not only does he see the first commandment as the most important and as expressed throughout all the

24. Heiko Oberman, "Immo: Luthers reformatorische Entdeckungen im Spiegel der Rhetorik," in *Lutheriana: Zum 500. Geburtstag Martin Luthers von den Mitarbeitern der Weimarer Ausgabe,* ed. Gerhard Hammer and Karl-Heinz zur Mühlen (Cologne and Vienna: Böhlau, 1984), 17-38.

commandments, but he also argues that there is a distinction to be made among the remaining commandments. They are given in descending order of importance. Thus, honoring one's parents or others in authority has an automatic limit: the first three commandments. When parents or other authorities command things that contradict faith in God, prayer, worship, or God's Word, Christians must not obey.

In a similar fashion and by virtue of their office, parents and other authorities may "break" the commandments that follow the fourth. Thus, governments wield coercive power (breaking the fifth commandment either literally in capital punishment or in more general ways through imprisonment). They (or the church) can pronounce a couple divorced (breaking the sixth commandment and the dominical command in Matthew 19:6).[25] They can expropriate property through taxes or the right of eminent domain (breaking the seventh commandment). And they can even speak evil of persons, as when a judge pronounces sentence (breaking the eighth commandment). This last example was a particularly sensitive one for Luther, who took the time to explain to his congregation why he could speak evil of the pope and not break this commandment — he did it by virtue of his office as teacher of the church![26]

Before jumping to the conclusion that such an approach to the commandments would foster tyranny, one should note that such lawbreaking was allowed only to the office of good governing (or good parenting, where even moderate discipline also "breaks" some commandments). Luther describes such governance not only in his appeals for good schools but also in his explanation to the fourth petition of the Lord's Prayer. Those in authority are to see to it that bread gets placed on their subjects' tables. The special place of the fourth commandment could never excuse selfishness or tyranny.[27] However, the office of parent or magistrate or pas-

25. Luther one time declared a woman divorced from her husband who constantly beat her. The council in Wittenberg (whom no one liked and whom Luther often threatened with excommunication) tried to exonerate the man and force the woman back to him (arguing that if wife beating were grounds for divorce, every woman in Wittenberg could do it). Luther appealed to the elector. See Hermann Kunst, *Evangelischer Glaube und politische Verantwortung: Martin Luther als politischer Berater* (Stuttgart: Evangelisches Verlagswerk, 1976), 86.

26. LC, Ten Commandments, 284 (BC, 424).

27. See especially Luther's comments in LC, Ten Commandments, 167-78 (BC, 409-10).

tor does wield authority. Otherwise, there is the tyranny of anarchy. Against those who think that taxation is evil or no judge can be a Christian, for example, Luther's discovering of the Mosaic ordering of the commandments speaks a firm "No!"

Moreover, in a reverse of this process, but consistent with it, Luther also realized that the poor and oppressed had a special place in the commandments. This becomes especially clear in the seventh commandment. There, Luther (interpreting the commandment positively) insists that we are to see to our neighbors' bodily needs. What if we and the government do not? The poor will cry to God (the only authority higher than neighbor or prince in Luther's world), and God will assuredly hear their cry. Then, look out! There will be hell to pay.[28]

Moses' Silence and Luther's Loquacity

In one interesting case involving the fourth commandment, Luther has expressly more to say than Moses.[29] Moses, after all, simply commands obedience to parents with no questions asked. In our own day, no one could in good conscience simply tell children to obey their parents no matter what. So, too, Luther makes two important exceptions. First, as we have stated above, he realizes what many teachers of the commandments forget: that Moses gives the commandments in order of importance. This means that Luther expressly excludes the first three commandments, which have to do directly with one's relation to God, from any discussion of obedience to parents or others in authority. For someone who had to defy pope and emperor and whose fellow Christians had even perished for confessing the gospel, this is no small matter. "If God's Word and will are placed first and are observed, nothing ought to be considered more important than the will and word of our parents, provided that these, too, are subordinated to God and are not set in opposition to the preceding commandments."[30]

Second, Luther realizes that — despite Moses' silence — he must say

28. LC, Ten Commandments, 246-47 (BC, 419).

29. The same can be said of the other Reformers. See David C. Steinmetz, "Calvin and Melanchthon on Romans 13:1-7," *Ex Auditu: An Annual of the Frederick Neumann Symposium on Theological Interpretation of Scripture* 2 (1986): 67-77.

30. LC, Ten Commandments, 116 (BC, 402).

something about parental responsibilities for children (and governmental responsibilities for their subjects). Even though his brief paraphrase of the fourth commandment in the Small Catechism omits such material, his preface to that work mentions such responsibilities expressly, as does the Large Catechism.[31] Luther has good authority to go on; Paul himself did the same thing in Ephesians. Moreover, every chance he gets to talk about such matters, Luther urges all authorities to support the education of children — something we could easily apply directly to our own day, where the importance of schools and learning is still under attack.

Moses' Loquacity and Luther's Silence

Luther does not always say as much as his text does about certain sins. In the Small Catechism his explanations of both the first and the sixth commandment break the normal paraphrastic nature of the work. Here are two negative commandments ("No other gods!" and "No adultery!") that receive only positive explanations: "We are to fear, love, and trust in God above all things" and "We are to fear and love God so that we lead chaste and decent lives, and each love and honor his or her spouse."[32]

The Large Catechism makes clear that Luther had plenty to say about the breaking of the first commandment. However, the explanation of the sixth commandment contains very few specifics. Luther first generalizes the command to mean (explicitly) the dishonoring of another person's marriage partner. He points out that Moses particularly mentions adultery because the Jewish people married young, celibacy was not commended, and prostitution and lewdness were not tolerated. After complaining about the "shameless mess and cesspool of all sorts of immorality and indecency," he points out that this commandment forbids not only outward acts but also "every kind of cause, provocation and means."[33] He immediately points out that sins against this commandment include not helping one's neighbor in preventing unchastity. What he does not do is provide

31. SC, Preface, 19-20 (BC, 350). He spends most of the 1520 *Treatise on Good Works* (LW 44:80-100) describing the responsibility of the authorities.

32. The woodcuts for these two commandments do demonstrate the breaking of these commandments: the Israelites and the golden calf, and David and Bathsheba.

33. LC, Ten Commandments, 202 (BC, 414).

descriptions of such activity. For Christians in a society bombarded with implicit and explicit talk about sex, Luther's reserve may come as a breath of fresh air.

The Commandments and "Self-Chosen Spirituality"

For Luther, the commandments are important not only for what they say but also for what they do not say. When he comes to translate Paul's strictures against certain kinds of pious (and misguided) behavior in the congregation at Colossae, Luther renders their problem in Colossians 2:23 "self-chosen spirituality," an expression particularly pertinent for a society infected by new-age religion. Against such stuff (Luther had in mind especially the monks),[34] Luther placed the Ten Commandments and other portions of Scripture that give us a much better idea of what God has in mind for humanity.

In contrast to modern attempts to bless or condemn the status quo, Luther describes as good works those things that have good biblical precedent. Otherwise, without a Word of God, as in the case of how one receives communion or other such matters, the conscience would remain uncertain. Luther is properly suspicious of folks who think they can soothe people's consciences by their own authority. When their last day comes, the devil will laugh at them if they say, "Well, Dr. Luther told me this was all right."[35] Of course, the devil is also not impressed when someone says, "They did it this way in Moses' day."[36] Certainty comes from the sure encounter with God's Word in the real world, where all the hard decisions arise out of God's Word for the sake of the conscience.

34. On occasion, such as in his sermon on the wedding at Cana, he rails against certain sourpusses who want to forbid people having fun at weddings. If it is not a sin to sit or to walk, it is not a sin to dance. At this point in the text, a pious editor noted that in Luther's day dances were not as lascivious as they are now. See *Dr. Martin Luthers sämtliche Schriften*, ed. Georg Walch, 2nd ed., 23 vols. (St. Louis: Concordia, 1892-1910), 11:467-68. Clearly, the editor had not seen Bruegel's late-sixteenth-century paintings of peasants dancing at a wedding.

35. See, especially, his Invocavit Sermons of March 1522. See LW 51:79-80.

36. See Luther's attack on Andreas Karlstadt in *Against the Heavenly Prophets*, 1525 (LW 40:84-90).

Equality in the Sixth Commandment

One of the most surprising things about Luther's explanation of the sixth commandment is the equality that Luther implies throughout. Despite his use of texts from Genesis 3 and Ephesians 5 in his marriage service (where even there he tones them down through his use of the promises in Genesis 1–2) and his use of Colossians 3 and 1 Peter in the so-called Table of Duties ("Household Chart," where his point is to prevent women from being fearful), Luther never mentions any inequality in his exposition of this commandment.[37] Even his paraphrastic explanation in the Small Catechism seems to imply (for both the 1959 and the 2000 editions of English translations of *The Book of Concord*) that he had men and women equally in mind.

This outspoken equality was no small feat for a thinker whose entire social life was marked by inequalities. However, for Luther such inequalities have nothing to do with the marriage bed. Here the man and woman get to fulfill God's blessing of the first couple. Rather than read inequality into the text (and thereby interpret Moses using [deutero-] Paul), Luther follows the lead of Paul in 1 Corinthians 7 (a passage he had interpreted at length in 1523)[38] and looks equally to the partners in a marriage. Whatever else they are, sexual relations are not an invitation to exploitation.

> Thus God wants to guard and protect every husband or wife through this commandment against anyone who would violate them. However, because this commandment is directed specifically toward marriage as a walk of life and gives occasion to speak of it, you should carefully note, first, how highly God honors and praises this walk of life, endorsing and protecting it by his commandment. . . . [God] has established [marriage] before all others as the first of all institutions, and he created man and woman differently (as is evident) not for indecency but to be true to each other, to be fruitful, to beget children, and to nurture and bring them up to the glory of God. God has therefore blessed this walk of life most richly, above all others, and, in addition, has supplied and endowed it with everything in the world in order that this walk of

37. See SC, A Marriage Booklet, 10-15 (BC, 369-71) and SC, The Household Chart, 6-7 (BC, 366).

38. LW 28:1-56.

> life might be richly provided for. Married life is no matter for jest or idle curiosity, but it is a glorious institution and an object of God's serious concern.[39]

In the same vein, Luther concludes his remarks on this commandment by stressing mutual cherishing and love in marriage.

> [T]his commandment requires all people not only to live chastely in deed, word, and thought in their particular situation (that is, especially in marriage as a walk of life), but also to love and cherish the spouse whom God has given them. Wherever marital chastity is to be maintained, above all it is essential that husband and wife live together in love and harmony, cherishing each other wholeheartedly and with perfect fidelity. . . . Under such conditions chastity always follows spontaneously without any command.[40]

In this positive assessment Luther takes direct aim at the "self-chosen" spirituality of monastic and clerical celibacy. Men and women of all walks of life, who have been created for it, shall be found in marriage. While allowing for some God-given exceptions (unsuitability or the gift of chastity outside marriage), Luther insists that the rest cannot resist these "natural inclinations and stimulations" of their own flesh and blood.[41] This he contrasts, in no uncertain terms, to the "papal crowd" of monks, priests, and nuns who, while abstaining from acts of fornication, have hearts filled with unchaste thoughts and evil desires. "In this regard, even if the monastic life were godly, still it is not in their power to maintain chastity."[42] His reason for giving such warnings, Luther states, is to foster a desire for marriage among the young and thereby lessen the "filthy, dissolute, disorderly conduct that is now so rampant everywhere." And Luther had never been to a rock concert or subscribed to HBO!

39. LC, Ten Commandments, 205-8 (BC, 414).
40. LC, Ten Commandments, 219 (BC, 415).
41. LC, Ten Commandments, 212 (BC, 415).
42. LC, Ten Commandments, 216 (BC, 415).

An Ought Never Implies a Can

Why does Luther spend half of the text of the Large Catechism talking about the commandments? Part of the reason may have to do with the proto-antinomian talk of his former student John Agricola.[43] However, Luther also provides an even more important answer to that question in the rest of the Large Catechism. The chief function of the law is not to show us an easy way to heaven, which (with a little hard work) we can reach, but to show us our sin — how infinitely far we are from heaven, God, and our neighbor (who is Christ in our midst!).

The Christian life, like baptism, goes from drowning to rising, from death to resurrection, from confession of sin to forgiveness. Thus, Luther writes against those who think the commandments are easy and who therefore think they have time to fulfill God's counsels. "They fail to see, these miserable, blind fools, that no one is able to keep even one of the Ten Commandments as it ought to be kept. Both the Creed and the Lord's Prayer must come to our aid, as we shall hear later. Through them we must seek and pray for help and receive it continually."[44]

Whatever else we do with the Ten Commandments, we can do nothing worse than to ignore their main function: to put us to death by showing our sin and driving us to the one place where there is help: the gospel. It is in Jesus Christ alone, who is the mirror of the Father's heart and whom the Holy Spirit reveals to us by faith alone, that we have our hope. This is not a matter of declaring a wrong right or of telling others to buck up and try harder. This is a matter of the gospel alone, that good news of forgiveness, life, and salvation that comes to us freely, as God's gracious word in Christ.

This brings us back to the beginning, to the heart. Luther begins and ends the commandments with their clear demand for faith. He only finds the commandments' fulfillment in the work of the Holy Spirit, who through the Word gives faith in Christ and thus, in him, fulfills all the commandments. The commandments — all of them — keep their rightful place in Christian theology only when they are in first place — that is, as

43. See Timothy J. Wengert, *Law and Gospel: Philip Melanchthon's Debate with John Agricola of Eisleben over* Poenitentia (Grand Rapids: Baker, 1997), 148-53.

44. LC, Ten Commandments, 316 (BC, 428). See also LC, Creed, 1-3 (BC, 431), and LC, Lord's Prayer, 2 (BC, 440-41).

the Word of death that drives us inexorably to our crucified and risen Lord Jesus. Perhaps, whatever else we say about sexuality in the coming years, we need most of all to remind one another of this.

CHAPTER 7

Luther on the Creed

Charles P. Arand

The Apostles' Creed has served as the baptismal creed for expounding the trinitarian faith to countless catechumens within the Western church for over fifteen hundred years. During that time it has been the subject of some of the most profound catechetical lectures, theological orations, and devotional writings ever produced by the church. Within the history of the Western church, however, no exposition of the creed for catechumens has yet matched the treatment given it by Martin Luther in his two catechisms of 1529. The Small Catechism's explanations possess a unique combination of theological depth and literary beauty that remains unsurpassed.[1] In the Large Catechism, those explanations are given a fuller theological amplification while remaining rooted in the earthiness of everyday life. In dealing with Luther's treatment of the creed, it would be a serious mistake to comment on it in isolation from its relation to the Decalogue and the Lord's Prayer, that is, within the larger framework of the catechisms themselves. When taken in their totality, they provide the Christian with a handbook for the "art of living by faith."

Within the overall structure of Luther's catechisms, the Decalogue diagnoses the fundamental human condition in terms of the need for faith in God within every situation of life. Yet even as the Decalogue requires us

1. Luther's expositions of the Apostles' Creed in the SC and LC will be cited from the BC (with slight emendations by the author), in parentheses according to the marginal paragraph number. Thus, "LC, Creed, 14-16" refers to those paragraphs in that translation.

to have no other gods, it does not divulge the identity of God. That is the task of the creed. In addition, if the first commandment makes known our fundamental nature as receivers, the creed underscores it by drawing out the nature and essence of God as the Giver of all good things. And so Luther consistently expounds the creed as the confession of Christians in response to the first commandment.[2] In his May 1528 sermons on the catechisms, Luther introduced the creed with the question, "What kind of God do you have? What do you expect from him?"[3] In answer to that question, the creed shows what we can expect from God (LC, Creed, 1). In the creed we learn that God has "given himself to us all wholly and completely, with all that he is and has."[4] Luther's keynote and theme can be stated simply: God gives; we receive. Knowing who God is, what God is like, Christians can then pray confidently the next chief part of the catechism, the "Our Father."

The Threefold Work of the Trinity

The Christian answers the question, "What is your God like?" by confessing the threefold name and work of God. To that end, Luther deliberately reorganized the creedal material, without altering the wording, by reducing the twelve articles (corresponding to the twelve apostles) common in the late Middle Ages to the three articles common in the early church. More than a desire for historical accuracy on Luther's part accounts for this rearrangement. He wanted to concentrate the catechumen's attention on the saving work of the triune God and further emphasize the *pro nobis* character of God's work "for us" in all aspects of our life. In doing so, he refocused the church's attention on the Trinity and the triune structure of salvation.

This restructuring of the creed occurred in two stages. First, in 1520, Luther correlated the three articles to the three persons of the Trinity. Each article tells about one of the three persons of the holy and divine Trinity. The first speaks of the Father, the second speaks of the Son, and the third speaks of the Holy Spirit.[5] This trinitarian ordering gave the entire explana-

2. LW 43:25.
3. WA 30I:9, 18.
4. LW 37:366.
5. *Ein kurze Form der zehn Gebote, eine kurze Form des Glaubens, eine kurze Form*

tion of the creed a theocentric perspective, since the Trinity now became the foundation of the catechisms' explanation of the creed. Girgensohn suggests that one ramification of this change is that the object of our faith no longer consists primarily of dogmatic statements about various theological subjects. Instead, the object of faith becomes the person of God, and so faith becomes viewed interpersonally and relationally.[6] Second, in the latter half of the decade, Luther correlated the three articles of the creed not only to the three persons but also to the particular gifts and works of each person. This theme comes out most prominently in his 1528-29 catechetical sermons. During this period Luther attaches the captions "creation, redemption, sanctification" to the articles and thereby makes them their leading motifs.[7] These captions are firmly in place by the December Sermon Series of 1528.[8] At that point Luther summarized the creed with the words "I believe in God the Father, who created me; I believe in God the Son, who redeemed me; and I believe in the Holy Spirit, who sanctifies me."[9]

Luther's restructuring of the creed allows him to teach the language and vocabulary of faith in a way that avoids turning faith into purely a matter of the head *(fides quae creditur)* or purely a matter of the heart *(fides qua creditur)*. When the former becomes the exclusive understanding

---

des Vaterunsers, 1520 (WA 7:214.25-28). This is also found verbatim in Luther's *Personal Prayer Book,* 1522 (LW 43:24).

6. Herbert Girgensohn, *Teaching Luther's Catechism* (Philadelphia: Muhlenberg, 1959), 121.

7. The captions for the first and second articles are fairly obvious, but less so for the third article. Luther first uses the caption "sanctification" in the Visitation Articles. In the third article, Luther had to contend with five disparate items and bring them into an organic unity. The second article seems to have provided the key as seen in his sermon on 10 December 1528. As the individual items of the second article dealt with the person and work of Christ, so Luther took the individual items of the third article and identified them with the work of the Spirit. Albrecht Peters, *Kommentar zu Luthers Katechismen,* ed. Gottfried Seebaß, vol. 2, *Der Glaube* (Göttingen: Vandenhoeck & Ruprecht, 1991), 36-37.

8. "The Creed has three articles, the first concerning the Father, the second concerning the Son, the third concerning the Holy Spirit. What do you believe about the Father? Answer: He is the Creator. What do you believe about the Son? He is the Redeemer. What do you believe about the Holy Spirit? He is the Sanctifier" (LW 51:162).

9. The first article teaches creation, the second redemption, and the third sanctification (LW 51:162, 163). The third article was the last to receive such a superscription. Here and elsewhere in Luther, the terms "sanctify" and "sanctification" include all aspects of being made holy, including forgiveness of sins.

of faith, faith becomes little more than an intellectual assent to the correctness of facts and thus devoid of any personal commitment to that which is confessed. It is akin to saying, "I believe that two plus two equals four." On the other hand, when the latter becomes the exclusive understanding of faith, we end up in the situation too common in the United States: "It doesn't matter what you believe as long as you believe sincerely." The key to faith becomes one's personal passion or depth of commitment apart from the object of that commitment. The subjective experience of faith becomes detached from the message of the gospel and degenerates into some form of sentimentality. Luther's exposition avoids falling off on either side of those two positions and provides a way to hold the head and the heart together in a most intimate unity. At every mention of God's gifts we must speak of their reception, that is, faith. At every mention of faith, we must mention the gifts received.

The Father Creates

Even as the entire creed was given to provide us with the gift of faith, so each article individually moves toward the same goal. In his earlier catechetical works, Luther placed more emphasis on the phrase "Father Almighty" than on "Creator of heaven and earth" in the Apostles' Creed.[10] In this context, he stressed the dynamic interaction between the omnipotence of God and the love of the Father. Because God is almighty he can help us; because he is our Father, he wants to help and will help.[11] In his later writings he shifts the focus to the words "Creator of heaven and earth." And so in the Small Catechism, Luther takes the opening line of the Apostles' Creed, "I believe in God the Father Almighty, Creator of Heaven and Earth," and capitalizes the word CREATOR, thereby bringing to the foreground the theme of the article and making it the point of reference for his entire exposition.[12]

In the case of the first article, Luther's goal is to arouse faith in God's

10. Peters, *Kommentar zu Luthers Katechismen,* 2:56-57.

11. This is especially true of Luther's *Brief Explanation* of 1520 (see LW 43:26) and his sermon on the creed of 4 March 1523 (WA 11:49.27ff.).

12. The Kolb-Wengert edition (BC) has helpfully brought this out through its capitalization of these words as well.

creaturely and providential care. In Luther's wording, the first article teaches that "we should know and learn where we come from, what we are, and to whom we belong."[13] In brief, we are to perceive ourselves as creatures and we are to recognize God as the exclusive giver of our lives and the whole context of created reality. We belong not to ourselves, and therefore also the course of our lives belongs not to ourselves.[14] By stressing God's creaturely care, the first article provides the basis for the Christian to pray the concluding words of the Small Catechism's morning and evening prayers, "I commend myself, my body and soul and all things into your hand." As Luther expounds on the theme of Creator in the catechisms, he addresses both the *creatio prima* (initial creation) and the *creatio continua* (continuing creation).

When the Apostles' Creed repeats the scriptural declaration that God created "the heavens and the earth," it utilizes a device called *merismus* by which two opposites are used to convey a larger whole. It names the highest point you can imagine and the lowest point you can imagine, thereby including everything in between. It is like saying that God created everything from A to Z.[15] To confess that God has created heaven and earth indicates by means of extremes that everything from the largest galaxy to the smallest microbe owes its existence to the divine will.[16] In this way the creed emphasized that the distinction between creator and creation was more fundamental than any other distinction in the universe. It is more fundamental than the distinction between body and soul, humans and angels, or matter and spirit. This distinction makes it clear that as Creator, God alone is independent and self-sufficient. The creation is by definition dependent and contingent. Thus the relation is established between God as absolute giver and the human person as absolute receiver. Luther captures this emphasis of the Apostles' Creed by replacing "heaven and earth" with the more personal phrase "me together with all creatures." He then reinforces the point that God is responsible for the totality of existence by stressing the little particle "all" nine times. God has made "all that exists,"

13. WA 45:12.16f.

14. Michael Beintker, "Das Schöpfercredo in Luthers Kleinem Katechismus," *Neue Zeitschrift für Religionsphilosophie* 31 (January 1989): 16.

15. Scott E. Hoezee, "A Sermon: The End in the Beginning," in *Exploring and Proclaiming the Apostles' Creed,* ed. Roger E. Van Harn (Grand Rapids: Eerdmans, 2004), 50.

16. Gordon J. Wenham, *Word Biblical Commentary: Genesis* (1:15) (Waco, Tex.: Word, 1987), 36.

given me "all my limbs and all my senses," "all my mental faculties," "all my property," and "all the necessities for body and life." He "protects against all danger," "defends me from all evil," and does this "all out of fatherly goodness." "For all of this it is my duty to thank and praise . . ." God has complete and total claim upon my life. Thus I am completely dependent upon God, as is all creation. The first article in turn provides the ontological foundation for the first commandment. "You shall have no other gods" because God alone is the Creator, he alone has given all that exists. In other words, there are no other gods beside him!

Luther does not proceed to expound the *creatio prima* of the first article by first dealing with the vastness of the universe and only at the very end arriving at my existence, in which context I will perceive something of my insignificance.[17] Instead, he introduces God's creative activity by beginning with the fact of my personal existence (body and soul), proceeds outward to the basic necessities of life (house and home), and then goes on to help the Christian embrace the entire world as God's good creation (LC, Creed, 14-16). This may seem somewhat anthropocentric, but in fact Luther's goal is to teach me to perceive all of life as a gift from God. And so he begins at the point where I most directly encounter God's creative activity (my very existence) and leads me by the hand out into the world in order to embrace the entire creation as God's gift.

The main focus of Luther's explanation, however, is on God's ongoing care for creation, what the dogmaticians refer to as the *creatio continua.* Here Luther expands the notion of creation beyond the Apostles' Creed.[18] The verbs ("give," "preserve," "provide," "protect," "shield," and "defend") are all explications of the word "create." In this way Luther picks up central themes of the biblical witness (Ps. 104; Job 38–40) where God does not stand apart from his creation after he brought it into existence. To the contrary, God remains actively involved in the here and now by continuing his work of creation for us. Whereas in the *creatio prima* God created

17. Our insignificance and place within the universe can be gained from a picture in Carl Sagan's book *Pale Blue Dot.* The picture is of Earth as taken from the *Voyager* spacecraft as it sped past Saturn.

18. In a sense, however, Luther is simply picking up and developing that which was implicit in the title *pantokrator* (all ruling or almighty) of the early Christian creeds. The title did not stress so much an abstract attribute of God as the active government of God within the world. It captures what that popular song declared, "He's got the whole world in his hands."

ex nihilo, "out of nothing," in the *creatio continua* he works through his "masks." In a sense, "God together with all creatures" has created me! Creatures are the "hands, channels, and means through which God bestows all blessings" (LC, Ten Commandments, 26).

In his catechisms Luther personalized creation in a different way than do contemporary New Age philosophers or radical environmental theologians. The Creator is not in, or equated with, the creature. Instead, he stands behind his gifts as the good giver. By viewing creation as a mask or coworker with God, creation is personalized and freed from being seen as godless material with which humans can do whatever they want.[19] Luther wants us to see the One who has given all things by having us look beyond the mask to where God works. Thus he exhorts, "When you see a tree bearing fruit, you see God the Creator at work."[20] Luther wants to open our eyes and ears that we may perceive how God is constantly at work around us. He shows how to cultivate the eyes and ears of faith in a simple and straightforward manner in a sermon from 1538. He exhorts that if we would only open our eyes and ears, we could hear the corn speaking to us: "Please rejoice in God, eat, drink, use me and serve your neighbor! I will fill the granary." In a similar way, the cows are also speaking to us. If we were not deaf, we would hear them say: "Rejoice! We bring you butter and cheese from God. Eat, drink, and share it with others. . . ." Likewise when we see the chickens lay their eggs, we would hear them saying, "Rejoice; we hatch new chicks." Continuing the theme, Luther points out that we should be able to hear the pigs grunt that they bring us brats and wurst from God. In brief, "all of the creatures are speaking to us."[21] And so whoever "disgraces the creature, violates the creator, who is in them for us there."[22]

The Son Redeems

The second article shows what we receive from God, above and beyond all the good things of creation mentioned in the first article (LC, Creed, 26).

19. Beintker, "Das Schöpfercredo in Luthers Kleinem Katechismus," 14.

20. Sermon, 10 December 1528; WA 30II:87.6-9; 88.5-6, 10-11; WA 30I:87f., 33ff., *Katechismuspredigten,* 1528.

21. WA 46:494.15ff., see also 45.

22. Beintker, "Das Schöpfercredo in Luthers Kleinem Katechismus," 15.

As he does in the first article, Luther selects a single theme by which he illumines the entire article. In the Apostles' Creed, Luther had three options around which he could have centered his explanation: (1) Jesus Christ; (2) his only Son; (3) our Lord. In the history of catechetical interpretation, the expression "our Lord" is pressed into service first by Luther and made the focal point of the interpretation. From the time of Augustine to Aquinas, it remained relatively unstressed. Indeed, Peters contends, "Nowhere was there an attempt to acquire a grasp of the entire article with the help of this expression."[23] And so the entire explanation of the second article centers our entire attention on the statement: Jesus Christ "is my Lord."[24] These three words fall heavily like a deep bell striking three times with the loudest strike on the word "Lord."[25] Why would Luther settle on the phrase "our Lord"? In part the language of lordship and kingship would have resonated with hearers living in a feudal society. But two further reasons suggest themselves. First, by means of it, Luther draws out the soteriological ramifications of the early church's Christology. Second, it also allows him to bring out the *pro nobis* character of Christ's work "for us," which in many ways was the chief contribution of the Reformation.[26]

With the phrase "our Lord," Luther pulls together the three centers of the Apostles' Creed, namely, the incarnation and birth, suffering and death, resurrection and exaltation of Christ. These three centers in turn raise three distinctive but related questions. Who is my Lord? How did he become my Lord? For what purpose did he become my Lord? For peasants in a medieval context, Luther accents what might be called a *Christus Victor* motif without ignoring the *Christus Victima* theme. This is especially true in the Large Catechism. Luther creates a "vivid miniature word painting" *(Kleinmalerei)*.[27] The picture painted before the eyes of the catechumen is a battlefield. On one side of the battlefield, stretched as far as the eyes can see, from horizon to horizon, stand Satan's armies and powers (sin, death, and the power of the devil). Behind enemy lines, the human

23. Albrecht Peters, "Die Theologie der Katechismen Luthers anhand der Zuordnung ihrer Hauptstücke," *Luther-Jahrbuch* 43 (1976): 16.

24. LC, Creed, 26, 27, 31.

25. Peters, *Kommentar zu Luthers Katechismen,* 2:100.

26. See Peters's lengthy treatment of this point, *Kommentar zu Luthers Katechismen,* 2:116ff.

27. M. Reu, *Dr. Martin Luther's Small Catechism: A History of Its Origin, Its Distribution, and Its Use* (Chicago: Wartburg Publishing House, 1929), 148.

race lies captive under the power of the devil, condemned to death, and "entangled in sin and blindness" (LC, Creed, 27). Christ the champion appears on the field for battle (like David against Goliath) and defeats sin, death, and the power of the devil by means of his blood and death.[28] Having routed the jailers and tyrants (LC, Creed, 30), Christ frees us, takes us as his own possession, and takes us home to his kingdom where we live in everlasting innocence, blessedness, and righteousness.

As Luther expounds the concept of Lord, he does so in a soteriological direction. The catechism does not speak in such a way that we first need to "accept Jesus as savior and then receive him as Lord." In the context of that phrase, "Lord" can sound like a taskmaster. In other words, accepting him in that way as our Savior is step one; putting him then in charge of our lives would be step two. Luther, by contrast, declares that "the little word 'Lord' simply means the same as Redeemer, that is, he who has brought us back from the devil to God, from death to life, from sin to righteousness and keeps us there" (LC, Creed, 31). In addition to the catechisms, this soteriological emphasis on Jesus as Lord appears in Luther's 1533 Torgau sermons on the creed. "See, thus shall we learn to know Him, that He is such a Lord who helps us, protects us and saves us." Luther proceeds to define Christ's lordship in terms of a gracious self-giving. As my Lord, Jesus gives himself in such a way that he is mine and I am his. He has given his life to us that we might find our life in him. Such gracious self-giving becomes and remains the trademark for the type of lordship by which Christ reclaims us and takes us under his care.[29] Christ does all this "for me." Here both elements belong together for Luther. All christological expressions are expressions *pro me,* and every phrase *pro me* must be interpreted in a christological fashion. The *pro me* emphasis on Christ's work again comes out in the Torgau sermons of 1533; "with 'our Lord' we confess that all that man is and does has occurred for us, that he was born for this purpose, has suffered, died and is risen that he may be OUR Lord."[30] Put more directly and bluntly, he became a human being in order to be my

28. For these motifs, see *The 1529 Holy Week and Easter Sermons of Dr. Martin Luther,* trans. Irving L. Sandberg, annotated with an introduction by Timothy J. Wengert (St. Louis: Concordia Academic Press, 1999). These sermons appeared just prior to the publication of the catechisms.

29. James Arne Nestingen, "Preaching the Catechism," *Word and World* 10 (1990): 37.

30. WA 37:49.16-19.

Lord, he lived and died in order to be my Lord, and he rose from the dead in order to be my Lord.

The Spirit Sanctifies

As in the first article, Luther selects one word from the third article and organizes his explanation around it. But this article gave him the most difficulty, for the Apostles' Creed simply states, "I believe in the Holy Spirit," and then appends a series of five seemingly disconnected items, namely, "the holy Christian church, the communion of saints, the forgiveness of sins, the resurrection of the body and the life everlasting." It was not readily apparent how all these things related to the Holy Spirit. It was not until 1529 that Luther finally settled on a central theme. He takes the name "Holy Spirit" and focuses on the word "holy" in such a way that the Holy Spirit *(spiritus sanctus)* of the Apostles' Creed becomes the sanctifying Spirit *(spiritus sanctificator)* in Luther's explanation. The theme of the "sanctifying Spirit" enables Luther to weave the five disparate items of the Apostles' Creed (holy Christian church, communion of saints, forgiveness of sins, resurrection of the body, and life everlasting) into an organic unity based on and centered in the sanctifying work of the Holy Spirit — as the title of the article indicates.[31] In other words, instead of using the word "holy" to describe a personal attribute of the Spirit, Luther uses it to describe what the Holy Spirit does for us and to us!

What does it mean to say that the Spirit sanctifies? The key lies in the opening words of Luther's explanation in the Small Catechism: "I believe that I cannot by my own reason or strength believe in Jesus Christ my Lord or come to Him." The Spirit sanctifies us by bestowing upon us the righteousness of Christ (second article) and thus making us holy. In the Large Catechism "sanctify" is treated initially as a synonym for justification. It means to bring us to "the Lord Christ to receive this blessing [the treasures of salvation won by Christ]" (LC, Creed, 39). So to be "sanctified" or to "be made holy" means "to be made a believer."[32] To be sure, later in his treatment of the third article Luther also deals with the idea of sanctification as we have become accustomed to considering it, namely, as growth in holi-

31. Girgensohn, *Teaching Luther's Catechism,* 178.
32. Girgensohn, *Teaching Luther's Catechism,* 180.

ness or growth in faith (LC, Creed, 57-59). The Spirit accomplishes this in two simultaneous actions: by bringing us to Christ and by gathering us into the church.

In the Small Catechism Luther first begins with the individual Christian. As in the first article, where Luther amplified the activity of "creating" to include "preserving" and "protecting," so here he unfolds the meaning of "sanctify" to encompass the activity of "calling," "enlightening," and "sustaining." It is not entirely clear what Luther packs into these words or precisely what is their relation to each other, for he does not deal with them at any length in the Large Catechism. It would seem best, however, not to take them as describing different, successive steps in the saving work of the Holy Spirit,[33] but as depicting the one work (bringing to faith) from different vantage points in order that we might appreciate the magnitude of this work. In other words, to say that the Spirit brings me to faith is to say that he has called me (an effective, successful calling and not merely an unheeded invitation), enlightened[34] me (not merely an intellectual process, but a kindling of faith within the heart),[35] sanctified me (bestowed upon me the righteousness of Christ), and sustained me in the true faith. As in the first article where God provides for our bodily needs through divinely designated "means of preservation" (reason, food, clothing), so the Spirit sanctifies through divinely designated "means of grace." The Spirit calls through the gospel, enlightens with his gifts,[36] and sanctifies and sus-

33. As in Erik Pontoppidan's pietistic catechism, which treated these as an *ordo salutis*, a series of distinct but successive steps. See, for example, H. U. Sverdrup, *Explanation of Luther's Small Catechism/Based on Dr. Erick Pontoppidan*, trans. E. G. Lund, abridged ed. (Minneapolis: Augsburg, 1900).

34. Perhaps the word "enlightened" refers to baptism and the catechumenate of the early church. See Robert I. Bradley, *The Roman Catechism in the Catechetical Tradition of the Church* (Lanham, Md.: University Press of America, 1990). He points out that in the early church the catechumens were referred to as the "enlightened" when the priest handed to them the creed and the Lord's Prayer, the two sources of their "enlightenment" (14).

35. Girgensohn, *Teaching Luther's Catechism*, 185.

36. "Enlightened with His gifts" is set in contrast to our natural or created gifts (*dona creata:* Solid Declaration VIII, 55, in BC, 626), especially "my own reason or strength." The same distinction is in the Large Catechism, Creed, 23. These *dona creata* are individual and are not the same in each person, whereas the gifts of the Holy Spirit are given to every Christian, the same gift, which creates faith, makes a Christian, and brings him to completion when there will be no more need of forgiveness. Norman E. Nagel, "The Spirit's Gifts in the Confessions and in Corinth," *Concordia Journal* 18 (1992): 230-43.

tains me by means of the one true faith *(im rechten Glauben; recta fide)*.[37] In every instance the entire emphasis "lies upon the Gospel. In this central idea lies the key to the understanding of the activity of the Holy Spirit."[38]

The Spirit brings me to faith in the same way that he gathers the entire Christian church. Thus Luther opens this section with the word *gleichwie,* the same word he used in the second article to describe that we will live with Jesus "even as *(gleichwie)* he has risen from the dead." So here he calls me to faith "even as *(gleichwie)* he gathers the entire Christian church." What does this mean? In brief, the Spirit does not call us to faith in isolation from the church. He brings us to faith by bringing us into contact with the church. So the Spirit brings me to faith in precisely the same way as he has always brought people to faith. Hence I should not look for a special or unique revelation from God. Similarly, the Spirit gathers us into the church; we do not "join" the church any more than we decide to come to faith. Just as "I cannot by my own reason or strength believe in Jesus Christ or come to him," so also I cannot by my own reason or strength join the holy Christian church. And so Luther does not hesitate in the Large Catechism to speak of the church as the mother that begets every believer. As Martin Marty once noted, this is not a picture of the American, idolatrous understanding of the church as a voluntary society of like-minded people.[39] Believers do not and cannot live a solitary existence apart from other believers. They cannot survive on their own. To think that we can is to commit spiritual suicide. The believer exists only within the community where the Spirit daily and richly forgives the sins of me and all other believers.

The Unity of the Trinitarian Persons and Works

In expounding the threefold name and work of God, the Small Catechism appears to distinguish the works of the Trinity so sharply that the Father

37. Note the ablative of means in the Latin translation. Also, *rectá* has the sense of "correct," as in the correct thing, the right stuff in contrast with right believing. Although the Latin translation should not trump the German, it may suggest one way in which a particular interpretation could be pursued. In this sense, the German *(im rechten Glauben)* could be understood as keeping me in the true faith *(fides quae creditur),* that is, keeping me in the gospel as opposed to keeping me simply in a state of truly believing.

38. Girgensohn, *Teaching Luther's Catechism,* 182.

39. Martin E. Marty, *The Hidden Discipline* (St. Louis: Concordia, 1962), 59-61.

appears exclusively as the Creator, the Son exclusively as the Redeemer, and the Spirit exclusively as the Sanctifier. This correlation of the three articles to the three persons does not come with an explicit discussion of the unity of the three persons, which has prompted some to suggest that the Small Catechism leaves itself susceptible to the charge of a "naive tritheism."[40] So how does Luther handle their unity? This is a difficult question given the purpose and function of catechesis. After all, catechesis provides a basic instruction in the faith. Yet the Trinity is arguably one of the most difficult teachings to convey. It is of considerable interest to note that Luther does not draw upon the traditional language and categories of dogmatics for his discussion of the Trinity in his catechisms. The Small Catechism contains no introduction to the Trinity and no treatment of God's attributes. It does not mention, let alone discuss, such classical terms as "person," "essence," and "Trinity." The Large Catechism offers little more. After a brief rationale for organizing the creed into three articles, Luther launches into the first article without a prior discussion of God's being, attributes, or unity. He provides no formal or extensive discussion of the Trinity in its unity in either catechism. Their explanations appear rather truncated precisely at this juncture and in need of supplementation.

Practically, however, the question might be asked, what does a young person or a recent convert need to know about the church's trinitarian formulations? Perhaps Luther here simply sets forth what was most needful and manageable for the people in the pew. He himself noted that catechists could go into greater depth on these subjects when their students were ready to leave the milk of the Scriptures for solid meat. "For the present, this is enough concerning the Creed to lay a foundation for the common people without overburdening them. After they understand the substance of it, they may on their own initiative learn more, relating to these teachings of the Catechism all that they learn in the Scriptures, and thus advance and grow richer in understanding" (LC, Creed, 70). Here perhaps lies a difference between dogmatic formulations and catechetical expres-

40. Francis Pieper, *Christian Dogmatics I* (St. Louis: Concordia, 1950), 422 n. 56, refers to Horst Stephan, *Glaubenslehre* (Berlin: Töpelmann, 1921), 193. Others have accused Luther of the opposite extreme, namely, a trinitarian monotheism. As Schlink points out, this probably indicates that Luther got it right. Edmund Schlink, *Theology of the Lutheran Confessions*, trans. Paul F. Koehneke and Herbert J. A. Bouman (Philadelphia: Muhlenberg, 1961), 60-66.

sions. It may well be that Luther avoided all technical, theological, and philosophical language in his catechetical expositions, preferring instead to state the faith in the language that the parishioner could understand.

Luther's pedagogical purpose alone, however, does not suffice to explain the relative absence of any discussion of the Trinity in terms of classic formulation: three persons and one divine essence. Even in the Large Catechism, where Luther instructs pastors and teachers, he does not provide any extended or detailed treatment on the subject. But there at the conclusion of his explanation of the third article, an important clue is provided for how he would handle the topic of the Trinity.

> In these three articles God himself has revealed and opened to us the most profound depths of his fatherly heart, his sheer, unutterable love. He created us for this very purpose, to redeem and sanctify us. Moreover, having bestowed upon us everything in heaven and on earth, he has given us his Son and his Holy Spirit, through whom he brings us to himself. As we explained before, we could never come to recognize the Father's favor and grace were it not for the Lord Christ, who is a mirror of the Father's heart. Apart from him we see nothing but an angry and terrible judge. But neither could we know anything of Christ, had it not been revealed by the Holy Spirit. (LC, Creed, 64-65)

In other words, Luther first presents the scriptural witness about the three persons and their works of creation, redemption, and sanctification. Having done that, he turns briefly to the question of their unity. "Luther did not go into detail on the formal doctrine of the Trinity because, like the Biblical writers, he was focusing more on God's works and actions in our behalf rather than on the mystery of God's person, which he never hoped to fathom. The *Catechism* is not a speculative treatise on the Godhead; it instead proclaims what he has done and is doing in our behalf."[41] Put another way, Luther places the doctrine of the Trinity within the narrative of salvation history, which corresponds well with Scripture's own approach.[42] "Through the leading concepts, creation, redemption, and sanctification,

41. Robert Kolb, *Teaching God's Children His Teaching* (Hutchinson, Minn.: Crown Publishing, 1990), 4-2.

42. Albrecht Peters, "Vermittler des Christenglaubens: Luthers Katechismen nach 450 Jahren," *Luther: Zeitschrift der Luther-Gesellschaft* 51 (1980): 38.

the Reformer was able to carry sufficiently the unity as well as the differences of the Trinity."[43]

Luther's Appropriation of the Creedal Tradition

In order to appreciate Luther's catechetical approach to the Trinity, it will help to see how Luther appropriated and adapted the catholic heritage bequeathed to him. In some ways he reaches behind the Thomistic-Augustinian tradition and links up with the trinitarian picture as it unfolded in the church up through the time of the Cappadocian Fathers.[44] Trinitarian reflection in the New Testament and in the three centuries leading up to Nicea as a rule focused its attention on what is considered to be the economic Trinity, which centered on the way in which the three persons were manifested soteriologically in the world. More precisely, the economic Trinity is manifested externally in the world through the work of creation, redemption, and sanctification.[45]

The so-called economic approach to the Trinity has several characteristics. First, discussion begins with the three persons and then proceeds to their unity. It begins with the revelation of the Father, Son, and Holy Spirit and then asks, "How are they one?" Second, one of these three persons provides the focal point for understanding their unity. This was always the Father. The names "God" and "Father" were generally used interchangeably. Third, the unity of the Trinity is found in the Father, in that the triune work begins and ends with the Father. All things proceed *a Patre ad Patrem,* from the Father to the Father. The one God/Father was understood as related to us *through* Christ and *in* the Spirit. These thoughts accord with the Cappadocian tradition, which emphasizes that "All action which comes upon the Creature from God . . . begins with the Father and is present through the Son and is perfected in the Holy Spirit."[46] This ap-

43. Reiner Jansen, *Die Trinität in Luthers Auslegungen des Apostolikums 1520-29: Studien zu Luthers Trinitätslehre* (Frankfurt: Peter Lang, 1976), 84.

44. Peters, "Vermittler des Christenglaubens," 40.

45. See Charles P. Arand, "Confessing the Trinitarian Gospel," *Concordia Theological Quarterly* 67 (2003): 203-14.

46. Also attributed to Gregory of Nyssa, *That There Are Not Three Gods,* in *Post-Nicene Fathers,* ser. 2 (reprint, Grand Rapids: Eerdmans, 1978), 5:334.

proach is apparent in the early *regulae fidei,* the Apostles' Creed, and the doxologies and prayers of the church.

In the early fourth century Arius changed the entire discussion by shifting the question of unity from the economy of salvation to the ontology of God's existence. He took statements made about God's work within the world and turned them into statements about God's eternal being apart from the created world. Since the Father sent the Son into the world, and since the Son obeyed the Father, the Son must be less than the Father in his being. The Nicene Creed dealt with the issue raised by Arius in a way that continued to reflect the economic Trinity but in a way that also opened the door to a new way of confessing the Trinity, namely, the immanent or ontological Trinity. In particular, the language of *homoousios* paved the way for a shift of focus from the Father to reflection on the one divine essence that is common to all three persons. And so the so-called immanent or ontological Trinity would concentrate attention on the inner life of God. The Athanasian Creed provides a good example of this approach to confessing the Trinity.

The immanent Trinity has several characteristics that can be seen in the thought of Western theologians such as Augustine and those that built upon his thought like Aquinas and Anselm. First, for Augustine, God and Father are not synonyms. The title "God" primarily refers to the Godhead, the divine essence shared equally by the three persons.[47] Second, the divine essence rather than the person of Father becomes the highest ontological principle and the locus of unity for the three persons. Third, this allows theologians to consider the topic of God somewhat independently of the particular revelation of Father, Son, and Spirit. It is at this point that we begin to see a separation in dogmatics between *De Deo* and *De Trinitate.* The former would deal with the attributes of God while the latter would deal with the specific relations of the three persons. Fourth, at times the ontological approach to the Trinity blurred distinctions between the three persons so that the problem became one of threeness.[48]

47. Catherine Mowry LaCugna, *God for Us: The Trinity and Christian Life* (San Francisco: HarperCollins, 1991), 98. Starting from unity tends to blur distinction between persons (any incarnate; all three in each work).

48. In other words, it does not matter who does what since it is all the work of one God (theoretically the Father could have become incarnate), nor does it matter to which person we address our prayers since they are all addressed to the same God. Here LaCugna suggests that the West began to develop a "compensating strategy" with its doc-

Both the economic and immanent approaches to the Trinity capture important biblical thoughts. Both approaches deal with the same God: the one in his works and his relation to the world, the other in his essence and his relation to himself.[49] In the revelation of his name and work (economic Trinity) God reveals his nature and essence (immanent Trinity). The economic Trinity preserves God's relationship to creation. It assures us that God is not simply a detached, ambivalent divine being who stands aloof from the world. The immanent Trinity presupposes the economic Trinity. It serves as the safeguard against any subordinationist tendencies in the latter. It also preserves God's freedom lest he become too much a part of this world that he cannot break in from outside and free it.

Both approaches to the Trinity are evident in Luther's catechetical writings. We can see them within two paragraphs of Luther's *Brief Explanation* of 1520 where Luther first makes an immanent-trinitarian statement and follows it with an economic-trinitarian statement: I believe "not only" (immanent-trinitarian statement), "but also" (economic-trinitarian statement). According to this pattern, Luther develops his thinking in the second article concerning Jesus as the Son of God in the following way: "I do *not only* believe that this means that Jesus Christ is the one true Son of God, begotten of him in eternity with one eternal divine nature and essence — *but* I also believe that the Father has made all things subject to him, that according to his human nature he has been made one Lord over me and all things which he created together with the Father in his divinity."[50] The same thought and formula carries over into the third article with reference to the Spirit: "I believe *not only* what this means — that the Holy Spirit is truly God together with the Father and the Son — *but* also that except through the Holy Spirit's work no one can come in and to the Father through Christ and his life, his suffering and death, and all that is said of him, nor can anyone appropriate any of this to himself."[51]

Of the two approaches to the Trinity, the catechisms of 1529 focus more exclusively on the economic than on the immanent contours of trin-

---

trine of appropriations. That is to say, while each person is involved in creation, it is appropriate to ascribe that activity particularly to the Father. See LaCugna, *God for Us*, 99-102.

49. Jansen, *Die Trinität in Luthers Auslegungen des Apostolikums 1520-29*, 62.

50. LW 43:26; WA 7:217.6-10.

51. LW 43:28; WA 7:218.25-28.

itarian thought. Instead of focusing on the intratrinitarian relations of the three persons within the one divine essence, Luther concentrates on the Trinity's self-turning toward the world.[52] For Luther this does not exclude the immanent Trinity, for the knowledge of God's works leads us to a knowledge of God's nature.

A Patre ad Patrem: The Father as Source and Goal

By adopting the economic approach to the Trinity, Luther's discussion of the unity of the Trinity begins with the Father who is identified preeminently with God.[53] In doing so, Luther follows the overall pattern of the New Testament Scriptures and the Apostles' Creed. Thus in the first article, Luther asks the question, "What kind of God do you have? What does he do?" He answers, "My *God* is the *Father* . . . apart from him I have no other *God*" (LC, Creed, 11). He concludes by observing that in this article we see all that we have and receive from *God.* For we see how the *Father* has given himself to us (LC, Creed, 24). Much of the same comes through with even greater clarity in the second article. Luther opens by stating that in Christ we see what we receive from *God* over and above temporal goods (LC, Creed, 26).[54] Here Jesus is called the Son of *God* and the Son of the *Father* (LC, Creed, 27). Luther observes that after we had been created by *God* the *Father,* Satan led us into sin so that we lay under *God's* wrath. But through his work Christ has restored us to the *Father's* favor and grace (LC, Creed, 30, 31, 43). There are fewer statements in the third article, but the thesis

52. Peters, "Vermittler des Christenglaubens," 39.

53. The Christian tradition has generally identified three possible referents for the appellation "God." First, "God" can refer to the divine being *in abstracto.* In this sense, it can apply to all religions that claim a deity. Second, Luther can use the word "God" as a cipher for the entire Godhead of the Trinity. This generally occurs when Luther refers to God apart from any specific person or work. Third, "God" can refer primarily to the first person of the Trinity, namely, the Father. In the catechisms, Luther interchanges "God" with "Father" much more frequently than with the other two persons of the Trinity. When "God" is used in juxtaposition with another person of the Trinity, it is always with reference to the Father.

54. This sentence is a reference back to the final sentence of the first article (LC, Creed, 64), where Luther states that the Father has showered us "with inexpressible eternal treasures through his Son and Holy Spirit."

holds also here. In order that the treasures of the gospel might be proclaimed, "*God* has caused the Word to be published, in which he has given the Holy Spirit" (LC, Creed, 38). Later Luther notes that forgiveness is constantly needed, for although *God's* grace has been won by Christ (LC, Creed, 54), it has yet to be delivered.

The identification of God with the Father allows Luther to identify the Father as the *terminus a quo* and *terminus ad quem*, that is, the source and goal of all the works and gifts confessed in the creed. In other words, all things proceed *a Patre ad Patrem*. Again, the key passage:

> In these three articles *God* himself has revealed and opened to us the most profound depths of his *fatherly* heart, his sheer, unutterable love. *He* created us for this very purpose, to redeem and sanctify us. Moreover, having bestowed upon us everything in heaven and on earth, *he* has given us his Son and *his* Holy Spirit, through whom he brings us to himself. As we explained before, we could never come to recognize the Father's favor and grace were it not for the Lord Christ, who is a mirror of the Father's heart. Apart from him we see nothing but an angry and terrible judge. But neither could we know anything of Christ, had it not been revealed by the Holy Spirit. (LC, Creed, 64-65, emphasis mine)

This highlights a twofold movement between the persons of the Trinity. The first movement *(a Patre)* expresses the soteriological self-giving of God to us. It follows the structure of salvation in Scripture. Salvation comes *from* the Father *through* his Son and *by* the Holy Spirit.[55] The second movement *(ad Patrem)* expresses our response of faith whereby we are brought *to* the Father, *through* the Son, *by* the Holy Spirit.

The movement that proceeds from God's gifts of creation through redemption to consummation follows the sequence of world and salvation history as well as personal experience.[56] It suggests that each work builds upon the former and presupposes the one before it. "The inner connection between the gifts of the Father, the Son, and the Holy Spirit are thereby in-

55. To use Luther's words, "the Father through his Son Jesus Christ our Lord and with the Holy Spirit let all this happen to me" (Conclusion to Creed, 1520: p. 29). See also Luther's *Predigt über das Symbolum*, 6 Marz 1520 (WA 11:53.7-11).

56. Peters, "Vermittler des Christenglaubens," 43.

dicated that each person does not give something for himself, but the Son adds something to the gifts of the Father, and the Spirit to the gifts of the Son respectively."[57] And so each successive article presupposes the previous article. Only the first article presupposes no other article. The first article lays the foundation and provides the setting for the other two articles. Were it denied, the second and third articles would crumble. The early church recognized this fact in its confession of the first article against all Gnostic and dualistic schemes. By confessing the Father as Creator, it confessed the goodness of creation. It establishes God's modus operandi of working through the created orders in the first article, so he also works through the incarnation of his Son in the second article. Similarly, the Holy Spirit makes use of creaturely gifts and means, namely, words, water, bread, and wine, in order to sanctify us. One should also add that the creation of our body in the first article and the resurrection of our body in the third article provide a nice *inclusio* to the entire creed.

Luther gives the narrative a soteriological thrust by noting that God has created us in order to redeem us and sanctify us. The purpose for which God continues to create and sustain us, continues to protect and defend us in spite of sin, is that we might be saved. In a sense the first article, like an emergency medical technician (EMT), stabilizes the patient and wheels her into the operating room of the second article, where the disease is diagnosed and destroyed. The patient then moves to the recovery room to regain her strength and health. The second and third articles presuppose the introduction of sin into God's creation and thus focus on God's gift of his Son for the world to rescue us from the domination of sin. Finally, the third article presupposes the work of Christ, particularly his death and resurrection. The Holy Spirit carries out the work of implementing, administrating, and bringing to fulfillment the reign of Christ.

The movement of God toward us (first article to second article to third article) has a counterpart movement that brings us to God by stressing the way in which faith comes to know and receive the gifts of God (third article to second article to first article). This ordering answers the question, "For what purpose did God carry out his work in all three articles?" What is the goal of creation, redemption, and sanctification? Simply put, all three persons, together with their works, bring us back to the Father. All three works — creation, redemption, and sanctification — lead us

57. Jansen, *Die Trinität in Luthers Auslegungen des Apostolikums 1520-29*, 69.

to the fatherly heart of God. We find God's gracious fatherly heart only through the Son, to whom the Spirit alone leads us.[58] The Spirit leads us to the Father through Christ, who has reconciled us to the Father. Luther gives this idea its classic formulation in his conclusion to the creed in the Large Catechism, as already cited above: "We could never come to recognize the Father's favor and grace were it not for the Lord Christ, who is a mirror of the Father's heart. Apart from him we see nothing but an angry and terrible judge. But neither could we know anything of Christ, had it not been revealed by the Holy Spirit" (LC, Creed, 65).[59] This theme is borne out by an examination of each article.

In the first article, the purpose for which God has given us all creation is that we might look to him for all things, as the first commandment requires. In the Large Catechism, Luther states, "He gives us all these things so that we may sense and see in them his fatherly heart and his boundless love toward us" (LC, Creed, 23). He gave us all of creation that we might thereby grasp the Father, namely, in the outward works, that he creates heaven and earth, that is, believe in him. After the Father had given us all of creation according to the Great Confession (1528), those gifts became obscured by Adam's fall and our sin. After we had received all sorts of good things from the Father, the devil led us into disobedience so that we lay under God's wrath. And so Christ's work is oriented to the Father; Christ has "snatched us, poor lost creatures, from the jaws of hell, won us, made us free, and restored us to the Father's favor and grace" (LC, Creed, 30). He has taken us as his own and "brought us back from the devil to God" (LC, Creed, 31).[60] The Spirit brings us to the Father by bringing us to Christ. Except through the

58. Peters, "Vermittler des Christenglaubens," 39.

59. This approach is a consistent theme throughout Luther's writings, especially his catechetical ones. For example, Luther's teaching on the Psalms, "The Son through the Spirit of the Father unites me with himself" [Filius per spiritum patris sui uniat me sibi] (WA 3:553.28). His *Brief Explanation* of 1520 states: "Everything, what we confess in the Creed, above all else the eschatological fulfillment, that gives us the Father through the Son Jesus Christ, our Lord, with and in the Holy Spirit."

60. He continues in the Great Confession: "Therefore the Son himself subsequently gave himself and bestowed all his works . . . and reconciled us to the Father, in order that restored to life and righteousness, we might also know and have the Father and his gifts" (LW 37:366). Again, Luther states: "Thus there is no other way of coming to God than through this Son and because through him (Son), his incarnation, we come to the Father" (WA 11:51.28).

Holy Spirit's work, "no one can come in and to the Father through Christ and his life, his suffering and death."[61] Luther notes that under the papacy, "No one believed that Christ is our Lord in the sense that he won for us this treasure without works and merits and made us acceptable to the Father. What was lacking here? There was no Holy Spirit present to reveal this truth and have it preached" (LC, Creed, 44).

By means of the *a Patre ad Patrem* approach, the catechism binds the works of the Father, Son, and Holy Spirit into a unity. The works of the Trinity cannot be lined up alongside one another in such a way that they stand as three isolated and disparate events. "Their work possesses at most a relative, not an absolute distinction. Instead, the work of any given person is always seen in relation to the work of the other two persons. And so the work of the Father, Son, and Spirit are not considered in themselves, but are seen entirely in the light of the Trinitarian faith."[62] There is an intimate interdependence, one might even say a mutual dependence, between the three gifts of creation, redemption, and sanctification. In any one divine person, we confront simultaneously the other persons and their work. "The certainty of this faith rests on this, that in Christ and the Spirit we have to do entirely and certainly with God himself, who will and can cause all things to serve for the best. But this God is for Luther the Father."[63]

The Godhead of the Trinity

What about the immanent Trinity? Following the pattern that all things proceed *a Patre* and return *ad Patrem*, the catechisms bring us to the one true God. Proceeding from the unity of their work (and presupposing the unity of God), Luther stresses that God has given himself entirely to us. In other words, although there are three subjects of the three works in the creed, there is yet one subject, namely, God. Here the subject of the action ("God") is not divided up among the plurality of actors.[64]

Thus, when referring to the works of the three persons in their totality, Luther identifies "God" as the single subject of that threefold work.

61. LW 43:28.

62. Jansen, *Die Trinität in Luthers Auslegungen des Apostolikums 1520-29*, 84.

63. Jansen, *Die Trinität in Luthers Auslegungen des Apostolikums 1520-29*, 63.

64. Karl Rahner, *The Trinity* (New York: Herder and Herder, 1970), 127.

When he does designate "God" as the subject, the work of God is identified in the general terms of God's self-giving and not in the specifics of creation, redemption, and sanctification. This logic of moving from the abstract to the concrete is seen in Luther's Great Confession of 1528 where he concludes,

> These are the three persons and one *God, who* has given himself to us all wholly and completely, with all that he is and has. The *Father* gives himself to us with heaven and earth and all the creatures, in order that they may serve and benefit us. But the gift has become obscured and useless through Adam's fall. Therefore the *Son* himself subsequently gave himself and bestowed all his works, sufferings, wisdom, and righteousness, and reconciled us to the Father, in order that restored to life and his righteousness, we might also know and have the Father and his gifts.[65]

Again, Luther names "God" as the subject of the whole creed, namely, God gives himself. Here he shows the move from the one God who is the Giver of all to the specification of the three persons together with the gifts proper to each.[66]

The most complete statement about the Godhead of the Trinity in the Large Catechism is found in his conclusion to the three articles. "God [unity of the Godhead] gives himself completely to us, with all his gifts and his power, to help us keep the Ten Commandments: the Father gives us all creation, Christ all his works, the Holy Spirit all his gifts" (LC, Creed, 69). Note how "God" is first named as the subject of all the works of the creed and then the Father, Son, and Spirit are identified with the particular works that each carries out.

It is at this point, at the conclusion of his treatment of the creed, that Luther makes the point that the creed's teaching on the Trinity in its two-

65. WA 26:505.38–506.3; LW 37:366, emphasis mine.

66. In his May 1528 catechism sermons, Luther first explains, "The Father creates everything, Christ redeems us from all evil, the Spirit directs us through his word and gives his church various gifts." After describing these three works of the three persons, he then proceeds to ask, "Do you not perceive that these are exceptional works? Do you not perceive that our God is great? He who creates heaven, earth, and everything? He who thereafter is able to redeem us with his blood? He who then creates faith and directs and raises us from the dead?" (WA 30I:10, 11-17).

fold movement *(a Patre ad Patrem)* distinguishes Christians from all other peoples on earth. "All who are outside the Christian church, whether heathen, Turks, Jews, or false Christians and hypocrites, even though they believe in and worship only the one, true God, nevertheless do not know what his attitude is toward them. They cannot be confident of his love and blessing. Therefore they remain in eternal wrath and damnation, for they do not have the Lord Christ, and, besides, they are not illuminated and blessed by the gifts of the Holy Spirit" (LC, Creed, 66). And so the creed brings us back to the first commandment. The creed has made known the identity of the one God to whom we entrust our lives, and that one God is none other than the Father, Son, and Holy Spirit.

Conclusion

Luther's catechisms not only provide a catechumen with easy-to-understand expositions of the faith, they also provide a pattern and basis for interpreting life theologically in light of God's Word. That is especially true in his treatment of the creed. Here Luther provides the catechumen with a "big picture" perspective by which she can glimpse God's work from the creation of the world to the consummation of the world. In addition, he assists the catechumen to see how she is an integral part of that great sweep of creation and salvation history so that it becomes her own personal history as well. The strength of Luther's presentation of the Trinity in the catechism lies in how each person of the Trinity plays an active and vital role within our lives. By connecting the three articles to the three persons and their works, the catechisms show that the "Giver and gift belong together; neither can be understood without the other."[67] Each plays a role that together they embrace the totality of our life in such a way that we cannot treat the Trinity as a piece of data that we are to know about, but as three persons who give us a true knowledge of God himself. This is true whether we consider each person of the Trinity individually or consider them together in their unity.

67. Girgensohn, *Teaching Luther's Catechism*, 129.

CHAPTER 8

Luther on Prayer in the Large Catechism

Timothy J. Wengert

"For whenever a good Christian prays, 'Dear Father, your will be done,' God replies from above, 'Yes, dear child, it shall be done indeed in spite of the devil and the entire world.'"[1] In this way, Martin Luther brought to a close his most trenchant exposition of prayer: a brief introduction to the subject in the Large Catechism. As important as other writings by Luther are for showing how to pray or for what to pray,[2] the LC penetrates to the heart of Luther's theology of prayer, doing it in simple terms for his intended audience. Yet, as the first part of this essay will show, the discourse in the LC on prayer takes on new focus in light of Luther's own experience.[3]

1. Martin Luther, LC, Lord's Prayer, 32, in BC, 444 (BSLK, 669). For a more traditional understanding of the petition from Luther, see, for example, WA TR 2:119 (no. 1510, dated 1-7 May 1532), where he contrasted God's will to human desire.

2. See especially *A Simple Way to Pray for a Good Friend,* 1535 (WA 38:351-75; LW 43:187-211); *A Personal Prayer Book,* 1522 (WA 10II:339-406; LW 43:3-45).

3. Bibliography for this topic is endless. Some of the more recent resources include: Rudolf Damerau, *Luthers Gebetslehre,* 2 vols. (Marburg: Im Selbstverlag, 1975-77); Martin E. Lehmann, *Luther and Prayer* (Milwaukee: Northwestern, 1985); Gunnar Wertelius, *Oratio continua: Das Verhältnis zwischen Glaube und Gebet in der Theologie Martin Luthers* (Lund: Gleerup, 1970); D. F. Wright, "What Kind of 'Bread'? The Fourth Petition of the Lord's Prayer from the Fathers to the Reformers," in *Oratio: das Gebet in patristischer und reformatorischer Sicht,* ed. Emidio Campi et al. (Göttingen: Vandenhoeck & Ruprecht, 1999), 151-61; Martin Brecht, "'Und willst das Beten von uns han': Zum Gebet und seiner Praxis bei Martin Luther," in *Frühe Reformation in Deutschland als Umbruch,*

The Praying Luther

Fascination with Luther and prayer began already long before his death. Not only did his barber, Master Peter Beskendorf, request Luther's instruction on how to pray,[4] but already Veit Dietrich, Luther's companion at the Fortress Coburg during the 1530 Diet of Augsburg, described to Philip Melanchthon the effect of Luther's praying.

> One time I had the opportunity to hear him praying. Good God, what spirit, what faith was in his words! He prayed for things with such reverence — as befits God — and with such hope and faith that he seemed to be holding a conversation with a father or a friend. "I know," he said, "that you are our Father and God. Therefore I am sure that you will destroy the persecutors of your children. If you do not do this, the result will be disaster for us. The whole affair is yours. We are constrained to implore you for this. Therefore, defend us, and so on." I was standing nearby and heard him praying in a clear voice using words to that effect. My soul was set on fire with such a singular passion to hear him speak with God in such a friendly, serious, and reverent manner. And throughout the prayer he interjected psalms, so that he was quite certain that everything for which he prayed would come about.[5]

---

ed. Bernd Moeller (Gütersloh: Gütersloher Verlagshaus, 1998), 268-88; Mark Sander, "Cyprian's *On the Lord's Prayer:* A Patristic Signpost in Luther's Penitential Theology," *Logia* 7 (Epiphany 1998): 13-18; George Tavard, "Luther's Teaching on Prayer," *Lutheran Theological Seminary Bulletin* 67 (Winter 1987): 3-22; Friedemann Hebart, "The Role of the Lord's Prayer in Luther's Theology of Prayer," *Lutheran Theological Journal* 18 (May 1984): 6-17; David P. Scaer, "Luther on Prayer," *Concordia Theological Quarterly* 47 (1983): 305-15; Vilmos Vajta, "Luther als Beter," in *Leben und Werk Martin Luthers von 1526 bis 1546,* ed. Helmar Junghans (Göttingen: Vandenhoeck & Ruprecht, 1983), 279-95; Gerhard Ebeling, "Beten als Wahrnehmen der Wirklichkeit des Menschen, wie Luther es lehrte und lebte," *Luther-Jahrbuch* 66 (1999): 151-66; Albrecht Peters, *Kommentar zu Luthers Katechismen,* vol. 3, *Das Vaterunser,* ed. Gottfried Seebaß (Göttingen: Vandenhoeck & Ruprecht, 1992).

4. *A Simple Way to Pray for a Good Friend* (1535).

5. *Melanchthons Briefwechsel: Kritische und kommentierte Gesamtausgabe: Regesten,* ed. Heinz Scheible, 10-plus vols. (Stuttgart-Bad Cannstatt: Frommann-Holzboog, 1977-), no. 949 (henceforth MBW). The text is in *Corpus Reformatorum: Philippi Melanthonis opera quae supersunt omnia,* ed. Karl Bretschneider and Heinrich Bindseil, 28 vols. (Halle: A. Schwetschke and Sons, 1834-60), 2:159 (henceforth CR), dated 30 June 1530. See also

This section examines three different experiences of Luther with prayer as a way of grounding the discussion in the LC within Luther's own life as a Christian.

Raising the Dead Melanchthon in 1540

By far the most famous example of Luther praying occurred in 1540.[6] In June 1540 Philip Melanchthon had taken sick on his way to the religious Colloquy in Haguenau. He stopped in Weimar on 12 June, unable to travel farther and too weak to return to Wittenberg. By the time his concerned colleagues, including Martin Luther and Justus Jonas, arrived in Weimar on 23 June with Melanchthon's son Philip, the poor man was in a semiconscious state.[7] After assessing the situation, Luther walked over to a window and started praying. As Luther later described it (according to Matthäus Ratzeberger), "There [in Weimar], the Lord God had to stretch out his hand to me. For I threw the entire sack in front of his door and rubbed his ears with all the *promissiones to hear prayers* that I was able to recall from the Holy Scripture, so that he had to hear me, were I to believe all those other promises."[8]

Julius Köstlin and Gustav Kawerau, *Martin Luther: Sein Leben und Schriften*, 5th ed. (Berlin: Duncker, 1903), 2:219, translated in H. G. Haile, *Luther: An Experiment in Biography* (Garden City, N.Y.: Doubleday, 1980), 278; also quoted in Ebeling, "Beten," 154.

6. For a dramatic reconstruction of these events, see Haile, *Luther*, 277-80. See also, Martin Brecht, *Martin Luther: The Preservation of the Church, 1532-1546*, trans. James Schaaf (Minneapolis: Fortress, 1993), 209-10.

7. WA TR 5:129 (no. 5407, dated Spring 1542): "Wir habe drey todt wiederumb lebendig gebethen, mich, meyne Kethe vnd Philippum, welchem zu Weinbeer schon die augen gebrochen waren." See also the much more detailed description by the physician, Matthäus Ratzeberger, in CR 28:67-70. (Cf. Matthäus Ratzeberger, *Die handschriftliche Geschichte Ratzeberger's über Luther und seine Zeit/mit literarischen, kritischen und historischen Anmerkungen*, ed. Christian Gotthold Neudecker [Jena: Mauke, 1850].) "Denn die Augen waren ihm gleich gebrochen, aller Verstand gewichen, die Sprache entfallen, das Gehör vergangen, und das Angesicht schlaff und eingefallen, und, wie Lutherus sagte, 'facies erat Hippocratica' [in need of a physician?]. Dazu kannte er niemand, aß und trank nichts."

8. CR 28:69-70 (the italicized portions in Latin). Cf. Haile, *Luther*, 278f. Luther had already begun to pray before leaving Wittenberg. See WA TR 5:95 (no. 5364, dated June 1540).

Luther's chutzpah toward God in that moment was not so much a sign of hubris (although it may at first glance appear as such) as it was of faith. "Throwing sacks" and "rubbing ears" were almost playful ways for Luther to express the urgency of the situation, the necessity of God's help, and the joy of being answered. Thus, upon entering the room, Luther had exclaimed, "May God protect us! Look how the devil has mistreated this *instrument* of mine."[9] The inordinate joy Luther derived from this answered prayer and Melanchthon's recovery may be seen in Luther's letter to his wife, Käthie, ten days later. There, however, we also hear less of Luther's faith and more of God's surprising mercy.

> Grace and Peace! Dear Maiden Käthie, gracious Lady von Zolsdorf[10] (and whatever other titles that pertain to Your Grace)! I wish to inform You and Your Grace most submissively that I am doing well here. I eat like a Bohemian and drink like a German. Thanks be to God! Amen! This is because Master Philip was truly dead and has arisen from the dead just like Lazarus! God, the dear Father, hears our prayer — that we see and experience — even though we still do not believe it. Let no one say "Amen" to our terrible unbelief![11]

This remarkable experience continued to echo in Luther's later comments on prayer. In spring 1543, discussion around Luther's table turned to the question of *fides aliena* (the faith of another) and whether it could

9. CR 28:69-70 (the italicized word is Greek: *organon*, a sense organ).

10. A plot of land recently purchased by Luther from his brother-in-law, Hans von Bora.

11. WA Br 9:168, dated 2 July 1540. Justus Jonas's account to Johannes Bugenhagen (CR 3:1060, dated 7 July 1540 from Eisenach, where they had brought their still weakened colleague) also mentioned answered prayer of the church. "Quod attinet ad D. Philip. Melan. certe hic e media morte, in qua profecto Wimariae luctabatur, oratione Ecclesiae et piorum revocatus est ad vitam." He also noted the encouragement of Luther, himself, and the other brothers (including Paul Eber, later pastor in Wittenberg, and Melanchthon's son Philip, Jr.). See Gustav Kawerau, ed., *Der Briefwechsel des Justus Jonas,* 2 vols. (reprint, Hildesheim: G. Olms, 1964), 1:398, no. 504. Melanchthon, in a letter to Bugenhagen written the next day in a still shaky hand, underscored this belief. MBW 2459 (CR 3:1061): "Si vixero, vere praedicare potero, me divinitus ex ipsa morte in vitam revocatum esse. Id omnes, qui una fuerunt, testantur. Utinam igitur possim deo gratias agere et ad laudem ipsius vivere."

save someone else. Luther burst out, "Absolutely!" Paul himself, Luther thought, had been saved on account of Stephen's prayer — not that Paul was saved by Stephen's faith but rather that out of his faith Stephen prayed for Paul to have faith. "Thus, prayer has preserved many, just as we prayed Philip back to life."[12] He continued, "It is impossible that God would not hear the prayer of faith. Whether he always does what we ask, that is another matter. *'God does not give according to the measure prescribed'* [Luke 6:38]. Instead, 'he gathers up and shakes out,' as he says."[13] He included the example of Augustine's mother, who prayed for her son's conversion and received instead "such an Augustine" that he is now called *"lumen ecclesiae"* (light of the church). "For this reason James says, *'Let us pray for the sick . . . the prayer of the righteous person can do much.'* That is one of the best lines in the whole letter. There is a powerful thing surrounding prayer, if only I could believe it, because God has bound and tied himself to prayer."[14]

Of course, the notion that God hears prayer did not mean for Luther that absolutely everything was answered according to human expectations. Already in the fall of 1532 he could exclaim: "We have this advantage: that our prayer is always heard. Even if it is not heard according to our will, nevertheless it is heard according to the will of God, which is better than our will. If I did not know that my prayer would be heard, it would be the devil praying in my place."[15]

12. WA TR 5:244 (no. 5565, dated Spring 1543; LW 54:453f.).

13. WA TR 5:244 (no. 5565, dated Spring 1543; LW 54:453f.). Italicized portion in Latin. Another example of God's inability to ignore such prayers, especially those in dire straits, comes in WA TR 2:261f. (no. 1912; according to no. 1812 [WA TR 2:222f.], dated September/October 1532): "Von herczen bitten vnd armer leut klagen richten ein geschrey an, das es alle Enngel muessen horen im himell. Winseln, zittern, beben [WA TR: leben, other mss. beben] in Gottes beuehl vnd in der noth ist ein gewiß zeichen eines Christen [WA TR: einner kranncklheitt, other mss.: eines Christen]." (Translation: "The petition of the heart and the complaint of the poor make so much noise that all the angels in heaven must hear it. Wimpering, shaking, and quaking in the presence of God's command [to pray] and in need is a sure sign of a Christian.") No. 1812 refers the "wimpering, shaking and quaking" to Moses before the Red Sea.

14. WA TR 5:245 (no. 5565, dated Spring 1543; LW 54:453f.).

15. WA TR 2:628 (no. 2742a). The context is clear from WA TR 2:629 (no. 2742b), where before saying this, Luther described his experience ministering to a woman dying in childbirth. "Si enim semper nostris votis respondere deberet, so were er vnser gefangener, vnd hette mir dies weib auch mussen wieder geben, aber er wuste es besser."

The notion that God promises not only to hear but also to answer prayer stood at the center of Luther's approach to prayer already in 1529, when he wrote the catechisms. His explanation of "Amen," a phrase that occurs in three different places in the Small Catechism, bears this out. To apply the creed's "amen" to each article, Luther concluded with the phrase, "das ist gewißlich wahr" (this is most certainly true). In the third question on holy baptism, Luther translated the end of Titus 3:5-8, "das ist [je] gewißlich wahr" (this is [surely] most certainly true). But it is in the Lord's Prayer that his confidence in God's self-binding and self-tying explodes onto the page. "That I should be certain [*gewiß*] that such petitions are acceptable to and heard by our Father in heaven, for he himself commanded us to pray like this and has promised to hear us. 'Amen, amen' means 'Yes, yes, it is going to come about just like this.'"[16]

The other side to God's promise for Luther is faith. Thus, in a not well-documented comment at table, he may have said, "As a cobbler makes shoes and a tailor sews clothes, so should a Christian pray. The handiwork of a Christian is prayer."[17] Nevertheless, this faith in prayer is hard to come by. Already in the 1530s he stated, "No one believes such power and efficacy is in our prayer, unless we learn by experience. But it is a tremendous thing when someone feels the press of necessity and, driven by its enormity, can then seize hold of prayer. I know this because I have so often prayed earnestly when faced with a matter of real earnestness. Thus, I have certainly been richly answered and have received more than I desired. Our Lord God may have put something off for a while, but he still heard."[18] As we shall see below, the link between faith, need, and earnestness, as something

16. SC, Creed, 2, 4, and 6; Baptism, 10; and Lord's Prayer, 21, in BC, 355f., 359, and 358 (BSLK, 511f., 516, 515). In the question on baptism, the "surely" *(je)* was added in 1536. Similarly, the 1531 addition of an explanation to the words "Our Father in heaven" showed the centrality of God's gracious promise (SC, Lord's Prayer, 2, in BC, 356; BSLK, 512). "With these words God wants to entice us, so that we come to believe he is truly our Father and we are truly his children, in order that we may ask him boldly and with complete confidence, just as loving children ask their loving father."

17. WA TR 6:162 (no. 6751, only in Aurifaber's collection).

18. WA TR 1:442 (no. 886). On 8 June 1532 (WA TR 2:155 [no. 1625]), he remarked, "If I were as devoted to prayer as Peter Weller's dog is to eating in the morning, then I would want to beg that the end of the world would come soon. For the dog thinks about nothing but his dish." For a prayer of Luther for the end of the world, see WA TR 5:349f. (no. 5777).

coming through external necessity and experience, was crucial to Luther's approach to prayer in the LC.[19]

In one remarkable comment, delivered in the summer of 1533, Luther combined Aristotle's causes[20] to the question of the relation in prayer between human need, faith, and God's promise. "The efficient cause *per se* of prayer is faith; the accidental [secondary] cause is necessity; the form[al cause] is the apprehension of undeserved mercy; the material [cause] out of which [prayer is formed] is the promise and command to pray; the final [cause] is the hearing and liberation."[21] This is not so much an example of Luther using Aristotle's causes to understand prayer as it is Luther analyzing his own understanding of prayer using the familiar dialectical categories of Aristotle (and Melanchthon). At the same time, this comment summarized many of Luther's key insights from the LC.

Praying in 1537 for the Electress of Brandenburg, Elizabeth of Denmark

Another concrete incident in Luther's life, this time involving unanswered prayer, shows how consistent Luther's understanding of the interaction of God's promise and faith was. In the summer of 1537, the electress of Brandenburg, Elizabeth von Dänemark, fell sick and ended up in Luther's home.[22] Several insights into prayer come from this stressful time in the Luther household. On 18 August, Luther prayed, "Dear Lord God, now

19. See also WA TR 5:437f. (no. 6013). Speaking about the Lord's Prayer, Luther noted that outside of temptation *(Anfechtung)* there is no true prayer, only blabbering: "dorinne [in the Lord's Prayer] begrieffen omnem necessitatem in omnibus tentationibus, nam extra tentationem non potest vere orari. Ideo Dauid dicit [Psalm 50:15]: Invoca me in die tribulationis etc. Alioqui ista βαττολογια friget." This passage from Ps. 50 also figured in his exposition in the LC.

20. For a table, the efficient cause is the carpenter (with the instrumental cause being his tools, and other accidental [secondary] causes including feeding one's family and the like), the formal cause is the design, the material cause is the wood, and the final cause is the purpose or goal, namely, to have something upon which to write (or, in a lecture hall, upon which to rest one's head).

21. WA TR 3:280 (no. 3353 a and b).

22. For details of the illness and her later move to Lichtenburg, see Brecht, *Martin Luther*, 239.

hear our prayer according to your promise! Do not let us throw the keys at your feet,[23] so that in the end we get angry at you and do not give you proper honor and what is your due.[24] Where will you be then? Ach, dear Lord, we are yours. Do what you will, only give us patience."[25] Two days later Anton Lauterbach recorded another prayer. "Dear God, you possess this name, that you are the Answerer of prayers, as David said [Ps. 145:19], 'He fulfills the desire of those who fear him and hears their groans.' Ach Lord, we are not praying for anything evil! Do not make us throw the keys at the door."[26] Thus, Luther's comment about prayer for Melanchthon, preserved by Ratzeberger, was typical of the way his faith understood God's promise to hear prayer. What he refused to do was to pray timidly.

Around the same time, in the summer of 1537, he again reflected on prayer and faith, but this time with a sense of awe that God even bothers to

23. According to the Grimms's *Deutsches Wörterbuch,* 15:856, this refers to the custom of a widow, who, when she cannot pay her deceased husband's debts, places the house keys either at the foot of the grave or on the bier, to show that she is no longer beholden to him and thus free of her debts. Thus, it means something akin to "washing one's hands of the whole affair." However, another possible source might be *2 Baruch* 9.18, where the text describes the priests' reaction to the destruction of Solomon's Temple. "Moreover, you priests, take you the keys of the sanctuary, and cast them into the height of heaven, and give them to the Lord and say: 'Guard Your house Yourself, For lo! We are found false stewards.'" Luther could scarcely have known this particular book of the Pseudepigrapha, but the parallel is striking. See Rivka Nir, *The Destruction of Jerusalem and the Idea of Redemption in the* Syriac Apocalypse of Baruch (Atlanta: Society of Biblical Literature, 2003), 83-100, where references in the Talmud are also discussed. I am grateful to Matthias Henze of Rice University for this reference.

24. German: *Zinsgutter,* literally, the tax owed a lord on a piece of property.

25. WA TR 5:438 (no. 6015). For Luther's prayers in English, see Andrew Kosten, ed., *Devotions and Prayers: Martin Luther* (Grand Rapids: Baker, 1956).

26. WA TR 5:438f. (no. 6015). Luther uttered a similarly direct prayer on 9 June 1532 in the face of a drought (WA TR 2:157f. [no. 1636]), where he again cited Ps. 145:18f. He also said that if God was not going to give rain, he would give something even better: peace and tranquility. He also warned God that if the prayer was not answered, ungodly people would say that God and God's Son were liars, concluding with these words: "Ich weis, das wir von hertzen zu dir schreien vnd bitten mit senlichem seufftzen; warum wiltu vns den nicht erhörn?" See also WA TR 4:99 (no. 4046), dated 10 October 1538, where Luther encouraged people to pray for daily bread against an outbreak of mice. The inflation of grain prices came also because of greedy farmers and merchants. "Let us pray for the godly paupers, who have to bear this the most, so that they may have daily bread and God's blessing. Amen."

hear a believer. "Ach, what a great thing the prayer of the godly is! How powerful it is before God, that a poor soul should talk with God and not be frightened in his presence, but instead know that God smiles at him in a friendly manner because of Jesus Christ. The conscience must not run away on account of its unworthiness or be overwhelmed with doubts or let itself be frightened."[27] This, too, was one of Luther's foci in the LC, where he used both law and gospel to solve the problem of the conscience fleeing prayer.

At the same time, Luther contrasted late-medieval piety and uncertain prayers to the saints to faith based upon Christ's promise. Moreover, he admitted the human tendency, which he himself had shared as a monk, to turn prayer into a work, an ascent of the soul that human beings can accomplish. As will become clear, such contrasts also played a role in the LC. As the following shows, with respect to prayers for the electress, Luther simply refused to pray, as late-medieval piety taught, "conditionally and hypothetically."

> Thus, the ancient [Christians] well defined prayer: "*Oratio est ascensus mentis ad Deum*" (prayer is the ascent of the mind to God).[28] It is well said, but I and everyone else did not understand that definition. We boasted about the ascent of the mind, but we missed out on the syntax, that we have to bring the *ad Deum* to it. On the contrary, we fled from God. We could not freely and with certainty pray to God through Christ, in whom the certainty of prayer exists, but we always prayed conditionally and hypothetically, not categorically. Therefore, my brothers, who can pray, pray without ceasing, that is, from the heart and also at certain times orally. For, in the presence of our dear God, prayer upholds the world; otherwise things would be quite different.[29]

27. WA TR 3:447 (no. 3605).

28. See CR 24:830, where Melanchthon attributed the saying to Pseudo-Dionysius.

29. WA TR 3:447f. (no. 3605). He concluded on a personal note that at home he did not pray as well as in the local church, where prayers are "from the heart and penetrating." For another discussion of the contrast of true prayer and works that pass for prayer, see WA TR 5:228 (no. 5545, dated late February/early March 1543).

Mixing Prayer and Politics in 1539

A third specific incident reveals yet another aspect of Luther's understanding of prayer. In the spring of 1539 the imperial princes gathered in Frankfurt am Main in an attempt to avoid what seemed by then to be inevitable: armed conflict over religion, exacerbated by the growing dispute between Philip of Hesse and Henry of Braunschweig-Wolfenbüttel. The result was the Frankfurt Truce *(Stillstand)* of 1539 that set in motion the religious colloquies of the 1540s and prevented all-out war until 1547. Philip Melanchthon, part of the Saxon entourage, was in Frankfurt from 13 February until 20 April, returning home on 9 May, when he dined with Luther.[30]

Luther, as always, remained at home and stewed about the prospects for peace in the face of political rumors and papal machinations. Throughout this time his companions recorded his prayers, especially in worship[31] but also upon the receipt of a letter from Melanchthon.[32] As he had already expressed in his exposition to the fourth petition of the Lord's Prayer, "civic peace is the highest gift of God on earth,"[33] the only defense

30. See his itinerary in MBW 10:483-85.

31. WA TR 4:450 (no. 4722), on 6 January 1539 (in worship service for the Feast of the Epiphany), praying for the conversion of Charles V; WA TR 4:464f. (no. 4744), 2 March 1539 (in Sunday service), prayer for peace; WA TR 4:293 (no. 4396; LW 54:335-36), 15 March 1539 (at Saturday vespers?), a prayer for peace against the papal raging, etc.; WA TR 4:466 (no. 4758), 11 May 1539 (in worship service), a prayer of thanks for God's continued protection and for peace (and the miraculous death of Duke George of Saxony).

32. See WA TR 4:308f. (no. 4430, dated 23 March 1539); upon the receipt of a letter from Melanchthon (MBW 2160 [WA Br 8:392-94], written from Frankfurt/Main on 14 March 1539; Luther's answer MBW 2168 [WA Br 8:397f.], written on 26 March 1539), Luther prayed for peace. See also his comments on 25 December 1538 in WA TR 4:196f. (no. 4200) and his public prayers against the "bloodthirsty papists" and encouragement to pray: "Ergo vos pii orate, poenitentiam agite, non tantum audite verbum sed secundum illud etiam vivite. Das wir doch vnserm Hergott eine trutzischk [from the Latin, trochiscus: a sweet perfume or breath freshener] oder weirach anlegten." Regarding prayers against the Turks, in WA TR 5:152 (no. 5437, dated Summer/Fall 1542), he recalled the legend of Jacob of Nisibis (cf. Gennadius, *De viris illustribus* 1), who was said to have prayed against Persian invaders in the fourth century. "So God can take away the heart of the Turk, if we pray constantly and in faith."

33. WA TR 2:659 (no. 2786, dated Fall 1532).

against such warlike enemies was prayer.[34] Here, as in the other cases, there was nothing that could not be brought before God's throne. Faith and God's promises again combined to encourage Luther even in the midst of his own pessimism. Luther also voiced this attitude in the introduction to prayer in the LC.

Not only at table but also in his letters Luther viewed the discussions in Frankfurt as needing prayer. Thus, at the beginning of negotiations, in a letter to Jakob Propst in Bremen, dated 21 February 1539, Luther wrote that "the prayer of the church hopes with us for peace."[35] Several weeks later, in a letter to Franz Burkhard in Frankfurt with the Saxon elector, Luther gave more content to these prayers. "We boldly pray for our convocation against Satan, especially against that fox from Mainz, lest his tail tickle and deceive you."[36] In his letter to Melanchthon on 26 March, he commented that, despite his own deep reservations, "We hope that our prayers have been heard."[37] Although the negotiations did not resolve the underlying tensions in the empire, they do reveal the role that prayer played for Luther in political matters. As personal as prayer could be for Luther, it was never caught in the kind of solipsism that so often marks teachings about prayer in the twenty-first century.

The Large Catechism[38]

The LC arose out of Luther's catechetical sermons of 1528, especially the set produced in late November and early December. The introduction to the section on prayer, which is the chief concern here, had direct connection to these sermons and to the Visitation Articles of 1527 and 1528.[39] In the LC,

34. WA TR 4:374f. (no. 4555, dated 1 May 1539). "Oratio piorum fuit arma contra ipsos, ut illorum fraudes sint revelatae."

35. WA Br 8:371.14 (no. 3300).

36. WA Br 8:382.13-15 (no. 3306). The "fox from Mainz" was Archbishop Albrecht.

37. WA Br 8:397.6-7 (no. 3314).

38. For this section, see Peters, *Das Vaterunser*, 13-41, especially the literature cited on 39-41.

39. WA 30I:95-98 (sermon on 14 December 1528) and CR 26:13-15, 54-56. The Latin version of 1527, written by Melanchthon, had a separate section on the prayer, including a very brief exposition of the petitions of the Lord's Prayer. The 1528 German version, worked on by Luther, Melanchthon, Bugenhagen, and even John Agricola, dropped mate-

Luther used substantial space to give a more detailed overview of the topic, something that he also did in a less expansive way to begin the creed. Here, however, Luther sensed how important prayer was for the Christian's daily life, much as he did later in the LC when he added a lengthy admonition on the reception of the Lord's Supper and, in a section added to the second edition, on private confession.[40]

In his exhaustive analysis of Luther's catechisms, Albrecht Peters lists five parts to this admonition. A more careful examination of Luther's grammar and his intention, however, reveals but three, plus a short opening transition from the preceding sections of the catechism. This will serve here as an appropriate outline for the following analysis.

Luther's Catechetical Order: Diagnosis, Treatment, Medication

Already in the introduction to his *Personal Prayer Book (Betbüchlein)* of 1522, Luther dealt with the question of the catechism's order. He used an Augustinian metaphor of sickness and healing to explain his reordering the parts of the catechism (moving from law to gospel to prayer).[41] Although his language was still much more in keeping with late-medieval piety, it demonstrates clearly how important the catechism's order was for Luther.

> Three things a person must know in order to be saved. First, he must know what to do and what to leave undone. Second, when he realizes that he cannot measure up to what he should do or leave undone, he needs to know where to go to find the strength he requires. Third, he must know how to seek and obtain that strength. It is just like a sick person who first has to determine the nature of his sickness, then find out what to do or to leave undone. After that he has to know where to

rial on the Lord's Prayer and subsumed a general discussion of prayer under the second commandment, reducing Melanchthon's four admonitions (command, promise, specific needs, persistence) to three by subsuming the fourth under the third. This corrects Peters, *Das Vaterunser,* 15-16.

40. LC, Lord's Supper, 39-84, in BC, 470-75 (BSLK, 715-24).

41. Werner Krusche, "Zur Struktur des Kleinen Katechismus," *Lutherische Monatshefte* 4 (1965): 316-31.

> get the medicine which will help him do or leave undone what is right for a healthy person. Third, he has to desire to search for this medicine and to obtain it or have it brought to him. Thus the commandments teach human beings to recognize their sickness. . . . The Creed will teach and show them where to find the medicine — grace — which will help them to become devout and keep the commandments. The Creed points them to God and his mercy, given and made plain to him in Christ. Finally, the Lord's Prayer teaches all this, namely, through the fulfillment of God's commandments everything will be given him.[42]

This movement from diagnosis of the human condition (sin) through the Law, to treatment through the announcement of God's mercy and grace, to the reception of medication through prayer marked all of Luther's catechesis and even his private prayer.[43] In fact, it was so important that already the Wittenberg catechism of 1525, composed of excerpts from the *Prayer Booklet,* included a portion of these introductory remarks.[44]

Thus, it is hardly surprising that Luther's comments on prayer in the LC began with a brief recitation of the relation between the Lord's Prayer and the earlier sections of the catechism.[45] The catechism began with "what we are to do." However, as tempting as it may be to turn the commandments into a project for the old creature to achieve, it is important to note the force of the verb *sollen,* translated here "are to." We should do this but, as Luther said to Erasmus, an "ought" never implies a "can." Earlier in the LC, Luther took this hubris head-on, as expressed by those who, thinking the Ten Commandments easy to fulfill, wanted to graduate to "Christian counsels." "They fail to see, these miserable blind fools, that no one is able to keep even one of the Ten Commandments as it ought to be kept. Both the Creed and the Lord's Prayer must come to our aid."[46] Not only

42. LW 43:13-14; WA 10III:376-77.

43. See *A Simple Way to Pray,* LW 43:193-95 (WA 38:358-59) and WA TR 5:209f. (no. 5517), dated Winter 1542/43, where Luther spoke of praying the Ten Commandments, the Lord's Prayer, and one or two passages from the Bible at night. "Thus, I fall asleep."

44. See "A Booklet for Laity and Children," trans. Timothy J. Wengert, in *Sources and Contexts of* The Book of Concord (Minneapolis: Fortress, 2001), 3-4. See also Timothy J. Wengert, "Wittenberg's Earliest Catechism," *Lutheran Quarterly* 7 (1993): 247-60.

45. LC, Lord's Prayer, 1-2, in BC, 440-41 (BSLK, 662).

46. LC, Ten Commandments, 316, in BC, 428 (BSLK, 640).

did Luther reiterate this very point in introducing the Lord's Prayer: "no one can keep the Ten Commandments perfectly," but he also added an even more devastating blow to the old creature, "even though he or she has begun to believe."[47] The faith created through the gospel as confessed in the creed does not fix the illness. Instead, the believer as believer is driven to prayer. Luther added to this the big three: devil, world, and flesh. This medieval and patristic trio combined in Luther's view to fight the gospel tooth and nail.[48]

In the light of humanity's deep illness and the creedal gospel (treatment), Luther was driven to prayer: that desperate call to the pharmacy in the middle of the night. The chutzpah of his prayer for Melanchthon already found expression in the LC. "Consequently, nothing is so necessary as to call upon God incessantly and to drum into his ears our prayer."[49] What is the content of this ear rubbing? "That he may give, preserve, and increase in us faith and the fulfillment of the Ten Commandments and remove all that stands in our way and hinders us in this regard." This need for faith and fulfillment of the commandments drove Luther finally to the Lord's Prayer itself, which provided him with "what and how to pray."[50] In this way the Christian finally demands from God, the Great Physician, the very medicine without which one cannot live in faith.

The Command to Pray

As in the catechism overall, Luther structured his very comments on prayer in the LC under the rubrics of diagnosis (law), treatment (gospel), and medicine (Lord's Prayer). Thus, paragraphs 4-18 examine Christ's command to pray. Here, Luther's comments are so much richer than many later discussions of "law and gospel," because for him they were encounters with God's word, which was working on Luther as he wrote.

As in the German version of the Visitation Articles, Luther first discussed prayer under the second commandment. Luther never saw a text of Scripture where he did not immediately think of its opposite. As he once

47. LC, Lord's Prayer, 2, in BC, 440 (BSLK, 662).
48. See Peters, *Das Vaterunser,* 28f.
49. LC, Lord's Prayer, 2, in BC, 440 (BSLK, 662).
50. LC, Lord's Prayer, 2, in BC, 440f. (BSLK, 662).

said: "When I preach, I make antitheses."[51] If a text forbids something, it means God is promoting the opposite. If a text promises something, it also means it is excluding something harmful. Regarding the explanations to the commandments in both the SC and LC, this meant for Luther that negative commandments had a positive side and vice versa.[52] Specifically, the second commandment for Luther did not only forbid the misuse of God's name but included the proper use of it.

Here the explanation of the second commandment in the SC is particularly instructive. "We are to fear and love God," Luther began, thus tying this and every other commandment to the first and its demand for faith, fulfilled expressly in the third article of the creed and the second petition of the Lord's Prayer.[53] The result of such faith in the light of the second commandment was, positively speaking, "so that we . . . instead use that very name in every time of need to call on, pray to, praise, and give thanks to God."[54] Already here Luther linked need with prayer. He also separated prayer from praise and thanksgiving, something that an English-speaking audience may not readily appreciate, where prayer is often defined as a general term for "words thrown in God's direction," thus including praise and thanksgiving. This is unfortunate if for no other reason than that the original, nonreligious meaning of the word "pray" in English, etymologically related to the German *fragen* (to ask) and the Latin *precare* (to beg), meant "to ask."[55]

The explanation in the LC also considered this positive side.[56] Luther

51. WA 36:183.20-21, cited in Fred Meuser, *Luther the Preacher* (Minneapolis: Augsburg, 1983), 50 n. 26. The original, a comment from a sermon on the Gospel for Pentecost Monday, 1532, reads: "Quando facio praedicationem, accipio Antithesin, ut hic Christus facit." Regarding the commandments, this was hardly Luther's invention, since it was related to sins of omission and commission.

52. In the SC, the two exceptions are the first commandment, spoken of only in its positive side (demanding faith in God), and the sixth commandment, where Luther (perhaps for cultural reasons) refused to list sexual sins.

53. SC, Ten Commandments, 4, in BC, 352 (BSLK, 508). See also LC, Ten Commandments, 324-29, in BC, 429-30 (BSLK, 642-44).

54. SC, Ten Commandments, 4, in BC, 352 (BSLK, 508).

55. In German, scholars now assume that there was always a difference between *bitten* and *beten*. However, each petition of the Lord's Prayer is not called *Gebete* but, as in English, *Bitte*.

56. LC, Ten Commandments, 70-77, in BC, 395-96 (BSLK, 578-80).

even provided some examples of good prayers for children. "One must urge and encourage children again and again to honor God's name and to keep it constantly upon their lips in all circumstances and experiences."[57] Here is where the Christian receives consolation (par. 70) and where the devil gets chased away (par. 71-72). In the same way, each day should be commended to God (par. 73).[58] But Luther also had in mind making the sign of the cross in danger and uttering short prayers in dire need or blessing. "'Lord God, save me!' or 'Help, dear Lord Christ!' . . . 'God be praised and thanked!' 'God has bestowed this upon me' etc."[59] In a world where religious gurus and experts overspiritualize everything and where only pietists seem willing to write on prayer, Luther's "simple and playful methods," as he called them (par. 75), come as a breath of fresh air. This advice was coming from someone who, according to Veit Dietrich, could spend three hours in prayer a day! Yet, as Luther understood it, the Christian life could not become a burden (par. 77), "for when we preach to children we must talk baby talk [German: *lallen*]."[60]

In the LC's introduction to prayer, Luther initiated the discussion of the command to pray with a look back at this discussion on the second commandment.[61] Again the command *not* to take God's name in vain led Luther immediately to the opposite (par. 5): "we are required to praise the holy name and to pray or call upon it in every need. For calling upon it is nothing else than praying."[62]

However, Luther's emphasis on the command to pray also arose out

57. LC, Ten Commandments, 70, in BC, 395 (BSLK, 578).

58. Luther was thinking here of the daily prayers in the SC, Blessings, 1-11, in BC, 363-64 (BSLK, 521-23).

59. LC, Ten Commandments, 74, in BC, 396 (BSLK, 579).

60. See also WA TR 5:202f. (no. 5508), Winter 1542/43. Dr. Jonas talked about how his children prayed against the Turks, even though they did not really understand what Turks were. Luther responded: "The prayer of children is good, because they still have pure voices and have not yet encountered opposition in their lives."

61. LC, Lord's Prayer, 4-6, in BC, 441 (BSLK, 662-63).

62. Luther also thought in antitheses when it came to the petitions of the Lord's Prayer. Thus, his comments in *A Simple Way to Pray* included both prayers and curses. Similarly, he even could imagine that praying to hallow God's name implied a curse on such teachers as Erasmus. See WA TR 3:147 (no. 3128), 13-28 March 1533: "Omnes, qui orant, maledicunt; velut cum dico: Sanctificetur nomen tuum, maledico Erasmo et omnibus contra verbum sentientibus."

of his pastoral experience and his desire to contrast true prayer with what passed for prayer in late-medieval piety. One senses this already in his insistence that prayer meant "calling upon God's name." This meant clearly that it was not simply a matter of reciting proper religious formulas, creating the proper religious attitude, or observing the proper religious exercises. Later in this section he addressed this problem directly.

The commandment, however, also eliminated all the old creature's excuses for not praying. In the LC, Luther focused first on "vulgar people" and their delusions that others would pray for them. This, too, arose from certain aspects of late-medieval piety, where thousands of masses, to say nothing of other prayers, could be purchased from "the religious" (professionals), whose spiritual exercises kept them closer to God. Luther's comments at table included at least one concrete example of this attitude. Johann Aurifaber, in a comment of Luther recorded nowhere else, preserved a story about the pastor of Holsdorf (a village near the town of Schweinitz). When his peasant parishioners demonstrated no knowledge of the basic catechism (the Ten Commandments, the Apostles' Creed, and the Lord's Prayer),[63] he refused them the Lord's Supper. When they complained to the official church visitors, the pastor admitted to having done this and explained that they could not pray. "We do not have to pray," a farmer responded. "That is why we hired you and pay you a salary, so that you would pray for us."[64] Even the LC (par. 6) echoed this attitude: "vulgar people who say in their delusion, 'If I do not pray, someone else will.'" The gross antinomianism against which Luther reacted in other sections of the LC also shows up here. "Thus they fall into the habit of never praying, claiming that because we reject false and hypocritical prayers, we teach that there is no duty or need to pray." Against such contempt, Luther could only preach the law as judgment.[65]

As with all his comments on late-medieval piety, Luther faced a

63. This word rarely referred to Luther's SC but simply to the chief parts themselves.

64. WA TR 6:163 (no. 6752). The same story is assumed in WA TR 5:183 (no. 5486, dated summer and fall of 1542). The pastor in question may have been Michael Stieffel, formerly pastor in Lochau (where he predicted that the end of the world would come on 19 October 1533). See MBW 1498 (CR 2:790f., a letter to Gabriel Zwilling, dated September 1534), MBW 2:110 (concerning the dating of MBW 1364), and WA 37:xvi n. 5.

65. Similarly, see Luther's comments in LC, Lord's Supper, 45-54, in BC, 471-72 (BSLK, 716-19), where he clobbered the "cold and indifferent" with the law.

problem. He had to preach the law in such a way that did not, to use his words elsewhere in the LC, "[institute] a new slaughter of souls."[66] Here he had first to reject (using rather gruff terms) "the kind of babbling and bellowing that used to pass for prayers."[67] Recitation of words — even beautiful or meaningful words — could not be prayer for Luther because it did not come from the heart and its deepest needs. Of course, Luther knew this practice firsthand from the monastery. In later life, he even admitted that he continued to try to recite the daily office after the Reformation had begun until Nicholas von Amsdorff and others convinced him to desist.[68] Despite his bad experience, however, Luther did not fully reject such recitation in the LC. It was good practice for children and the illiterate, but for Luther this was not yet prayer. True prayer, as he repeated throughout this introduction, was born of deep-felt need.

The command to pray also defined the Christian life. To be Christian and not to pray (now in the sense of crying out in our need to God) was plainly logically impossible. After all, a true Christian was someone who had been worked over by the law and driven to the gospel. Refusing to pray was as unthinkable for Luther (to borrow an earlier analogy) as refusing to fill a prescription for the life-giving medicine after hearing the diagnosis and learning the treatment. Luther used a variety of images to get his point across. First, he likened the command to pray to the command to obey authorities (the fourth commandment). Second, he made clear that prayer has to do with God, not with us. It is a matter of glorifying God's name. The law, then, functioned for Luther to "silence and repel" (par. 8) the old creature's excuses and allow faith the victory. Thus, he returned to the fourth commandment in paragraph 9, now to describe the relation between father and son. Luther, who at this time was both father and son, could speak with some authority out of this analogy. Thus, the obedience accorded the command arose not out of some slavish notion of compliance, but from the relation of faith. No wonder that in 1531 Luther added to the SC an explanation to the introduction of the Lord's

66. LC, Lord's Supper, 42, in BC, 471 (BSLK, 716).

67. LC, Lord's Prayer, 7, in BC, 441 (BSLK, 663).

68. WA TR 3:485f. (no. 3651, dated 21-25 December 1537), where practices included locking himself in his cell and trying to catch up on his prayers. Von Amsdorff and others finally got him to stop by laughing at him. See also WA TR 2:11 (no. 1253, 14 December 1531), where Luther dated this event to 1520. For another reflection on monastic praying, see WA TR 4:654 (no. 5094, dated 11-19 June 1540).

Prayer and emphasized the loving relationship of parent and child out of which true prayer arises.[69]

At this point in the explanation, namely, in the second edition, also printed in 1529, Luther inserted two paragraphs (par. 10-11). He still focused on the same issue (par. 10: "as though it made no difference if we do not pray, or as though prayer were commanded for those who are holier and in better favor with God"). However, in the additional comments (the only important addition to the LC outside of a completely new section on confession and a new preface), he delved even deeper into the commandment, finding at its center God's gracious heart. Here, Luther expressed his pastoral concern for the damaging effect of the law on the weak by turning the law inside out.

One time Johannes Schlaginhaufen, whose serious spiritual struggles in 1531-32 were well documented in his own version of the *Table Talk*, blurted out at table, "Whenever I think about God and Christ, this immediately comes into my mind: 'You are a sinner; therefore God is angry with you. For this reason your prayer will amount to nothing.'" Luther replied, "If I waited to pray until I was righteous, when would I pray? Now, then, whenever Satan suggests to you: 'You are a sinner; God does not listen to sinners,' you should boldly turn that argument inside out and say, 'Therefore, because I am a sinner, I pray, and I know that the prayers of the afflicted are effective in God's sight.'"[70]

In the LC Luther managed to address the same issue by finding gospel in the center of law. The human heart always flees from God (par. 10), "thinking that he neither wants nor cares for our prayers because we are sinners." Instead of pitting God's promise to be father against such fears, Luther turned to God's command to pray (par. 11). First, Luther thought that the command would make us pray out of fear ("so that we may not increase his anger by such disobedience"). More surprisingly, however, Luther insisted that "by this commandment [God] makes it clear that he will not cast us out or drive us away, even though we are sinners; he wishes rather to draw us to himself so that we may humble ourselves before him, lament our misery and plight, and pray for grace and help." Underneath the command "Call on me" sounds the voice of the ever-inviting Love of

69. SC, Lord's Prayer, 2, in BC, 356 (BSLK, 512). See also Birgit Stolt, "Martin Luther's Concept of God as a Father," *Lutheran Quarterly* 8 (1994): 383-94.

70. WA TR 2:115 (no. 1492, 7 April to 1 May 1532).

the sinner's life. Even the anger is that of a spurned love, not simply of an angry judge. "Therefore we read in the Scriptures that [God] is angry because those who were struck down for their sin did not return to him and through prayer set aside his wrath [for their sin] and seek grace."[71]

Returning to the original text of the LC, Luther made the same point, though in a less radical way, by focusing not on God's heart but on the prayer itself (par. 12-13). The command to pray, like the fourth commandment, actually gives meaning and worth to something that has no worth in itself. Obedience to parents gains worth only from God's commandment (not from the worth of either parent or child), because the commandment, as Word of God, is the only thing on which the person "can rely and depend." In the same way, the one praying can trust the Word of God, now in the form of a commandment, to turn what is unworthy into something worthy. Thus, those praying "should think, 'On my account this prayer would not amount to anything; but it is important because God has commanded it.'"[72]

Under this aspect of the commandment, Luther again criticized earlier practices. In the first place (par. 14), he attacked the notion that prayer was effective *ex opere operato,* by using a German equivalent of this Latin technical phrase "if the act were performed" ("daß das Werk getan wäre"). Prayer became thereby a matter of luck and a completely uncertain occurrence, reduced to aimless mumbling. No wonder Luther could tell Master Peter in *A Simple Way to Pray* that the Lord's Prayer was the greatest martyr on earth![73] God, on the contrary, had commanded human beings to pour out their needs to him, in the expectation that he is actually listening to what they say and mean.

In the second place (par. 15-16), the focus of prayer in late-medieval piety was always on one's own worthiness — as reflected in the case involving poor Johannes Schlaginhaufen. The command to pray also overturned spiritual pride and its mirror image, despair; no one is worthier than another. The famous spiritual, for all of its beauty, might need some correction by Luther's lights, when it sings, "If you cannot pray like Paul." Instead, Luther stated, one "should say, 'The prayer I offer is just as precious, holy, and pleasing to God as those of St. Paul and the holiest of saints. The

71. LC, Lord's Prayer, 11, in BC, 442 (BSLK, 664), revised by the author.

72. LC, Lord's Prayer, 13, in BC, 442 (BSLK, 665).

73. WA 38:364.25, cited in Peters, *Das Vaterunser,* 36.

reason is this: I freely admit that he is holier in respect to his person, but not on account of the commandment.'" The command, understood in this faith-filled light, leaves room for neither boasting nor despair and again functions for Luther as good news.

Thus, Luther walked a tightrope between arrogance and despair, using the command of God to keep the balance. On the one side, he insisted (par. 17) that "our person" had no effect on God. Whether spoken by a sinner or a saint, any prayer uttered in obedience to the command to pray is heard by God. Moreover (par. 18), the commandment guaranteed for Luther that God will not "allow our prayers to be futile or lost." Unlike much of what passes for lessons in elementary school, praying is not "busywork." "If [God] did not intend to answer you, he would not have ordered you to pray and backed it up with such a strict commandment." On the other side, Luther also insisted that God's command revealed the seriousness of the situation — especially in the face of the vulgar tomfoolery of the old creature. "God is not joking" (par. 18) and is angry and threatens punishment "if we do not pray."

The Promise to Hear and Answer Prayer

Luther spent only two paragraphs (19-20) on God's promise to hear and answer prayer and then a paragraph (21) summarizing his arguments in the first two sections of his introduction. However, as the examples above demonstrate, God's promise to answer prayer formed one of the central motivations (or: material causes) for his praying. For Luther, God's promise was best summarized in Psalm 50:15 ("Call on me in the day of trouble; I will deliver you") and Matthew 7:7-8 ("Ask, and it will be given you . . . for everyone who asks receives"). Perhaps one of the most playful attempts to apply the latter verse to prayer came in 1542. Here Luther revealed both the ground of his confidence in asking God and the way in which the promise itself drove a person to pray.

> Up until now, prayer has preserved the church. Thus we must continue to pray. That is why Christ says, "Ask, seek, knock!" First we are to ask. Now, as soon as we start asking, God sneaks away somewhere and doesn't want to hear or to be found. So, a person has to start searching, that is, keep on praying. When a person seeks for him, God shuts himself

> up in a closet. If someone wants to get in, that person has to start knocking. Of course, if someone knocks only once or twice, God ignores it. Finally, when the knocking gets to be too much, God opens the door and says, "Whatever do you want?" "Lord, I want this or that." Then God says, "All right! Go ahead and have it." Thus, you have to wake God up. I'm of the opinion that there are still a lot of godly people here [who pray this way], as sure as there are also a lot of evil jerks [who do not]. Thus, the verse "Ask . . ." implies nothing less than: "Ask, shout, cry, search, knock, bang!" Moreover, a person has to keep it up without stopping.[74]

Despite Peters's implication that Luther's comments on prayer in the LC are somewhat domesticated and lack any hint of the problem of theodicy with which other comments wrestle,[75] this section on God's promise in its very brevity places the problem of unanswered prayer squarely where Luther always placed it: in the promise of God. On the one hand, the promises work faith in us and "ought to awaken and kindle in our hearts a longing and love for prayer." Here, too, Peters misconstrues the *sollen* and imagines that this is simply more law. Luther did not say here that the one praying "should" but that the promise "should" have this effect. Its failure to do this may be a result of human sin (and thus God's promise to hear works as law, showing human unbelief), but it may also be a problem in God. Luther magnified the problem by adding, "For by his Word, God testifies that our prayer is heartily pleasing to him and will assuredly be heard and granted, so that we may not despise, cast it to the winds, or pray uncertainly." Rather than using theology to solve the problem of unanswered prayer, Luther rested his case in the certain promise of God. It is his very silence about theodicy in the face of God's promise that allowed him room to pray with such chutzpah. What Peters does not realize is that the problem of unanswered prayer must always remain unanswered in theology, lest one abandon God's promises and, thus, faith itself for explanation.

The conclusion of the first two sections bears this out. Here, Luther ex-

74. WA TR 5:123 (no. 5392, dated Spring 1542). For a different translation, see Haile, *Luther*, 278.

75. Peters, *Das Vaterunser*, 32-34. His unconsidered comment about the "melanchthonische Richtung" of article 11 of the Formula of Concord misses completely the fact that, except when dealing with "an unbeliever" like Erasmus, Luther always grounded comments about predestination in God's promise, especially when dealing with the conscience under attack.

pressed clearly his confidence and allowed his simple German pastors and people, the intended readers of this catechism, permission to do the same. "You can hold such promises up to [God] and say: 'Here I come, dear Father, and pray not of my own accord nor because of my own worthiness, but at your commandment and promise, which cannot fail or deceive me.' Those who do not believe such a promise should again realize that they are angering God, grossly dishonoring him, and accusing him of lying."[76] To "hold up such promises" (German: *ihm aufrücken;* literally "throw back at God") expresses far more profoundly the heart of faith's struggle against unanswered prayer. Luther refused to allow an unresponsive God to send humanity back into itself, wondering whether it had done something wrong. Instead, everything rests on God's command and promise, the ground and "material" of faith. Believers could even tell God that if it were up to them, they would not be there praying. It is God's fault for commanding them to pray and for promising to "hear and grant" (German: *gewähren,* "fulfill," used in Luther's translation of the Bible only in Ps. 20:5) their requests.

The Words to Say

Luther introduced the final section of his remarks with a simple "furthermore."[77] In addition to the command and promise, Luther wrote (par. 22), "God takes the initiative and puts into our mouths the very words and approach we are to use." He immediately described the two reasons for God's actions: our needs and our certainty.[78] With every prayer human beings cook up on their own, the question will always arise whether it was done correctly. The issue of such "self-chosen spirituality," as Luther translates Colossians 2:23, has been dealt with by others.[79] Here it is enough to realize

76. LC, Lord's Prayer, 21, in BC, 443 (BSLK, 667). This same combination as an introduction to confident prayer occurs in *A Simple Way to Pray* (LW 43:194-95; WA 38:359-60) and in the explanation of "Amen" in the SC, Lord's Prayer, 21, in BC, 358 (BSLK, 515).

77. LC, Lord's Prayer, 22, in BC, 443 (BSLK, 667). The Latin translator, too, understood that the singular German *(Über das)* implied the first two sections and translated with the plural *(Praeter haec).*

78. LC, Lord's Prayer, 22, in BC, 443 (BSLK, 667): "In this way we see how deeply concerned he is about our needs, and we should never doubt that such prayer pleases him and will assuredly be heard."

79. Scott Hendrix, "Martin Luther's Reformation of Spirituality," now in *Har-*

that for Luther the Lord's Prayer is a treasure direct from Christ's lips to Christian hearts. "God loves to hear it." The motif of "treasure" (German: *Schatz*) figures significantly in the LC, particularly in his description of the benefits of the Lord's Supper.[80] This highly affective language also marks paragraph 23, where Luther used words like *edler* (here translated "noble" but which also has deep association to jewels) and the phrase "trade for all the riches in the world [German: *der Welt Gut*]."

What clearly caught Luther's imagination in this third section (especially par. 24-32), however, was human need and its reflection in the petitions of the Lord's Prayer. This concern, already expressed in opening comments on the command to pray, now takes center stage. Even though he called such needs accidental causes, that was only because they varied in his mind according to the individual's plight. However, they were intimately connected with faith itself. Need was simply another, poignant way for Luther to express the (eschatological) *Anfechtungen* (assaults), under which believers all live.

Now it becomes clear that for believers the *sollen* of Luther's discussion is out of their hands. God's Word (command and promise) and human need conspire, in Luther's words, "to drive and compel us to pray without ceasing." Now, as Peters also points out, it was no longer a matter of some mechanical mantra that allowed monks to pray without ceasing (and also without thinking), but prayer had become for Luther the very breath of a Christian living under the cross, in the midst of attacks, at the end of the world.[81] "Therefore we have rightly rejected the prayers of monks and priests, who howl and growl frightfully day and night, but not one of them thinks of asking for the least little thing [literally: a hair's breadth]."[82] The final break with late-medieval piety and its insistence that prayer or the sacraments were effective *ex opere operato* (by the mere performance of the rite) occurs here. The lie of this form of piety is revealed not only through God's Word but also on the basis of human experience. If

vesting Martin Luther's Reflections on Theology, Ethics, and the Church, ed. Timothy J. Wengert (Grand Rapids: Eerdmans, 2004), 240-60.

80. LC, Lord's Supper, 20-37, in BC, 468-70 (BSLK, 711-15). See also WA TR 1:183 (no. 421, dated Christmas 1532), where Luther compared the Lord's Prayer and the Psalms but finally admitted that he prayed the Lord's Prayer more avidly (German: *lieber*) than any psalm.

81. Peters, *Das Vaterunser,* 28-31.

82. LC, Lord's Prayer, 25, in BC, 443 (BSLK, 667).

prayer is not asking and begging God out of true human needs, it is simply howling and growling, unwilling or unable to ask (par. 25) "even for a droplet of wine." Worse yet, it is one more form of works righteousness, so twisted that it never even occurs to the worker to ask God for anything.

Having broken with this late-medieval (and modern!) piety concerning prayer, what remains to the one praying (outside of the "material" of command and promise) is his or her need. Here, finally, Luther resolved the pastoral problem of turning prayer into one more "must" with which to slaughter souls. In one of the most paradoxical statements in the LC, Luther described human need this way. "But where there is to be true prayer, there must be utter earnestness. We must feel our need, the distress that drives and impels us to cry out. Then prayer will come spontaneously, as it should, and no one will need to be taught how to prepare for it or how to create the proper devotion."[83] In language strikingly similar to his later comments at table described above, Luther mixed human need and earnestness in such a way as to eliminate the "ought" of prayer and turn it into spontaneity. Whereas religious people tend to deny needs (and look down at anyone who suddenly begins to pray or comes to worship as a result of deep-felt needs), Luther reveled in them. Needs — one might say "God's law in the flesh" — drive and impel with the opposite result that one might expect. Literally in German, "prayer just comes forth from itself, as it should." Now, finally the *sollen* is quieted in the face of desperate, real earnestness. This *gemitus* (groaning) was for Luther the heart of all prayer.[84]

To reveal our needs, the Lord's Prayer comes to the believer's rescue and provides a complete listing of all human need (using the SC as a guide): for God's Word, for the Holy Spirit and faith, for victory over evil, for all the necessities of daily life (especially peace), for forgiveness (especially in the face of conscience, which always thinks it has no business praying), for strength in *Anfechtung*, and for final deliverance from all evil

83. LC, Lord's Prayer, 26, in BC, 444 (BSLK, 668).

84. See WA TR 3:79 (no. 2918, 26-29 January 1533): "Christianus semper orat, sive dormiat sive vigilet. Cor enim eius orat semper, et suspirium est magna et fortis oratio. Sic enim dicit: Propter gemitum pauperum nunc exurgam, Esa[iae] 11 [actually Ps. 12:6]. Sic christianus semper fert crucem, licet non semper eam sentiat." For Luther's early use of this phrase and its importance in his theology, see Heiko Oberman, "'Simul gemitus et raptus': Luther and Mysticism," in *The Reformation in Medieval Perspective,* ed. Steven Ozment (Chicago: Quadrangle Books, 1971), 219-51.

in the "vale of tears."[85] Luther realized, of course, that the human heart was more devious than simply to fall to its knees in the midst of needs. The listing of needs in the Lord's Prayer aids human weakness. "For we are all lacking plenty of things: all that is missing is that we do not feel or see them. God therefore wants you to lament and express your needs and concerns, not because he is unaware of them, but in order that you may kindle your hearts to stronger and greater desires and open and spread your apron wide to receive many things."[86] This self-induced ignorance or denial finally comes to an end in the Word of God, this time in the words of the Lord's Prayer itself, which sets the heart on fire — the very affective language Dietrich himself used to describe Luther's praying. Then, God shakes loose more than humanity's outstretched ponchos can hold.[87] God knows human needs but allows our prayers, grounded in faith, to be the ground of that very faith.

It would seem that paragraphs 28-29 mark a fitting peroration for Luther's admonition. However, as is often the case, a last remark caused him to expand this section to include several other points. For one thing, here is the only place where Luther mentioned what otherwise was central to his understanding of prayer: that it never takes place in isolation from others.[88] So (par. 28), when he went to list needs, he mentioned "anything that affects us or other people around us." Pastors, magistrates, neighbors, and servants come in for special mention. In the same breath, Luther reiterated his point in paragraph 21, that those praying needed to remind God of his commands and promises. The point of the admonition, Luther concluded (par. 29), was to prevent crude and cold prayers. People were daily becoming more inept in praying.

Luther clearly had summarized his chief arguments. But wait! An offhand mention of the devil caused him to break off the end of the admo-

85. SC, Lord's Prayer, 3-20, in BC, 356-58 (BSLK, 512-15). See also WA TR 5:57 (no. 5317-18, dated 19 October to 5 November 1540) for an explanation of the grammar of the Lord's Prayer.

86. LC, Lord's Prayer, 27, in BC, 444 (BSLK, 668).

87. Here, the German word *Mantel* designated the common cloak worn by either sex.

88. For a fine summary of this point, see Peters, *Das Vaterunser,* 37-39. See also WA TR 1:340 (no. 700, from the first half of the 1530s), where Luther linked the Lord's Prayer especially to this common praying. See also WA 6:237.33–239.19 (LW 44:64-66) and WA 2:114.3-31 (LW 42:60). I am indebted to my student, Gary Steeves, for this reference.

nition. Finally, the reader glimpses the end of the world. The ineptness in prayer was not simply a human foible; it matched exactly the devil's own desires, since he knows what damage proper prayer could do to him. Here, in language that modern readers of Luther all too often ignore, Luther stated the serious, eschatological struggle in which prayer is caught up.[89]

Paragraphs 30-32 suddenly showed the other side of coin, so to speak. This appearance of the devil, a very important part of the language in both the SC and LC, illustrates to the reader just how much more is at stake in prayer than academic or mystical conversations with God. The God who commanded Luther to pray, promised to answer, and gave him the words to pray is the very God who redeemed him with his holy and precious blood "from sin, death, and the power of the devil."[90] Here, Luther brought the entire Reformation and all the struggles over church into focus with the comment about the devil. Here, the political Luther was praying in ways not unrelated to his later prayers in 1539. The only weapon the Christian has to wield against Satan is "prayer alone," a *sola* worth adding to Reformation stained-glass windows — but understood now not as mere howling or magic but as arising out of God's Word and human need and thus in line with the "little word" *(Wörtlein)* of "A Mighty Fortress." The only thing that had prevented a collapse of the Reformation movement itself was prayer (par. 31): "a few godly people intervened like an iron wall on our side." Otherwise, "the devil would have destroyed all Germany in its own blood." Enemies of the gospel might laugh and sneer, "But by prayer alone we shall be a match both for them and for the devil." There follows (par. 32) Luther's brief synopsis of the third petition, with which this essay began. With respect to prayer, everything, finally, rests in God's hands. "Yes, dear child, it shall be done indeed." It is on this eschatological note that Luther concluded his remarks, rejecting all babbling, howling, and growling, and concentrating instead on actual, concrete asking — "a great and precious thing."[91] It was on this remarkable canvas that Luther could then paint his exposition of the Lord's Prayer in the LC.[92]

89. See, especially, Heiko Oberman, *Luther: Man between God and the Devil* (New Haven: Yale University Press, 1989).

90. SC, Creed, 4, in BC, 355 (BSLK, 511). See Peters, *Das Vaterunser*, 28-34.

91. LC, Lord's Prayer, 33, in BC, 444-45 (BSLK, 670).

92. For an analysis of his exposition, see Peters, *Das Vaterunser*, 42-188, and, in English, Charles P. Arand, "Battle Cry of Faith: The Catechism's Exposition of the Lord's Prayer," *Concordia Journal* 21 (1995): 42-65.

CHAPTER 9

The Last Supper: The Testament of Jesus

Reinhard Schwarz

Luther defined the Last Supper very precisely as the making of a testament by Jesus. He finds all the determining marks of this activity in the New Testament witness to Jesus' Last Supper with his disciples "in the night in which he was betrayed" (1 Cor. 11:23). By the very action of making a testament himself, Jesus at one and the same time instituted his testamental activity as a sacrament. This is to be carefully observed in the doctrine of the Supper, since in the sacraments we have to do with actions, which in turn, to be accorded their particular character, must be described as actions.

In his critique of the sacrifice of the Mass Luther did not simply cut out the action character of the sacrament without replacement. For him, the action of making a testament is the heart of the sacrament. Testament-making activity therefore replaces the sacrificial activity, because in the testament Jesus turns to his disciples in a saving act, simultaneously establishing a particular bond between himself and them.

This essay, in the English translation by Gerhard Forde, was originally published as "Abendmahl: die Testament Handlung," *Luther* 59 (1988): 13-25, and is reprinted by permission of Vandenhoeck & Ruprecht.

The Idea of Testament in Luther, 1519-1521

In the decisive years 1520-21 every work in which Luther deals with the problem of the Mass sets the idea of testament in the center. First in *A Treatise on the New Testament, That Is, the Holy Mass,*[1] then in *The Babylonian Captivity of the Church,*[2] and further in the two treatises paralleling each other written at Wartburg Castle, *On the Abolition of the Private Mass* and *On the Misuse of the Mass.*[3] Already on his exegesis of Galatians 3:15-18[4] in the Galatians commentary of 1519, Luther had so expounded the concept of testament as to make it fruitful for the interpretation of the Supper. To every legacy as a "last will and testament" there belongs, Luther observes, a testator who makes the legacy, one person or an entire group to whom it is to be distributed, the testamentary promise itself, and finally the inheritance bequeathed in the testament. Thus God promised a testament to Abraham and his posterity when he bequeathed him a saving possession that would include all peoples. Luther, with Paul, interprets that possession as the righteousness of faith. In Jesus Christ, Abraham's descendant and Son of God, indeed through his very death, this divine testament of promise is opened up so that ever since the legacy of salvation can be distributed. For with Hebrews 9:17 one must say that a testament goes into effect only with the death of the testator; only then can the legacy be appropriated by the one intended in the testament.

Luther can bring the concepts covenant *(pactum)* and testament into agreement in this context, even though they do not denote the same things.[5] Whoever makes a covenant must remain alive; for a testament to go into effect, however, the one who makes it must die. But in Jesus Christ both come together. In him God, over whom death has no power, has made a covenant with humanity. And Jesus Christ himself issued his testa-

1. WA 6:357ff.; LW 35:79-111.

2. WA 6:513.4ff.; LW 36:11-26.

3. WA 8:44.3ff. and 521.32ff.; LW 36:179-80, 181-82. None of the German editions of selected works of Luther in this century outside of the six-volume edition *Ausgewählte Schriften* edited by Karin Bornkamm and Gerhard Ebeling (Frankfurt am Main: Insel, 1983) have taken up this important writing of Luther's. The Insel-Ausgabe contains a shortened version of the German in 3:85-164.

4. WA 2:519.3ff.; 521.25ff.; LW 27:264, 268.

5. WA 2:521.33ff.; LW 27:268.

mentary legacy in the face of death. Just as Jesus Christ is "both God and Man, so Testament and Covenant are in this case the same."[6]

No big step is needed to apply these ideas from the exegesis of Galatians to the understanding of the Supper. Luther took this step early in 1520, first in the *Treatise on Good Works,* briefly indicating it in a short exposition on the meaning of the Mass as the Testament of Christ,[7] and more extensively and for the first time thematically a bit later in the *Treatise on the New Testament, That Is, the Holy Mass.*[8] The enumeration of the individual aspects of testament making varies in the above-mentioned thematic treatments of the question of the Supper. The four points already named in the Galatians commentary are expanded by Luther in the *Treatise on the New Testament,* first by the "seal or warranty *(Wahrzeichen)*" of bread and wine, under which Christ is present with his body and blood,[9] and further by the duty enjoined upon us to hold Christ in memory or commemoration,[10] as Paul indicates in 1 Corinthians 11:26. For "this is what an earthly testator does, who bequeaths something to his heirs, that he may leave behind him a good name, the good will of men, and a blessed memory, that he should not be forgotten."[11] In *The Babylonian Captivity,* when he deals with the question of the essence of the Supper, Luther proceeds from the premise that it is the very testament Christ has given for believers to participate in after his death.[12] On this "immovable foundation" Luther sets three points: the death of the testator, the promise of the inheritance, and the designation of the heir.[13] All three points are contained in the words spoken at the Supper, which, taken as a whole, form the last will and testament promised by Jesus.[14] In 1521 Luther returns to the four-point distinction as set forth in the Galatians commentary.[15] Here he sets a definition: "A testament is nothing but the last will of one who is dying, telling

6. WA 2:521.36ff.; LW 27:268. "Sicut idem Deus et homo, ita idem pactum et testamentum."

7. WA 6:23ff.; LW 44:55-56.

8. Above, n. 2.

9. WA 6:359.18ff.; LW 35:86-87.

10. WA 6:359.30ff.; LW 35:87.

11. WA 6:359.30ff.; LW 35:87.

12. WA 6:513.14ff.; LW 36:87.

13. WA 6:513.25ff.; LW 36:38.

14. WA 6:513.24ff.; LW 36:38.

15. WA 8:444.18ff., or 521.6ff.

how his heirs are to live with and dispose of his properties after his death."[16]

Since Luther in general perceives the promise of salvation to be the fundamental content of the sacraments, it is important for him to bring the promise of salvation into internal agreement with the explanation of the Supper as testament. In the words of the Supper Jesus had promised the saving gift of the forgiveness of sins to all believers as the legacy of his death.[17] However, from the perspective of the donor there is a difference between a promise or offer and the making of a testament. "A testament is made by one who is going to die. A promise, however, is made by one who will continue to live."[18] In the person who in this instance is the donor of both promise and testament, however, the difference disappears. When "God now and again in the scripture calls his promise a 'testament' he wants thereby to indicate that he would die. And again when he calls it a promise he wants to indicate that he would live. And thus he would give us to understand with his own words that he would become human, die, and nevertheless live eternally."[19] These expositions find their parallel in Luther's reflections on the relation between covenant or covenantal pact *(pactum)* and testament in the Galatians commentary. Here, as there, the difference in the concepts is mirrored in the difference between the humanity and the divinity of Jesus Christ. The situation in the Supper is determined by the impending death of Jesus. But the content of the legacy that Jesus bequeaths in this situation has its telos in the eternal life that God guarantees. The testament of Jesus is in its content testament and covenantal pact, a promise of life in community with God. Luther finds the entirety of salvation in the testamental promise of Jesus. In the Small Catechism he explains later with reference to the Supper: "Where there is forgiveness of sins, there is also life and salvation." He understands the promise of the Supper in the same sense already in 1520-21.[20]

We can clarify further. God's forgiving love restores humans out of the lostness of sin and death into communion with God once again, so

16. WA 8:521.14ff.; LW 36:179. Cf WA 8:444.18ff.: "Est igitur testamentum nuncupatio morituri, qua disponit suam hereditatem certis heredibus."

17. WA 6:513.34ff.; LW 36:38.

18. WA 8:521.4ff.; LW 36:179.

19. WA 8:521.10ff.; LW 36:179. Cf WA 6:513.36ff.; LW 36:38.

20. WA 6:358.14ff.; LW 35:85; and WA 6:513.34ff.; LW 36:38. See also WA 8:436.18ff.; or 511.27ff. (LW 36:169), and 518.18ff. (LW 36:176).

that humans thereby receive for themselves eternal life and complete salvation. The divinity of Jesus encompasses his full authority to declare God's grace to humans in their sin and separation from God. This full authority gave to the public works of Jesus the peculiar power that unleashed faith in some but caused offense in others because they could not tolerate such divine authority in this man. In the face of his impending condemnation for blasphemy, Jesus once again confirmed the full authority of the forgiveness of sins to his disciples. He did that expressly in view of the threat of death hanging over him. He accepts his death for the sake of the forgiveness of sins so that the confirmation of his full divine authority becomes itself the declaration of his testament. The reality of this situation in the face of the impending death demonstrates the humanity of Jesus. He demonstrates it himself. For in that he confirms his full divine authority to forgive unto his death, he identifies himself with his earthly life in flesh and blood. He affirms the fact that he had shared his earthly life with those who had received the grace of God through his address. At the same time, he underlines his word of testament by giving his disciples bread and wine and designating it as his body and blood, which he will surrender into death. Bread and wine, which Jesus identifies with his body and blood in his testamental word, become in this situation the "pledge" and "seal" of the testamentary promise.[21]

Exegetical, Christological, and Sacramentological Foundations

Luther puts all his emphasis on the claim that in the words of the testament Jesus applies God's grace to us. It is therefore a complete perversion to celebrate the Supper as a sacrifice in which something is presented to God. But rather than interpreting Luther's critical exposé of the explanation of the sacrifice of the Mass in detail and testing its validity through a comparison with the theology current in the church in his day, it is more important to me first of all to insist that for Luther the entire activity of the Supper is determined by the idea of testament. That is demonstrated already in the fact that in the writings of 1520-21 he consistently, even if with slight omissions, keeps adding more elements that go together to make up

21. WA 6:359.18ff.; LW 35:86-87. See above, n. 10. Cf. WA 6:518.10ff. (LW 36:44), WA 8:440.24ff.

the testamental activity of Jesus. That has exegetical, christological, and sacramentological importance.

Peter Stuhlmacher[22] has recently shown from the texts of the Supper that according to the original witness of the New Testament the Supper is rooted in a farewell meal. The meal was connected with a Jerusalem Passover meal of Jesus and his disciples but was already overshadowed by the anticipated death sentence on Jesus. The origin of the Supper accordingly lies in a quite uniquely determined meal celebration and not in a regular custom of meal celebrations of Jesus with his disciples during the time of his earthly activity. Already in the traditions of the New Testament witnesses, the farewell meal had separated itself from the Passover meal, shifting the points of view. The farewell meal activity could be separated from the Passover meal because the twofold act in which Jesus distributed bread and wine to his disciples with the word of promise had taken on an importance of its own even over against the Passover meal itself.

To be sure, Luther's understanding of the Supper as the testamental activity of Jesus is not found as such (as an explicit form) in any of the various New Testament Supper texts. But Luther's interpretation is not simply an arbitrary selection of isolated themes from the New Testament texts or a collation of such themes. Rather what comes to light in Luther's interpretation is a plumbing of the depths of the Supper's action to which all the New Testament witnesses point.

The underlying test for every conception of the Supper is the manner in which it can align itself with the situation of Jesus "in the night in which he was betrayed," even though the history of the liturgy of the Supper shows that the connection with this situation has not always been preserved. In the late-medieval doctrine of the Supper, the act of consecration, the central part of the sacrifice of the Mass, was expressly connected with the last meal of Jesus with his disciples. In that meal celebration, therefore, Jesus had ostensibly acted out a sacramental rite of sacrifice, in a sense a previewing of his own sacrificial death. He was thereby supposed to have transferred to his disciples themselves the priestly duty of redoing retrospectively a sacramental representation of his sacrificial death. In a sense, the sacrificial rite at the Last Supper of Jesus with his disciples therefore relates to the church's sacrifice of the Mass in mirror-image-like fash-

22. Peter Stuhlmacher, "Das neutestamentliche Zeugnis vom Herrenmahl," *Zeitschrift für Theologie und Kirche* 84 (1987): 1-35.

ion. The symmetrical axis lies, so viewed, in the sacrificial death of Christ, whose sacramental representation, once previewed by Jesus, is now again retrospectively celebrated. The sacramental activity of Jesus among his disciples therefore finds its meaning in the supposition that Jesus intended to institute the churchly celebration of the sacrifice of the Mass.

It is a quite different matter when the Last Supper of Jesus with his disciples is understood as his making of a testament. Then this activity itself commands its own place within the passion story because therein Jesus, in the form of a testament given to his disciples, reinforces his divine authority as proclaimer of grace. The testamental promise of forgiveness fits exactly the situation of the impending death of Jesus. As has been established above, the testamental activity of Jesus itself brings the true divinity as well as the true humanity of Jesus to expression. Contrariwise, it is questionable whether the christological dimensions would be thus established if the Last Supper of Jesus were to be understood as an anticipatory sacramental representation of his sacrificial death. Would not the overwhelming power with which death also strikes Jesus be depotentiated? In any case, for Christology it means something quite different if Jesus "in the night in which he was betrayed" views his death as a sacramental act than if he already in this moment represents his death as a sacrificial death.

Ecclesiastical theology in Luther's day had, as indicated briefly above, interpreted the Last Supper of Jesus with his disciples as the rite of institution for the Sacrament of the Altar. With this view came the assumption that Jesus with his words "Do this in remembrance of me" had given to his apostles and their successors, according to the example of the rite here celebrated by him, the commission to offer the sacrifice of the Mass in perpetuity to God, and that he had simultaneously with these words ordained the apostles as priests and bestowed on them the full power to consecrate and sacrifice. This interpretation gave the meal activity of Jesus the character of a sacramental sacrifice-celebration, which was the basis for the ecclesiastical sacrament of the sacrifice of the Mass.

Our comparison shows that exegetical and christological points of view shift when Luther interprets the Last Supper of Jesus as his testamental action. Luther strongly emphasized the difference for sacramental theology over against the ecclesiastical teaching of the time. In the testamental action of Jesus, what occurs exclusively for Luther is the turning to us humans of God's forgiving love. There is no place here for the offering of something of worth to God and for God, not even in the highest form of the bringing of a sacrifice, as happened in the death of Jesus. Whatever the death of Jesus may mean for faith, even should faith grasp it as a sacrificial death, remains completely the mystery of this death event itself. The testamental activity, like every testamentary declaration, does indeed have death in view. Nevertheless, as the act of testament making, it has its own weight even over against the event of death itself.

Exegetical, Christological, and Sacramentological Applications

Luther's new understanding of the Supper was quickly appropriated by other Reformation preachers. Urbanus Rhegius in Augsburg provides a good example as early as 1521. Not only was he, it appears, the first preacher outside of Wittenberg to provide evidence of the new understanding of the Supper, but there are also brief printed works from the years following in which he interprets the Supper, albeit with variations, as the making of a testament. As preacher of the Augsburg Cathedral Church, he said on the Corpus Christi festival in 1521 (30 May)[23] that "the holy and most venerable Sacrament of the Altar" is from its very origin "a Testament of Christ" just as other testaments are a promise of those who are under the threat of death and about to die who announce a heritage and designate heirs (A 3v1). What Jesus has promised to his disciples and "through them also to us all" (A 4r) in the words of the Supper as "an incomparable inheritance" (A 3v), is indulgence (*Ablass* — "forgiveness") from sin, an eternal joy (A 3v1), and "eternal life" (A 4r), an immeasurable treasure, "the true treasure of grace" (A 4v), not to be exchanged for the "indulgence *(Ablass)* from punishment" that the church offers in her prayer and indulgence *traffic.* "We will not be unchristian Christians who don't want to bear the cross with the Savior, but ask only that he forgive us our sin" (A 4v).

One year later Urbanus Rhegius coupled the idea of testament with the idea of communion *(Gemeinschaft).*[24] For with the forgiveness of sins Jesus established a communion of all believers with himself and with one another. "All the spiritual benefits of Christ and his saints are yours in

23. *Ain Sermon von dem hochwirdigen sacrament des Altars, gepredigt durch Doctor Urbanum Regium, Thuombprediger zuo Augspurg, am tag Corporis Christi* (1521).

24. *Underricht wie sic ein Christenmensch halten sol das er frucht der Mess erlang und Christlich zue gotz tisch ganng* (1522).

common" (A 2v), and, to be sure, all the suffering as well. It is similar to the situation in the civil community when someone gives a handwritten sign or some such as certification "that he is a citizen of the same city, a member of the same community so that he has everything that affects the city in common with his fellow citizens, happiness and suffering, the useful and the harmful. Everything, name, honor, freedom, business, mores, custom, help, counsel" (A 2v), is common to him in the same city.

In his next treatise on the Supper in 1523, Rhegius did not put the idea of testament so prominently in the center, but it still makes its appearance. In this instance he puts all his emphasis on the insistence that the devotion of the Supper be carried by faith in the promise of grace given by Jesus in the words of the Supper. Rhegius reissued this tract in 1525[25] with the addition of some short texts — in part, prayers — all intended to foster an evangelical piety vis-à-vis the Supper. For our purposes the second addition is worth mentioning ("The five main articles of this most blessed Testament"). He makes five points according to which the Supper is to be viewed as the Testament of Jesus. This summary has a tradition of its own that I cannot go into here. I must content myself with the indication that with the handing on of this text one finds two woodcuts that depict the new evangelical understanding of the Supper in telling fashion. At least one of them could be reproduced in somewhat reduced size in the original essay.[26]

In both woodcuts the scene of the Last Supper of Jesus is combined with the distribution of bread and wine as the body and blood of Christ to the faithful. The room of the Last Supper of Jesus with his disciples has opened itself up for all who in faith wish to participate in the inheritance given by Jesus. It is simply assumed that the promises of Jesus to his disciples are valid for all believers because the Word of Jesus transcends space and time. The idea of distribution of the testament transposes the Supper communicants directly into the situation in which Jesus had spoken the

25. *Von dem hochwirdigen Sacrament des altars underricht, was man aus heyligergeschrift wissen magk . . . zu Augspurg gepredigt corporis Christi bis auf den achtenden* (1525).

26. It is the title-page woodcut of the treatise *Wie ein Christenmensch ein tegliche beicht und bekantnus gegen got von hertzen sol thuen, gezogen auss der geschrifft. Mit was gestalt und glauben wir uns sollen halten gegen dem Testament und disch Christi* that appeared anonymously without indication of printer, place, or year. For the woodcut, see the original essay in *Lutheran Quarterly* 9 (1995): 391-403.

words of the testament. To put it differently, the words of Jesus, which had made his Last Supper with his disciples into a testamental action, also make the Supper in the Christian congregation into the testamental action of Jesus.

In later years Luther never surrendered the idea of testament even though the discussion of the question of the presence of the body and blood of Christ in the bread and wine then repressed all other points of view. The basis for the treatment of the passion texts during Holy Week in Wittenberg, and also for Luther's passion sermons, had since the mid-twenties been Bugenhagen's combining and harmonizing of the passion texts from the four Gospels.[27] According to Bugenhagen's exposition, the Supper event is clearly distinguished from the Passover meal. The Passover lamb must be eaten perpetually, whereas Jesus and his disciples sat down[28] to the activity that became the origin of the Christian Last Supper. Jesus "makes a Testament" in this action; he does not institute a sacrifice.[29] When Bugenhagen writes that we Christians should remember that the body of Christ was given over to death and the blood of Christ poured out on the cross for our sins, he does not therewith interpret Christ's death on the cross so as to collapse it into the action of the Supper itself. He adds, furthermore, that that remembrance of the death of Jesus is faith, which already makes blessed "alone without the sacrament" and without which the external partaking of the sacrament is nothing.[30] Nevertheless, Christians know how to treasure the Supper: "Troubled consciences use this sign happily from the heart as Christ has instituted it because therewith the conscience is comforted and faith is strengthened."[31]

As the making of a testament by Jesus, the Supper unambiguously has Jesus as the acting subject. Who the acting subject is in the Supper was among other things a controversial issue between Luther and Zwingli. In Zwingli's view the Supper is a communal action of convinced believers who thereby remember thankfully Jesus' death on the cross and commit

27. The first printing of the Latin edition came in 1524. The German version appeared for the first time in 1526; it was included in Luther's so-called *Winter Postil* from 1528 without Bugenhagen's commentary. See WA 21:165-80.

28. *Die Historia des leydens und der Auferstehung unseres Herrn Jhesu Christi aus den vier Evangelisten* (Wittenberg, 1526), Bl. C 1^v.

29. *Die Historia,* Bl. C 2^v.

30. *Die Historia,* Bl. C 2^v.

31. *Die Historia,* Bl. C 2^v–3^r.

themselves therewith to the duty that goes with it. Therefore Luther could say of the representatives of the Zwinglian doctrine of the Supper: they "make of the Supper a symbol, that is, a memorial, by which one can identify Christians externally . . . so that it is simply to be a memorial among Christians themselves, not with respect to God, by which they practice and maintain love among themselves."[32]

Against that Luther maintains:

> We know however, that it is and is called the Lord's Supper, not the Christians' Supper. Because the Lord has not only instituted it, but also makes it and hosts it himself and is the cook, waiter, food and drink himself. . . . So Jesus does not say when he commands and institutes it, "Do this as your password so as to recognize and love each other," but rather, "Do this in remembrance of me." If we are to do it in remembrance of him it is therefore instituted in his service, to his glory. But how do we serve him? . . . I esteem him in that faith is strengthened and we learn to know him.[33]

The drastic words insist that Jesus himself administers the Supper, he acts himself expressly through the words of the Supper. Therewith he himself sets forth food and drink as his gift and portions it out. But in the Supper food and drink serve the purpose of confirming the essential promises of the inheritance, the promise of the forgiveness of sins and eternal life. Through his bestowal of the inheritance Jesus as the acting agent turns the meal activity into the making of a testament.

In May of 1536 when several cities from South Germany that had earlier tended toward Zwingli's doctrine of the Supper adopted the Wittenberg doctrine under the leadership of Bucer, the conviction was expressed in the Wittenberg Concord that "the grace and benefit of Christ . . . was appropriated."[34] In Luther's conception such appropriation occurs in that Christ himself acts through his Word of Grace. His will to be gracious in the institution of the Supper — not a priestly act of consecration — also preserves, according to the Wittenberg Concord, the presence of his body

32. WA 23:269.19ff.; LW 37:141.

33. WA 23:271.8ff.; LW 37:142. Cf. WA 45:200.11: Christ as host of the Supper is the *Speisemeister.*

34. WA Br 12:207.26ff.

and blood in bread and wine. Therefore since Jesus' Words of Institution are taken as the making of a testament, this presence of body and blood is given only as long as the Supper is celebrated and does not last beyond this situation.[35]

When Luther repeatedly contents himself by grounding the essence and significance of the Supper in the institution by Jesus, so to him the Last Supper of Jesus is the permanent ground for the insistence that the Lord is the acting subject in every Supper through his Words of Institution. In these words the Lord makes himself present, as he does everywhere where his gospel is preached. But he makes himself present through the Supper also in the particular manner of his body and blood. His presence in bread and wine has its salvific meaning in the promise of grace of the Words of Institution. Thus also for the older Luther the action of the Supper has its spiritual center in the promise of the forgiveness of sins. Therefore it is no wonder that in a 1537 sermon, similarly to those of 1520-21, he says that Christ in his words at the Supper has bequeathed "his Testament" — "last Word and Will."[36]

Significance for Present Understanding of the Supper

For some years now in the churches of the Reformation a new quest for the meaning of the Last Supper has been evident, for its power to create community and to strengthen hope. In ecumenical dialogues agreement on the Supper has been sought through recourse to the anamnesis of God's saving activity in the cross of Christ or through the idea of the remembrance of the sacrifice. In every contemporary concern for a renewal of understanding in the Supper one ought to attend to two questions that pose themselves out of Luther's interpretation of the Supper as the making of a testament by Jesus: the question of the acting subject in the Supper and the question of what character the Supper has *in nuce* from its very origin. Luther provided clear answers to these questions. He is able to defend his understanding of the Supper not only according to sacramental theology but also exegetically and christologically in precise regard for the situation of

35. WA Br 12:206.11ff. Cf. WA 7:327.13ff. (LW 32:18), to Martin Schalling and dated 27 February 1535.

36. WA 45:200.25ff.

Jesus "in the night in which he was betrayed." In that situation Jesus, in full authority to proclaim to humanity God's saving grace, had instituted the Supper as his testamental action. From this theological center much that is sought in the modern quest for the meaning of the Supper opens up of itself. For as testamental action the Supper strengthens both the consciousness of community and eschatological hope. God's forgiveness in the promise of Jesus, which he confirms through his bodily presence, renews above all community between God and humanity and also thereby establishes the community of Christians with one another. The grace of God, commonly received and equally valid for all, is the true basis of communal life. The promise of forgiveness of sins gives eternal life just as the love that God in Jesus Christ gifts to humans mediates eschatological certainty (Rom. 8:38f.), which will not be surpassed or at the most imagined by the idea of a heavenly communal Supper. Jesus' making of a testament points in itself to his death, which the community is called to remember, even if the Supper in its essence is not a remembrance activity. For this reason also a remembrance of the sacrifice in the anamnesis of the Supper cannot transform itself into a sacrificial memorial. Amid all the concern for enrichment in the understanding of the Supper, we must remain in this theological center, true, according to the measure of our knowledge, to the Founder in his will to establish his testament.

CHAPTER 10

Luther on Private Confession

Ronald K. Rittgers

Most students of the Reformation are familiar with Martin Luther's assault on the sacrament of penance, how he insisted that it promoted works righteousness, clerical tyranny, and reliance on human doctrine. In *The Babylonian Captivity of the Church* (1520) Luther asserted, "The promise of penance . . . has been transformed into the most oppressive despotism, being used to establish a [clerical] sovereignty that is more than merely temporal."[1] In *On Confession: Whether the Pope Has Power to Command It* (1521), the reformer accused the pope of using the sacrament of penance to invade vulnerable lay consciences with his false gospel of human achievement. He castigated the pope as the Antichrist who "breaks open the bridal chamber of Christ and makes all Christian souls into whores."[2] Luther's own experience of the "dark side"[3] of sacramental confession played an important role in his Reformation breakthrough.[4] His discovery of justifi-

1. WA 6:544.12-13; LW 36:83.

2. WA 8:152.6-8.

3. It should be noted that Luther's experience of sacramental confession as a monk was not entirely negative. Especially while Staupitz was his confessor, Luther found great consolation in the sacrament of penance. Staupitz's emphasis on divine love and grace as the source of contrition rather than the end of contrition proved quite liberating for the young Luther, who had been led to believe just the opposite by his reading of late-medieval nominalists like Gabriel Biel. See David Curtis Steinmetz, *Misericordia Dei: The Theology of Johannes von Staupitz in Its Late Medieval Setting* (Leiden: Brill, 1968), 101.

4. In a table talk Luther acknowledged that on account of such abuses in confession

cation by faith was motivated, at least in part, by a desire to find a remedy for the struggles of conscience he believed were occasioned by the sacrament of penance. Luther came to believe that God neither expected nor needed penance; God required only faith in the divine promise of forgiveness in Christ as sheer gift.

Most students of the Reformation also realize that in spite of Luther's opposition to the sacrament of penance, he was actually a strong advocate of private confession. He thought a properly reformed version of the traditional rite provided an extremely effective way of applying the Word to individual consciences and thus of conveying the vital *pro me* aspect of the gospel to believers. In 1522, when his colleague Andreas Bodenstein von Karlstadt sought to abolish private confession in Wittenberg, Luther returned from hiding in the Wartburg and declared in a sermon: "I will allow no one to take private confession from me and would not give it in exchange for all the wealth of the world. For I know what consolation and strength it has given me. No one knows what it can give unless he has struggled much and frequently with the devil. I would have been strangled by the devil long ago if confession had not sustained me."[5]

Luther wanted no one to be forced to confession, but neither would he allow anyone to deny him access to it. "We must have much absolution," he argued, "so that we may strengthen our fearful consciences and despondent hearts against the devil. Therefore no one should forbid confession."[6] He conceded that those with strong faith had no need of private confession: they could simply receive absolution directly from heaven. But he observed that few, including himself, possessed such unwavering trust in God.

Owing in large part to Luther's strong support for the practice, Lutherans developed a reformed version of private confession that appeared in nearly every evangelical church order of the sixteenth century. This new rite was directly influenced by Luther's prescriptions in his Maundy Thursday sermon (1523)[7] and his *Form for the Mass and Communion*

he had become "a poor wretch" *(ein armer Tropf)* as a monk. WA TR 1:269.17-19 (no. 582 from 1533); LW 54:104.

5. WA 10III:62.1-2; LW 51:98.

6. WA 10III:62.9-10; LW 51:99.

7. Luther assured his listeners in his Maundy Thursday sermon that they could go to communion without confessing their sins to a priest beforehand, but he also advised them that measures would have to be taken in the future to curb "the evil abuses" that were threatening the worthy reception of the sacrament (WA 12:478a.1-2). The prospect of

(1523).[8] Drawing on these sources and others, Luther and his fellow evangelical reformers developed a version of private confession that consisted of the following parts: an examination of faith (that is, knowledge of the catechism) and outward moral conduct, an acknowledgment of one's depravity, and a voluntary confession of private sins followed by pastoral counsel and absolution. Gone was the traditional distinction between mortal sins and venial sins. Gone also was the priestly examination of conscience and the concomitant requirement of a full or complete confession (that is, one in which the penitent confessed all his mortal sins). There was no attempt to assess degrees of sorrow for sin, and there was no assigning of penances to reduce time in purgatory, as purgatory itself was rejected, along with the entirety of penitential piety, including indulgences.[9] The

laypeople participating in the Lord's Supper without sufficient preparation frightened Luther and his colleagues. The apostle Paul had promised divine reprisal for such negligence (1 Cor. 11:26-32); the religious leaders of Wittenberg believed him. Luther's proposed measures included an interview with a pastor in which each communicant would be asked about the moral condition of his heart, whether he knew what the Lord's Supper was, and why one should want to partake of it (WA 12:477a.11–478a.1; 479a.5–480a.1). The confession of sins was still strictly voluntary.

8. Toward the end of 1523, Luther took formal measures to institute the precommunion interview he had discussed in his Maundy Thursday sermon. According to the reformer's *Form for the Mass and Communion,* a priest was to know the names and conduct of those who wanted to receive the Eucharist from him. He was to admit to the Lord's Supper only those who had given an account of their faith and evidenced adequate understanding of the sacrament (WA 12:215.18-23; LW 53:32). This examination was to take place annually for most people, but only once in a person's lifetime, or even never, if he possessed sufficient understanding. Luther reasoned that those who were educated and of high social standing were presumably aware of the rudiments of Christian faith (WA 12:215.29-31; LW 53:32-33). Priests were to exclude only those who were living in open sin and refused to repent. Immediately before participating in the Lord's Supper, communicants were to stand in front of the congregation to gain its confirmation of their fitness to partake of Christ's body and blood. Private confession continued to be voluntary and was treated separately in the treatise.

9. See Craig Koslofsky, *The Reformation of the Dead: Death and Ritual in Early Modern Germany, 1450-1700* (New York: St. Martin's Press, 2000), 34-39. Koslofsky demonstrates that Luther did not finally condemn the doctrine of purgatory until 1530. But he also shows that already late in the second decade of the sixteenth century and in the third decade the reformer had transferred the sufferings of purgatory to this life. In other words, while Luther was slow to reject purgatory, from an early point on he made little use of the doctrine as traditionally conceived.

confessor was no longer a judge in the courtroom of conscience; he was now a servant *(Diener)* of the Word. In fact, any Christian could act as confessor, because the authority to forgive now resided in the Word, not in a person.[10] The crucial corollary of this understanding of authority was that believers could be certain of forgiveness, because the divine promise to forgive was utterly trustworthy; God could not lie.

In spite of Luther's support for this reformed version of private confession, he was ambiguous about the sacramental status of the new rite. Throughout *The Babylonian Captivity of the Church* Luther treated confession as a third sacrament, but then reversed himself in the conclusion. He wrote, "it has seemed proper to restrict the name of sacrament to those promises which have signs attached to them. The remainder, not being bound to signs, are bare promises. Hence there are, strictly speaking, but two sacraments in the church of God — baptism and the bread. . . . The sacrament of penance, which I added to these two, lacks the divinely instituted visible sign, and is, as I have said, nothing but a way and a return to baptism."[11] For Luther, private confession was a kind of pseudosacrament, a means of returning to the inexhaustible supply of grace one received in baptism. Private confession was salutary but not sacramental.

Luther's famous reversal on the sacramental status of private confession had important consequences for the plight of the new practice in the early decades of the German Reformation. While most Lutheran reformers supported the new rite, there was no consensus as to its theological justification. Luther had said in 1520 that penance was not a sacrament, but in the 1531 Apology of the Augsburg Confession, Melanchthon, using a different definition of sacraments, asserted that it was,[12] a position held by several

10. For a discussion of how Luther dismantled the sacrament of penance late in the second decade of the sixteenth century and early in the third decade, see Ronald K. Rittgers, *The Reformation of the Keys: Confession, Conscience, and Authority in Sixteenth-Century Germany* (Cambridge: Harvard University Press, 2004), 52-58. For more general treatments of Luther's theology of confession, see Laurentius Klein, O.S.B., *Evangelisch-Lutherische Beichte: Lehre und Praxis* (Paderborn: Bonifacius-Druckerei, 1961), 11-81, and Ernst Bezzel, *Frei zum Eingeständis: Geschichte und Praxis der evangelischen Einzelbeichte* (Stuttgart: Calwer, 1982), 11-25.

11. WA 6:572.10-34; LW 36:124.

12. Melanchthon asserted in Article XII, "we must believe the voice of the one absolving no less than we would believe a voice from heaven. Absolution can properly be called the sacrament of repentance, as even the more learned scholastic theologians say." BSLK,

other important reformers.[13] In keeping with the Augsburg Confession,[14] most Lutheran church orders required confession before participation in the Lord's Supper,[15] but few referred to it as a sacrament. Lutheran private confession thus became institutionalized before evangelical theologians had settled on a coherent and unified theological explanation for it. This fact contributed directly to the German Reformation's most important debate about private confession, the so-called Nuremberg Absolution Controversy, a conflict that is little known among Reformation students.[16] As no other debate of the early Reformation, the Nuremberg conflict revealed both the defining concerns and the unresolved problems of Luther's mature version of evangelical private confession.

259.15-20; BC, 193. In Article XIII, Melanchthon asserted, "Therefore, the sacraments are actually baptism, the Lord's Supper, and absolution (the sacrament of repentance). For these rites have the command of God and the promise of grace, which is the essence of the New Testament." BSLK, 292.24-29; BC, 219. (Here and in n. 14 below, I have followed the translation in BC.)

13. Brenz held private absolution to be a sacrament, as did most of Osiander's colleagues in Nuremberg, including Luther's close associate, Wenzeslaus Linck. See Rittgers, *Reformation of the Keys,* 143 and 149.

14. With regard to private confession, Melanchthon asserted in Article XI that Lutherans "teach that private absolution should be retained in the churches, although an enumeration of all sins in confession is not necessary. For this is impossible according to the Psalm [19:12]: 'But who can discern their errors?'" (BSLK, 66.1-7; BC, 145).

15. According to Thomas Tentler, the Lutheran version of private confession appeared in fifty evangelical church orders between 1525 and 1591. See his article "Confession," in *The Oxford Encyclopaedia of the Reformation,* ed. Hans J. Hillerbrand, 4 vols. (New York: Oxford University Press, 1996), 1:401.

16. The discussion of the Nuremberg Absolution Controversy below draws on Rittgers, *Reformation of the Keys,* 139-58. See also Gunter Zimmermann, *Prediger der Freiheit: Andreas Osiander und der Nürnberger Rat 1522-1548,* Mannheimer Historische Forschungen, vol. 15 (Mannheim: Palatium, 1999), 309-41; and Gottfried Martens, "'Ein uberaus grosser unterschiedt': Der Kampf des Andreas Osiander gegen die Praxis der allgemeinen Absolution in Nürnberg," in *Festhalten am Bekenntnis der Hoffnung: Festgabe für Professor Dr. Reinhard Slenczka zum 70. Geburtstag,* ed. Christian Herrmann and Eberhard Hahn (Erlangen: Martin-Luther-Verlag, 2001), 145-64. For older treatments, see Bernhard Klaus, *Veit Dietrich: Leben und Werk,* Einzelarbeiten aus der Kirchengeschichte Bayerns, vol. 32 (Nürnberg: Selbstverlag des Vereins für Bayerische Kirchengeschichte, 1958), 147-68; and Gottfried Seebaß, *Das reformatorische Werk des Andreas Osiander,* Einzelarbeiten aus der Kirchengeschichte Bayerns, vol. 44 (Nürnberg: Verein für Bayerische Kirchengeschichte, 1967), 254-62.

The Nuremberg Absolution Controversy

The immediate occasion for the Nuremberg debate was the decision of the city's famous — and infamous — preacher, Andreas Osiander, to oppose general confession, that is, the congregational recitation of a confession of sin followed by a clerical absolution spoken to the whole assembly. Osiander and the Schwäbisch Hall reformer Johannes Brenz were the authors of the 1533 Brandenburg (Ansbach)-Nuremberg Church Order, one of the most influential guides for worship and belief in early Lutheranism.[17] They had deliberately chosen not to include a form for general confession in their church order, thinking it unbiblical. This move constituted a liturgical innovation, as a reformed version of the traditional practice *(Offene Schuld)* had been in use in Nuremberg since the mid-1520s, when the city officially adopted the Reformation.[18] (Nuremberg was the first imperial city to convert to the evangelical faith.) Osiander had also preached against general confession on several occasions, despite the city council's repeated warnings to the contrary.[19] (The city council supported general and private confession, insisting both had a legitimate role to play in evangelical Christianity.) Osiander was concerned that laypeople would not attend private confession if general confession were practiced, because they would think the individual encounter with a pastor redundant. The laity would thus forfeit the great consolation that private absolution offered and the clergy would lose a crucial opportunity to promote moral discipline. Osiander had good reason to be concerned: all extant sources indicate that Nurembergers were not going to confession, despite what the church order stipulated.[20]

In an attempt to gain further support for its position, the Nuremberg city council wrote to Wittenberg for advice. In a letter dated 18 April 1533, Luther, along with Melanchthon, recommended that the imperial city should retain both forms of absolution because both constituted a valid

17. Emil Sehling dubbed the 1533 Brandenburg-Nuremberg Church Order the *Stammutter* of a whole family of Lutheran church orders. Emil Sehling, ed., *Die evangelischen Kirchenordnungen des XVI Jahrhunderts* (Tübingen: J. C. B. Mohr–Paul Siebeck, 1961), 11:125. Brandenburg here refers to the principality of Brandenburg-Ansbach-Kulmbach near Nuremberg.

18. Rittgers, *Reformation of the Keys,* 92.

19. Rittgers, *Reformation of the Keys,* 145-46, 148-49.

20. Rittgers, *Reformation of the Keys,* 171.

means of preaching the gospel. The Wittenberg reformers wrote, "the preaching of the holy gospel is also in essence an absolution in which forgiveness of sins is proclaimed to many people in common and publicly or to one person alone, whether in public or in secret."[21] (The Augsburg Confession suggested the same.)[22] Because there was scriptural precedent for proclaiming the good news to both crowds and individuals, Luther and Melanchthon argued that it was appropriate for evangelical churches to practice both general and private absolution. If some who heard general absolution did not receive it in faith, this did not constitute adequate grounds for abolishing it. Absolution of any kind was always dependent upon faith for its efficacy. The Wittenberg reformers asserted that "all absolution, whether general or private, must be understood to require faith and to help those who believe in it."[23] Forgiveness in Christ still had to be preached, regardless of whether those who heard it believed it or not.

The Wittenberg reformers shared Osiander's concern to protect private absolution. As in Nuremberg, the new rite was part of the mandatory preparation for communion in their churches,[24] the only difference being

21. WA Br 6:454.6-9. Luther had similarly argued in an Easter Tuesday sermon, "Hie solten wir auch von der Beicht sagen, welche wir behalten und loben als ein nützlich heilsam ding, Denn wiewol sie (eigentlich zu reden) nicht ist ein stück der Busse, auch nicht nötig und geboten ist, So dienet sie doch dazu, das man die Absolutio empfahe, welche ist nichts anders denn eben die Predigt und vekündigung der vergebung sünden, welche Christus alhie befilhet beide, zu predigen und zu hören. Weil aber solche Predigt von nöten ist, in der Kirchen zu erhalten, so sol man auch die Absolution behalten, Denn es ist hierunter kein ander unterscheid on das solch wort (so sonst in der Predigt des Euangelii allenthalben öffentlich und in gemein jeder man verkündigt) dasselb wird in der Absolution einem oder mehren, die es begeren, in sonderheit gesagt, Wie denn Christus geordnet, das solche Predigt der vergebung der sünden allenthalben und all zeit nicht allein in gemein uber ein gantzen hauffen, sondern auch einzelen Personen (wo solche Leute sind, die es bedürffen) gehen und schallen sol, Wie er in des folgenden Sontages Euangelio sagt: 'Welchen ir die sünde vergebt, den sind sie vergeben.'" This sermon was part of Caspar Cruciger Sommerpostille (1544). WA 21:262.32–263.8.

22. In the article on repentance (XII), the Augsburg Confession calls upon truly penitent Christians to believe in the forgiveness offered through the "gospel or absolution" *(ex evangelio seu absolutione).* It should be noted that the German version has "the gospel and absolution" *(das Evangelium und Absolution),* BSLK, 67.5; BC, 44-47. See also Zimmermann, *Prediger der Freiheit,* 310.

23. WA Br 6:454.13-15.

24. Although Luther and Melanchthon opposed Osiander's position on general ab-

that Wittenbergers actually participated in it.[25] Luther and Melanchthon displayed a clear preference for private absolution because of the way it allowed for the gospel to be applied to individual consciences. In fact, the Wittenberg reformers could not conceive of general absolution apart from private absolution. According to them, it was the experience of the latter that taught the laity how to receive the former properly: "Very few people would know how to use or receive general absolution if they did not remember along with this application *(applicatio)* that they should receive general absolution as if it were for each individual and that the actual office and work of the gospel is assuredly to forgive sin by grace."[26] For Luther and Melanchthon, general absolution was valid, but only in relation to private absolution, clearly the more desirable medium of divine forgiveness from their point of view.

The Wittenberg opinion did little to mollify Osiander.[27] At stake for him in this debate was nothing less than the status of private absolution as a third sacrament. According to Osiander, general absolution was an abuse

---

solution, it should be noted that the 1533 Wittenberg Church Order also contained no form for general absolution. See Sehling, *Kirchenordnungen,* vol. I/1, 701ff. (However, there was a form for general absolution in the 1533 Visitation Articles. See Zimmermann, *Prediger der Freiheit,* 336 n. 99.) According to Bernhard Klaus, Luther preferred an exhortation to worthy participation in the Lord's Supper over general confession, exactly what Osiander had provided in the 1533 Brandenburg-Nuremberg Church Order. Luther thought general confession had gradually replaced the exhortation in the Middle Ages. See Klaus's article, "Die Rüstgebete," in *Leiturgia: Handbuch des evangelischen Gottesdienstes,* ed. Karl Ferdinand Müller and Walter Blankenburg, vol. 2 (Kassel: J. Stauda, 1955), 539-41. Despite their similar liturgical preferences, Luther and Osiander still had very different views on the validity of general confession. (See below.) Klaus argues that Luther excluded general confession from his church orders because he thought it represented an incursion of the private and personal into a worship service that emphasized the communal. See Klaus, 542.

25. See Rittgers, *Reformation of the Keys,* 184-85.

26. WA Br 6:455.30-34.

27. Osiander wrote a letter to Luther and Melanchthon defending his position, though it is not extant and we do not know if the Wittenberg reformers ever read it. See Nürnberg Staatsarchiv, Handschriften 415, fol. 10. Luther did concede later in a letter to the Nuremberg city council that he had not been properly informed of Osiander's position. See WA Br 6:527.9-10. Nevertheless, Luther and Melanchthon adopted the same position on general absolution when asked for another written opinion by the Nuremberg council in 1536. See WA Br 7:594.11–595.20.

of this status and therefore had to be opposed. In a lengthy treatise entitled *On the Keys,*[28] Osiander articulated his argument that like baptism and the Lord's Supper, absolution was a divinely instituted means of grace accompanied by a divinely specified sign, the laying on of hands,[29] that could be applied only to individuals. Other means of grace were intended for use with crowds in order to inform people about God's wrath and mercy. Here the Nuremberg reformer had in mind the preaching of the law and the gospel.[30] But absolution — or the loosing key — was a sacrament, and for Osiander this meant something very specific.[31]

According to the Nuremberg preacher, a pastor's word of forgiveness was valid regardless of the faith or moral condition of the person who received it. As a sacrament, clerical absolution reliably conveyed what it signified, God's judgment or forgiveness.[32] According to Osiander, God did not simply offer grace to the penitent through clerical absolution, as the Nuremberg preacher's opponents — including Luther — maintained; God actually communicated grace to the individual, quite apart from her prep-

28. Gerhard Muller and Gottfried Seebaß, eds., *Andreas Osiander d.A., Gesamtausgabe,* vol. 5 (Gütersloh: Gütersloher Verlagshaus–Gerd Mohn, 1983), 412-91. Hereafter referred to as GA.

29. GA 5:489.26-30. See n. 32 below.

30. Osiander could refer to the preaching of the law and gospel collectively as "a key of knowledge" *(einen schlussel des erkanntnus oder des wissens),* as could Luther. See GA 5:429.14 and WA 30II:491.18-20; LW 40:357.

31. Osiander defined a sacrament as "a transaction *(handel)* in which God's promises and truth are by divine command presented to an individual, accepted and personally appropriated *(in busem gesteckht),* so that the person is consecrated, sanctified, and received into the kingdom of God and eternal life." GA 5:485.1-4. He argued that both Luther in the *Babylonian Captivity* and Melanchthon in the *Apologia* for the Augsburg Confession had clearly stated that absolution was a sacrament. GA 5:482.29–483.2. As we have seen, Luther equivocated on this issue in the *Babylonian Captivity,* at first calling absolution a sacrament and then concluding that, strictly speaking, it was not. Melanchthon was clearer on the issue, but not all Lutherans accorded the same authority to his *Apologia* as they did to the Augsburg Confession itself, which was less precise.

32. When comparing private absolution to the real presence of Christ in the elements of the Lord's Supper, Osiander asserted, "thus also in absolution the word spoken with the laying on of hands is not a sign of the loosing but the loosing itself. For as truly as the servant speaks to and touches the confessant physically, so God himself truly speaks to and touches him with his Word and Holy Spirit in and with the absolution and laying on of hands" (GA 5:489.26-30).

aration or desire to receive it.[33] The keys worked *ex opere operato.*[34] The confessor had considerable power in this scheme, and with it, a responsibility to exercise his office properly.[35] Osiander therefore concluded that a pastor should pronounce absolution only to those whom God wanted to forgive, and the only way to determine this with certainty was to examine each penitent privately. Those who declared or received absolution in an unworthy manner would be punished by God for their abuse of his sacrament. As Osiander explained, "if the person who is absolved does not have sufficient sorrow or faith, the keys do not for this reason lie or deceive. What is loosed on earth is certainly loosed in heaven. If the absolved person remains without sorrow or faith . . . he will be damned on account of his hardness and unbelief. But the sin from which he has been released is truly forgiven him."[36] For Osiander, general absolution simply posed too great a risk for abuse of the keys; he was not willing to jeopardize the souls of pastors and penitents by allowing it to continue in Nuremberg.

Though Osiander stressed the importance of the confessor assessing the confessant's spiritual condition, it should be noted that he did not conceive of the confessant's faith and sorrow meriting absolution. Indeed, one of the main reasons he opposed general confession was that he felt it made forgiveness dependent upon the worthiness of the confessant. The form for general confession in use in Nuremberg at this time included a pastoral exhortation that called upon confessants to acknowledge their sins to God "with heartfelt love and a desire for his divine help [and] with firm belief and trust in his gracious promise." It then urged confessants to forgive all those who had sinned against them and stated, "If you do this, I will then

33. For a discussion of the connection between Osiander's soteriology — according to which Christ's divine nature was infused into believers — and his theology of the keys, see Dietrich Stollberg, "Osiander und der Nürnberger Absolutionsstreit: Ein Beitrag zur Geschichte der Praktischen Theologie," *Lutherische Blätter*, 17 Jahrgang, 85 (17 July 1965): 153 and 165-66.

34. On this point see Martens, "'Ein uberaus grosser unterschiedt,'" 159.

35. Osiander advised confessors to respond in the following way to confessants who had doubts about their worthiness to receive absolution: "you do not need to worry about whether or not I should speak and pronounce God's mercy to you. You need only hear and believe the word of absolution that you are truly forgiven in heaven. For it has been commanded to me — not you — to determine whether I should absolve you or not" (GA 5:465.35–466.2).

36. GA 5:448.30–449.2.

release you from all of your sins on behalf of the holy Christian Church and by the command and promise of our Lord Jesus Christ."[37]

Osiander argued that this formula left confessants in a worse state than had the sacrament of penance. He wrote, "The pope and those who belong to him make everything depend upon sorrow. This absolution expects even more. Who can believe that he has been absolved [according to this teaching]? Truly, no one, unless he believes and knows beforehand that he possesses all the above-mentioned virtues."[38] Osiander wanted to protect lay consciences from the burden of works righteousness and thought the best way to do so was to stress the completely unconditional nature of absolution. His rather awkward conclusion that a person could actually incur guilt while being absolved followed from his belief that confessants were totally passive in sacramental absolution.

Osiander and Luther on the Keys

Throughout his treatise on the keys Osiander maintained that Luther agreed with his understanding of absolution. The Nuremberg preacher frequently referred to Luther's treatise *The Keys* (1530) to support his own argument. There was something to Osiander's claim. Luther asserted in his treatise that the keys worked by "pure grace" and were in no way dependent on the sorrow of the confessant for their efficacy.[39] The Wittenberg reformer assailed the "Papists" for robbing the laity of the immense consolation the keys offered by making absolution contingent upon the confessant's degree of sorrow, something that was impossible to measure. Similar to Osiander, Luther maintained that "an uncertain absolution is the same as no absolution at all."[40]

Luther even maintained in his treatise that confessants could be bound or loosed apart from faith. When arguing against certain "factious spirits and sophists" — Anabaptists and spiritualists — who believed that the Spirit forgave sins directly, Luther insisted that absolution was always conveyed through the spoken word alone; not even faith affected the effi-

37. Rittgers, *Reformation of the Keys*, 92.
38. Rittgers, *Reformation of the Keys*, 153.
39. WA 30II:496.40; LW 40:364.
40. WA 30II:480.24-25; LW 40:344.

cacy of the keys. The Wittenberg reformer asserted, "Do you believe that he is not bound who does not believe in the key which binds? Indeed, he shall learn, in due time, that his unbelief did not make the binding vain, nor did it fail in its purpose. Even he who does not believe that he is free and his sins forgiven shall also learn, in due time, how assuredly his sins were forgiven, even though he did not believe it. St. Paul says in Romans 3[:3], 'God will not fail on account of our unbelief.'"[41] Osiander cited this passage in his own treatise on the keys to demonstrate that Luther supported his understanding of absolution.[42] This claim, however, was problematic.

Throughout Luther's *The Keys* he repeatedly stated that absolution had to be received by faith to be efficacious for the individual. Immediately following his assertion that people could be bound or loosed from their sins apart from faith, the Wittenberg reformer explained,

> We are not talking here about whether people believe in the efficacy of the keys or not. We fully realize that few believe. We are speaking of what the keys accomplish and give *(thun und geben).* The one who does not accept what the keys give receives, of course, nothing. But the keys do not fail on this account. Many do not believe the gospel, but this does not mean that the gospel fails or lies. A king gives you a castle. If you do not accept it the king has not failed or lied. Rather, you have deceived yourself and the fault is yours. The king certainly gave it.[43]

Despite what Luther asserted about a person being bound or loosed apart from faith, here he clearly maintained that the keys gave nothing *(nichts)* to the person who lacked faith.[44] His point was that the objective working of the keys was in no way dependent on faith, or any other subjective foundation, but the actual appropriation by an individual Christian of what the keys offered did require faith. Luther may have been unclear, perhaps even inconsistent, but Osiander also ignored the numerous state-

41. WA 30II:498.31–499.1. I have used the LW translation (LW 40:366-67) except for the quotation from Romans, which has a mistake in the LW. For a similar passage see WA 30II:499.16-28 (LW 40:367), where Luther emphasizes the objective working of the keys against a Roman Catholic interlocutor.

42. GA 5:449.4-10.

43. WA 30II:499.1-8; LW 40:367.

44. Osiander also cited this excerpt from Luther's treatise in his own work, but failed to see how it undercut his argument. GA 5:449.10-14.

ments in the Wittenberg reformer's treatise that contradicted his own embattled position. As we have seen, Luther had also clearly stated in his letter to the Nuremberg city council — which Osiander had heard read — that faith was essential to reception of absolution, a position he had championed over a decade earlier in his *Sermon on the Sacrament of Penance* (1519).[45]

Like Osiander, Luther maintained that because the efficacy of the keys was based on God's promise (Matt. 16:18-19; 18:18; John 20:23), they could always be trusted to offer divine forgiveness (or punishment), regardless of the confessant's moral disposition. But, unlike Osiander, Luther insisted that a layperson could receive the divine offer of forgiveness only if he had faith. Luther asserted in his treatise, "[f]or [the keys] demand faith in our hearts, and without faith you cannot use them with profit. But if you believe in their judgment they recover for you the innocence you received in baptism."[46] Or again, "the one who believes [in the loosing key] has done enough to satisfy this key before and apart from all works. [This key] requires no work, though afterward such faith will produce works."[47] And finally, "the keys require no work, only faith."[48] Far from demanding perfect faith from penitents, the keys called for simple trust that God would honor the pastor's word of forgiveness. Although Osiander also wanted confessants to receive absolution in faith, he did not think such belief was necessary to the sacrament's efficacy for the individual.

For Osiander, the contention that absolution was an offer that had to be received by faith posed a direct threat to the validity of the keys. Luther was aware of this threat, but did not consider it particularly serious. To those who charged that his version of the keys rendered absolution uncertain, the Wittenberg reformer responded, "Well, friend, if you call this a failure [i.e., that the keys do not accomplish their purpose unless met with faith], then God fails in all his words and works. After all, very few people believe or accept what he constantly speaks and does for everyone."[49] The

45. In the *Sermon on the Sacrament of Penance* (1519), Luther insisted that faith was essential for the reception of forgiveness, and even made faith one of the three constitutive elements of his version of confession, along with grace and absolution. WA 2:715.21-39; LW 35:11.

46. WA 30II:505.28-30. I have used the LW translation (LW 40:375).

47. WA 30II:505.42–506.4; LW 40:375-76.

48. WA 30II:468.21-22; LW 40:329.

49. WA 30II:499.9-13; LW 40:367.

point, again, was that God's offer of grace was valid quite apart from human responses to it, but only those who received the divine mercy in faith benefited from it. This faith was not a human work — on this point Osiander and Luther were agreed. It was a gift of God created in individuals by the Word.[50] But only Osiander thought this required complete passivity on the part of the confessant; Luther believed it implied receptivity.[51] Neither man wanted to ascribe agency to confessants, but whereas Luther could still allow — even require — a divinely caused human response in confession, Osiander permitted nothing of the sort, at least not in the initial reception of absolution. Even if Luther had agreed with Osiander that absolution was a sacrament, he would have argued that faith was necessary to receive forgiveness. The reformers still would have been at odds on how the keys worked.

But Luther did not agree with Osiander's contention that the keys were a sacrament. Indeed, although the Wittenberg reformer clearly regarded absolution as a means of grace, he was still not willing to refer to it as a sacrament and never did so directly in his 1530 treatise. Absolution was still a pseudosacrament in his mind, and it would remain so throughout the remainder of his career. Luther would not place absolution on the same level with baptism and the Lord's Supper. Osiander, by contrast, saw the keys as a third sacrament, and maintained that just as communicants received the body and blood of Christ regardless of their worthiness, so too confessants were bound or loosed apart from considerations of faith or sorrow. In both cases the sacrament conveyed what it promised: grace to those who believed and spiritual poison to those who did not.[52] As we have seen, Luther could say that the keys worked apart from faith,[53] but he did not speak of confessants incurring divine wrath for receiving absolution

50. Osiander asserted in his treatise, "we are not able to produce faith, it is a work of God." GA 5:426.26-27. See also GA 5:472.1-2.

51. Another way of stating this difference would be to say that while both men conceived of the word of absolution calling forth faith, Luther thought the actual reception of forgiveness depended on the cleric's words being met with the faith that those same words had created. Osiander thought the cleric's words effected forgiveness regardless of the confessant's response to them, although he clearly wanted faith to follow.

52. It should be noted that Osiander did not conceive of clerical absolution itself acting as spiritual poison, for he was clear that the unworthy confessant's sin was forgiven. But this impious reception of absolution would then provoke divine wrath.

53. To my knowledge, Luther nowhere made this claim for general absolution.

unworthily, something he openly asserted of the Lord's Supper.[54] Luther conceived of absolution as a return to baptism; it was this sacrament that governed his thinking on the keys. (Here Luther was opposing the traditional view that saw penance as a "second plank" to which a lapsed Christian could turn, having exhausted the supply of grace given in baptism. For Luther, baptismal grace never ran short.)[55] The baptized required faith to receive grace from baptism, although the promise of grace was not dependent upon this faith and could even benefit the person who came to belief years after his actual baptism.[56] The same was true of the keys. Osiander also related the keys to baptism, but his understanding of how they worked was based on the model of the Lord's Supper: grace was conveyed to the worthy and the unworthy alike, in the latter case with harmful consequences. Thus, Luther and Osiander disagreed both on the sacramental status of absolution and on its relationship to the undisputed sacraments of baptism and the Lord's Supper.

There was another even more important difference between Luther and Osiander on the keys. Luther showed little of Osiander's confidence in the ability of human confessors to determine with certainty whom God wanted to forgive (or not). Although Luther was a strong advocate of the precommunion interview, especially as the evangelical movement matured,[57] he thought there were limits to what a confessor could discern in such an encounter. His thinking here was shaped by his view of the so-called key of knowledge.

Luther rejected the traditional belief that Christ had given a third key to the disciples that enabled them to use the binding and loosing keys properly by granting them supernatural knowledge of a penitent's inward moral condition.[58] In his 1530 treatise on the keys, he asserted, "It is certainly true that one must know and be certain whom and what one should bind and

54. See Paul Althaus, *The Theology of Martin Luther,* trans. Robert C. Schultz (Philadelphia: Fortress, 1966), 400.

55. See Klein, *Evangelisch-Lutherische Beichte,* 57-59.

56. See Althaus, *Theology of Martin Luther,* 368-69.

57. In a table talk from 1540, Luther asserted that the primary reason for retaining private confession was so that one could determine whether laypeople knew the catechism. WA TR 4:694.14-16 (no. 5175).

58. On the key of knowledge see Henry Charles Lea, *A History of Auricular Confession and Indulgences in the Latin Church* (Philadelphia, 1896), 1:158-59, 161-65. For Luther's discussion of the key of knowledge, see WA 30II:490.27–491.32; LW 40:357-58.

loose. For one should not play blind-man's buff with God's order. . . . But the knowledge to which they refer in this key — namely, that one should know how a person stands before God — does not exist *(das ist nichts)*. . . . Therefore we do not wish to possess or to endure such a key of knowledge. . . ."[59]

Luther opposed clerical claims to epistemological privilege in both the sacrament of penance and the new version of private confession; neither the Roman Catholic confessor nor his evangelical counterpart possessed divine insight into a penitent's soul. Osiander held a different view in that he promoted a version of the key of knowledge. To be sure, the Nuremberg preacher did not wish to return to the late-medieval interrogation of conscience; he simply wanted confessants to exhibit adequate knowledge of the evangelical faith and a measure of sorrow for their sins.[60] He had nothing more in mind than the examination of faith and conduct prescribed in evangelical church orders. Still, owing to his unique theology of the keys, Osiander placed greater stress on the role of the confessor in the precommunion interview than Luther did. Both men believed that Christ acted through the human confessor to absolve penitents,[61] but only

59. WA 30II:492.8-15; LW 40:358.

60. Osiander insisted several times in his treatise that a confessant simply had to come to his confessor and say, "I am sorry for my sins" *(es reuet mich)*, to be worthy of absolution. See GA 5:454.9 and 481.25.

61. In a table talk from 1540, Luther asserted, "Wiewohl ich sie (Ohrenbeichte) mein Leben lang nicht unterlassen will; denn da absolvirt und spricht mich von Sünden lost nicht ein Mensch, sondern Gott selber. Auch soll man die Leute fur allen Dingen wohl lehren und ihnen einbilden, daß man nicht einem Menschen, sondern Gott und dem Herrn Christo beichte; item daß nicht ein Mensch, sondern Christus absolviere. Aber das verstehen und gläuben jtzt die Leute nicht. . . . Darum soll man die Leute lehren, daß man Christo beichte, daß Christus absolvire durch den Mund des Dieners. Denn des Dieners Mund ist Christus Mund, des Dieners Ohre ist Christus Ohre. Aufs Wort und Befehl Gottes soll man sehen und sich verlassen, nicht auf die Person; Christus sitzt da Beichte, Christus hörets; Christus Wort sinds, nicht Menschen Wort, so da gehort und geredt werden aus des Beichtvaters Munde." WA TR 4:694.16-28 (no. 5175). ("As much as I do not want to neglect it [oracular confession] during my entire life, since God and not a human being absolves me and frees me from sins — moreover, one should teach and instruct the people above all else that one confesses not to a human being but to God and the Lord Christ and likewise that not a human being but Christ absolves — still the people now do not understand this. . . . Therefore one ought to teach the people that a person confesses to Christ and that Christ absolves using the mouth of the minister. For the minister's mouth is Christ's mouth; the minister's ear is Christ's ear. One must look to and rely on

Osiander concluded from this that pastors had to discern whom God wanted to forgive. Luther's 1530 treatise flatly rejected the kind of evangelical sacerdotalism present in Osiander's theology of the keys. We have already seen the same opposition to clericalism in the letter Luther and Melanchthon sent to Nuremberg in 1533. By insisting on the validity of general confession and the necessity of faith to receive all absolution, Luther undermined all priestly hegemony in the communication of forgiveness and thus underscored the primacy of the Word, his driving concern in the reformation of private confession.

The Nuremberg city council sent a copy of Osiander's treatise on the keys to the Wittenberg theologians, asking them for their opinion of it.[62] On 8 October Luther confirmed via letter to the council that he and his colleagues had diligently studied the treatise.[63] In the same letter, Luther informed the council that he had also written directly to Osiander,[64] and that he hoped his letter would help restore peace and unity among the Nuremberg clergy, as he believed all were motivated by noble concerns.[65] Luther again expressed his strong support for private absolution, although he maintained that Christians could obtain forgiveness outside of an individual encounter with their pastor.[66] (As it later became clear, Osiander believed the same, although he thought private absolution provided the surest source of forgiveness for serious sins. Osiander's central concern was about clergy using the keys properly.)[67] Luther also repeated his support for general absolution and the necessity of faith to receive all forgiveness.[68] Such faith was not based on a person's worthiness; it was simply the way a person accepted or said "Yes" to the offer of forgiveness.[69]

God's word and command not on the person [of the minister]. Christ sits there in the Confession; Christ hears it; they are Christ's words not human words that are heard and spoken from the father confessor's mouth.")

62. WA Br 6:520.65-71.

63. WA Br 6:527.12. Luther also confirmed in a letter to Osiander that he had read the Nuremberg preacher's treatise on the keys. WA Br 6:531.1-3.

64. WA Br 5:530-32; LW 49:395-98.

65. WA Br 6:528.14-17.

66. WA Br 6:528.18-49.

67. Rittgers, *Reformation of the Keys*, 160-63. See also, Martens, "'Ein uberaus grosser unterschiedt,'" 157.

68. WA Br 6:528.50–529.68.

69. WA Br 6:529.79-84.

Luther responded to Osiander's claim that general absolution constituted an unworthy exercise of the keys by distinguishing between *predigen* and *Jurisdiction*.[70] Luther conceded that evangelical clergy had authority over open or public sins, but not over hidden or secret ones. Pastors could only bind the latter through the preaching of the gospel, in which case the Word, if met with unbelief, effectively retained the sins of the unbeliever (or loosed the sins of the believer). The same preaching could also extend forgiveness to a person separated from the Lord's Supper because of open sin, provided the person had faith. (Luther argued that such a person should then seek formal reconciliation with the church.)[71] As we have seen throughout, Luther would not allow any human being — be he pope or an evangelical preacher — to enter the inner sanctum (that is, the conscience) of the individual Christian; here only the Word was to reign. The Word was the primary agent in Luther's version of private confession: it alone bound or loosed sin and also created the faith necessary to receive the forgiveness it mediated.

Luther concluded his letter to the Nuremberg city council by suggesting an interim measure to keep the peace: allow Osiander not to practice general absolution in his church, while his colleagues continued to practice it in theirs.[72] Luther gave identical advice to Osiander.[73] The same day, 8 October, Luther wrote to his friend Wenzeslaus Linck, also a preacher in Nuremberg, urging him to regard Osiander as a sick person *(aegrotum)* who would only recover from his malady — *pertinacia* —[74] if treated with discretion, intelligence, and patience.[75]

Conclusion

Osiander never recovered. The debate about absolution continued for several years in Nuremberg and was finally resolved only in the mid-1540s, when the city took decisive action toward requiring private confession,

70. WA Br 6:529.69-73.
71. WA Br 6:529.69-79.
72. WA Br 6:529.90–530.100.
73. WA Br 6:531.16-20.
74. WA Br 6:533.20.
75. WA Br 6:532.5–533.10.

though it continued to allow general confession, much to Osiander's chagrin.[76] Luther entered the debate at least one more time, providing another written recommendation to the city council in 1536 in which he repeated his earlier position about the validity of general absolution and the condition of faith. (Osiander had again preached against general confession in direct defiance of the city council's orders.)[77] Osiander left Nuremberg in 1548 as a means of protesting the city's adoption of the Augsburg Interim and eventually wound up in Königsberg, where he would soon become involved in a debate about soteriology that would permanently tarnish his reputation as an authentically evangelical theologian.

The value of studying Osiander on the power of the keys lies not so much in the answers he provided as in the questions he raised for Luther and others about the new rite. As we have seen, the institution of private confession as a formal practice in Lutheran Germany took place before evangelical theologians had reached consensus on its theological justification. Osiander was trying to provide such a justification. He was unsuccessful in this endeavor largely because his proposal sounded (and was) too Roman Catholic. But the question he posed about the practical difficulty of attracting people to private confession while general confession remained was valid.[78] More importantly, the need he perceived in the evangelical movement to provide a more robust theological defense of private confession as a *mandatory* practice was entirely legitimate.

Luther was in favor of mandatory private confession for communicants, although he wanted the actual confession of (secret) sins within the new rite to be voluntary. He justified the examination of faith and conduct as being necessary to ensure worthy reception of the Lord's Supper.[79] He could not provide a similarly compelling reason for the second part of the evangelical rite, private confession of sin followed by private clerical abso-

76. Rittgers, *Reformation of the Keys*, 170-92.

77. WA Br 7:594-95, no. 3108; Luther, Jonas, Cruciger und Melanchthon an den Rat von Nürnberg, Wittenberg, 28 November 1536.

78. Gottfried Seebaß observed, "Es muß aber festgestellt werden, daß Osiander die praktische Aufhebung der Privatabsolution durch den Gebrauch der allgemeinen Absolutionsformel richtig vorausgesehen hat." See *Das reformatorische Werk des Andreas Osiander*, 262.

79. It should be noted that Luther allowed confessants whose knowledge of the catechism and conduct of life were already known to their confessor to forgo the examination of faith and conduct. See n. 8 above.

lution. Had Luther believed that absolution was a sacrament, he might have been able to set the new rite on firmer theological footing. But he thought Scripture taught otherwise and, as we have seen, consistently resisted locating the authority to forgive sin in any human being, cleric or not. This meant that Luther could provide no strictly theological rationale for a Christian to prefer private confession over general confession, or even over confession to a fellow brother or sister in Christ, for all conveyed the same grace.

Mandatory private confession did become a prominent feature of evangelical religious life in the early modern period,[80] although largely for pastoral and political reasons. Lutheran clergy continued to stress the consoling effects of private confession for troubled consciences. Lutheran rulers saw in the new rite an effective means of planting the evangelical creed in the minds of the faithful as part of their larger efforts to "confessionalize" the common folk. (This was owing to the examination of faith.)[81] The question of the new rite's sacramental status was never finally decided, although Lutheran theologians continued to debate it for decades — even centuries — to come.[82] Luther contributed directly to Lutheranism's uncertainty about the status of private confession. For better and for worse, the new rite was his rite.

80. Klein, *Evangelisch-Lutherische Beichte,* 174.

81. On this point see Susan C. Karant-Nunn, *The Reformation of Ritual: An Interpretation of Early Modern Germany* (New York: Routledge, 1997), 100.

82. Klein, *Evangelisch-Lutherische Beichte,* 81-85, 97-99, 151-53; Bezzel, *Frei zum Eingeständnis,* 52-54.

PART IV

The Pastor and the People's Piety

CHAPTER 11

Luther regarding the Virgin Mary

Beth Kreitzer

Luther's early reformation insights and insistence on doctrinal reform based on his christological understanding of the gospel had far wider implications than he at first imagined, and the Protestant Reformation transformed Christian thought and practice in many areas of Europe. One such area that received a critical reevaluation was the role of the Virgin Mary and the saints in the Christian community. Luther transformed the notion of sainthood, ridding the church of much of what he considered to be superstition and idolatry, but he continued to find a positive role for the saints in Christian history and pedagogy.

Mary, as the mother of God's Son, holds a unique place among the saints, and Luther was concerned to articulate clearly her importance to Christian tradition. His reform of doctrine and piety was not intended to push Mary aside, but rather to reorient the understanding of Mary and her role, namely, as a necessary but subordinate figure to Christ. From the medieval portrait of the heavenly Queen and intercessor, Mary was transformed by Luther into a complex, but far more human, image of the pious mother who paradoxically remained a virgin, charged with the honored task of bearing and raising the Son of God.[1]

1. A number of authors have addressed Luther's views on Mary; some useful texts in English are P. N. Brooks, "A Lily Ungilded? Martin Luther, the Virgin Mary, and the Saints," *Journal of Religious History* 13 (1984): 136-49; W. J. Cole, "Was Luther a Devotee of Mary?" *Marian Studies* 21 (1970): 94-202. More general studies of Mary among the re-

Mary in the Late-Medieval Period

As a young man, Luther was steeped in the religiosity of his day. This piety was dominated by Mary and the saints, who were central to the system of merit and the search for salvation that so occupied late-medieval Christians. The church year itself was punctuated by the great Marian festivals as well as other saints' days, while Marian hymns such as the Magnificat were integrated into the church's liturgy. Prayers such as the rosary were the foci of both personal and corporate devotion, and holy objects associated with Mary, especially candles and wax blessed on Candlemas, were thought to have power to assist women in childbirth and Christians on their deathbed.[2]

The theology surrounding Mary had reached a high level of complexity by the beginning of the sixteenth century. While most Marian doctrine was based on authoritative Scriptures, rather than apocryphal texts such as the second-century *Protevangelium of James,* which provides information on Mary's conception and childhood, such extracanonical legend was highly influential in the development of Marian piety, and thus indirectly influenced theological statements about her. In the early church, most Marian theology was developed in response to christological questions. Mary's role in maintaining Christ's fully human nature was central, and explains to a large extent Mary's importance in the early councils. The use of the title *Theotokos* (literally "God-bearer," but more

---

formers include Heiko Oberman, "The Virgin Mary in Evangelical Perspective," *Journal of Ecumenical Studies* 1 (1964): 271-98; David F. Wright, "Mary in the Reformers," in *Chosen by God: Mary in Evangelical Perspective,* ed. D. F. Wright (London: Marshall Pickering, 1989), 161-83. Also see Jaroslav Pelikan, *Mary through the Centuries: Her Place in the History of Culture* (New Haven: Yale University Press, 1996). For further bibliography and a study of the development of the image of Mary across the first several generations of Lutheran preachers, see Beth Kreitzer, *Reforming Mary: Changing Images of the Virgin Mary in Lutheran Sermons of the Sixteenth Century* (New York: Oxford University Press, 2004).

2. A number of works treat devotion to Mary in the medieval period; some recent texts include Rachel Fulton, *From Judgment to Passion: Devotion to Christ and the Virgin Mary, 800-1200* (New York: Columbia University Press, 2002); Donna Spivey Ellington, *From Sacred Body to Angelic Soul: Understanding Mary in Late Medieval and Early Modern Europe* (Washington, D.C.: Catholic University of America Press, 2001), which is a study of Mary in Catholic sermons; Mary Clayton, *The Cult of the Virgin Mary in Anglo-Saxon England* (Cambridge: Cambridge University Press, 1990); Dominique Iogna-Prat et al., eds., *Marie: Le culte de la Vierge dans la société médiévale* (Paris: Beauchesne, 1996).

commonly translated "Mother of God") was the main controversy behind the council at Ephesus (431), which defined Christ's two natures, fully God and fully human. The council of Chalcedon (451) reaffirmed Christ's hypostatic union, and also affirmed Mary's virginity both *in partu* and *post partem.* Mary's paradoxical position as mother and virgin dominated both thought and devotion, allowing her to serve as a model both of motherhood and also of female asceticism, the latter having a particularly high place within the Catholic tradition.

Theological debates surrounding the Virgin continued in the medieval period. Because Mary was the person most closely and directly associated with Jesus' humanity — in the common medieval theory of the atonement, it is through our kinship with Jesus' humanity that we are able to be saved — she was thought to be worthy of a great deal of respect and adoration. This adoration, along with the perceived connection between sexuality and sin and thus conversely between virginity and purity, led to the greatest Marian debate of the later medieval period, that over her immaculate conception. The feast of Mary's conception had been celebrated in the Eastern church for centuries, and the popular legend of her miraculous conception stemming from the *Protevangelium* was a popular theme in art. The feast was gradually transported into the West, where it began to generate controversy among theologians. In the early twelfth century Bernard of Clairvaux wrote his famous letter to the canons of Lyon in opposition to the feast, while the first treatise promoting Mary's immaculate conception was written by one of Anselm's students to honor the feast's celebration in England.[3] The eleventh century saw other Marian prayers and hymns come into common usage: the *Salve Regina,* the *Alma Redemptoris Mater,* and most especially the *Ave Maria.* This prayer, which had appeared in briefer form in the East from at least 600, quickly became popular for both personal devotion and liturgical use.[4]

The debate over the immaculate conception continued to rage into

3. Hilda Graef, *Mary: A History of Doctrine and Devotion,* vol. 1, *From the Beginning to the Eve of the Reformation* (New York: Sheed and Ward, 1963), 217-18. For more information on the developments leading up to the proclamation of the dogma of the immaculate conception, see Edward D. O'Connor, ed., *The Dogma of the Immaculate Conception: History and Significance* (South Bend, Ind.: University of Notre Dame Press, 1958).

4. The history of the rosary, which received its final form only in the sixteenth century, is detailed in Anne Winston-Allen, *Stories of the Rose: The Making of the Rosary in the Middle Ages* (University Park: University of Pennsylvania Press, 1997).

the fifteenth century. Thomas Aquinas, while teaching the common notion that Mary was free from any actual sin, denied the immaculate conception on the grounds that Mary could not have been purified from sin until the animation of her soul (the "quickening"), and even then her purification was redemption through Christ. Even the highly devotional *Mariale super missus est,* mistakenly attributed to Albert the Great until the twentieth century, which promotes Mary as "the helper of redemption through her compassion," holds the view that Mary was sanctified in the womb at some point after conception.[5] The banner of the immaculate conception was taken up by the Franciscan order, especially the theologians William of Ware and his student Duns Scotus, who argued that the most perfect redemption, which is what Christ would have wanted for his mother, was to be preserved from sin rather than only purified from it.[6] The council of Basle (1431-49) declared in favor of the feast and the doctrine in 1438, but the council had already been dissolved by the pope, so this declaration had no legal force.

The acrimonious nature of the debate led the pope to forbid discussion of the issue first in 1482, then again in 1483 and 1503. Theologians continued to write on the matter, including the nominalist theologian so influential on Luther, Gabriel Biel. Biel argued for Mary's eternal predestination as the *Theotokos,* and stressed three Mariological "rules": the "superlative rule," which accords the highest possible privileges to Mary that do not contradict Scripture or tradition; the "comparative rule," which gives Mary a position second only to God and higher than all the other saints; and the "rule of similitude with Christ," which stresses Mary's cooperation with Christ through her humility.[7] We find a number of common Marian titles in Biel: she is co-redemptrix and mediatrix along with Christ, the Mother of the Church, and the Queen of Heaven who practices

5. Graef, *From the Beginning,* 273.

6. The dogma of the immaculate conception, pronounced by Pius IX in 1854, essentially follows Scotus's arguments: "the Blessed Virgin Mary at the first moment of her conception by a special grace and privilege of Almighty God, in view of the merits of Christ Jesus, the Savior of the human race, by preservation was pure of all stain of original sin." See the bull *Ineffabilis Deus VII,* cited in Thomas O'Meara, *Mary in Protestant and Catholic Theology* (New York: Sheed and Ward, 1966), 58.

7. See Heiko Oberman, *The Harvest of Medieval Theology: Gabriel Biel and Late Medieval Nominalism* (Cambridge: Harvard University Press, 1963; reprint, Durham, N.C.: Labyrinth Press, 1983), 304-8.

continual intercession with Christ: "as mediatrix to the mediator she completes the work of salvation, she pleads the case of mankind and balances by her *misericordia* the *iustitia* of her Son."[8]

The view of Mary as the Queen of Heaven and the Mother of Mercy is a strong element of popular devotion to Mary — her significance in the church's "treasury of salvation" cannot be overestimated — but the late-medieval devotion to the humanity and suffering of Christ also led to the increased focus on the human motherhood and suffering of Mary. Devotion to Mary as the sorrowing mother, the *Mater Dolorosa,* was especially common, and Mary's role at the death of the Christian was emphasized. In the writings of Luther's older contemporary, the Augustinian Johann von Paltz, we find a special focus on the *mitleiden,* or "co-suffering" of Mary at the cross. In our hour of need, Paltz suggests that we pray not only to Christ that our sins might not be counted against us, but also to Mary that she not see our great unworthiness, but come to help us: "I ask you through your eternal election, your holy conception, and your vigil at the cross, come to help me at my final end."[9] In Paltz's work we see the most elemental aspect of late-medieval Marian piety and devotion: although it is Christ whose sacrifice saves us, it is Mary that brings us to Christ and the salvation he provides.

Luther's Critique of Marian Devotion

Students of the Reformation are familiar with the story Luther recounted of his impetus into the monastery: out of fear for his life during a thunderstorm, young Martin called out to Mary's mother, "Help, St. Anne, I will become a monk!"[10] His rash vow led him into the Augustinian friary in Erfurt and put an end to his father's dream of seeing his eldest son a prominent and wealthy lawyer. Later in life he berated himself not only for not properly honoring and obeying his father, but also for placing such trust in a saint rather than in Christ. He recalls with disdain other practices of his youth, such as "vowing to fast on bread and water on Saturday for the

8. Oberman, *Harvest of Medieval Theology,* 310.

9. Johann von Paltz, "Die himlische funtgrub," in *Johannes von Paltz Werke,* vol. 3, ed. Heiko Oberman (Berlin: De Gruyter, 1983-89), 246.

10. WA TR 4:440.9f., no. 4707 (1539).

Blessed Virgin," and calling on Mary and the saints for help.[11] This vow, he insists, was made "not to God, or to Mary, but to the devil, because it was not commanded," while he called upon Mary because he feared Christ as an angry judge.[12] Luther questioned not only the abuses and excesses into which Marian devotion had fallen in the late-medieval period, but also the theological structure that placed Mary in such a high and unique position of power. To Luther, the official church teachings that posited Mary as an intercessor or mediator or focused on her merit and virtues were suspect and needed to be discarded in the light of the gospel.

We find in Luther's early lectures on the Psalms his first criticisms of the invocation of the saints and Mary, where he suggests that they detract from faith in the power of God and Christ.[13] While he did not reject invoking the saints for several years, his growing belief in the christocentric nature of the gospel led him to retreat from the idea that Christians should call upon Mary and ask her and the saints to pray for them. In a sermon from 1519, Luther could still suggest that at the hour of death the Christian should "invoke all the holy angels and especially his angel and the mother of God," since God has commanded "that the saints should love and assist all who believe."[14] But by the 1521 treatise on the Magnificat, Luther insisted that even if Christians call upon Mary for help, they should recognize that the power belongs to God and not to Mary: "We ought to call upon her, that for her sake God may grant and do what we request. Thus also all other saints are to be invoked, so that the work may be in every way God's alone."[15]

Soon after this treatise was published, Luther became even more conclusive on this issue: the centrality of Christ and the fact that he alone is responsible for our salvation leads to the realization that the cult of the saints and Mary is superfluous. While she continues to deserve respect and honor, Christians cannot call upon Mary as an advocate or intercessor, as though through her own merit or her close connection as his mother she somehow deserves that Christ do her bidding; this, Luther insists, makes her into an idol or goddess. In the Smalcald Articles of 1537, Luther bluntly

11. WA 25:510; WA 34I:38.

12. WA 25:210.

13. WA 1:150.412ff.

14. WA 2:696.

15. LW 21:329; WA 7:575.

states that the invocation of the saints "is neither commanded nor recommended, has no precedent in the Scripture," while the associated festivals, masses, sacrifices, prayers, and churches and altars dedicated to the saints are in fact idolatry: "Such honor belongs to God alone."[16]

Along with the mistaken notion that Christians should ask the saints and Mary for their prayers, Luther condemns the common medieval notion that Mary as the merciful mother can somehow mediate for and protect sinners from her wrathful son. Not only does this make Mary into a goddess, as suggested by the popular image of Mary as the "Madonna of the Protective Cloak" who towers over and shelters her supplicants under her mantle, but it also mistakenly represents Christ as a harsh and fearsome judge. Luther especially blames the otherwise venerable Saint Bernard for repeating his vision of Mary baring her breasts to Christ in intercession for sinners, reminding him of what he owes to her as his mother.[17] This is, in Luther's view, both an insult to Mary and incorrect teaching about Christ: Christ is the author of mercy through the grace of God and his sacrifice on the cross. Mary herself believed this, and would have been ashamed and upset to be so mistakenly represented.

Not only did Luther reject the idea that Mary takes an active role in salvation and has power over Christ to obtain favors for her devotees, he also rejected the complementary notion that she was worthy of grace and meritorious through her virtues and her acceptance of the incarnation. If she could not be a goddess with great powers in heaven, neither should she be an idol who is worshiped and adored.

Luther frequently criticized the belief that Mary somehow merited her role as the mother of God. In his discussion of the Magnificat, Luther attacks the idea that Mary's humility earned her the privilege of bearing God's Son. Rather, he insists, her humility means that not only did she consider herself unworthy of this great blessing, but she also came from a poor family with low social status. He stresses her *niedrigkeit,* her "lowliness," rather than her humility. She does, however, exhibit true humility, in that she does not become proud at receiving such a great honor, but remains simple and humble in heart. But we should be careful of praising Mary for this great virtue, and Luther insists that she would prefer to be addressed in this manner: "O Blessed Virgin, Mother of God, you were

16. Smalcald Articles II.ii.25-28, in BC, 305-6.

17. See, among others, WA 21:65.31; WA 7:568.29; WA 10III:325.5.

nothing and all despised; yet God in His grace regarded you and worked such great things in you. You were worthy of none of them, but the rich and abundant grace of God was upon you, far above any merit of yours. Hail to you!"[18] She would not be offended by such a remark, but is rather offended by those who see merit and honor in her, and thereby take away honor from God. Hymns such as the *Regina coeli laetare* inappropriately call her "worthy" to bear Christ: she was worthy only in that she was suitable as a young virgin and appointed to the task by God.

Likewise, other aspects of her character that had been held as meritorious were now reevaluated. Although Luther retains the significance of Mary's virginity, both as a necessity for orthodox Christology and also for stressing proper morals and behavior, it again is not a virtue that "earns" her grace. The pope and his followers glorify Mary's virginity, but in fact, Luther comments, it was important only "because it was needful for the conceiving and bearing of this blessed fruit." Her virginity helped Christ avoid "the corruption of our flesh," and thus the taint of sin.[19] But her virginity should not be made into a virtue in itself, or be used to promote a life of avowed virginity or celibacy, as the pope has done. Instead, Christians should realize that God values marriage above celibacy, which is not commanded by Scripture for anyone: the presence of Jesus and his mother at the wedding in Cana, the site of his first miracle, shows the higher value God has placed on marriage. In fact, Luther asserts, God would have chosen a married woman rather than simply a betrothed virgin to be Jesus' mother if he could, "since virginity is contrary to the physical nature within us [and] was condemned of old in the law."[20]

To help avoid the problems caused by excessive adoration of Mary and the tendency of "the pope and his monks" to "make a god out of the Virgin," Luther corrects what he sees as a mistake in the Vulgate translation of the New Testament. In his own translation of the angel's salutation to Mary in Luke 1:28, Luther replaces the phrase *"Ave Maria, gratia plena,"* or "Hail Mary, full of grace," with "Hail gracious one, or blessed one," which he felt not only more accurately translated the Greek term, but also avoided the problems associated with *"gratia plena."*[21] This last phrase

18. LW 21:322; WA 7:568.

19. LW 45:202, *That Jesus Christ Was Born a Jew* (1523); WA 11:314-36.

20. LW 45:202; WA 11:314-36.

21. WA 52:626, sermon on the annunciation (1532). See also Heinz Bluhm, "Luther's

somehow suggested that she was filled with grace, and could, through her own will and power, bestow it upon others. The terms *holdselige* and *begnadete* more accurately convey the passivity of the original: she is blessed by God through his unmerited and gracious attention to her. In light of this, Luther warns against using the *Ave Maria* as a prayer, which in fact it is not: "it is no prayer; it is a formula of praise," and since it has been misused so greatly in the past, "it were best that the Hail Mary should entirely be laid aside."[22] It can be used as a meditation on God's grace and an expression of our respect for her who is "blessed among women," but must only be used with a right understanding and proper faith.

Mary: Teacher by Word and Example

Along with his critique of "papist" superstition and the abuses associated with Marian veneration, Luther had an abundance of positive comments to make about the Virgin Mary. She was as great an example of faith as the patriarch Abraham, and modeled other important virtues as well. She served to teach all Christians about the theological virtues of faith, humility, and love, but could also model the social value of obedience to authority, and teach especially to women the virtues of modesty and propriety.

Mary's faith is most clearly displayed in her response to the angel at the annunciation. Her fiat, her trusting acceptance of the message of the angel and the truth of God's grace to her, shows for Luther the essence of faith: "That is a high and excellent faith, to become a mother and remain an uncorrupted virgin; that truly surpasses sense, thought, and all human reason and experience."[23] Mary had to rely completely on God, and discount anything her own reason and experience could tell her: this is the true nature of faith. This faith and trust that she had been chosen to be the mother of God was, according to Luther, an even greater miracle than the incarnation itself.[24]

Translation and Interpretation of the Ave Maria," *Journal of English and German Philology* 51 (1952): 196-211, and Birgit Stolt, "On Translating Ave Maria as 'Hello, There, Mary,'" *Lutheran Quarterly* 12 (1998): 105-7. Luther's main treatise on translating is in WA 30II:632-46; LW 35:177-202.

22. WA 11:59-60, sermon of 11 March 1523.

23. WA 17II:399, sermon on the annunciation (1522).

24. WA 15:478.

Once she accepted in faith that she would give birth to God's Son, Mary's humility kept her from the sin of pride. Her humility was not a virtue that somehow merited her position as Jesus' mother, but rather a belief in her own lowliness and unworthiness. Mary recognized that all the blessings given to her came from God's grace, and responded in the beautiful words of the Magnificat, "My soul magnifies the Lord . . ." In his treatise on the Magnificat, Luther insists that the lessons of humility and trust found in this text should be well learned "by all who would rule well and be helpful lords."[25] Those in leadership positions, whether in the church or in the state, need especially to be reminded to avoid the sin of pride, to avoid thinking that all the blessings they have received have somehow been deserved. Through her teachings on faith and humility in the Magnificat, Mary can be rightfully called a "great doctor and prophet, more learned than all the apostles and prophets."[26]

In response to her faith, and through her recognition of her own unworthiness in humility, Mary also becomes a great example of Christian love, which lives through service to others. After receiving the message that she would be the mother of God's Son, she hurried to visit her elderly relative Elizabeth. Her loving service to Elizabeth and her work as nursery maid to the baby John clearly model Luther's view of faith that is necessarily active in works of love. Mary expressed God's love to her neighbor, as all Christians are called to do.

As an outgrowth of both her humility and her love, Mary serves as a profitable example of obedience, both to God and to earthly authorities. Despite her advanced pregnancy, Mary and Joseph were obedient to the command of the emperor and journeyed to Bethlehem, displaying their piety. She was even obedient to the law requiring her purification after giving birth to Jesus, although technically as a virgin she was not impure under the law. Her example, Luther remarks, shames all of us who are guilty under the law but remain disobedient.[27] Perhaps even more importantly, she shows that obeying laws in order to avoid offending or scandalizing others is even more important than flaunting one's freedom from these laws: the needs of the community and the good of others require Christians to act selflessly.

25. LW 21:298; WA 7:544.

26. WA 52:691, *Hauspostille* (1544).

27. WA 52:148-49, sermon on Mary's purification, *Hauspostille* (1544).

Along with her importance as an example to all Christians, Luther stresses that Mary was also a good example for "all women and virgins." Along with the majority of earlier interpreters, Luther insists that Luke wanted rather to indicate that Mary went "chastely" or "modestly" *(züchtig* or *endelich),* rather than quickly, to see Elizabeth. Her good behavior and chaste conduct again reveal the restrictions upon Christians: Christian freedom does not mean licentiousness, but in fact the Christian is duty-bound to act in a socially proper and inoffensive manner. For women especially, Luther promotes the virtue of proper behavior, including it as one of the "three especially beautiful and lovely roses" in the rose garland of virtues displayed by Mary. The three roses — the virtues of faith, humility, and "fine and chaste conduct" — are more precious than any fine jewels or silks.[28] Mary's faith in God's Word teaches women that they should spend time in church or at prayer rather than at the market or dancing, while her humility teaches women to avoid pride, which is their particular downfall. The third rose, chaste conduct, shows women that they should not be irresponsible and nosy, gossiping with their friends in the street, but should rather stay at home focusing on their chores.

Mary was not always perfect, however, and on at least two occasions she showed her humanness.[29] Her mistakes also provided Luther with an opportunity to present Mary as an example to his audience. When searching for her twelve-year-old son in Jerusalem, she first looked among her friends and acquaintances, and only eventually sought out the temple where Jesus was impressing his elders. For Luther, these "friends and acquaintances" represent the councils and church fathers, but Jesus will be found only in "that which is his father's," that is, in the Word of God.[30] If Mary herself could not find Jesus, why should we trust other human authorities? Likewise at the wedding at Cana, although Mary approached her son in faith and in loving concern for the bride and bridegroom, she erred in trying to impose her will upon Christ. If Mary, who had "a greater,

28. WA 52:682-83, sermon on the visitation, *Hauspostille* (1544).

29. Although Luther considered Mary to be without sin, through God's grace of course, as we will see in the following section, that did not mean that she never made mistakes. Luther's willingness to ascribe error to Mary was amplified by his followers, who eventually (and quite remarkably, considering the weight of authority against the idea) decided that Mary was in fact a sinful human being. See Kreitzer, *Reforming Mary,* especially chapters 4 and 5.

30. WA 12:414, sermon on the Sunday after Epiphany (1523).

stronger faith than any other saint," can err, it is foolish to insist that the church and the holy fathers cannot err.[31] Her example proves for Luther that the only true and abiding authority is in God's Word.

Doctrine concerning Mary

Luther continued to accept a number of the traditional doctrines concerning Mary, in particular those teachings that expressed Mary's importance for orthodox Christology. And while he eventually rejected many of the titles that had been given to Mary during the medieval period, such as Queen of Heaven and Mother of Mercy, he was not unwilling to accept some other Marian doctrines, even her sinlessness, despite their lack of scriptural proof. His proviso for such teachings was that since they did not rest upon the evidence of Scripture, they could not be made into mandatory beliefs.

Mother of God

The title *Theotokos,* the God-bearer, was declared at the Council of Ephesus in 431, in response to controversy over popular devotion to Mary and confusion over Christology. Luther also was concerned to express clearly his orthodoxy on issues of Christology, and to counter those who were suggesting what he considered to be heretical positions. Mary is of the highest importance for establishing the humanity of Christ: Luther stresses frequently that Christ is a "true and natural son of the Virgin Mary, from whom He inherited flesh and blood as any other child does from its mother."[32] This is what the creed teaches in the phrase "born of the Virgin Mary": Christ's human nature is utterly genuine, given by his mother. However, as the incarnation of the divine and the promised Savior, Christ was also without any sin. Following Augustine, Luther insisted upon Mary's virginal conception of Christ, in order to avoid any possibility of sin entering through the sexual act. Luther balanced the need to stress that Jesus was a "natural son" and Mary his "natural mother," with

31. WA 21:64, *Winterpostille* (1528).

32. LW 22:23, sermons on the Gospel of John.

the desire to protect Christ's sinlessness through this unnatural, but pure, means of conception.[33] Christ's sinless birth was necessary for human sanctification: "God sent another birth that had to be pure and immaculate [in order] to make the impure sinful birth pure. That is the birth of the Lord Christ, his only-begotten son, and therefore he did not want to allow him to be born out of sinful flesh and blood, but he should be born from a virgin alone."[34] Luther was also willing to accept the traditional conditions that followed from such an unusual conception: "[Mary] gave birth without sin, without shame, without pain and without injury, as she also conceived without sin."[35] She was thus free from the "curse of Eve," that she should bear her children in pain.

While Mary is the guarantor of Christ's humanity, and thus most definitely the mother of Jesus the man, Luther does not hesitate to reject the heretical Nestorian view that Mary is not also the mother of God. There is only one Son, Luther insists, although he has two natures, and Mary is the mother of this one Son who is both fully God and fully human: "Mary bore [both] God and man," making her truly the *Theotokos*.[36] And although this title serves to maintain the orthodoxy of Luther's Christology, he recognizes that it also has further implications for Mary: "[F]or on this [becoming the mother of God] there follows all honor, all blessedness, and her unique place in the whole of mankind, among which she has no equal, namely that she had a child by the Father in heaven. . . . Hence men have crowded all her glory into a single word, calling her the Mother of God."[37] However, as the title stresses her relationship to Christ, so also Luther insists that she herself wants all the attention to go to Christ; she ascribes all her blessings to God's grace and none to her own merit.

Perpetual Virginity

Despite Luther's many publications in the early years of the Reformation, rumor and misinformation about his teachings abounded. One particu-

33. WA 10I/1:67, sermon on Christmas, *Weihnachtspostille* (1522).
34. WA 17II:304, sermon on Christmas Eve, *Festpostille* (1527).
35. WA 10I/1:67, sermon on Christmas, *Weihnachtspostille* (1522).
36. WA 40III:708.
37. LW 21:326, the Magnificat; WA 7:572.

larly dangerous charge against him was that he taught that Jesus was the natural son of Joseph and that his mother Mary was in fact not a virgin, but had many sons. To combat this charge, Luther published *That Jesus Christ Was Born a Jew* in 1523, which clarified his teachings about Christ's birth and about the Virgin Mary. In this text he insisted that Mary conceived Jesus as a virgin, making the traditional connection between sexuality and sin: "the flesh is tainted and its built-in physical nature cannot bestow her fruit except by means of an accursed act."[38] Mary's virginity was necessary so that her son could avoid this taint.

Luther goes further than this to express a belief in the continuation of Mary's virginity beyond Jesus' birth; although he would not want to praise Mary's perpetual virginity as a model for a life of avowed celibacy, he did want to support the belief in Mary's virginity *ante partum, in partu,* and *post partem* expressed by the Council of Chalcedon in 451.[39] However, this doctrine had received too much attention in the past, so Luther suggests that "we should be satisfied simply to hold that she remained a virgin after the birth of Christ because scripture does not state or indicate that she later lost her virginity."[40] In this case, Luther was content to rest with tradition, even to the extent of explaining the presence of Jesus' "brothers" in the New Testament as a reference to cousins or other relatives. He suggests that phrases such as "before they came together" (Matt. 1:18) and "Joseph knew her not until she brought forth her first-born son" (Matt. 1:25) do not necessarily indicate that she became a regular wife to Joseph after Jesus' birth.

Immaculate Conception

As we have seen, the status of Mary's conception was still contested in Luther's time. Theologians agreed that Mary was indeed free from original sin, and furthermore from all actual sin, but they disagreed over the point at which she was purified (or in the Franciscan tradition, preserved) from sin. In Luther's final sermon on the holiday of Mary's conception, preached in 1520, he complains that the debate about her conception has

38. LW 45:205.

39. For Luther's support of Mary's virginity *in partu* see WA 17II:457; 7:549; 11:320; for *post partem* see WA 11:320; 49:174 and 182; 51:176; 54:207.

40. LW 45:206.

caused a great deal of trouble among the monks, even though "there is not a single letter about it in the gospels or otherwise in the Scriptures."[41]

In this sermon Luther outlines his views on Mary's conception and clearly leans toward the immaculist side of the debate, but takes the middle position favored by most theologians. His explanation rests on the common medieval division of generation into two conceptions: the "first conception," that of the body, is during the act of intercourse, necessarily infected by concupiscence and thus sin; the "second conception" is at a later point when the newly formed soul enters the fetus, also called animation. Christ, because he was not the result of generation between a man and a woman, clearly avoided any connection with original sin even in the first conception. Mary, on the other hand, was born through the usual means of a father and a mother, and thus experienced a physical conception tainted with sin. It was at the second conception, when her soul entered her body, that she was "purified from original sin and decorated with God's gifts."[42] Because this second conception is more important than the first, and is the moment at which one is said to live, Luther can say that "from the first moment that she began to live, she was without all sin," placing Mary in the "middle between Christ and other men."[43] However, Luther insists that no required doctrine can be made about Mary's conception, as it is not expressly mentioned in the Bible.

The Assumption

Mary's assumption was not a defined dogma in the sixteenth century, although it was a very popular holiday in the late-medieval period. Her bodily assumption into heaven allowed for the continuing development of her honors and titles, and also supported her role as the most powerful advocate for humankind before her Son. It was thought to provide even more comfort to sinners than Christ's own resurrection and ascension, since she

41. WA 17II:280, *Festpostille* (1527).

42. WA 17II:288. The words Luther uses, "von der erbsünnde sey gerainniget worden," clearly indicate the idea of cleansing Mary from sin rather than preserving her from it.

43. WA 17II:288. Some scholars have doubted whether Luther maintained this belief throughout his life, and there are several ambiguous statements in later texts. He did not comment directly on the matter again.

was completely human and thus more representative of the Christian hope of eternal life in heaven.

Not surprisingly, Luther did not long preach on this holiday, for it is also not mentioned in Scripture. In his last sermon on this holiday, preached in 1522, Luther remarks that we cannot know how Mary is in heaven, nor is it necessary to discover everything about the saints in heaven. All we can know, based on certain biblical passages, is that they live in Christ, but not how: "the Scriptures say clearly that Abraham, Isaac, Jacob and all the faithful live, therefore it is necessary that you believe that the Mother of God lives; but how this happens, that one must entrust to our loving God."[44] Luther stresses that it is also important to avoid any idolatrous notions based on her presence in heaven: she cannot serve as an advocate or intercessor "as the pope teaches . . . with the result that he has made the mother like her Son in all things."[45] He suggests rejecting the feast not only on the grounds that it is without biblical foundation, but also because of the idolatrous notions that have been attached to it.

Conclusion

Although the role of the Virgin Mary and the saints in the Protestant Reformation has not been of central interest to scholars of the period, it is in fact one of those topics that has continued to define clearly the differences between Protestants and Roman Catholics.[46] The definition of the dogmas of the immaculate conception (1854) and the assumption (1950) highlighted major barriers between the confessions, regarding not only Mary's significance but also papal power and the equal authority of Scripture and tradition. Devotion to Mary and the continuation of her titles and privileges have been an important area of discussion in the ecumenical movement.[47] It remains a stumbling block to mutual understanding between Protestants and Roman Catholics.

44. WA 10III:269.

45. WA 52:681, sermon on the visitation (1544).

46. One prominent exception is Robert Kolb, *For All the Saints: Changing Perceptions of Martyrdom and Sainthood in the Lutheran Reformation* (Macon, Ga.: Mercer University Press, 1987).

47. Two documents that have stemmed from such discussions are Anderson, Stafford, and Burgess, eds., *The One Mediator, the Saints, and Mary: Lutherans and Catho-*

Luther's views on the Virgin Mary are an interesting combination of new and old. While his changed conceptions of grace, justification, and authority along with his christocentric approach to all aspects of Christian faith transformed his presentation of Mary, he also accepted a number of traditional doctrines concerning Mary, especially those defined at the early ecumenical councils. The resulting new and unique picture of Mary reveals a tension that Luther had difficulty resolving: How can Christians properly praise and appreciate Mary as the mother of God, who did after all announce that "all generations shall call me blessed" (Luke 1:48), while nevertheless avoiding the pitfalls into which late-medieval Roman Catholicism had fallen, especially what he characterized as the idolatrous worship of Mary as queen and mediator with Christ?

Clearly Luther decided to err on the side of caution. Although he was quick to point out Mary's virtues — her faith, humility, and love — he constantly reaffirmed that in no way did she merit God's grace or have any power to intercede for sinners with Christ. Along with all the saints, Luther insists that Mary in her own faith and behavioral ways points to God, praising God and his blessings but never herself. Even her lifelong sinlessness and virginal purity, two doctrines that Luther maintained without scriptural evidence and that set Mary apart from the rest of the human race, were for him primarily due to her unique role as the mother of God. They were signs of God's grace and not intended to concentrate attention on the woman herself.

Mary's most important role for Luther was that of exemplar. In her faith and trust in God's promises, her love and service to others, her humility and lack of pride, she is one of the foremost models of true Christian virtue in the entire Bible. And because for Luther the good Christian is also a good citizen and member of the community, Mary provides a positive example of obedience to both civic government and church law. Her chaste and modest behavior and lack of frivolity make her an ideal model for women and girls, and Luther promoted especially those aspects of her story that fit his preconceived image of the pious Christian woman. What he considered to be unusual characteristics — her lifelong virginity, her preaching and teaching, her role as a "doctor of the church" — were care-

lics in Dialogue VIII (Minneapolis: Augsburg Fortress, 1992); and A. Blancy and M. Jourjon and the Dombes Group, *Mary in the Plan of God and in the Communion of Saints,* trans. M. J. O'Connell (New York: Paulist, 2002).

fully noted as part of her unique role as the mother of God's Son. But despite any tension he might have felt in explaining Mary and her role in the life of the church, Luther clearly retained a love and respect for the woman who bore the Savior of the world.

CHAPTER 12

Luther on Eve, Women, and the Church

Mickey L. Mattox

Was the Reformation "good" for women? Did the Protestant reformers somehow promote the cause of women in church or society? There have been considerable debate and discussion on such questions in recent years, and rightly so.[1] The theology and (less often) the practice of the Protestant reformers have both come in for close analysis. Do we find there the source of long-standing errors and misunderstandings that we must now abandon, or support for continuing traditional practices that exclude women from some of the churches' public ministries?[2] One source in this debate is the theology of Martin Luther[3] and his own life and practice, especially in

1. For general studies of the problem, see Steven E. Ozment, *When Fathers Ruled: Family Life in Reformation Europe* (Cambridge: Harvard University Press, 1983); Merry E. Wiesner, *Women and Gender in Early Modern Europe* (Cambridge: Cambridge University Press, 1993). Helpful summaries of the state of research may be found in Carter Lindberg, *The European Reformations* (Oxford: Blackwell, 1996), 363-66; Euan Cameron, *The European Reformation* (Oxford: Clarendon, 1991), 402-5; and Lyndal Roper, "Gender and the Reformation," *Archiv für Reformationsgeschichte* 92 (2001): 290-302.

2. See, for example, Jane Dempsey Douglass, "The Image of God in Women as Seen by Luther and Calvin," in *The Image of God: Gender Models in Judaeo-Christian Tradition,* ed. Kari Elisabeth Børresen (Minneapolis: Fortress, 1995), 236-66; for more on Calvin see John Lee Thompson, *John Calvin and the Daughters of Sarah: Women in Regular and Exceptional Roles in the Exegesis of Calvin, His Predecessors, and His Contemporaries* (Geneva: Librairie Droz, 1992).

3. A noteworthy example is Paul R. Hinlicky, "Luther against the Contempt of

relationship with his wife Katharina von Bora.[4] Luther has sometimes been portrayed as a champion of women's rights in the church, but his authoritative voice has also been invoked as a final bulwark against "feminist" claims.

As this essay will demonstrate, Luther developed a distinctive but nevertheless quite traditional and even restrictive theoretical understanding of the place and role of women in church, home, and society. There were aspects of his thought, however (on male-female relations, on the nature of the struggle for faith, and on the priesthood of believers), that seemed to suggest that women could or should preach. Indeed, these trajectories in Luther's thought attracted attention in the sixteenth century. As Gottfried Maron points out, the Roman Catholic polemicist Alfons de Castro (O.F.M.) accused Luther of making it possible for women to enter the church's priesthood and thus of reviving the Montanist heresy, largely

Women," *Lutheran Quarterly* 2 (1988): 515-30. Further specialized studies include Matthieu Arnold, *Les femmes dans la correspondance de Luther* (Paris: Presses Universitaires de France, 1998); Scott H. Hendrix, "Luther on Marriage," *Lutheran Quarterly* 14 (2000): 335-50; Kristen E. Kvam, "Luther, Eve, and Theological Anthropology: Reassessing the Reformer's Response to the *Frauenfrage* (Woman Question)" (Ph.D. diss., Emory University, 1992); Ingetraut Ludolphy, "Die Frau in der Sicht Martin Luther," in *Vierhundert-Jahre lutherische Reformation, 1517-1967,* ed. Helmar Junghans, Ingetraut Ludolphy, and Kurt Meier (Göttingen, 1967); Gottfried Maron, "Vom Hindernis zur Hilfe: Die Frau in der Sicht Martin Luthers," *Theologische Zeitschrift* 39, no. 5 (1983): 272-83; Birgit Stolt, "Luther on God as Father," *Lutheran Quarterly* 8 (1994): 383-95. Helpful for appreciating the further development of the Lutheran tradition is Scott H. Hendrix, "Christianizing Domestic Relations: Women and Marriage in Johann Freder's *Dialogus dem Ehestand zu Ehren,*" *Sixteenth Century Journal* 23 (1992): 251-66.

4. The scholarly literature on Katharina von Bora has expanded significantly in recent years. See, among others, Roland Bainton, "Katherina von Bora," in *Women of the Reformation in Germany and Italy* (Minneapolis: Augsburg, 1971), 23-44; Helmar Junghans, "Katharina Luther in the Light and in the Shadow of the Reformation," in *Ad Fontes Lutheri: Toward the Recovery of the Real Luther; Essays in Honor of Kenneth Hagen's Sixty-fifth Birthday,* ed. Timothy Maschke, Franz Posset, and Joan Skocir (Milwaukee: Marquette University Press, 2001), 86-103; Ernst Kroker, *Katharina von Bora: Martin Luthers Frau,* 16th ed. (Berlin, 1983); Jeanette C. Smith, "Katharina von Bora through Five Centuries: A Historiography," *Sixteenth Century Journal* 30 (1999): 745-74; Martin Treu, ed., *Katharina von Bora. Die Lutherin. Aufsätze anläßlich ihres 500. Geburtstages* (Wittenberg, 1999); Martin Treu, "Katharina von Bora, the Woman at Luther's Side," *Lutheran Quarterly* 13 (1999): 157-78.

on the basis of the priestly role he was willing to grant all Christians.[5] Yet Luther himself never drew that conclusion.

The breadth and scope of Luther's remarks on this topic — many of them eminently quotable — necessitate from the outset some narrowing of the subject field. This essay seeks only to lay out the general shape of Luther's thought on this complex topic, drawing especially on Luther's sermons and lectures on Genesis. Examination of Luther's extensive work on Genesis can help us understand how Luther viewed the created structure of human life and of woman's place in church, home, and society. As the nineteenth-century Luther scholar Julius Köstlin pointed out, the Genesis lectures in particular are an especially rich source for Luther's theology generally, as well as for his distinctive version of Christian practical wisdom.[6] Attention to these sources, moreover, sets us down in Luther's parish or classroom, showing us not only what he may have said in one or another context, but how he attempted to shape his parishioners' and students' understanding of crucial issues related to marriage, family, and sexuality.

It would be possible, as one might suspect, to come at this topic in quite another way. Maron, for example, lists three crucial changes Luther made in the Christian perception of gender and sexuality.[7] First, he emphasized the sheer predictability and regularity of Christian marriage over against the prior preference for the celibate life. This involved a revaluation of human sexuality: the desire by which the married love and seek one another is itself a created good.[8] This good was then connected to a second crucial change, namely, the elevation of the Christian household over the monastery or convent as the concrete sphere — a "holy order" — within which most would live out their faith. Here parents replaced abbots and

5. Maron, "Vom Hindernis zur Hilfe," 280. Maron cites the work of de Castro's *Adversus omnes haereses* (Cologne, 1549).

6. Köstlin-Kawerau, *Martin Luther: Sein Leben und seine Schriften*, 5th ed., 2 vols. (Berlin, 1903), here 2:425. See also Mickey Mattox, *"Defender of the Most Holy Matriarchs": Martin Luther's Interpretation of the Women of Genesis in the* Enarrationes in Genesin, *1535-1545* (Leiden and Boston: Brill, 2003).

7. Maron, "Vom Hindernis zur Hilfe," 277-81.

8. On this issue, note the remark of Heiko Oberman, *Luther: Man between God and the Devil* (New Haven: Yale University Press, 1989), 267: "For Luther, God is so vitally present in the power of attraction between man and woman that he inspires the conjugal union and Himself constitutes [*sic*] the sexual bond of marriage."

abbesses as those responsible for the spiritual health of the community. The Christian household itself thus came to stand under the cross, so to speak, with Christian parents carrying out the good work of begetting and bearing children, and of suffering, living, and dying together in faith, hope, and love.

Thirdly, according to Maron, Luther replaced the exclusively male priesthood with the common priesthood *(das allgemeines Priestertum)* on the basis of which all Christians have the right and duty to announce to one another God's forgiveness for Christ's sake through faith. As Maron observes, Luther distinguished between the public and private spheres within which this forgiveness should be announced, namely, the gathered Christian assembly *(Gemeinde)* and the Christian home. In the former, women may speak only when it is necessary for the sake of the gospel; in the latter, however, their speech is essential and routinely necessary. Relying on Ernst Wolf, Maron concludes that Luther's acceptance of women preaching *when necessary* demonstrates that they have been excluded from the public ministry only for the sake of social order and not on the basis of a divine law. By implication, in this view, the practice of women's ordination today in no way contradicts either Luther's understanding of the Scriptures or his most central theological convictions.

Helpful as it may be to weave together Luther's thought in this fashion, it seems more appropriate to approach Luther in a more historical fashion. Accordingly, this essay begins with a brief analysis of the historical development of Luther's understanding of the story of the creation of Eve and of her role in the fall into sin. This story was foundational for Luther's perception of matters ecclesial and familial, as well as for his understanding of the civil state and its role in fallen human society. A second section reaches out somewhat further, examining Luther's understanding of the female religious life. As is widely known, Luther was no friend of Christian monasticism. However, his emphasis on the goodness of sexuality and the givenness of married life as the proper sphere of God-pleasing existence for the vast majority of human persons did not at all entail the secularizing of the Christian life. Instead, it suggested a social transformation that rendered the domestic sphere a legitimate arena within which to fight the good fight of faith.[9] The Christian home, and with it the institution of

9. Roland Bainton's imaginative portrayal of this aspect of Luther's thought in his *Here I Stand: A Life of Martin Luther* (New York: Mentor, 1950) is still unsurpassed.

Christian marriage, became a religious order of God's own making.[10] Within this domestic sphere, moreover, women's distinctively religious duties were to be performed: bearing and raising up godly children, witnessing to God's faithfulness in their own heroic deeds of faith, and "preaching" God's Word faithfully within their own homes. This essay thus concludes with an examination of some cases where Luther explicitly identified faithful women "preaching" the gospel, including the significance of Luther's exegesis of these stories for the wider issue of women's service in the church. In the end, this research will not resolve the issue of gender relations for the present but instead will show what Luther said on this important topic and why he will remain an inspiration to gender progressives and traditionalists alike.

It may strike some as odd that one would attempt to answer the question of women and the church in Luther's theology by appeal to his exegesis of the Old Testament. Should one not instead look to his perception of the place of women in the New Testament or in the history of the church? Indeed, much could be learned by examining Luther's interest in the women of the New Testament, in the "virgin martyrs" of the early church, or by studying his personal contacts and correspondence with important women of his own day.[11] From Luther's perspective, however, things are today as they have always been. The saints of the Old Testament lived, as saints still do, by faith in the promise of God. Founded on the divine promise of redemption first announced in Genesis 3:15, the "church" of the Old Testament stands in fundamental continuity with that of the New. Or, as Luther bluntly put it, "from the beginning of the world, there have always been Christians."[12] Whether *ante* or *post adventum Christi*, the

10. Scott Hendrix observes that Luther makes marriage "the truly religious order [and] elevates it to the spiritual status that had been reserved for the celibate members of the priesthood and monastic orders." "Luther on Marriage," 338.

11. Something of the range of questions one might ask is suggested by the impressive variety of sources presented in the recently published *Luther on Women: A Sourcebook,* ed. Merry Wiesner-Hanks and Susan C. Karant-Nunn (Cambridge: Cambridge University Press, 2003).

12. WA 24:99-100. Latin text: "Atque hic vides Vetus testamentum cum novo convenire et vides Adamum Christianum fuisse ut nos, in eundem enim Christum credidit in quem nos credimus. Hoc tantum discrimen est: ipse prius, ego post ipsum sum. . . . Semper ergo fuerunt Christiani ab initio mundi. Iustificati igitur iam sunt Adam et Eva per Christum."

Christian lives by faith in the Word of God, and it is the struggle to abide in this faith that interests Luther as an exegete. The stories of the saints of the Old Testament showcase this struggle and thus function as case studies in authentic Christian existence.

Eve, in the Early Luther

The modern question of women's ordination was rarely on Luther's mind. But he thought about Eve often, certainly much more frequently than the few biblical references to her would suggest, and he found in her story the biblical charter for understanding gender relations as God intended them. As I have tried to show elsewhere, however, Luther's imaginative reading of Eve and her story changed over the years, particularly after his marriage in 1525.[13] The source for our knowledge of the younger Luther's thought on Eve is the so-called *Declamationes* on Genesis, sermons delivered in Wittenberg from 1523 to 1524 and published in Latin and German editions in 1527. Still wearing his Augustinian habit, Luther painted a remarkably traditional and socially conservative picture of Eve and her original positional relationship to her husband. In a crucial comment on the creation of Eve, Luther grounded woman's continuing subjection to man in Eve's subjection to her husband *prior to the fall.* Commenting on Genesis 2:24, Luther marveled at the mutuality that marked the first union of male and female. However, he noted one important limit: "'They,' therefore, 'will be one flesh,' that is, they will have one possession, one home, one family, field, conversation, education of sons, wealth, poverty, glory and all things in common, whatever pertains to life in the flesh, except that the husband ought to rule [*dominare debet*] in the wife."[14] On the younger Luther's reading, a familial hierarchy was intended from the beginning. He also found symbolic meaning in Eve's "birth" out of her husband's side; her literal derivation from Adam's substance stood as a sign not only of their mutuality and likeness, but also of her subordination to his *rule.*[15] For this reason, he claimed, the "woman" took her original name from the "man" (that is, Isha from Ish), just as German women in his own day took their

13. Mattox, *"Defender,"* chapters 1–2.
14. WA 24:79.
15. WA 24:80. Cf. WA 9:332.

names from their husbands. Women are literally *identified* by the men to whom they are related, and this reflects the divinely intended order of human life.

Thus, it is not surprising to find that in Luther's exegesis of Genesis 3 he also faulted the first woman, "talkative and superstitious," for speaking with the serpent in the first place. 1 Timothy 2:14 suggested to the younger Luther (probably based on what he had learned from Augustine) that Eve was liable to deception in a way that her husband was not. He imagined her as a woman "simple," "weak," and "little,"[16] who had no business engaging in a "disputation" that from the outset was over her head; instead, she ought to have referred the devil's questions to the man, her superior.[17] Following the lead of many in the antecedent Christian exegetical tradition, he also found in Eve's "neither shall we touch it" proof positive that she was a poor student of the Word of God, adding to it when she should instead have simply relied upon it. Luther did not shrink, moreover, from drawing out the wider implications of Eve's failure when faced with temptation, noting that women in general are known for being superstitious and prideful. In short, he half universalized Eve's failings, and applied them not to humankind in general, but to females alone.[18]

The younger Luther also connected Eve's failing in this case to her subjection to her husband's ecclesial authority. Addressing one of the stock exegetical questions related to this passage, he asserted that Eve had not heard the "divine command" (*mandatum divinum;* that is, the command concerning the tree of the knowledge of good and evil) directly, but was instead intended to learn it from her husband, to whom it had first been spoken by God. The Word of God, to which the woman was to be subordinate, was a Word she was to hear from her husband. The duty of preaching, in other words, was assigned to Adam alone, meaning that Eve was subordinated to her husband in their "church" as well as their home. Her fall thus involved for the young Luther, as it had for generations of exegetes, an element of subversion of divinely established order. She rebelled

16. WA 24:83-84.

17. WA 9:334.

18. Robert Bast finds something similar in his analysis of Luther's "Decem Praecepta," 1516-17 (WA 1:398-521). See Bast's *Honor Your Fathers: Catechisms and the Emergence of a Patriarchal Ideology in Germany, 1400-1600* (Leiden, New York, and Cologne: Brill, 1997), 78-92.

not only against God, but also against her husband and his divinely established authority over her.

In his examination of the internal mental and spiritual process by which Eve fell into sin, however, Luther emphasized not her differences from Adam, but their similarities. This was determined in large part by his distinctive convictions about the centrality and universality of the problem of faith and unbelief. As one might expect, the dynamic of faith and unbelief functioned throughout Luther's reforming career to inform his interpretation of the Bible.[19] As he noted in the preface to the Latin edition of his writings published in Wittenberg in 1545, he "ran through the Scriptures" to confirm and buttress his insight that God justifies sinners by means of the righteousness of faith.[20] This insight simply had to apply to every person equally, meaning that women and men went through the same internal process when dealing with temptation or coming to faith. The *equality* of every human person (in terms of the universal experiences of sin and grace, confession and absolution, the fall into unbelief and the restoration to faith) pushed Luther's exegesis in a direction that contradicted the harsh judgment on Eve he had just pronounced. Thus, the younger Luther also found in Eve a type of every Christian, female *and* male, and he made her temptation and fall archetypal not only for women, but also for men, even going so far as to compare Eve's fall from faith to that of the apostle Peter.[21] Adam therefore fell not, as Augustine had suggested, out of "excessive affection" for his wife, but simply because he, too, gave in to temptation and became an unbeliever. Likewise, when Eve and her husband heard the enigmatic promise of a coming redeemer who would crush the serpent's head (Gen. 3:15), they were united in a common faith.

Nevertheless, the younger Luther also confirmed his reading of Eve's original subordination by appeal to the notion of "headship" found in

19. Cf. Luther's own remarks in WA 24:15: "Aber das ist war, Moses schreibet neben den gesetzen schoene Exempel des glaubens und unglaubens. . . . Das Exempel aber yhres glaubens gehet mich an, das ich Christo auch, wie sie, gleube."

20. This is Luther's self-description of the zeal with which he returned to the Scriptures following his "evangelical breakthrough." See the "Preface to the Complete Edition of Luther's Latin Writings, 1545," WA 54:186; LW 34:337.

21. For this, see Luther's comments in the so-called "Scholia" on Genesis, WA 9:335: "Mox enim, ut vacillamus, ut mutamur in fide, succumbimus, cadimus quemadmodum et Petrus in mari." The reference is to Matt. 14.

1 Corinthians 11. He also connected the further subjection imposed on her in Genesis 3 — "and he shall rule over you" — to the establishment of the civil estate.[22] Although in the *Declamationes* he did not explore this connection in any detail, he did make clear that this text should not be read as if Adam had not ruled over the woman from the beginning. Instead, he claimed that Adam, who had previously ruled only within his own home, was given a new responsibility for ruling over the wider human community in all matters pertaining to their common life. The civil estate therefore appeared only as a consequence of the fall into sin, and the woman was excluded *ab origine* from ruling either within the home or beyond it.

Eve, in the Later Luther, and the "Three Estates"

In the later *Enarrationes* on Genesis, classroom lectures delivered between 1535 and 1545,[23] Luther's interpretation of Eve was structurally almost identical to that of the *Declamationes.* The divinely created structures of church, home, and (later) the civil estate still framed human existence as established by God. The fall still denoted most fundamentally a movement from faith to unbelief, and in this regard there is no difference between male and female. However, the elder Luther — a married man who had fathered six children — offered a strikingly altered and imaginative portrayal of Eve, making her a great saint, a woman whose heroic faithfulness merited attention and emulation. Rather than weak, superstitious, and talkative, she is now a "heroic woman" *(mulier heroica)* who engaged in conversation with the serpent because she recognized it instantly as one of the creatures over which she had been set, as a "partner in the rule" *(socia gubernationis)* with her husband, as ruler and keeper. She was, moreover, an excellent philosopher, "in no part, that is, neither in body nor in soul . . . inferior to her husband Adam."[24]

22. WA 24:102: "Tradita est his verbis homini potestas regendi non solum mulierem, sed etiam praeter eam omnia quae ad hanc vitam pertinent. Apostolus 1. Corinth. 11. virum vocat caput mulieris, item imaginem et gloriam Dei, id est praesidentem et regentem omnia humana etc. Atque hic vides ordinationem potestatis secularis a Deo esse, cui obedire vult Deus."

23. For the integrity of the *Enarrationes* as a source for the thought of the elder Luther, see appendix 1 in Mattox, *"Defender,"* 259-75.

24. WA 42:138; LW 1:185. Cf. WA 42:87; LW 1:115.

Of equal importance, she was not originally subordinated to Adam's *rule* within their home; instead, her subjection resulted from their fall into sin. Indeed, for the elder Luther, the unfallen Eve was subordinated to her husband only insofar as the office of preaching had been entrusted to him alone in the giving of the *mandatum divinum.* This tree "was *Adam's* church, altar, and pulpit."[25] Eve's subordination to the preached Word seems to have followed as a consequence of the temporal order of human creation; because Adam was created first, only he heard the original divine "sermon," and, as the older Luther imagined things, only he was charged with the duty of proclaiming it to his posterity. Thus, Eve's subordination to the Word of God preached by her husband came to symbolize not her original subjection to her husband's rule, but the subordination of Adam's posterity generally (including, naturally, his male heirs) to the Word of God. Eve prefigures the church's subjection in faith to the saving Word of Christ, both symbolically and literally.

Nevertheless, the elder Luther also clearly labeled Eve as in some other way her husband's "inferior." Jane Dempsey Douglass has argued that tensions such as this in Luther's exegesis show that he was divided between progressive ideas that lead in the direction of a full theory of original equality between the sexes and more traditional notions of an original hierarchy in which males had the upper hand.[26] Plausible as this argument may seem, it is probably better to think of Luther as holding these tensions together in his own mind, in such a way that it is possible — and not necessarily contradictory — for him to say that Eve both was and was not her husband's inferior. The conceptual framework within which Eve's alternating equality and inferiority were set is the so-called doctrine of the "three estates." Taking stock of this doctrine makes it possible to distinguish, just as Luther himself seems to have done, between ways in which Eve could have been her husband's equal, and ways in which she was his inferior. In addition, this doctrine helps make clear the distinction Luther made between the rule over the creation exercised by humankind before the fall and the coercive rule of one human being over another as made necessary by the fall.

In the *Enarrationes* and elsewhere, Luther applied and developed the traditional notion that God had structured human life by means of a series of created "orders" *(ordines).* Since he often spoke of three orders — eccle-

25. WA 42:72.20-21; LW 1:95, emphasis mine.

26. See her essay, "The Image of God in Women," 236-66.

siastical, domestic, and civil — the German term *Dreiständelehre* ("doctrine of the three estates") functions as the classical shorthand for this teaching. As Wilhelm Maurer explains, careful attention to the otherwise bewildering variety of terms Luther chose to express this concept goes a good distance toward explaining what he meant. Instead of the Latin *ordo,* he referred at times to "institutions" *(Stiffte),* to "hierarchies" *(Hierarchiae),* or, sometimes, to "estates" *(Stände).*[27] The notion of "order" or "estate" implied a created sphere of human and divine relations within which one could delineate a concrete set of benefits and/or mutual obligations. The *ordo* of the church, for example, denoted the divine-human relationship, within which humankind received — *gratis* — the blessings of life and discovered the duties of worship and obedience. Luther's talk of "hierarchies" was not intended in the Platonic sense of an ascent toward God, but denoted instead three different sets of relationships that overlapped one another like a series of concentric circles. Not surprisingly (given Luther's own vocation), the "ecclesiastical estate" took on a certain priority, as it encloses both the civil and the domestic estates, orienting humankind not only toward earthly relations and obligations, but also toward heavenly ones. Within the context of a fallen humanity, moreover, the notion of "hierarchies" functioned to draw attention to the three concrete arenas within which God preserves the world, inviting believers to participate in God's ongoing battle against the devil.

In the *Enarrationes,* Luther made clear to his students that the original creation included only two of these orders: the ecclesial *(sacerdotium, Priesteramt)* and the domestic *(oeconomia, domus, Ehestand).*[28] The civil

27. For the *Dreiständelehre,* see Wilhelm Maurer's *Luthers Lehre von den drei Hierarchien und ihr mittelalterlicher Hintergrund* (Munich: Bayerischen Akademie der Wissenschaften, 1970). According to Maurer (5), Luther prefers the terms *Stift* and *ordo,* but in the late 1530s turns increasingly to *hierarchien.* Although there is an element of anachronism in the term *Dreiständelehre,* Reinhard Schwarz observes that it can scarcely be avoided, even if it must be explained historically and factually. See his "Luthers Lehre von den drei Stände und die drei Dimensionen der Ethik," *Lutherjahrbuch* 45 (1978): 15-34, here 18. For some of the problems associated with the term, see Carl Braaten, "God in Public Life: Rehabilitating the 'Orders of Creation,'" *First Things* 8 (December 1990): 32-38; Edward Schroeder, "The Orders of Creation: Some Reflections on the History and Place of the Term in Systematic Theology," *Concordia Theological Monthly* 43 (1972): 165-78.

28. For Luther's exegetical reflections, see the *Enarrationes in Genesin,* WA 42:79; LW 1:104. Cf. his *Enarratio capitis noni Esaiae,* WA 40III:646.17-21.

estate *(politia, civitas, weltliche Obrigkeit)* is also an order, but in the state of original innocence as the elder Luther imagined it, civil government, that is, the rule of one human being over another, was simply unnecessary.[29] Underscoring the ad hoc character of this third order in characteristically hyperbolic language, he could even speak of the civil estate as a "kingdom of sin" *(regnum peccati)*.[30] Certainly, he did not intend in any way to undermine the civil estate's divinely given authority. Instead, he meant only to say that the divine ordinance that created and established it was given with a view to humankind's fallenness. As is clear from even a cursory reading of Luther's explanation of the fourth commandment in the Large Catechism, moreover, the civil estate's authority to rule *(potestas)* is distinctively paternal. Indeed, as Maurer notes, Luther grounded each of the orders in the *Vateramt,* which itself mirrors and expresses the fatherhood of God.

The paternal quality of authority in each of the estates does not necessarily mean, however, that the exercise of authority was intended to be an exclusively male prerogative. To the contrary, as *socia gubernationis,* Eve before her fall also exercised paternal authority over the creation. Indeed, the elder Luther defended the Vulgate's translation of Isha with "virago," explaining that Eve was created to be a "she-man," that is, a "heroic woman who acts in a manly way."[31] The provisional quality of the civil estate thus relates closely to Luther's understanding of Eve's positional relation to her husband before and after the fall. Since the civil estate's *potestas* is itself a consequence of the fall, it had no place in an unfallen world, certainly not in the relations between "manly" Eve and her husband.

The "inferiority" Luther ascribed to the woman he elsewhere described as "in no part" inferior therefore cannot mean that she was subor-

29. WA 42:79, "Moreover, there was no state [*politia*] before sin, for there was no need of it." (LW 1:104.)

30. WA 42:79.

31. WA 42:103, on Gen. 2:23. "Nos Ebraicae linguae elegantiam neutiquam possumus imitari. *Isch* significat virum: Hevam autem dicit vocandam *Ischa,* perinde ac si dicas a Vir Vira, quod sit uxor, heroica Mulier, quae virilia gerit." Cf. the discussion in Nicholas of Lyra, *Biblia latina, cum postillis Nicolai de Lyra et expositionibus Guillelmi Britonis in omnes prologos S. Hieronymi et additionibus Pauli Burgensis replicisque Matthiae Doering* (Nuremberg: Anton Koburger, 1487), comment *n* on Gen. 2:23, p. 32^{v}. See also the discussion in Jerome, *Hebraicae Quaestiones in Libro Geneseos,* Corpus Christianorum, Series Latina, vol. 72 (Turnhout: Brepols, 1953), 5.

dinated to his rule. Thus, the "heroic" Eve must have been somehow qualitatively or quantitatively "less" than her husband. But how? Eve was a "most excellent creature" *(praestantissima creatura),* Luther told his students; "nevertheless she was a woman." In addition, he observed, she "seems to be a somewhat different creature from the man, in that she has both *different members* and a *much weaker constitution.*"[32] Eve, as the elder Luther imagined her, thus had a certain constitutional inferiority to Adam — apparently in the sense that he was physically stronger — but she was not his inferior in terms of her partnership in the rule over the creation. In short, the unfallen Eve was both her husband's equal partner and his inferior. She was subordinated not to his "rule," but only to the Word of God he had preached to her. She was physically inferior, but this did not preclude her full partnership in the rule over the creation.

What is the significance of Luther's understanding of Eve for his position on the place and role of women in the church? Clearly, he did not think of Eve as a partner in her husband's duty to proclaim the Word of God. Moreover, given the divine imposition of the civil estate, beginning with Adam's rule over Eve, there is little room in Luther's social ethic for the full participation of women in the rule of the civil state. The consequence would seem to be that Luther would expect from faithful Christian women only silence and submission in church, home, and society.

It comes as something of a surprise, then, to read the remainder of Luther's exegesis of Eve's story, particularly his exposition of her final two reported utterances, first at the birth of Cain (Gen. 4:1), and later that of Seth (Gen. 4:25). Exiled from the garden but filled with faith in the promised "Seed" who would crush the serpent's head, Eve proclaimed, "I have gotten a man from the Lord," fully in expectation that she had already brought forth the promised Redeemer. Brokenhearted later at Cain's shameful fratricide, Luther explained, Eve remained "a most holy woman, full of faith and love" *(sanctissima mulier, plena fidei et charitatis).* Reading once again between the compact lines of her story with a distinctively theological imagination, Luther examined her seemingly matter-of-fact observation that "God has appointed for me another seed in place of Abel, whom Cain killed." In this "sort of little sermon," Eve heroically confessed her faith and proved herself a skilled theologian, joining her husband in excommunicating Cain. "Full of faith, love, and endless crosses," she rec-

32. WA 42:51; LW 1:69.

ognized that the ways of God sometimes contradicted "the wisdom of the flesh" and she saw that the promise of redemption would proceed not through their firstborn, but through Seth.[33] The heroic faith and Spirit-given wisdom evident in Eve's sermons mean for Luther that she should be remembered and numbered among the great biblical saints.

Women in the Household Church

In spite of his conviction that women have been excluded from preaching and from ruling in the church, home, or state, then, Luther nevertheless credited Christian women with a capacity for the active and even heroic confession of the faith.[34] Confined by their station in life to the estate of the home, they nevertheless witnessed to the faith within the household church of the Old Testament, both by their deeds and by their words. This conception of female Christian faithfulness also informed the elder Luther's further exegesis of the stories of Genesis. Lecturing to classrooms filled with the young men who would soon constitute the learned Lutheran ministry, he repeatedly lifted up the example of this or that faithful woman, simultaneously schooling his students in the pastoral discernment of the workings of law and gospel in the lives of the faithful and suggesting the kind of Christian heroism they might hope for in their own lives, and from their own wives and female parishioners.

This included the expectation that women would sometimes correct or instruct their husbands or pastors. Interpreting Genesis 21, for instance, he insisted that Saint Sarah asked her husband Abraham to expel the servant Hagar and her son Ishmael from their household not because she was jealous or prideful, but because she had more carefully reflected on the divine promise of redemption. Abraham should have remembered that redemption was to come not through his firstborn, Ishmael, but from Isaac, Sarah's boy, born according to the promise of God. The promise was the

33. WA 42:238-40; LW 1:324-26.

34. I intend "confession" here in the sense of giving living witness to the faith in the present and, therefore, not a mere recitation of the church's faith. On this issue, see Robert Kolb, *Confessing the Faith: Reformers Define the Church, 1530-1580* (St. Louis: Concordia, 1991). For further work on a biblical woman's heroic confession in Luther's Genesis exegesis, see my "*Defender*," chapter 6.

same; it applied equally to Sarah and Abraham and, as the elder Luther's interpretation of Eve had already shown, they had an equal capacity to believe it. Abraham, however, had not considered it carefully enough, perhaps because of his affection for Hagar and Ishmael. Thus, Abraham benefited from his wife's intervention, and, as Luther reads the story, her doing so in no way violated her subjection to his rule.[35] The implication was that Christian men, including young Lutheran pastors, could expect to learn Christian wisdom from their wives as their equals, and sometimes their superiors, in faith.

Luther's interpretation of this story also has strong Mariological undertones, a factor one must account for in any evaluation of the question of Luther on women and the church. Luther found in the stories of both Sarah and Hagar, for example, proleptic echoes of the story of Mary, labeling them "mothers of the church."[36] Moreover, the promise of redemption ultimately fulfilled through Mary's Son imparted to motherhood generally a kind of reflected glory, for the expectation of the coming "Seed of the Woman" meant that the devil stood in fear of every expectant woman. Eve and all the women of the patriarchal households greatly desired the "good of offspring," moreover, because they knew it was through this "work" that the devil would ultimately be overthrown. The Mariological, ecclesiological, and christological aspects of Luther's interpretation of these women imparted no small element of heroism to their stories. He recognized, moreover, that in literally going to the point of death in order to bring forth life, women somehow imaged and pointed to the coming Savior. To be sure, in itself this was little more than a reaffirmation of the Pauline assertion that women shall be saved through childbearing (1 Tim. 2:15), a text that had long been understood Mariologically. Moreover, there was a difference between the times. Not everything said of the patriarchs' wives and their place in the church could be said of Christian women generally in Luther's day. Obviously, they could not hope to bring forth the Savior. Nevertheless, they could identify both with the heroic and at times outspoken matriarchs and also with Christ himself in their own motherly work.

The example of Luther's reading of Sarah's story also reminds us of the kinds of changes the Reformation would effect in the lives of women: not a movement into the leadership of church and society, but one di-

35. WA 43:149-52; LW 4:20-24.

36. For this, see Mattox, "*Defender,*" chapters 3–4.

rected toward the further development of the Christian home. Women who might otherwise have been nuns or clerical concubines or even prostitutes became instead honorable Protestant housewives, supporting and sharing in their husbands' vocations, establishing what historians have labeled the Protestant "household workshop." The Protestant parsonage, the pastor's own household community of faith as Luther idealized it in the classroom and lived it with Katharina, would provide the model for the Protestant Christian home more generally. For the parsonage itself, Luther found fit examples aplenty in the stories of the Old Testament patriarchs and their wives.

Historians have frequently observed that in moving from convent and even from the public brothel to the Protestant household, women lost a measure of the freedom they had previously enjoyed. Both the convent and the brothel were to a certain extent arenas of female independence from male domination.[37] Some abbesses, for example, exercised considerable authority within and even outside their communities. From a modern perspective, the question whether the Reformation was "good" for women depends on whether one sees the domestication of women within the Protestant household as an improvement over their arguably more independent status beforehand. From Luther's perspective, however, prostitution was a social evil that should be prohibited, and the convent offered a false way of salvation through "self-chosen works." There could therefore be no real question about whether women's movement into the Protestant household was good or bad. Instead, it was a movement back toward what God had commanded and established, a reintegration into the concrete and divinely appointed sphere within which Christian men and women were called to live faithfully.

Women's "Preaching": Public or Private?

There were further instances of female speech in Genesis that impressed Luther enough for him to call attention to a woman's "preaching." Lowly Hagar, once a runaway and later an exile, is probably the most impressive example from the *Enarrationes.* As Luther told her story, she was trans-

37. For these issues, see the studies cited above, particularly Ozment, *When Fathers Ruled.*

formed by an unexpected confrontation (which Luther reads as an instance of confession and absolution) with the "angel of the Lord" by a spring in the wilderness. Afterward, she obediently returns to Abraham's household (Gen. 16), where "she acknowledges the mercy of God, preaches and calls upon God by a new name, in order to make known the benefit through which He had declared himself to her."[38] Indeed, Luther reads Hagar as a "mother of the church," the matriarch of a great Christian nation (the Hagarites), and he surmises that Ishmael, too, became a faithful preacher of the gospel. Clearly, however, Luther did not imagine Hagar or any other woman preaching and presiding over the sacraments in a Christian congregation at worship. Nor did he expect Christian women in his own day to follow Hagar's example by giving public witness to their faith. Or did he? Did he not imagine Hagar preaching the gospel to the gathered assembly of Abraham's household (who would presumably have confronted her on her return), including the patriarch himself?

Elsewhere, Luther had clearly acknowledged the legitimacy of a woman's preaching in some form of public assembly, particularly within female communities like that of the Christian convent where men were not allowed.[39] He also recognized that the question of women's preaching could be raised on the basis of his doctrine of the common priesthood, and even admitted its necessity when no suitable man could be found for the task.[40] "If the Lord were to raise up a woman for us to listen to," he once said, "we would allow her to rule like Huldah."[41] Remarks like these reflect Luther's conviction that no merely human reality, even the total lack

38. WA 42:598: "Nec id solum, sed agnoscit Dei misericordiam, praedicat et invocat Deum novo nomine ad celebrandum beneficium eius, quo se erga ipsam declaraverat." Cf. LW 3:69, which translates *praedicat* with "she praises."

39. *Epistel S. Petri gepredigt und ausgelegt* (1523), WA 12:308: "Darumb sind sie alle zu mal priester, muegen Gottis wort verkundigen, on das weyber nicht ynn der gemeyn reden sollen, sondern die menner predigen lassen, umb des gepotts willen, das sie yhren mennern sollen unterthan seyn, wie S. Paulus leret 1. Cor:14. Solch ordnung lesset Gott bleyben, macht aber nicht unterscheyd des gewallts. Wo aber nicht menner da weren, sondern eyttel weyber, als ynn nonnen kloestern, da moecht man auch eyn weyb unter yhn auff werffen, das da predigte." Cf. WA 8:498: "Wenn aber keyn man predigest, ßo werß von nöten, das die weyber predigten."

40. Cf. WA 7:166. For further examples, see Maron, "Vom Hindernis zur Hilfe," 280-81.

41. WA 26:48-49; LW 28:280. Cf. WA 8:251; LW 39:234.

of faithful male Christians to proclaim the Word, can finally stand in the way of the gospel. However, on the basis of 1 Corinthians 14 he also made it clear that women should be silent in church itself. In any case, he thought it clear that women were naturally unsuited for public speaking, typically arguing that the voice of a man was more appropriately fitted for the task.[42] In his comments on 1 Timothy (1527-28), he could even go so far as to say, in contrast to what he later taught in the classroom, that Adam was wiser than Eve and therefore intellectually better fitted for the task of preaching.[43] In sum, Luther's explicit answers to the question of women's preaching were grounded in his perception of women's natural fittedness for the task, as well as a reading of 1 Corinthians 14 as a divine positive law that simply forbade the practice without necessarily explaining why.

Nevertheless, when speaking of the duties of Christian parents in the context of a rather exuberant early explanation of his doctrine of the common priesthood, he insisted: "Most certainly father and mother are apostles, bishops, and priests to their children, for it is they who make them acquainted with the gospel."[44] Not surprisingly, then, in the *Enarrationes* on Genesis he pictured Saint Eve faithfully instructing her children in law and gospel based on her participation in the common priesthood.[45] This example is no less problematic, however, than that of Hagar. Did Luther think of Eve as teaching her children only on weekdays and not on the Sabbath? Only at "home" and not in their "church"? If the entire human family consisted of Adam and Eve and their few offspring, what difference could there be between the church as gathered community and the church as an extended family gathered at home?

Conclusion

Lingering questions such as these show why Luther will continue to inspire both those who oppose and those who support the full participation of

42. See, for example, WA 8:497.

43. WA 26:48-49; LW 28:280. Compare Douglass, "The Image of God," 249.

44. WA 10II:301: "Denn gewißlich ist vater und mutter der kinder Apostel, Bisschoff, pfarrer, ynn dem sie das Euangelion yhn kundt machen."

45. On this particular episode, see Ulrich Asendorf, *Lectura in Biblia: Luthers Genesisvorlesung (1535-1545)* (Göttingen: Vandenhoeck & Ruprecht, 1998), 323.

women in the ministries of the church. The issue of women's roles continues to divide the church. For example, the churches united in the Lutheran World Federation (LWF) are also internally divided over this issue of "church order," such that Federation statements that address the questions have to be crafted with considerable care in order to avoid causing offense.[46] There is little sign, moreover, that this issue will be resolved soon, in spite of the determination of the LWF itself to support the ordination of women. It is fair to say, then, that this remains an unresolved problem, one with which Lutherans on all sides of the issue ought to be concerned.

Luther himself did not support the ordination of women to the public ministry, and this is one of those stubborn historical facts one must simply accept. Despite Maron and Wolf, Luther did think the ordination of women to the pastoral ministry was a contradiction of divine law, namely, that given in 1 Corinthians 14. The divine origins of each of the three estates, moreover, left little room for a Christian movement for the emancipation of women, even if the elder Luther came to think of Eve's subjection to her husband's rule as a divinely imposed consequence of the fall and not as a reflection of what God had intended.

However, in terms of the systematic development of a version of Christian thought that could reasonably be construed as faithfully Lutheran, he clearly left the door open. He found in women heroic examples of faith and faithfulness, and discerned in their stories christological and Mariological resonances that rendered their deeds and words worthy of careful reflection. Moreover, he modeled just this kind of reflection in his own biblical exegesis, attending carefully to women's "sermons" and encouraging his followers to do likewise. He pictured them giving authentic witness to the faith in what were arguably public assemblies of the faithful (the church), and he seems equally to have imagined their menfolk giving heed to their word. From a modern perspective, of course, Luther's readings of the women of Genesis will strike many as fanciful, even excessively Christianized.[47] The significance of these readings today, however, does

46. Note, for instance, the cautious wording in "The Episcopal Ministry within the Apostolicity of the Church" (Geneva: Lutheran World Federation, 2003), par. 16-17 (pp. 13-14).

47. This has long been the case. Note, for example, the critical remarks of Otto Zöckler on Luther's interpretation of Hagar in his *Luther als Ausleger des Alten Testaments* (Greifswald, 1884), 60.

not depend on how one judges Luther's exegetical method or practice, but on his exemplary willingness to give ear to the voices of faithful women in recognition of their important roles in the church and in salvation history as a whole.

CHAPTER 13

Luther on Music

Robin A. Leaver

Luther's comments on music are many and varied. One, however, he repeated at different times and in different contexts: "Music is next to theology."[1] His letter to composer Ludwig Senfl, dated 4 October 1530, contains his most extended statement:

> I plainly judge, and do not hesitate to affirm, that except for theology there is no art that could be put on the same level with music, since except for theology [music] alone produces what otherwise only theology can do, namely, a calm and joyful disposition. . . . This is the reason why the prophets did not make use of any art except music; when setting forth their theology they did it not as geometry, not as arithmetic, not as astronomy, but as music, so that they held theology and music most tightly connected, and proclaimed truth through Psalms and songs.[2]

1. WA TR, no. 968: "Die Musik ist . . . nahe der Theologie"; WA TR, no. 3815: "Musica est . . . theologiae proxima" (see *What Luther Says: An Anthology,* trans. and ed. Ewald M. Plass [St. Louis: Concordia, 1959], hereafter cited as WLS, no. 3090); WA TR, no. 7034: "Ich gebe nach der Theologia der Musica den nähesten *Locum* und höchste Ehre" [I place music next to theology and give it the highest praise]. WLS, no. 3091; WA 50:370, preface to Rhau's *Symphoniae iucundae* (1538): "Experientia testis est, Musicam esse unam, quae post verbum Dei merito celebeat . . ." [Experience confirms that next to the Word of God, music deserves the highest praise]. LW 53:323.

2. LW 49:427-28; WA Br 5:639: "Et plane iudico nec pudet asserere, post theologiam

It is this distinctive statement — "music is next to theology" — that distinguishes Luther from his predecessors, as well as from many of his contemporaries, and has therefore been continuously quoted and commented upon. But it is a dictum that should not be considered in isolation: in order to understand what Luther meant, it needs to be set against the context of medieval views concerning music, compared with his other comments about music, and examined with regard to the way in which music was incorporated into his theological thinking.[3]

A Proposed Treatise on Music

The doctrine of justification is central to Luther's theological thought, and yet when one examines his tremendous literary output, it is surprising to find that there is not one work devoted to a full-scale presentation of the doctrine.[4] From a comment he made in his open letter *On Translating* (1530), he did, however, plan to write one;[5] nevertheless, although there are a few notes and outlines for such a work, it was never written. Similarly, there is no fully worked-out treatise from his pen on the subject of music, only prefaces and letters, together with many scattered references throughout his voluminous writings. But, like the doctrine of justi-

---

esse nullam artem, quae musicae possit aequari, cum ipsa sola post theologiam id praestet, quod alioqui sola theologia praestat, scilicet quietem at animum laetum. . . . Hinc factum est, ut prophetae nulla sic arte sint usi ut musica, dum suam theologiam non in geometriam, non in arithmeticam, non in astronomiam, sed in musicam digesserunt, ut theologiam at musicam haberent coniunctissimas, veritatem psalmis et canticis dicentes." See also WA 50:371, preface to Rhau's *Symphoniae iucundae* (1538): "Unde non frustra Patres et Prophetae verbo Dei nihil voluerunt esse coniunctius quam Musicam" [the fathers and prophets wanted nothing else to be associated as closely with the Word of God as music]. LW 53:323.

3. These issues are explored in my book, *Luther's Liturgical Music: Principles and Implications* (Grand Rapids: Eerdmans, 2007). What follows here is a slightly revised form of a section from chapter 3, "Luther's Theological Understanding of Music," in which a primary document concerning Luther's understanding of music is discussed within the context of some of his other writings.

4. See Robin A. Leaver, *Luther on Justification* (St. Louis: Concordia, 1975), 9.

5. "If God gives me grace, I shall have more to say about it in the tract 'On Justification,'" LW 35:198; WA 30II:643: "Weiter wil ich (so Gott gnade gibt) davon reden ym buchlin de iustificatione." See WA 30II:657-76.

fication, he did propose to write a treatise on music, though again, apart from a draft also dating from the same year (1530), it was another unfulfilled intention.[6]

The draft is partially in Greek, Περι της Μουσικης *(Concerning Music),* in essence a summary of the primary headings of the proposed study that reflects some of the medieval thinking Luther inherited, as well as his own distinctive perspectives, statements that were echoed many times in his various writings. In content it has many parallels with his letter to the composer Ludwig Senfl of October 1530, cited above, which suggests that this draft outline was written around the same time:

> I love music.
> Its censure by fanatics does not please me
> For
> 1. [Music] is a gift of God and not of man
> 2. For it creates joyful hearts
> 3. For it drives away the devil
> 4. For it creates innocent delight, destroying wrath,
> unchastity, and pride.
> I place music next to theology.
> This is well known from the example of
> David and all the prophets, who all
> produced poetry and songs.
> 5. For [music] reigns in times of peace.
> It will be difficult to keep these delightful skills after us, for they are of peace. The Dukes of Bavaria are to be praised in this, that

6. It is interesting to note that the evidence for Luther's intention to write a treatise on justification and another on music dates from 1530. It therefore seems likely that both of these ideas germinated during the six months he was in Coburg castle, during the Diet of Augsburg. Being removed from his day-to-day pressures in Wittenberg gave him the opportunity to think and write. See Martin Brecht, *Martin Luther,* trans. James L. Schaaf (Philadelphia: Fortress, 1985-93), 1:379-84. In his correspondence between Coburg and Augsburg there was much preoccupation with the doctrine of justification — Luther was concerned that Melanchthon would concede too much. But he also wrote letters to Senfl and Johann Agricola in which music was the primary topic, including references to chant melodies that were important to him, as was the song of the birds; see Robin A. Leaver, "Luther as Musician," *Lutheran Quarterly* 18 (2004): 125-83, now (revised) chapter 2 of *Luther's Liturgical Music.*

they honor music. Among our Saxon [dukes] weapons and cannons are esteemed.[7]

The following then is in the form of a commentary on the points raised in Luther's outline of a treatise on music.

Introduction

Luther's opening statement, "I love music,"[8] underscores his personal attachment and commitment to music, not just in theory but also in practice. For Luther is not here expressing an intellectual appreciation of the structures and forms of music but rather an experiential response to music as performed and heard. Many medieval treatises on music were primarily concerned with theory; Luther's proposed treatise would by contrast stress

7. WA 30.II:696:

Περι της Μουσικης
μουσικην εραω
Eciam damnantes non placent Schwermerii
Quia
1. Dei donum non hominum est
2. Quia facit letos animos
3. Quia fugat diabolum
4. Quia innocens gaudium facit irae
Interim pereunt libidines
Superbia
Proximum locum do
Musicae post Theologiam.
Hoc patet ex examplo David et omnium prophetarum,
qui[a] omnia sua metris at cantibus mandaverunt.
5. Quia pacis tempore regnat.

Durate ergo et erit melius arti huic post nos, Quia pacis sunt. Duces Bavariae laudo in hoc, quia Musicam colunt. Apud nos Saxones arma et Bombardae praedicantur.

For a German version, see WA TR, no. 7034 (= WA 30II:695), translated in Walter Buszin, "Luther and Music," *Musical Quarterly* 32 (1946): 88.

8. See also WA TR, no. 6248 (uncertain date): "Musicam semper amavi"; "Music I have always loved," WLS, no. 3092.

the fundamental practice of music.[9] In the same way that Luther discovered the doctrine of justification after an intensely personal struggle, by asking the biblical question, "What must I do to be saved?" and receiving the answer, "Believe on the Lord Jesus Christ" (see Acts 16:30-31), so Luther's theological understanding of music began with his personal involvement in and attachment to music. The doctrine of justification and music both can — and must — be objectively defined, but both are subjective in their effects. A purely intellectual appreciation of the doctrine — which Luther consistently dismissed as "historic faith" — is not enough; justifying faith is both practical and personal: "Oh, it is a living, busy, active, mighty thing, this faith. . . . Faith is a living, daring confidence in God's grace, so sure and so certain that the believer would stake his life on it a thousand times."[10] Similarly, an intellectual appreciation of music, its forms and structures as expressed in written notation on the page, is insufficient, for it cannot be experienced as music until its vibrations have excited the air and entered the outer ear. But even that is not enough, for the outward sound needs to be perceived within and move the inner heart:

> But to chant *(cantare)* means to praise with the mouth only, to jubilate *(iubilare)* is to do it in the heart, etc. [on Ps. 68:25].[11]

> Wherever the word "song" *(canticum)* is used in psalm titles, it must always be understood that such a psalm is one of joy and dancing and is to be sung with a feeling of rejoicing. For a song and singing spring from the fullness of a rejoicing heart. But a spiritual song, or spiritual melody, is the very jubilation of the heart [on Ps. 45].[12]

9. See the discussion in the Leaver article (cited in n. 6 above) dealing with the similar shift in emphasis in the teaching of music among the teachers and alumni of Wittenberg University.

10. LW 35:370, Preface to Romans, 1522, WA DB 7: "O es ist eyn lebendig, schefftig, thettig, mechtig ding umb den glawben . . . Glawb ist eyn lebendige erwegene zuuersicht auff Gottes gnade, so gewis, das er tausent mal druber sturbe."

11. LW 10:344; *Dictata super Psalterium* (1513-16); WA 3:405: "Cantare autem est ore tantum laudare, iubilare corde &c."

12. LW 10:208; WA 3:253: "Ubicunque 'Canticum' in titulis habetur, semper debet intelligi, talem psalmum esse gaudii et tripudii et cum affectu exultandi cantandum. Nam Canticum et cantus ex abundantia gaudentis cordis oritur. Est autem Canticum spirituale seu melodia spiritualis ipse iubilus cordis."

> Some people confess with their lips only. They are the ones who say one thing in the heart and another with the mouth, like the sinner who has evil intentions and sings to God nevertheless [on Ps. 9:1].[13]

> Note that there is a difference between singing and saying, as there is between chanting or saying a psalm and only knowing and teaching with the understanding. But by adding the voice it becomes a song, and the voice is the feeling. Therefore, as the word is the understanding, so the [singing] voice is its feeling [on Ps. 101:8].[14]

Luther can even make the extravagant correlation that if faith is real it will involve music, and the believer must needs sing. He therefore employs the same kind of language he used to describe justifying faith in his preface to the Epistle to the Romans (cited above) and applied it to the music of faith: "For faith does not rest and declare a holiday; it bursts into action, speaks and preaches of this promise and grace of God, so that other people may also come up and partake of it. Yes, his great delight impels him [David] to compose beautiful and sweet psalms and to sing lovely and joyous songs, both to praise and to thank God in his happiness and to serve his fellowmen by stimulating and teaching them."[15] Similarly, in his preface to the Bapst *Gesangbuch* of 1545, he wrote: "For God has cheered our hearts and minds through his dear Son, whom he gave for us to redeem us from sin, death, and the devil. He who believes this earnestly cannot be quiet about it. But he must gladly and willingly sing and speak about it so that others also may come and hear it. And whoever does not want to sing and speak of it shows that he does not believe and that he does

13. LW 10:92; WA 3:89: "Aliqui confitentur in labiis tantum. Hii sunt, qui aliud in corde, aliud in ore loquuntur, ut qui peccator est in proposito malo, psallens nihilominus deo."

14. LW 11:294; WA 4:139: "Nota, quod cantare et dicere differunt, quod psallere vel psalmum dicere et tantummodo intellectu agnoscere et docere. Sed vocem addendo fit cantus, que vox est affectus. Sicut ergo verbum est intellectus, sic vox ipsius affectus."

15. LW 15:273, *Treatise on the Last Words of David,* 1543 (WA 54:33): "Denn der glaub ruget und feiret nicht, Er feret heraus, redet und prediget von solcher verheissung und gnade Gottes, das ander Leute auch dazu komen, und der telhafftig werden, Ja fur grosser freude fehet er an, tichtet schöne susse Psalmen, singet liebliche lustige Lieder, damit zu gleich Gotte frölich zu loben und zu dancken, Und auch die menschen nützlich zu reitzen und zu lernen."

not belong under the new and joyful testament, but under the old, lazy, and tedious testament."[16]

Luther's love for music, therefore, is undergirded by theology, and his second premise in his draft outline of a treatise on music is the logical consequence of the first: "[Music's] censure by fanatics does not please me." Here a polarity of opposites is established: "I love music; fanatics hate it." The reason for Luther's displeasure is that for such *Schwärmerei* (enthusiasts) music is inherently biased toward evil, and must therefore be kept within strict limits. But nothing could be further from Luther's mind. If music is the creation and gift of God, then it should be cherished rather than despised, and Luther could not bring himself to undervalue such a precious gift. He already had to deal with Karlstadt, who had expounded a negative attitude toward music in Wittenberg with his *De cantu Gregoriano disputatio (Disputation on Gregorian Chant)* of 1521.[17] Thus when Johann Walter's set of part-books, known as the *Chorgesangbuch,* was published in 1524, Luther provided a preface in which he took aim against such negative views of music. He knew that music could be misused[18] and put to base ends, but would not concede that music itself was the problem — how could it be, if it is the gift from God? "These songs were arranged in four [to five] parts to give the young — who should at any rate be trained in music and other fine arts — something to wean them from love ballads and carnal songs and to teach them something of value in their place, thus combining the good with the pleasing, as is proper for youth. Nor am I of the opinion that the Gospel should destroy and blight all the arts, as some of the pseudo-religious claim."[19]

16. LW 53:333. WA 35:477: "Denn Gott hat unser hertz und mut frölich gemacht, durch seinen lieben Son, welchen er für uns gegeben hat zur erlösung von sunden, tod und Teuffel. Wer solchs mit ernst gleubet, der kans nicht lassen, er mus frölich und mit lust davon singen und sagen, das es andere auch hören und herzu komen. Wer aber nicht davon singen und sagen wil, das ist ein zeichen, das ers nicht gleubet und nicht ins new fröliche Testament, Sondern unter das alte, faule, unlustige Testament gehöret."

17. See the material cited in n. 6 above.

18. Luther's approach to the use and abuse of music is discussed at some length in Leaver, *Luther's Liturgical Music,* chapter 1.

19. LW 53:316. WA 35:474-75: "Und sind dazu auch ynn vier stymme bracht, nicht aus anderer ursach, denn das ich gerne wollte, die iugent, die doch sonst soll und mus ynn der Musica und andern rechten künsten ersogen werden, ettwas hette, damit sie der bul lieder und fleyschlichen gesenge los werde und an derselben stat ettwas heylsames lernete,

1. Music Is a Gift of God

Having stated his positive against the negative of the "pseudo-religious" enthusiasts, Luther then enumerates a sequence of statements concerning music, several of which sound very similar to the aphorisms of Johannes Tinctoris, or the poetic expressions of Jean Gerson.[20] Luther begins, however, with a categorical statement that is not found in either of the earlier writers, a statement that conditions the meaning of those that follow: "1. [Music] is a gift of God and not of man." Here again is the repeated antiphon of Luther's thinking about music. Variant forms of the statement can be found scattered throughout his writings, but here in this outline of the proposed treatise on music it takes on a special significance: its context underscores its content. Here it is not just a pithy saying that can be found elsewhere in Luther's literary output, it is the foundation stone on which his views of music are based. It is because music comes from God as a gift that it has dimensions of meaning, power, and effectiveness that far exceed any human art or science. Music is not an *inventio,* a work of humankind, but a *creatura,*[21] a work of God. Again there are parallels here with the doctrine of justification. In the same way as justification is God's gift of grace rather than the reward for human effort, so music is in essence God's gift of creation rather than a human achievement. Oskar Söhngen rightly points out that Luther's personification of music as "Frau Musica" in his vernacular poem is no mere allegory but rather the expression of the ontological reality that from the beginning of the world music has been an essential element within God's creation, and it — "she" — continues to inspire and influ-

---

und also das guete mit lust, wie den iungen gepürt, eyngienge. Auch das ich nicht der meynung byn, das durchs Evangelion sollten alle künste zu boden geschlagen werden und vergehen, wie etliche abergeystlichen fur geben."

20. Johannes Tinctoris (1435-1511) was a music theorist whose writings were widely studied in the late-medieval period; he wrote *Complexus viginti effectuum nobilis artis musices,* which includes twenty aphorisms on the use of music with commentary. The French theologian Jean Gerson (1363-1429) made a significant impact on Luther especially during his early theological studies, but the Reformer continued to refer to Gerson throughout his life. Gerson was also the author of a significant number of treatises on music, as well as a poem in praise of music in the second part of *De canticis* (written between 1424 and 1426): *Carmen de laude musicae.*

21. Preface to *Symphoniae iuncundae,* 1538; WA 50:373.

ence human lives.[22] Thus, Luther wrote in the preface to *Symphoniae iuncundae:* "Next to the Word of God, music deserves the highest praise. She is a mistress and governess *(domina et gubernatrix)* of those human emotions . . . which as masters govern men or more often overwhelm them. No greater commendation than this can be found — at least not by us."[23] The following headings in Luther's sketch are in a sense consequences of the first numbered statement. This is demonstrated by the fact that when one attempts to find illustrative citations in Luther's writings, what are distinct in his draft outline are frequently found overlapping and complementing each other in his commentaries and other writings.

2. Music Creates Joyful Hearts

Luther's second point in the draft is: "[Music] creates joyful hearts" *(facit letos animos).* Although this is a distant echo of Tinctoris's thirteenth aphorism *(Musica homines letificat),* Luther is not simply making an arbitrary list of attributes but rather is creating a sequential and interrelated structure for a proposed treatise. Thus the primary reason why music creates joyful hearts is because it is the gift from God. Thus commenting on Psalm 4:1 in his first lectures on the Psalms, he wrote:

> It is the function of music to arouse the sad, sluggish, and dull spirit. Thus Elisha summoned a minstrel so that he might be stirred up to

22. Oskar Söhngen, *Theologie der Musik* (Kassel: Stauda, 1967), 84-85. The poem "Frau Musica" is discussed in chapter 3 of *Luther's Liturgical Music.*

23. WA 50:371: "Musicam esse unam, quae post verbum Dei merito celebrari debeat, domina et gubernatrix affectuum humanorum . . . quibus tamen ipsi homines, ceu a suis dominis, gubernantur et saepius rapiuntur." Hermann Finck, who matriculated at Wittenberg University in 1545, reported some ten years after Luther's death: "Inter caeteras praeclaras artes quae uere DEI dona sunt, non infimum locum tenet Musica. . . . Et reuerendus pater dominus Martinus Lutherus piae memoriae saepe dicere solitus est, multa semina bonarum virtutum inesse animis ijs, qui Musica afficerentur" [Among all the other excellent arts that are indeed gifts of God, music is by no means the least. . . . the reverend father Herr Martin Luther, of pious memory, often used to say that many seeds of the finest virtues are sown in souls affected by music]; Hermann Finck, *Practica Musica* (Wittenberg: Rhau, 1556; facsimile, Bologna: Forni, 1969), A 1^{r-v}.

> prophesy [2 Kings 3:15]. Hence מנצח properly means stimulus, incitement, challenge, and, as it were, a spur of the spirit, a goad, and an exhortation. . . . For in all these the listless mind is sharpened and kindled, so that it may be alert and vigorous as it proceeds to the task. But when these are at the same time sung to artistic music, they kindle the mind more intensely and sharply. And in this manner David here composed this psalm למנצח, that is, as something inciting, stirring, and inflaming, so that he might have something to arouse him to stir up the devotion and inclination of his heart, and in order that this might be done more sharply, he did it with musical instruments. Thus in ancient times the church used to read psalms before Mass as an incentive. To the present day some verses remain in the Introit. And to the present day the church has the invitatory psalm in Matins, namely, "O come, let us sing to the Lord" [Ps. 95:1], whereby the people invite each other to praise God. And the psalm is rightly called "invitatory," because the psalmist summoned not only himself but also others to praise God. This is what St. Ambrose did with a chant, by means of which he dispelled the sadness of the Milanese, so that they might bear the weariness of the time more lightly. But it can, not without sense, also be called "invitatory" for the reason that the Holy Spirit is invited in the same way. For when we are challenged, God is soon aroused also. And therefore we learn from these words that whoever wants to arouse himself to devotion should take up the Psalms.[24]

24. LW 10:43. *Dictata super psalterium* (1513-16); WA 3:40: "Habet enim natura Musice, excitare tristem, pilgrum et stupidum animum. Sic Helizeus vocavit psalten, ut excitaretur ad prophetiam. Quare Mnazeah est proprie incitabulum, invitatorium, provocatorium ac velut calcar spiritus, stimulus et hortatorium . . . Quia in hiis omnibus acuitur et accenditur animus ignavus, ut vigil et strenuus eat ad opus. Quod si ista simul cantentur in Musica artificiali, vehementius et acrius accendunt animum. Et hoc modo hic David fecit hunc psalmum la mnazeah, i.e. pro invitatorio, excitatorio et inflammatorio, ut scilicet haberet, quo seipsum excitaret ad devotionem et affectionem cordis, et ut acrius hoc fieret, fecit in musicalibus. Sic olim Ecclesia solebat psalmos ante missam legere, scilicet pro incitatorio, cuius adhunc versus restant de introitu. Et adhuc in matutinis habet invitatorium psalmum, scilicet 'venite exaltemus,' quo sese mutuo invitant ad laudem dei. Et recte vocatur psalmus sic invitatorium, quia non solum se, sed etiam alios invitavit ad laudem Dei. Sicut Sanctus Ambrosius fecit cum cantu, quo Mediolanensium tristitiam depulit, ut levius ferrent tedium temporis. Sed et non vane potest invitatorium dici eo quod isto modo etiam spiritus sanctus invitetur. Quia cum nos sumus provocati,

Similarly, almost twenty years later, he wrote on Psalm 118:16-18: "A good song is worth singing twice. It is customary for people, when they are really happy or joyful, to repeat a word two or three times. They cannot say it often enough, and whoever meets them must hear it. This is the case here, that the dear saints are so happy and joyful over the miracles God does for them when He delivers them from sin and death, that is, from every evil of body and soul, that out of sheer joy they sing their song over and over again."[25] In the beginning of his poem on music, "Frau Musica" says:

> Of all the joys upon this earth
> none has for men a greater worth
> than what I give with my ringing
> and with voices sweetly singing.[26]

In his letter to Ludwig Senfl (1530) Luther states that "except for theology [music] alone produces what otherwise only theology can do, namely, a calm and joyful disposition."[27] But this joyful disposition is brought about by music that is more than just the human voice, individually or combined with others. Therefore in 1541 he could write in much the same way as he did in commenting on Psalm 4 in 1513-16 (see above): "The

---

mox etiam deus excitatur. Ex istis igitur discimus, quod qui vult seipsum ad devotionem excitare, apprehendat psalmos."

25. LW 14:83, *Das schöne Confitemini, an der Zahl der 118. Psalm* (1530); WA 31:145. "Denn ein gut liedlin mag man wol zwey mal singen, So ists auch aller menschen weise, wenn sie von hertzen frolich odder lustig sind, das sie ein wort, zwey, drey mal wider holen und konnen nicht gnug das selbige sagen, Was yhn begegenet, mus es horen. Also laut es hie auch, das die lieben heiligen so hertzlich fro und lustig sind uber den grossen wunder werckenm so Gott an yhn thut, das er sie von sunden und tod (das ist von allem ubel, beide leibs und seelen) erloset, das sie für freüden yhr lied ymer widder forne anfahen." "We often sing a good song over again from the beginning, especially one we have sung with pleasure and joy" (on Ps. 118:29); LW 14:105; WA 31:181: "So pflegt man die guten lieder, wenn sie aus sind, widder forn an zu heben, sonderlich wo sie mit lust und liebe gesungen sind."

26. LW 53:319, "A Preface to All Good Hymnals. Frau Musica," 1528; WA 35:483: "Fur allen freuden auff erden Kan niemand keine feiner werden, Denn die ich geb mit meim singen Und mit manchem süssen klingen."

27. LW 49:428; WA Br 5:639: ". . . quae musicae possit aequari, cum ipsa sola post theologiam id praestet, quod alioqui sola theologia praestat, scilicet quietem et animum laetum."

stringed instruments of the . . . Psalms are to help in the singing of this new song; and Wolff Heinz[28] and all pious, Christian musicians should let their singing and playing to the praise of the Father of all grace sound forth with joy from their organs, symphonias,[29] virginals, regals, and whatever other beloved instruments there are (recently invented and given by God), of which neither David nor Solomon, neither Persia, Greece, nor Rome, knew anything."[30] Observe Luther's parenthetical comment: the development of new and wonderful musical instruments is due to human skill, but the raw materials used to make them, together with music itself, are the prior gift of God in creation.

For Luther, therefore, musical instruments have a fundamental part to play in the praise of God. The many references to Luther's practice of singing at table should not be thought of as primarily an a cappella performance practice. Johann Mathesius reports in his autobiography that in the early 1540s Luther's regular after-dinner *Kantorei* was accompanied by instruments: "It is an authentic 'Musica' and Kantorei, in which one can sing and play to praise God with honorable people, and sing good Psalms, as David did with harps, a good Swiss hymn,[31] or a Josquin psalm, fine and gentle, together with the text, and also sung with instruments."[32]

28. Organist in Halle.

29. In medieval literature "symphonia" was used to designate a number of different instruments, usually those that produced more than one sound simultaneously, such as the bagpipe and hurdy-gurdy. Praetorius employs "symphonia" for all string keyboard instruments, which, given the context, seems to be Luther's meaning here; see Michael Praetorius, *Syntagma musicum II; De Organographia* (Wolfenbüttel: Holwein, 1619; facsimile, Kassel: Bärenreiter, 1958), 62.

30. WLS, no. 3100 (slightly altered). Dedication in a Bible presented to Wolf Heinz, 1541. WA 48:85-86: "Solch new Lied sollen auch des folgenden psalms Seitenspiel helffen singen. Und Wolff Heintz auch beide mit seiner Orgeln, Symphonien, Virginal, Regal, und was der lieden Musica mehr ist, Davon (als seer newer kunst und Gottes gaben) weder David noch Salomon, noch Persia, Grecia noch Roma ichts gewust, sein singen und spielen mit freuden gehen lassen, zu lob den Vater all gnaden."

31. A composition by Senfl is meant.

32. *Hrn. M. Joh. Mathesii . . . Lebens-Beschreibung/so da Seine Geburth/Aufferziehung/Studia, Beförderung/Tugenden/Ehestand/Priesterlich-Exemplarisches Ende/und was sonst zu seinem Lebens-Wandel gehöret,* ed. Johann Balthasar Mathesius (Dresden: Zimmermann, 1705), 32-33; cited in Wolfram Steude, *Untersuchungen zur mitteldeutschen Musiküberlieferung und Musikpflege im 16. Jahrhundert* (Leipzig: Peters, 1978), 90: ". . . eine ehrliche Musica und Cantorey, darinnen man von von ehrlichen Leuten singet und

The use of instruments in Wittenberg is confirmed by Martin Agricola, who wrote in 1545: "I have been astonished to see, when boys come to Wittenberg and especially to the university, how they fare with their fellow students, who when they sit down at table or get up from it, joyfully engage in singing and playing instruments such as lutes, fiddles and winds; or they pick up harps and other instruments."[33]

For Calvin instrumental music presented a theological problem, because it was so closely intertwined with the sacrificial cultus of the temple, a cultus that was abrogated by the sacrifice of Christ on the cross. Commenting on Psalm 92:4, Calvin wrote: "[T]he Levites who were appointed . . . singers . . . employ their instruments of music — not as if this were in itself necessary, only it was useful as an elementary aid to the people of God in these ancient times. . . . now that Christ has appeared . . . it were only to bury the light of the Gospel, should we introduce the shadows of a departed dispensation."[34]

---

klinget, Gott preiset, gute Psalmen singet, wie David in die Harffen, einen guten Schweitzersichen Choral oder Josquinschen Psalm, fein leise und gelinde, sammt den Text, auch in die Instrumenta singet."

33. *The "Musica instrumentalis deudsche" of Martin Agricola: A Treatise on Musical Instruments, 1529 and 1545*, trans. and ed. William E. Hettrick (New York: Cambridge University Press, 1994), 71; Agricola, *Musica instrumentalis deudsch* (Wittenberg: Rhau, 1545; facsimile, New York: Broude, 1966), sig. Biijr:

> Ich habe wunder vernomen
> Wenn sie gen Wittemberg kommen
> Und sonst zur Universitet
> Wie es jhn bey der Burse geht/
> Welche/wenn sie zu Tische gan
> Odder widder dar von auffstan/
> Sich üben frölich im singen
> Auch auff Instrumenten klingen
> Als Lauten/Geigen/und Pfeiffen
> Odder die Harffen angreiffen
> Und ander Instrumenta zwar. . . .

34. John Calvin, *Commentary on Psalms*, trans. James Anderson (Edinburgh: Calvin Translation Society, 1845-49; reprint, Grand Rapids: Eerdmans, 1949), 3:494-95; Johannes Calvin, *In librum psalmorum commentarius*, ed. August Tholuck (Berlin: Eichler, 1836), 2:153: "Levitas, quibus iniunctum erat canendi munus, proprie compellat, ut musica etiam instrumenta adhibeant: non quia per se hoc necessarium foret, sed quia utile erat rudimentum veteri populo . . . quia quum exhibito Christo. . . . Evangelii lucem

Luther has a different perspective; for him voices and instruments sounding together are a theological opportunity, the sound of joy of the redeemed as they glorify the God of grace. Commenting on Isaiah 5:11, Luther wrote: "Elisha says: [2 Kings 3:15] 'Bring me a minstrel, etc.' Amos 6:5 says: 'Like David [they] invent for themselves instruments of music.' Certainly if you make use of music as David did, you will not sin."[35] Similarly, in a letter to Prince Joachim of Anhalt, 16 June 1534, Luther wrote: "So Elisha was awakened by his minstrel [2 Kings 3:15] and David himself declares in Psalm 57[:8] that his harp was his pride and joy: 'Awake up, my glory; awake psaltery and harp.' And all the saints made themselves joyful with psalms and stringed instruments."[36]

3. Music Drives Away the Devil

Luther's third numbered point in the draft is "[music] drives away the devil" *(Quia fugat diabolum),* a sequence of words that is almost identical with Tinctoris's ninth aphorism *(Musica diabolum fugat).* The concept was a general one that Luther inherited, but it was a matter of great personal concern to him since his letters, table talks, and other writings contain frequent references to the personal onslaughts of the devil. But for Luther music was more than a means of distraction, in the hope that temptation would be forgotten. From his point of view, the corollary of music being the gift of God is that the devil, being opposed to God, must therefore abhor music. Thus this third heading is a logical consequence of the first, but it also follows on naturally from the second, since the devil is antagonistic to pure joy. In his table talks are recorded a number of similar statements,

suffocant qui adhuc Ecclesiam involvunt veteribus umbris." For further representative examples see Calvin's comments on Pss. 71:22; 81:3; 149:1; *Commentary on the Psalms* 3:98, 312; 5:312 respectively = *In librum psalmorum* 1:529-30; 2:76, 522.

35. LW 16:62; *Lectures on Isaiah* (1528); WA 31II:43: "Helizeus: 'adduc,' inquit, 'mihi psalten' etc. Amos 6. Sicut David putaverunt se etc. Certe si usus fueris musica ut David, non peccabis."

36. *Luther: Letters of Spiritual Counsel,* trans and ed. Theodore G. Tappert (Philadelphia: Westminster, 1965), 94; WA Br 7:78: ". . . wie Elisäus sich ließ durch seinen Psalter erwecken, 2 Kön. 3, und David im Psalter selbs sagt Ps. 57, seine Harfe sei seine Ehre und Freude: *Exurge, gloria mea, exurge, Psalterium et Cithera,* und aller Heiligen machen sich fröhlich mit Psalmen und Saitenspielen."

such as: "Satan is a spirit of sadness; therefore he cannot bear joy, and that is why he stays very much away from music."[37] In his letter to composer Ludwig Senfl, 4 October 1530, he wrote:

> For we know that music, too, is odious and unbearable to the demons. Indeed I plainly judge, and do not hesitate to affirm, that except for theology there is no art that could be put on the same level with music, since except for theology [music] alone produces what otherwise only theology can do, namely, a calm and joyful disposition. Manifest proof [of this is the fact] that the devil, the creator of saddening cares and disquieting worries, takes flight at the sound of music almost as he takes flight at the word of theology.[38]

Here Luther makes the profound connection between "the sound of music" and the "word of theology": both repel the devil. Thus Luther's view that "music is next to theology" is not just a formula of words but an important fundamental working principle: music is next to theology because both accomplish similar results. Like theology, music "serves to cast out Satan, the instigator of all sins, as is shown in Saul, the king of Israel [1 Sam. 16:23]."[39] Thus in Luther's poem in praise of music, "Frau Musica" is heard to say:

> But God in me more pleasure finds
> than in all joys of earthly minds.

37. WLS 3:983, n. 8; WA TR, no. 194 (1532): "Satan est Spiritus tristitiae. Ideo non potest ferre laetitiam, ideo longissime abest musica." See also WA TR, nos. 968, 2387, and 2545.

38. LW 49:427-28; WA Br 5:639: "Scimus enim musicen daemonibus etiam invisam et intolerabilem esse. Et plane iudico, nec pudet asserere, post theologiam esse nullam artem, quae musicae possit aequari, cum ipsa sola post theologiam id praestet, quod alioqui sola theologia praestat, scilicet quietem et animum laetum, manifesto argumento, quod diabolus, curarum tristium et turbarum inquietarum autor, ad vocem musicae paene similiter fugit ad verbum theologiae."

39. WA 50:371. Preface to *Symphoniae iuncundae* 1538: "Rursus per eandem expelli Satanam, id est omnium vitiorum impulsorem, ut in Saule rege Israel monstratur" [So you too must turn to your regal or gather some good companions about you and sing with them until you learn how to defy the devil]. Letter to Matthias Weller (7 October 1534). *Luther: Letters of Spiritual Counsel,* trans. and ed. Theodore G. Tappert (Philadelphia: Westminster, 1955), 97. WA Br 7:106: "also greift Ihr auch ins Regal, oder nehmet gute Gesellen und singet dafur, bis Ihr lernet ihn spotten."

> Through my bright power the devil shirks
> his sinful, murderous, evil works.[40]

4. Music Creates Innocent Delight

Luther's fourth heading in his outline for a treatise on music is the logical consequence of the third. If the devil is thwarted by music, then the evil he fosters must similarly be destroyed by means of music and good promoted instead: "[Music] creates innocent delight, destroying wrath, unchastity, and pride." So he can write in his treatise on the last words of David (1543): "For the evil spirit is ill at ease wherever God's Word is sung or preached in true faith. He is a spirit of gloom and cannot abide where he finds a spiritually happy heart, that is, where the heart rejoices in God and in His Word."[41] In the draft outline the fourth point is elaborated further. Luther adds: "I place music next to theology. This is well known from the example of David and all the prophets, who all produced poetry and songs." This parallels what Luther wrote in his letter to Senfl:

> Manifest proof [of this is the fact] that the devil, the creator of saddening cares and disquieting worries, takes flight at the sound of music almost as he takes flight at the word of theology. This is the reason why the prophets did not make use of any art except music; when setting forth their theology they did it not as geometry, not as arithmetic, not as astronomy, but as music, so that they held theology and music most tightly connected, and proclaimed truth through Psalms and songs.[42]

40. LW 53:320, "A Preface to All Good Hymnals. Frau Musica," 1528; WA 35:483-84:

Sondern auch Gott viel bas gefelt
Denn alle freud der gantzen welt.
Dem Teuffel sie sein werck zerstört
Und verhindert viel böser mörd.

41. LW 15:274. WA 54:34: "Denn dem bösen geist ist nicht wol dabey, wo man Gottes wort im rechten glauben singet oder predigt. Er ist ein geist der traurigkeit, und kan nicht bleiben, wo ein hertz Geistlich (das ist, in Gott und seinem wort)."

42. LW 49:428; WA Br 5:639: "Manifesto argumento, quod diabolus, curarum tristium et turbarum inquietarum autor, ad vocem musi dem cae paene similiter fugit ad verbum theologiae. Hinc factum est, ut prophetae nulla sic arte sint usi ut musica, dum

As passages already cited make clear, Luther makes frequent references to David banishing Saul's evil mood through music, Elisha's call for a musician to play so that he could prophesy, as well as general comments on the use of musical forms by various prophets. The following are other examples:

> The Holy Spirit himself honors her [music] as an instrument for his proper work when in his Holy Scriptures he asserts that through her his gifts were instilled in the prophets, namely, the inclination to all virtues, as can be seen in Elisha [2 Kings 3:15]. On the other hand, she serves to cast out Satan, the instigator of all sins, as is shown in Saul, the king of Israel [1 Sam. 16:23]. Thus it was not without reason that the fathers and prophets wanted nothing else to be associated as closely with the Word of God as music.[43]

> For by it [music] also the evil spirit of Saul was driven off [1 Sam. 1:23], and the prophetic spirit was given to Elisha [2 Kings 3:15].[44]

> And as David initiated the writing of psalms and made this a vogue, many others were inspired by his example and became prophets. These followed in David's footsteps and also contributed beautiful psalms; for example, the Sons of Korah, Heman, Asaph, etc.[45]

> That it is good and God pleasing to sing hymns is, I think, known to every Christian; for everyone is aware not only of the example of the

suam theologiam non in geometriam, non in arithmeticam, non in astronomiam, sed in musicam digesserunt, ut theologiam et musicam haberent coniunctissimas, veritatem psalmis et canticis dicentes."

43. WA 50:371: "Honorat eam ipse Spiritus sanctus, ceu sui proprii officii organum, dum in scripturis suis sanctis testatur, dona sua per eam Prophetis illabi, id est omnium virtutum affectus, ut in Eliseo videre est. Rursus per eandem expelli Satanam, id est omnium vitiorum impulsorem, ut in Saule rege Israel monstratur. Unde non frustra, Patres et Prophetae, verbo Dei nihil voluerunt esse coniunctius quam Musicam."

44. WLS, no. 3094. *Operationes in psalmos* (1518-21). WA 5:98 "Nam hinc et spiritus malus Saul pellebatur . . . et Heliseo spiritus propheticus dabatur" (on the superscription of Ps. 4).

45. LW 15:273. *Treatise on the Last Words of David* (1543). WA 54:33: "Und da solch tichten den Psalmen David anfieng, und in schwanck bracht, wurden dadurch viel andere erleucht und zu Propheten erweckt, die auch da zu helffen, und schöne Psalmen machten, als die kinder Korah, Heman, Assaph etc."

> prophets and kings in the Old Testament who praised God with song and sound, with poetry and psaltery, but also of the common and ancient custom of the Christian church to sing Psalms. St. Paul himself instituted this in 1 Corinthians 14[:15] and exhorted the Colossians [3:16] to sing spiritual songs and Psalms heartily unto the Lord so that God's Word and Christian teaching might be instilled and implanted in many ways.[46]

5. Music Reigns in Times of Peace

Luther's fifth heading is: "[Music] reigns in times of peace." To this he adds the observation: "It will be difficult to keep these delightful skills after us, for they are of peace. The Dukes of Bavaria are to be praised in this, that they honor music. Among our Saxon [Dukes] weapons and cannons are praised." Here Luther registers the irony that the Catholic Bavarian dukes, who opposed evangelical reforms, richly supported music while the Lutheran dukes of Saxony, patrons of Luther in other respects, had actually disbanded their musical foundations, refused to give financial support to the teaching of music in their university of Wittenberg,[47] and seemed more prepared for war than peace. He made much the same point in his letter to Senfl, who was, of course, composer to the Bavarian court:

> Even though my name is detested, so much that I am forced to fear that this letter I am sending may not be safely received and read by you, excellent Louis, yet the love for music, with which I see you adorned and gifted by God, has conquered this fear. This love also has

46. LW 53:315-16. Preface to Walter's *Chorgesangbuch* (1524). WA 35:474: "Das geystliche lieder singen gut und Gott angeneme sey, acht ich, sey keynem Christen verborgen, die wehl yderman nicht alleyn das Exempel der propheten und könige ym allten testament (die mit singen und klingen, mit tichten und allerley seytten spiel Gott gelobt haben) sondern auch solcher brauch, sonderlich mit psalmen gemeyner Christenheyt von anfang kund ist. Ja auch S. Paulus solchs 1 Cor. 14 eynfetzt und zu den Collossern gepeut, von hertzen dem Herrn singen geystliche lieder und Psalmen, Auff das da durch Gottes wort und Christliche leere auff allerley weyse getrieben und geübt werden."

47. On the Saxon fiscal policy that denied financial support to music foundation and the large amounts spent on other concerns, see WA TR, nos. 968, 2545a, and 2545b.

> given me hope that my letter will not bring danger to you. For who, even among the Turks, would censure him who loves art and praises the artist? Because they encourage and honor music so much, I, at least, nevertheless very much praise and respect above all others your Dukes of Bavaria, much as they are unfavorably inclined toward me.[48]

The previous statements in Luther's draft outline for a treatise on music are easily amplified by his comments in other writings, but on this last point[49] it is not exactly clear how he would have expounded it in the study had he completed it. The comparative reference to the dukes of Bavaria and Saxony would suggest that his primary thought was of civil peace rather than theological peace, that music tempers the warlike spirit. But does this mean that this fifth proposition is merely a continuation of the fourth, that Luther was simply illustrating music's power over one of the most significant "other excesses" by stating, in effect, that "music creates peace and destroys war"? That is possible, except that Luther will often link civil peace and theological peace. For example, in 1541 his response to the threat of the advancing Ottoman Empire across Europe was to call the people to prayer in public worship that had a significant musical content.

> The people need to be challenged to earnest devotion through public prayer in the churches. It has been my practice, with permission of the pastors and the congregation, to chant alternately with the choir, as is customary, Psalm 79 after the sermon on Sunday, either at the morning or at the evening service. Then a choirboy with a good voice, from his place in the choir, sings on his own the antiphon or tract, "Lord, not according to our sins" [*Domine, non secundum*, Ps. 103:10]. After that, a second choirboy may chant the other tract, "Lord do not remember the iniquities of our forefathers" [*Domine ne memineris,*

48. LW 49:427; WA Br 5:639: "Quamvis nomen meum sit invisum, adeo ut vereri cogar, ne satis tuto recipiantur a te et legantur, optime Ludovice, quas mitto literas, vicit tamen hanc formidinem amor musicae, qua te video ornatum et donatum a Deo meo. Qui amor spem quoque fecit, fore ut nihil periculi sint tibi allaturae literae meae; quis enim vel in Turca vituperet, si amet artem et laudet artificem? Ego sane ipsos tuos Duces Bavariae, ut maxime mihi parum propitii sint, vehementer tamen laudo et colo prae caeteris, quod musicam ita fovent et honorant."

49. Since the document is fragmentary, it is an open question whether this was the last point in his intended treatise, or whether he intended further sections.

> Ps. 79:8]. Following that the whole choir, kneeling, may sing, "Help us, O God" [*Adiuva nos, Deus,* Ps. 79:9]. . . . Thereupon, when desired, the congregation may sing, "Grant us peace" [*Verleih uns Frieden gnädiglich*] or the Lord's Prayer in German [*Vater unser im Himmelreich*].[50]

Luther had created a German version of the Latin antiphon *Da pacem domine in diebus nostris* (Grant us peace, Lord, in our time), *Verleih uns Frieden gnädiglich,* some years earlier, probably first appearing in the no-longer-extant 1529 edition of Klug's Wittenberg *Geistlicher lieder.*[51] Instead of the traditional melody Luther created a new one, closely related to *Nun komm der Heiden Heiland* and *Erhalt uns, Herr, bei deinem Wort. Erhalt uns, Herr, bei deinem Wort* was written around the same time as his *Appeal for Prayer against the Turks* (1541), though probably after he had penned the sentences cited above, because instead of the Latin antiphons Luther originally suggested, these two hymns based on the same melodic material, *Erhalt uns, Herr, bei deinem Wort*[52] and *Verleih uns Frieden gnädiglich,* were soon sung together at the end of Sunday services.[53] But

50. LW 43:231, slightly altered. *Appeal for Prayer against the Turks* (1541). WA 51:606-7: "Damit aber das Volck zur andacht und ernst gereitzet würde durch offentliche Gebet in der Kirchen, Leisse ich mir gefallen, wo es den Pfarherrn und Kirchen auch gefeile, das man am Feiertage nach der Predigt (Es sey morgends oder abends) den Lxxviiij psalm sunge ein Chor umb einander, wie gewonet. Darnach tret ein wol gestimpter knabe fur den pült ynn yhrem Chor, und singe allein die Antiphon oder tract, Domine Non secundum. Nach dem selben ein ander knabe, den andern tract, Domine ne Meminaris Und darauff der ganze Chor knyend, Adjuva nos Deus . . . . Darauff (wo man wil) mag der Leye singen, Verleyhe uns frieden oder das deutsche Vater Unser etc."

51. In the 1533 edition of the Wittenberg hymnal, following *Verleih uns Frieden* is a prayer for peace and good government, Luther's translation of the Collect from the *Missa pro pace; Geistliche lieder* (Wittenberg: Klug, 1533; facsimile, Kassel: Bärenreiter, 1954), fol. 51r-52r; see WA 35:233; LW 53:138.

52. On *Erhalt uns, Herr, bei deinem Wort,* see Robin A. Leaver, "Luther's Catechism Hymns. 1. 'Lord Keep Us Steadfast in Your Word,'" *Lutheran Quarterly* 11 (1997): 397-410, now chapter 4 of *Luther's Liturgical Music.*

53. See, for example, Johannes Spangenberg, *Kirchengesenge Deudsche* (Magdeburg: Lotter, 1545), fol. 26r-27r, the sequence being, Benediction, *Verleih uns Frieden,* Collect, *Erhalt uns, Herr.* Later practice was to sing the two hymns one after the other, *Erhalt uns, Herr,* then *Verleih uns Frieden,* following the Benediction. Singing a prayer for peace at this juncture may have been suggested by the earlier practice of singing the *Nunc dimit-*

even before this both Luther's *Formula missae* (1523) and his *Deutsche Messe* (1526) made significant use of chanted forms of prayer for peace with strong theological overtones. In their provisions for the Lord's Supper both liturgical orders indicate that the *Agnus Dei*, or its German version, with the final prayer, "*dona nobis pacem/gib uns deinen Frieden*" (grant us your peace), could be sung during the distribution of communion,[54] and both orders include the (chanted) Aaronic blessing (Num. 6), with its final words, "and grant you peace."[55] In the *Formula missae* Luther directs that the distribution of communion is to be introduced by *Pax Domini*, and in his explanation of its meaning equates peace with forgiveness: "'The peace of the Lord,' etc., which is, so to speak, a public absolution of the sins of the communicants, the true voice of the Gospel announcing remission of sins, and therefore the one and most worthy preparation for the Lord's Table, if faith holds to these words as coming from the mouth of Christ himself."[56]

For Luther, the liturgical greeting "the peace of the Lord be always with you" carries within it the proclamation of the gospel, the declaration of forgiveness. Given this understanding, it seems likely that in his exposition of the fifth point of his projected treatise on music he would have included some thoughts about music and peace, both theological and civil. Although we cannot be certain that he would have done so, it must be observed that there is a strong connection between Luther's words in the *Formula missae* about the *Pax Domini* being "the true voice of the Gospel announcing remission of sins," and his statements concerning the proclamatory function of music, such as "God has preached the Gospel through music."[57]

---

tis . . . in pace at the end of the Roman Mass. Luther had created his vernacular version of the *Nunc dimittis* in 1524: *Mit Fried und Freud ich fahr dahin.*

54. LW 53:29 and 82; WA 12:213 and WA 19:99.

55. LW 53:30 and 84; WA 12:213 and WA 19:102.

56. LW 53:28-29; WA 12:213: "Pax domini etce., quae est publica quaedam absolutio a peccatis communicantium, Vox plane Evangelica, annuncians remissionem peccatorum, unica illa et dignissima ad mensam domini preparatio, si fide apprehendatur, non secus atque ex ore Christi prolata."

57. LW 54:129. WA TR, no. 1258 (1531): "So hat Gott das Evangelium auch durch die Musik gepredigt." For further material, see the complete chapter 3, "Luther's Theological Understanding of Music," in *Luther's Liturgical Music.*

CHAPTER 14

Luther and Cranach on Justification in Word and Image

Christoph Weimer

To speak of Luther and the theme of justification, that is, to speak of the idea that Luther reawakened the awareness that a human being is justified before God by grace alone, seems to be nothing special. However, that Lucas Cranach expressed himself on this theme and did so in images, as the title of this essay suggests, may be more surprising and thus provides the thrust of the following deliberations.

Approach

There would be no Luther without Cranach, for whoever knows Luther knows him through the work of Lucas Cranach the Elder. Luther's countenance, whether as determined Augustinian monk, as scholar and preacher, or as the husband, has been fixed and created by Cranach, the painter and purveyor to the court of the Wettin electors in Wittenberg. In images of almost innumerable variation and compilation, the Reformer has been captured by his contemporary and friend, both in woodcuts and etchings suitable for reproduction, and also in paintings on tablets and altars. However, Cranach gained a name for himself not only through his work on portraits

---

Originally given to the Luther-Gesellschaft-Münster, 27 November 2000, appearing here with only minor changes as translated by Wilhelm Linss from *Luther* 74 (2003): 22-38.

and the wide public reach that came with it. With his abilities, he represented the thoughts of Luther and bestowed on particular biblical themes a new approach in the fine arts, making theological thoughts understandable, and contributing to the "laification of the task of visual persuasion."[1] He did not resist visual polemics against the established church. With all this involvement, Cranach's shop, with its many workers, could speedily fulfill the commissions of the elector's court. These commissions ranged from the decoration of various castles to the pictorial reporting of tournaments and hunts, to the manufacturing of horse blankets and the painting of a garden house.

Who is this man, who from 1504 on became part of the development of the Reformation in Wittenberg and from his position as court purveyor, respected citizen, and friend of the Reformer cleverly knew how to evaluate his opportunities? What is known concerning the painter Lucas Cranach, who had a close friendship with Luther and yet did not reject customers faithful to Rome, who furnished images for the Reformation at a time when the forces of the Radical Reformation were banning any and every kind of pictorial decoration from the church? Finally, who is this artist who through his images was an advocate of the Reformation and thus from his perspective forced an answer to the question of the significance of images and their use in the church of the Reformers?

Luther's Attitude toward Images

With these questions we come to the basis of the relationship between the theologian and the artist, the Reformer and the pictorialist. Does theology allow images, and if so, in what form? Have we forgotten that faith comes from hearing (Rom. 10:17) and has its source in the Word of Holy Scripture and in the Word of proclamation? What significance then can images have? "The Word, I say, and only the Word is the vehicle of God's grace."[2] This is Luther's famous statement of 1519. According to this, there is no need for images in the arena of the church and its proclamation. The iconoclasts were in the right, and the relationship of Luther to Cranach must be understood as a nonrelationship.

1. "Laisienung der visuellen Überzengungsarbeit." Martin Warnke, *Hofkünstler. Zur Vorgeschichte des modernen Künstlers* (Cologne: Dumont, 1985), 285.

2. WA 2:508f. (1519); LW 27:249ff.

Of course, for Martin Luther the question of images is first not a separate theme. The question of what one should think of images was imposed on him, and he saw himself forced by external circumstances to take a position on it. When he began his reforming activities and was summoned to the Diet of Worms (1521), and afterward had to hide in the Wartburg Castle, the Reformation threatened to slip from his hands. Others understood Luther better than he understood himself and went beyond him in their interpretations. Now the "old" was totally discarded, and in this storm, even that which was tried and true was being sacrificed. Images and objects of art were removed from church buildings and destroyed.

When Luther heard about it, he took a position on the events in an explicit essay and in sermons.[3] In his words we immediately realize what he emphasizes: "concerning [the images] . . . also it is true that they are unnecessary, and we are free to have them or not, although it would be much better if we did not have them at all. I am not partial to them."[4] The presence of images is not necessary, yet — and this is decisive — since the images are present, their usage is the determining factor. One must distinguish between having images and using images. When images are present, then the decisive criterion is how the viewer uses the images. With this, Luther turned a page in dealing with images and at the same time revealed the heart of his theology. In the question of usage (also in regard to images) the entire Reformation theology is at stake. How so? A retrospect on Luther's distinction of God's Word as law and gospel will aid us in our thinking.

The Word of God as Law and Gospel

As is generally acknowledged, the true theologian is proven by a correct distinguishing of God's Word as law and gospel. Luther makes the entire Holy Scriptures and the knowledge of theology dependent on the appropriate distinction of law and gospel.[5] "Both are the word of God, the law or

3. "Wider die himmlischen Propheten, von den Bildern und Sakrament" (1525), WA 18:62ff.; LW 40:79ff.

4. WA 10III:26.21ff. (1522); LW 51:81.

5. Cf. WA 7:502.34f. (1521).

the Ten Commandments . . . and the gospel which also is God's word, but here the important aspect is that one must rightly distinguish the two kinds of word and not allow them to be mixed, otherwise one of them will be lost, if not both of them."[6] It is therefore out of the question for Luther to consider the law as the word of human beings and the gospel as the Word of God, just as little as one could attribute the law as the Word of God to the Old Testament and the gospel as the Word of God to the New Testament. Rather, both are the Word of God. Exactly in order to make them recognizable as law and as gospel, both have to be clearly kept apart. But how does that happen? Law is "the word of God and command . . . that commands us what we should do and demands works from us."[7] Gospel, on the other hand, is the Word of God that does "not demand our works, does not bid us to act, but tells us to receive and to accept."[8] Or, in other words, "The Gospel and the Law, taken in their proper sense, differ in this way: The Law proclaims what must be done and left undone; . . . the Gospel, however, proclaims that sins have been remitted and that all things have been fulfilled and done."[9] However, this was not enough of a distinction. Within the law a twofold use has to be distinguished *(duplex usus legis)*. The first, the civil or political use of the law *(usus politicus legis)*, has to be mentioned. It is the Word of God as law that provides the external coordinates of peaceful living together under the conditions of sin. It does not make one good but rather deters and punishes the people[10] and prevents chaos that otherwise might arise. To be distinguished from this use is the "theological use of the law" *(usus theologicus legis)*. This use becomes effective when through the use of the law an individual is identified as a sinner, falls into despair, and strives for the gospel.[11] This is the true function of the law and is bestowed on it by the gospel.[12] The law, which is permeated by the gospel, makes it a teacher leading to Christ.[13]

In this extremely brief recollection of the theological heart of Luther, two items are noticeable: on the one hand there is the distinguishing

6. WA 36:9.33ff. (1532).
7. WA 36:12.19ff.
8. WA 36:14.22ff.
9. WA 2:466.3ff. (1519); LW 27:183-84.
10. Cf. WA 17I:123.29ff. (1525).
11. Cf. WA 54:82.18ff. (1543); LW 15:333.
12. Cf. WA 40I:480.13 (1531/35); LW 26:309.
13. Cf. WA 39I:445.21ff. (1537).

of God's Word as law and gospel, on the other that this distinction is, so to speak, enriched by the criterion of usage. Who decides whether the Word of God is now political law or theological law for me; or perhaps it springs into action as gospel here? Does the burden of this distinction rest with the preacher who has to proclaim and interpret the Word of God or only with the hearers themselves? Who decides whether now the gospel or now the law is to be heard? By indicating this problem, Luther directs attention entirely to "use and usage" as the "methodical means . . . of applying the basic insight of the Reformation in the entire realm of theology."[14] On the basis of linguistic data I believe I can say that Luther speaks of "use" only in reference to the law; the formulation of a *usus evangelii* does not appear in his works. Exactly when it is a question of the gospel, the human being as user is nullified. The gospel defines the human being in such a way that he or she can do justice to it only by "receiving."[15] Here no behavior of "using" is called for. Here, the human being, by what another (namely, Christ) has done, is subjected to a condition that does not allow a use that affects one's life in any other way except through "accepting and believing."

The Use of Images

This sketchy reminiscence of the center of the theology of the Reformation is enlightening for the question of images because Luther also treated them under the point of view of their use. He posits a difference between "having images" and "using images." In regard to their existence, images belong to *adiaphora*. They are not necessary but free; one may have them or not have them.[16] Because their existence is unobjectionable, their production

14. Gerhard Ebeling, *Word and Faith* (Philadelphia: Fortress, 1963); "Zur Lehre vom *triplex usus legis* in der reformatorischen Theologie," in his *Wort und Glaube*, 3rd ed. (Tübingen: Mohr, 1967), 62. "Remarkably, this question was never discussed in Protestant theology," 64. "*Uti* and *usus* are for Luther the category of the existential relationship to an object. . . . Understanding is proven first *in usu.*," 60. Cf. Ebeling's *Dogmatik des christlichen Glaubens*, III/3, 3rd ed. (Tübingen: Mohr, 1993), 282f. Cf. WA 40I:174.25f.; LW 26:95; WA 26:14.23f. (1528), LW 28:231.

15. Cf. WA 40I:168.20ff.; LW 26:91; WA 24:4.8ff. (1527) and WA 36:14.22f.

16. Cf. WA 10III:26.4ff. and 35.7ff (1522); LW 51:81-82 and 86; WA 18:73.14f.; LW 40:90.

also must not be rejected.[17] However, if one has images, then the use of images is decisive, and this determines the relationship to the image. Here also it is valid to say: "it is not a dispute about the essence but about the use and abuse of objects."[18] Consequently, Luther can speak of a misuse of images. Misuse appears in a veneration that worships stone and wood instead of God.[19] With some pictorial representations, the people no longer distinguish between reproduction and the person reproduced, and therefore they worship stone and wood. Sometimes Mary, for instance, is represented in images so exalted that people "come to her for help and comfort, as though she were a divine being."[20] The other abuse consists in the belief that donating cloisters and ecclesiastical furnishings is meritorious before God, "for who would place a silver or wooden image in a church unless he thought that by so doing he was rendering God a service?"[21] The donation of images is thus a variant of works righteousness. But the opposite is also true and is, according to Luther, an abuse; namely, when existing images are destroyed. He writes, "However, to speak evangelically of images, I say and declare that no one is obligated to break violently images even of God, but everything is free, and one does not sin if he does not break them with violence . . . not with the law in a Karlstadtian manner. For whoever acts in this manner, attempts to heap coals on his head with contrary behavior, but with his action alone despises the image without acting against the misuse."[22]

Luther was also aware of a positive usage of images. Basically, he began with the idea that pictorial representation helps understanding, "because we need to form thoughts and pictures of what is presented to us in words and cannot think or understand anything without images."[23] Images serve "as contemplation, as testimony, as memory, as a sign."[24] If evangelical preaching has made the hearer into one who "sees," who is free from misuse, then the viewing of images is an aid for understanding theological facts. Luther elucidates this in a sermon on the confessional state-

17. Cf. WA 10III:27.21ff.; LW 51:82-83; WA 18:69.1ff. and 70.4ff.; LW 40:86, 87.

18. *Non est disputatio de substantia, sed usu et abusu rerum.* WA 28:554.5f. (1529).

19. WA 6:211.12ff. (1520); LW 44:32.

20. WA 7:570.5f. (1521); LW 21:323.

21. WA 10III:31.10f.; LW 51:84.

22. WA 18:74.3ff.; LW 40:91.

23. WA 37:63.25f. (1533).

24. WA 18:80.9; LW 40:96.

ment "descended into hell, on the third day he rose again."[25] The very painting of this complex confessional point "beautifully shows the power and usefulness of this article" and "prevents quibbling." This quibbling consists in deliberating from what material the flag of Christ was made so that it cannot burn, what material the doors of hell are made of, and similar questions. The image prevents such speculation. Instead there are clues "to speak very clearly and distinctly of hidden things."[26] Even though Luther especially esteemed certain images, such as the image of John the Baptist pointing to Christ, or emphatically suffered under other images, like Christ as a judge, he tactfully refused to interpret an image, conceding this freedom to the viewer. From his own life experience, from the existential appropriation that is founded alone on the viewing, he can therefore call some motifs beautiful, or glorious paintings.[27] He speaks of a "fine painting"[28] or of a "comforting picture."[29]

It would be a brittle, dry exercise if we could not visualize Luther's doctrine of images. His understanding of images has not only a theoretical but also a perceptible side. His trusting relationship to the artist Lucas Cranach demonstrates how much the Reformer himself worked with images.

Lucas Cranach

Cranach's first years of life are in darkness. Indeed, the house of his birth is shown in the Franconian city of Kronach, but this is just as unauthenticated as the year of his birth, 1472. Before 1504 he frequented Vienna and may be considered a representative of the Danube Style.[30] Subsequently he was called to the court in Wittenberg, where he remained in the service of the Saxonian elector for the rest of his life. His workshop quickly became the operation of many people; without it he would not have been able to fulfill so many different commissions. After he was granted a coat of arms

25. WA 37:62.1ff.
26. WA 37:65.22f.
27. Cf. WA 46:683.35ff. (1537-38); LW 22:170.
28. Cf. WA 46:307.12f. (1537-38).
29. WA 49:772.7 (1545).
30. Together with Albrecht Altdorfer and Wolf Huber.

in January of 1558, Cranach's works carried the well-known signature of the winged serpent with a ring in its mouth. Cranach increased his renown and his fortune, acquiring a pharmacy and entering into the paper and book trade. In subsequent years he became a treasurer and mayor of the city and followed his elector John Frederick into imprisonment after the Smalcald War. After release from confinement, he moved to Weimar in 1552, and "almost reaching the 81st year of his age, he concluded his glorious life on October 16, 1553,"[31] and is buried in the Cemetery of St. James in Weimar.

To understand Cranach's life and work means to understand him in his own time. With him, "the history of his social career becomes the history of his life. Restlessly, without painful violence, his internal fate is integrated in his external fate. Without being a servant to the economic cycles of his time, he is always its product. He proceeds securely and in a dignified manner on the way to his success and dies as a brightly shining embodiment of all civil virtues."[32] Cranach's position in Wittenberg, undisputed but also free from stimulation, is the entryway for the artistic judgment of his work. The span of such judgments ranges from the estimation that remaining in Wittenberg introduced a decline from his original quality,[33] all the way to the quite opposite observation that his work, exactly because of this decision, became the work of "a fully creative seeker and finder of his own style."[34] Indeed, Cranach's stereotyped, repetitive figures suggest viewing him as a supplier of requested art. The flood of commissions he managed makes it difficult to draw a line between handicraft and art. Nevertheless, it cannot be denied that the theme of images, to which we now turn, in deepening these expositions, presupposes a high level of reflection, as well as an intensive occupation with Luther's theology.

31. C. E. Reimer, *Historisch-critische Abhandlung über das Leben und die Kunstwerke des berühmten deutschen Mahlers, Lucas Cranach* (Hamburg and Leipzig: Grunds Witwe und Holle, 1761), 14.

32. Wilhelm Worringer, "Lukas Cranach," in *Klassische Illustrationen,* vol. 3, ed. Kurt Bertels (Munich and Leipzig: R. Piper and Co., 1908), 3f.

33. Cf. Max J. Friedländer, "Einführung," in *Die Gemälde von Lucas Cranach,* ed. Max J. Friedländer and J. Rosenberg, 2nd ed. (Basel: Birkhäuser, 1979); see also Georg Dehio, *Geschichte der deutschen Kunst,* text-volume 3, 2nd ed. (Berlin: De Gruyter, 1931), 112.

34. H. Esswein, "Die Kunst des Lukas Cranach und ihre Wurzeln im Eros," *Ganymed,* no. 4 (Münich, 1922): 51.

Luther and Cranach

When Luther moved permanently to Wittenberg in the fall of 1511,[35] Cranach, who was eleven years his senior, already held a solid position in both court and city. The first traces of the friendship between the two men point to the year 1520 when Luther inquired of Cranach about lodging for a friend (Matthew Adreanus). The friendship quickly deepened, as is evident in the etchings of Luther created during this period by Cranach. From Frankfurt Luther informed Cranach that he needed to "go into hiding" after the Diet of Worms.[36] Since both Cranach and his wife are addressed by Luther as *Gevatter* and *Gevatterin* in this letter, we may conclude that all three were connected through godparenting relations. When Luther temporarily and secretly stayed in Wittenberg in the first week of December 1521, Cranach impressed into memory the appearance of Luther as "Squire Jorg." In the spring of 1522 he published this "disguised Luther" both as a woodcarving and as a painting.

Luther also used the print shop of Cranach just as Cranach was making a concerted effort to distribute the writings of Luther. In 1523 Luther seemed to have housed the "unmarried and destitute Katharine von Bora first in the large household of Lucas Cranach."[37] Cranach was a witness at the engagement of Luther to Katharine and furnished the official wedding pictures after the wedding. He always chose to make the cutout of Katharine larger so that she would be portrayed as more dainty. Cranach was among the table guests in Luther's house and, in turn, invited into his house the participants of the discussion of the Wittenberg Concord in 1536.[38] Matters concerning the city played an important role between the two men. The councilors Cranach and Döring no longer retained Luther as a guarantor of the common treasury because of his inability to handle financial matters.[39] Furthermore, Cranach discussed in Luther's house the reasons for the temporary scarcity of food, and when their son Hans Cranach died in 1537 in Bologna, Luther found comforting words for the

35. Cf. R. Schwarz, "Luther," in *Die Kirche in ihrer Geschichte,* vol. 3, ed. Bernd Moeller (Göttingen: Vandenhoeck & Ruprecht, 1986), 21.

36. Luther to Cranach on 28 April 1521, WA Br 2:305f.; LW 48:201.

37. Martin Brecht, *Martin Luther,* vol. 2, trans. James L. Schaaf (Philadelphia: Fortress, 1985-93); *Martin Luther,* vol. 2 (Stuttgart: Calwer-Verlag, 1986), 194.

38. Cf. Brecht, *Martin Luther,* 3:60.

39. Cf. Luther to Brisger on 1 February 1527; WA Br 4:164.6ff.

mourning parents. Despite this close tie between the two men, it was only after Luther's death that an altar painting portrayed them together in the same picture. Even if Cranach did not himself live to see the installation of the Weimar altar painting in 1555, the composition goes back to him. The work shows Luther next to Cranach and John the Baptist under the cross.

The Cooperation of Theologian and Artist

To limit the cooperation between the theologian and the artist to the images of justification would narrow the exchange they had with each other and its mutual influence. A broad palette of Cranach's creations shows how Luther's thoughts were visualized by Cranach, or how Cranach put existing subjects into a new context.

Here should be noted the *Passion of Christ and Antichrist,* which appeared in 1521 after the Diet of Worms. In two rows with thirteen antithetical woodcuts each, the life of Christ is contrasted critically with the papacy and the curia. As Christ ascends to heaven, the pope descends into hell; as Christ heals invalids, the pope is observing a tournament, and so on. The sheets, each signed by Cranach, include texts in part derived directly from Luther. Cranach expressed his opinion just as clearly in regard to church politics by a cycle of images on the book of Revelation in Luther's September testament of 1522.

Here one can also detect darts of criticism against the curia, indicated by the dragon being crowned with a tiara. It is noteworthy that through the compilation of biblical texts with these anti-Roman motifs, the observant reader is without words silently induced to draw the conclusion that the papacy is the power in Revelation that acts against Christ's kingdom. Thus "the visual agitation surpasses the verbal one and appeals also to political sentiments."[40] With the illustration of Karlstadt's freight wagon of 1519, Cranach operated in a similar church-political way. This cartoon shows a wagon in the upper zone of the picture on which a pious penitent rides toward the suffering Christ. Paul and Augustine are the drivers who keep the wagon moving forward despite the stones on the road and the hindering devil on the wheels. Antithetically, in the lower

40. Berthold Hinz, *Lucas Cranach d. ä und seine Bildmanufaktur* (Munich: Bayer, Vereinsbank, 1994), 67.

zone a second wagon, well lubricated and without obstacles, goes forward with a holy fighter in the figure of Saint George toward the wide-open throat of hell. With a monk seated on the wagon, all theological topoi, from which one thought to be separated, go into the hellish throat.

Two examples may clarify how themes of existing images take on a different meaning, and first under the influence of Melanchthon, and then Luther, Luther's texts modify the familiar use of an image. One is the wood carving *Holy Kinship* (1510?). This motif is a favorite portrayal of the relatives of Jesus. The picture shows Anna and Mary in the center with the child Jesus; on the right, next to them, are the three husbands of Anna, deep in conversation. From the left approaches Joseph, and in the foreground are the children. Under the influence probably of Melanchthon, the significance and use of this motif both change. If originally Saint Anna was to be seen in connection with the indulgence of 1510, so now a verse is added to the carving that encourages sending children to school.

The other example is the heavenly ladder of Saint Bonaventure. Here two versions are clearly distinguished. The pre-Reformation version has on the banners and rungs inscriptions regarding disdain for the world, considering oneself as low. The ladder is an aid for Christians to ascend (to heaven). "Altogether it is an image that warns and admonishes the viewer and reader, wanting to impress on them . . . that they should turn to God over the seven rungs with God's help."[41] The Reformation interferes here in changing the image in such a way that the progress becomes a journey from God to humans. Now on the rungs can be read: baptism, Lord's Supper, and forgiveness of sins. "The ladder thus does not consist of steps one has to climb but indicates the means of salvation which God uses to come to the people and to lead them to God."[42]

Just as these are examples of a subsequent reorientation of existing images, so other works advocate a new emphasis in pictorial art. At least fourteen variations of the *Blessing of the Children* are known to be from Cranach's workshop. The portrayal is also found before Cranach's time but not in large mural paintings. All the works of Cranach on the theme have

41. G. Seebass, "Die Himmelsleiter des hl. Bonaventura von Lukas Cranach d. ä. . . Zur Reformation eines Holzschnitts," in the series of the Sitzungsberichte der Heidelberger Akademie der Wissenschaften, Philosophical-Historical section, report no. 4 (1985), 50.

42. Seebass, "Die Himmelsleiter," 52.

in the upper part of the image the fitting quotation from Mark 10. The earliest dated piece comes from 1538-39 and thus belongs to the period of the separation of the Reformation from the Anabaptists. While the latter rejected infant baptism, Luther emphasized, "he [Christ] is now present in baptism as he was then; we Christians know that for certain: therefore we must not refuse to baptize children."[43] With the cheerful group of children and the blessing gesture of Jesus, Cranach underscored this opinion of Luther. At the same time, the compact crowd of people stresses the significance of the family and thereby the directing of the children to Christ by the parents. These are two issues to which Luther had already devoted special attention in the catechisms. The theme of *Christ and the Woman Taken in Adultery,* according to John 8:3ff., receives a similar enhancement of meaning. Alongside all known variations, the Weimar version is attractive because Jesus takes the accused woman by her hand and points with his other hand in the direction of the questioners and so turns their challenge back on to them.

The Image of Justification

With this brief retrospective, the foundation is ready for Cranach's images of justification. If there is one theme from the "Cranach workshop" that "consisted of a working together with Luther and the other Wittenberg theologians,"[44] it is the Cranachian depiction of law and gospel. In this work the teamwork of artist and theologian finds its most compressed expression. The subject appeared on different canvases of the workshop in Wittenberg around the end of the 1520s, and then was also taken up by Lucas Cranach the Younger; it further appeared beyond the work and time of the Cranachs in a variety of canvases.[45] The difficulty of finding an appropriate title for this image becomes apparent in the assortment of summaries for the one theme. The titles that come close are "Law and Gospel," "The Fall and Redemption," and "Law and Grace." However, in the carry-

43. WA 17II:84.1ff. (1525).

44. Oskar Thulin, *Cranach-Altäre der Reformation* (Berlin: Evangelisches Verlag-Anstalt, 1995), 126.

45. Cf. Christoph Weimer, *Luther, Cranach und die Bilder* (Stuttgart: Calwer-Verlag, 1999), 79.

ing out of their content, such titles must be careful to counteract a formulaic "contrasting of the main points of the Old and New Testaments."[46] The work is handled in a more nuanced manner under the title of "religious-dogmatic compositions" in order then to speak more precisely of an "old and new covenant."[47] The use of the concept of allegory comes up not only in the German literature in the form of the title "allegory of law and grace"[48] but also in English treatments of it. There the description is "Allegory of Law and Grace"[49] or "The Law and the Gospel."[50] The theme is further judged under the keywords of typology (Ohly), or the antithetical character is underscored with the identification "Antithesis of 'Law and Gospel,' or of 'Old and New Testament.'"[51] Next to these titles are those that take the human and faith into consideration in their formulations. Thus, "major evangelical dogmas of 'the fall and redemption through faith'"[52] can be spoken of, outlined in a subtitle "the human in the decision before God: the fall into sin — redemption; law — gospel,"[53] and comprehensively "justification through faith,"[54] or finally in a balanced manner, "justification of the sinner before the law through the grace of God and faith."[55]

Judgment regarding the way Cranach worked with the theme of justification is not always favorable. Some see in this picture "Protestant alle-

46. Ernst Grohne, *Die bremischen Truhen mit reformatorischen Darstellungen und der Ursprung ihrer Motive, Abhandlungen und Vorträge der Bremer Wissenschaftlichen Gesellschaft* 10/2 (Bremen: Geist, 1936), 14.

47. K. E. Meier, "Fortleben der religiös-dogmatischen Kompositionen Cranachs in der Kunst des Protestantismus," *Repertorium für Kunstwissenschaft* 32 (1909): 415.

48. Helga Hoffmann, *Die deutschen Gemälde des XVI. Jahrhunderts,* Kunstsammlungen zu Weimar (introduction and catalogue), no. 16 (1988), 52, etc.

49. Craig Harbison, *The Last Judgement in Sixteenth Century Northern Europe: A Study of the Relation between Art and the Reformation* (New York: Garland, 1976), 94.

50. Carl C. Christensen, *Art and the Reformation in Germany* (Athens: Ohio University Press, 1979), 124.

51. P.-K. Schuster, "Abstraktion, Agitation und Einfühlung," in *Luther und die Folgen für die Kunst,* Ausstellungskatalog Hamburger Kunsthalle, ed. Werner Hoffmann (Munich: Prestel, 1983), 210.

52. Hans Posse, *Lucas Cranach d. ä.* (Vienna: Schroll, 1942), 36.

53. Thulin, *Cranach-Altäre der Reformation,* 126.

54. Hinz, *Lucas Cranach d. ä und seine Bildmanufaktur,* 117ff.

55. Dieter Koepplin and Tilman Falk, *Lucas Cranach. Gemälde, Zeichungen, Druckgraphik,* Katalog zur Ausstellung im Kunstmuseum Basel II (1976), 505.

gories overburdened with thoughts,"[56] with which the "shallow fantasy" of Cranach is unable to lift "the religious thought world of the Reformers it intends to portray to an artistic height."[57] It is overweighted with "dry, didactic propagandistic content,"[58] with a meaning that is difficult to understand. They indeed marked the height of his creativity, but do not contribute to Cranach's fame, for he did not "get beyond some pedantic allegories."[59] Finally, we stand with these pictures before "sad conglomerations of a tasteless external symbolism."[60]

Cranach's works on the theme have clear dichotomal structures and are separated in the middle by a dried-out tree on the left and a greening one on the right. In the left half of the image, motif scenes from the Old Testament are shown, for example, the fall, Moses and the prophets, and the presentation of the sinful mortal who is driven by death and the devil toward hell. On the opposite half one can see motifs such as the proclamation to the Shepherds, the annunciation, the brazen serpent, Christ triumphant, the paschal Lamb, as well John the Baptist directing a praying person to the crucified Jesus. From the wound in the side of Christ, blood pours out on the praying person. These make up the base stock of the breadth of the motifs in these portrayals.

It is now necessary to distinguish between two differing renditions of this image. They are designated, according to their place of preservation of a protagonist of the series, as Gotha or Prague type.[61] The criterion for the distinction is the person pictured, and primarily how often that person appears. The variation is clearly recognizable. Thus all the works that show a human being both in the left and the right half belong to the Gotha type. On the left the person is driven into condemnation, and on the right the individual is directed by the Baptist to the Crucified. In the structure of the picture, the scene of the brazen serpent can be on either side. All the works

56. J. Jahn, "Der Weg des Künstlers," in *Lucas Cranach der ältere. Der Künstler und seine Zeit,* ed. Heinz Lüdecke (Berlin: Henschel, 1953), 80.

57. Hubert Janitschek, *Geschichte der deutschen Malerei in Geschichte der deutschen Kunst,* vol. 3 (Berlin: De Gruyter, 1890), 495.

58. Posse, *Lucas Cranach,* 36.

59. Georg Dehio, *Geschichte der deutschen Kunst,* text-vol. 3, 2nd ed. (Berlin: De Gruyter, 1931), 118.

60. Worringer, "Lukas Cranach," 116.

61. This chapter, as it appeared originally, was accompanied by two photos, one of the Gotha type, one of the Prague type. These are not reproduced here.

that portray only a (sitting) person at the trunk of the dividing tree belong to the Prague type. This person is directed by the Prophet on the left side and also by the Baptist on the right side to the Crucified in the right half.

If the figure in question, who is driven into condemnation or is directed toward Christ or is seated at the tree, is considered more closely as a criterion, a further distinguishing detail appears. For it is not always the case that Adam, in the picture of the fall, is identical with the person who is driven into death and the one pointed to Christ or the one seated at the tree. All presentations of the theme portray different figures in the different parts of the picture, as seen in their physiognomy, especially in their style of beard. This breadth of variation makes it possible to understand the Prague version as a more extensive presentation of the theme of justification. Because this figure is not identical with the Adam of the fall and is not prejudiced by a biblical motif, the attitude of the viewer toward the figure is held open. He is a cipher for "the common man" into whom the viewer slips;[62] he is the undefined placeholder for the viewer. In this way the picture's historical elements (such as the fall) and its dogmatic elements (such as John pointing to the cross) are entwined. The (Gotha) altar painting in Weimar, however, transforms the potential present moment into a unique moment from back then: Cranach takes the place of "the common man." Thus, the work takes on the character of a confession because Cranach himself is standing there. It makes the potential process of identification for the viewer of another time period difficult (the place is already occupied).[63] The Prague type expands the possibility of identification. At first sight it offers only the possibility of the reception of the viewer, but the viewer is claimed by both sides of the picture *at the same time.* The Gotha type admits only a pale either-or. It is the *one* person, stretched between law and gospel, who is affected by justification. This more widely extended interpretation of the theme is confirmed by examining the tradition of the pictures standing behind the Prague type.

The motif Hercules at the Crossroads stands as the pictorial tradition behind the Prague type.[64] The story reports that Hercules goes to a

62. Cf. Friedrich Ohly, *Gesetz und Evangelium: Zur Typologie bei Luther und Cranach: Zum Blutstrahl der Gnade in der Kunst* (Münster: Aschendorff, 1985), 32.

63. Where the identification becomes impossible, there the boundary to a cult-image is overstepped.

64. Cranach occupied himself (however, first from 1537 on) with this theme. Cf.

lonely place, contemplating the way of life he should take. Figures full of vice and of virtue appear to him. After some discussion, each side tries to win him over using corresponding statements. Hercules has the choice to go either to the left or to the right. This is underscored by the contrasting pointing of the fingers of the female figures. Most of the time the way of virtue leads up a mountain; that of vice into a (shallow) river landscape. Hercules makes his well-known decision. In the Prague composition Cranach indeed takes up the subject, but with an incisive alteration. The person at the tree can turn to the left, but the pointing of the Prophet points him in the same direction as that of the Baptist. Prophet and Baptist are symmetrically portrayed. The person is met with the same message, given by each of them. With this "artifice," Cranach changes the traditional motif; it is not a crossroads. The Prophet instructs the person in the same way as the Baptist. The motif of Hercules is only conditionally used in the Prague type because through the artifice of Cranach it is no longer an option for the person, or the option is limited, because both pointing fingers direct the individual to the cross. The Gotha type does not allow an option for the person in the image. There the individual is destined to the one or the other side.

With the Prague type, Cranach achieves various goals. First of all, he brings into the picture that which characterizes the Mannerist epoch in which he is to be counted. Against the background of the Reformation and the revolutions connected with it ("the unrest and confusion of the Mannerist epoch"),[65] he breaks through a given image pattern and makes the "problematic human"[66] his theme. The architecture in the painting of Hercules at the Crossroads is left behind or only brought in to such an extent that it shines through for the viewer. Upon the investigation of the new image structure, the viewer not only encounters familiar image structures but also has a new experience of seeing beyond the original motif. The *one* person between God's demanding and comforting Word, as Old and New Testament show them equally,[67] is the theme of the Prague type.

Erwin Panofsky, *Hercules am Scheidewege und andere antike Bildstoffe in der neueren Kunst,* in *Studien der Bibliothek Warburg,* 18 (Leipzig: Teubner, 1930), fig. 47a.

65. Jacques Bousquet, *Malerei des Manierismus. Die Kunst Europas von 1520-1620,* 3rd ed. (Munich: Bruckmann, 1985), 10.

66. C. Grützmacher, "Manierismus heute. Umrisse eines Stilproblems," in *Malerei des Manierismus,* 274.

67. Cf. WA 10I/2:159.7ff.

The human problematic consists in being exposed to the claim of the Word of God as law and gospel in the same way. Theoretically, law and gospel can be clearly distinguished. But in reality, this distinction is difficult to establish, and the person remains caught in the tension between the two. The Gotha type offers various situations into which the viewer can look. In doing so, the tension of law and gospel — a tension that concerns the same person — is lost; it is weakened to its disadvantage.

With the Prague type, Cranach succeeds in giving a true representation of Luther's insight that law and gospel are not to be schematically distributed to the two Testaments.[68] Luther did not doubt "for a moment . . . that one could find the Christ of the New Covenant already in the Old Covenant, promised and sensed in overwhelming riches."[69] With the symmetrical correspondence of Prophet and Baptist, this insight is visualized. The Prophet already points to the cross. However, noticing this is left to the viewer. The person in the picture does not become aware of this matter. The person is seated indeed turned toward the Prophet, but his head is turned to the Baptist. He sees only the Baptist and his instruction. However, with this portrayal the viewer of the composition can approach a statement that is communicated in words only with difficulty. The composition thus achieves a meaning that the word alone cannot achieve.[70]

Finally, we should here call attention to one further factor. With his Prague type, Cranach has found a middle way between a sentimental immersion, as imitation suggests, and the correct representation of accurate proportions and perspective always involving a sober character, familiar from the Renaissance. Between imitative experience and sobriety, the one person represents a figure that is not prejudiced by (familiar) image motifs, and that by its location between God's demanding and God's comfort-

68. Cf. Heinrich Bornkamm, *Luther and the Old Testament,* ed. Eric W. Gritsch, Ruth C. Gritsch, and Victor I. Gruhn (Philadelphia: Fortress, 1969), 81-87; *Luther und das Alte Testament* (Tübingen: Mohr, 1948), 69ff.

69. Bornkamm, *Luther and the Old Testament,* 82. The Gotha type with its strict division suggests a division between law and gospel in each Testament.

70. We intentionally did not mention all the different inscriptions in the paintings. In my opinion they do not contribute anything to the understanding of the image, since these Scripture verses were affixed to the painting afterward (except for a depiction in Königsberg). The painting can be interpreted without the texts. The text may vary or can be left out completely. Some inscriptions are in Latin and would have had a smaller readership.

ing word is not alien to the viewer. Because this situation is not strange to us, the message of the picture affects us in an incomparable way, reflecting our situation, and we as viewers can easily imagine ourselves in the theme of the picture.

Whether the Gotha version of the theme (which meanwhile has moved somewhat to the background) was influenced more by Melanchthon deserves its own separate study. Melanchthon was rather inclined to bring the definition of law and gospel into handy formulas. The dynamic character of the event of justification, as Luther saw it, receded in Melanchthon in favor of a methodical settlement. With the Prague version of the theme, Cranach successfully visualized the theme of justification in a way congenial to Luther, and so brought the central theme of the Reformation to expression in an image.

CHAPTER 15

Luther's *Fourteen Consolations*

Jane E. Strohl

Luther began work on *Tessaradecas consolatoria pro laborantibus et oneratis*[1] in August 1519 at the suggestion of Georg Spalatin, the court chaplain of Frederick the Wise. The elector had fallen gravely ill upon his return from the imperial diet in Frankfurt am Main at which Charles of Spain had been chosen to succeed his grandfather as Holy Roman emperor. Luther, keenly aware of his indebtedness to the Saxon prince, readily embraced the opportunity to express his gratitude through this work of consolation.

On 22 September he sent the Latin manuscript to Spalatin, who was to make a free translation of the treatise into German and present it to the elector. This task was completed and the manuscript returned to Luther by the beginning of December. Again at Spalatin's urging, Luther allowed the *Consolations* to be published in both languages in February 1520. In 1535-36 he oversaw the preparation of a new edition, including the letter of dedication that had inadvertently been omitted from the first Latin version, and adding a preface, in which Luther stated that successive editions from strange hands had so mutilated the original text that he felt compelled to try to restore it. He declared, moreover, that he had not taken advantage of this opportunity to alter or embellish his thoughts as he might have done. Rather, he left the whole, which he characterized as representative of his

1. WA 6:99-134; LW 42:119-66. Page citations refer to the American Edition unless otherwise noted. I have used the translation as is. Emendations have been made on the basis of the Weimar Edition.

views at the beginning of the reform movement, untouched, so as both to demonstrate the progress he had made in the interim and to provide matter for his opponents' malice.

The *Fourteen Consolations* are modeled on a popular cult of medieval Germany. According to legend, in 1446 a Franconian shepherd had a vision of the Christ child surrounded by fourteen saints. In time each of the fourteen acquired a name and an office as the guardian against specific diseases and calamities or as the patron for certain classes of people. These figures often served as the subject for altar paintings. Luther, who in the course of the treatise criticizes those who observe the cult of the saints "only to escape the very evil which the saints, by their example and memory, teach us should be borne" (138), offers his own altar screen of images designed to "strengthen the pious heart" (123) in the acceptance of suffering rather than to encourage the sufferer in superstitious attempts to ward it off. In this Luther espouses a position already well established in medieval theological literature. Pope Gregory, for example, had advised admonishing the sick to recognize their status as children of God in the discipline being exercised upon them.[2] The chastisement was viewed as edifying, making for spiritual health, and thus to be accepted as a sign of God's love and not simply as the work of divine wrath.

As Luther and numerous medieval theologians before him point out, many saints suffered disease or physical affliction. God thereby taught these chosen ones patience, crowning their faith with virtue, while manifesting God's own majesty by perfecting power in weakness. For the great saint as for the least of these, the church's little ones, illness served to wean one from earthly things and fill one with concern for, and all too often apprehension of, one's eternal destiny. The people of medieval Europe, ravaged repeatedly by the plague, had great grounds for fear and little hope of healing and recovery. When it came to considering the world to come, they expanded their terror rather than rekindling a hope for wholeness. The ferocity of God as evidenced in pestilence was regarded as a foretaste of the judgment to come and a potent reminder to every Christian to do all he or

2. The source for much of the following summary is Darrel W. Amundsen, "The Medieval Catholic Tradition," in *Caring and Curing: Health and Medicine in the Western Religious Traditions,* ed. Ronald L. Numbers and Darrel W. Amundsen (New York: Macmillan, 1986), 65-107. Those interested in Christian attitudes toward healing and health issues will find this collection of essays most informative.

she could to insure escape from that far more terrible condemnation. Thus, while illness could appear as a grace when it advanced the perfection of holiness in the saints, it was also a manifestation of God's wrath intended to scare some spiritual sense into the unbeliever or worldly Christian. Such persons too could turn illness to their own advantage.

In the collection of prints that constitutes the most popular form of the medieval *Ars Moriendi,* one finds a portrayal of the temptation of impatience. The dying man is shown beset by demons who make him angry at his fate and suspicious of the motives of the family and friends who watch at his bedside. In this way, the devil seeks to rob him of the merit to be won by patient endurance and the humble acceptance of God's will. In the companion picture there appears an angel who consoles the afflicted man with the thought that suffering, if properly borne in life, proves to be a blessing in that it lessens one's pains in purgatory after death. God inflicts misery now so as to be able to offer rewards in eternity. The picture shows God the Father holding an arrow and a whip, Christ as the man of sorrows, and various saints with the instruments of their martyrdom, all surrounding the deathbed to remind the sufferer of the necessity and value of patience.

Luther shares this understanding of the positive role suffering, particularly illness, can play in the life of the Christian. It can drive the sinner out of self-satisfaction to the very border of despair and then ultimately to Christ. It can render the believer more susceptible to the divine activity, which as sheer grace can transform the emptiness of deprivation into the fullness of God. However, Luther diverges from certain tendencies in medieval Christianity. He does not let the wrath of God, which he too intuits behind the ills befalling sinful humanity, eclipse the kindness made known in Christ and transform the Savior into a judge. Nor does he let believers find something of their own to build upon and cling to even in the midst of the dissolution illness entails. Patient endurance of suffering is a virtue pleasing to God, but it is not a means by which one may improve one's position at the last judgment.

Given the clear allusion to the cult of the saints made by the framework of Luther's treatise, it is striking that the author finds no source of consolation in the appeal to saints and relics, the most popular religious practice of his time. Frederick the Wise, for whom Luther wrote the work, possessed one of the largest and most prestigious collections of relics in Europe. Luther never suggests that he avail himself of this resource. Here, as with a number of other medieval practices, it is not for Luther a question of distinguishing between an abuse and a proper use. He allows no legitimacy to acts of piety that seek to avert suffering so that one might return unscathed to one's temporal concerns. Moreover, to depend upon the saints and their relics to restore one to bodily health is to make far too much of earthly well-being and far too little of the mercy of Christ.

Luther's *Fourteen Consolations* consist of two parts or panels, the consideration of which should put one's present condition in proper perspective. Luther writes in the introduction:

> The Holy Scriptures approach the matter of comfort in a twofold manner, insofar as they represent to our view both blessings and evils, wholesomely intermingled. This is in accord with the word of the Preacher, "In the day of evil be mindful of the good, and in the day of the good be mindful of the evil" (Eccles. 11:25). The Holy Spirit knows that a thing has only such value and meaning to a man as he assigns to it in his thought. Whatever he regards as trivial and of no value will affect him only slightly, whether it be love when it comes to him or pain when it goes away. Therefore, the Spirit tries with great effort to draw man away from thinking about things and from being affected by them. When the Spirit has accomplished this, then all things, whatever they may be, are indifferent. Therefore, the diversion is best effected through the Word, by which our present thought is turned from the thing that moves us at the present moment to something that is either absent or does not move us at the moment. It is thus very true that we shall find consolation only through the Scriptures, which in the days of evil call us to the contemplation of our blessings, either present or to come, and in the days of blessing, point us to the contemplation of the evils. (124; translation emended)

This programmatic statement is somewhat misleading, for Luther follows two tacks in his work of consolation. Often he relativizes the reader's suffering with reminders that the present ills could be much worse and are always susceptible to improvement in the future. This consciousness of the ceaseless vicissitudes of human existence can foster an attitude of almost Stoic indifference toward one's current tribulation. However, at significant points in the treatise Luther does not diminish this suffering but transfigures it, making of the very *malum* a *bonum* and generating not indifference, which neither seeks nor avoids, but a passion that actively rejoices in its burdens.

Luther begins with the evil within, the depth of which, by God's mercy, is seen only by faith and never fully experienced. The evil we actually suffer is only the tip of the iceberg, and so at any given moment our freedom from pain is greater than the pain we ought rightfully feel. This true evil, though hidden from us, does nonetheless make itself known in the troubled conscience when faith falters and in our recurrent awareness that nothing we do in this world is whole and perfect. These experiences of evil are blunted, however, by familiarity, which, according to Luther, is another effect of God's providential care. They "do not cease being evils just because they are less sharply felt by us" (127), but "we measure, feel, or do not feel our evils not on the basis of the facts, but on the basis of our own thoughts and feelings" (127). Our very insensitivity is our salvation.

The second image, that of the evil before us, enumerates the tragedies, indignities, and diseases that may yet befall any one of us. Thus, in regarding our present trouble we should be thankful that we have been spared all these other possible afflictions. Yet even if one should remain unscathed by any of the calamities listed, one evil, and that considered the greatest of all, is inevitable — death. "Because death is such a great evil, we see many who would rather live with all the evils mentioned above than to die once and have them ended. Disdaining the other evils, this is the one to which the Scriptures ascribe fear. . . . There is no one who would not choose to submit to all other evils if thereby he could avoid the evil of death. Even the saints dreaded it, and Christ submitted to it with trembling fear and bloody sweat" (129). However, Christians face an even more dreadful threat in the future, that is, the possibility of falling from grace. "What true Christian will not want death and even sickness when he sees that as long as he lives and is healthy, he is in sin and always likely to fall, yes, daily does fall into more sins, thus constantly thwarting the loving will of his loving Father? . . . The man who does not prefer the evil of death to the evil of sin loves God his Father but little. God has ordained that this evil be brought to an end by death and that death be the minister of life and righteousness" (130). Here the misery of death is not only diminished by comparison to something worse, the fall into sin, but is as a consequence transformed from an evil into a blessing. Death, when set against sin, becomes the minister of life and righteousness.

Consideration of the past evil or the evil behind us in the third image and of the evil beneath us in the fourth image returns to the method of minimizing the sufferer's present trouble. In the former case he is exhorted to weigh this single affliction against the manifold instances of God's providential care in his past. "These and other exhortations are all intended to teach us that since God was with us when we did not think so, or he did not seem to be with us, we should not doubt that he is always with us, even when it seems that he is absent from us. He who upheld us in many times of need, even without our request, will not forsake us in a smaller affliction, even though he seems to do so" (131). Instead of focusing on the evils that befall him, he should rejoice that God has not allowed countless others to strike home. One has only to consider the thousands suffering eternal damnation in hell for sins not a thousandth of one's own to dismiss as minor the evil one currently endures. "I ask you, what are all the sufferings life can bring compared with the eternal punishment which they indeed suffer justly because of one sin, while we go free and unpunished for our many sins which God has covered?" (134). Whatever evil befalls us in this life is barely a fraction of what we have deserved, and this restraint on God's part is a sign of God's mercy toward us.

Again, in comparison to the agents of evil on our left hand, that is, wicked people, we should marvel at the limited damage God permits them to inflict rather than bemoan the pain we must endure now and again from them. Moreover, these persons are to be pitied when their situation is contrasted to that of Christians.

> You see how deep is the abyss of evils that is here opened up, and how it is an opportunity for pity and compassion and for overlooking our own paltry ills, if the love of God abides in us. What God permits us to suffer is nothing compared to what they suffer. . . . Who is so hard of heart as not to sicken at the wretched sight of those lying at the doors of the churches and in the streets, with disfigured faces, their noses, eyes, and other members so hideously consumed with festering sores that the mind is terrified and the senses recoil from the sight? What else does God intend with these lamentable specimens of our flesh and common humanity but to open the eyes of our mind so that we might see even more horrible forms in which the sinner's soul shows forth its disease and decay, even though he himself may live in purple and gold among roses and lilies like a child of paradise? . . . Even in regard to bodily ills, these people are worse off than we are. How can they, I ask

> you, find sweet and pure joys, even if they have obtained everything their heart desires, as long as their conscience can find no peace? Can there be an evil more dreadful than the unrest of a gnawing conscience? (136; translation emended)

Luther here dismisses the horrors of physical pain and disfigurement as pale reflections of the spiritual decay within the ungodly. True suffering is the conscience at enmity with God. For Christians, who bear their ills "while in the faith, in the kingdom of Christ, and in the service of God" (135), their evil, when compared to that of the ungodly, will seem as nothing at all.

Contemplation of the evil on our right hand, which is the evil endured by the saints both living and dead, again humbles us. There is, asserts Luther, no lack of persons who suffer more seriously and bitterly both in spirit and body than we do.[3] He offers as an example John the Baptist, whose humiliating and undeserved death shames those who would make much of their sufferings or who would try to escape them. Luther chastises those who honor the saints in the hope that they will preserve them from pain and sorrow. He also answers those who object that they cannot be expected to imitate the saints, for the latter suffered for their innocence

3. In his *Ein Sermon von der Betrachtung des heiligen Leidens Christi* (1519), Luther exhorts his readers always to measure their own sufferings against the sorrows of Christ. Just as true devotion to the saints results in an imitation of their patience and endurance, so proper contemplation of the passion of Christ, having embraced him as a sacrament, now takes him as an example (WA 2:141.12-29): ". . . Nu bedencken wyr es [das ley den Christi], das wir auch wircken, Nemlich also: Sodich ein weetag oder krankheyt beschweret, dencke, wie gringe das sey gegen der dornenn kronen und negelnn Christi. Szo du must thunn adder lassenn, was dir widdert, denck, wie Christus gepunden und gefangen hyn und her gefurt wirt. Ficht dich die hoffert an, sieh, wie deyn herr vorspottet und mit den schechenn vorachtet wirt. Stost dich unkeuscheyt und lust an, gedenck, wie bitterlich Christus zartes fleysch zurgeysselt, durchstochen und durchschlagen wirt. Ficht dich hass und neyt an, ader rache suchst, denck, wie Christus mit vielen threnen und ruffen fur dich und alle seyne feynde gpeten hat, deß wol billicher gerochen hette. Szo dich trubsal adder wasserlei widderwertickeyt leyplich adder geystlich bekummert, sterck dein hertz und sprich: Ey worumb solt ich dan nit auch eyn klein betrubnis leyden, szo meyn herr im garten blut vor angst und betrubnis schwitzt, Eyn fauler, schendlicher knecht were das, der auff dem bett liegenn wolt, wan seyn herr in todts noeten streytten muss." Note that here once again the principle applied is that of diminishment of the believer's trials by comparison to a situation more dreadful.

whereas common mortals are tormented for their sins. That, writes Luther, is a very stupid statement. "If you are a sinner, good! The thief was also a sinner, but by his patience he merited the glory of righteousness and holiness. Go and do likewise. Whenever you suffer, it is either because of your sins or your righteousness. Both kinds of suffering sanctify and save *[beatum facit]* if you will but love them" (140). The two causes of suffering become one, and the sinner is transformed into the saint by the act of confession. "[A]s soon as you have confessed that you suffer justly for your sins, you are righteous and holy as the thief on the right hand. Confession of sin, which is truth, justifies and sanctifies, and thus in the very moment of this confession you suffer no longer for your sins but on account of your innocence" (140; translation emended). The acknowledgment of the justice of God's judgment engenders in the sinner a proper righteousness so that his or her sufferings are meritorious rather than punitive. Luther does not suggest that such confession will bring deliverance from tribulation. Indeed, the purpose of this sixth image is to convince believers that evils can and must be borne.

In the introduction to the *Fourteen Consolations* Luther extols the power of the Word to direct our thoughts to the contemplation of evils in times of blessing and to the consideration of our blessings when times are bad. In the seventh image of evil, the evil above us, the Word accomplishes far more than the diversion of our thoughts from our sufferings.

> Thus the bride says, "His lips are lilies, letting sweet-smelling myrrh fall in drops" (Song of Sol. 5:13). What resemblance is there between lilies and lips, since lips are red and lilies white? It is said in a mystical sense, as if to say that Christ's words are clear and pure, without even a vestige of blood red bitterness or malice, but only sweetness and mildness. Yet into them he drops precious and chosen myrrh (that is, the most bitter death). These purest and sweetest lips have the power to make the bitterest death sweet and fair and bright and dear, for death (like precious myrrh) removes all of sin's corruptions at once. (141)

Here Luther develops the theme introduced in the second image that death changes from an evil to a blessing by delivering us finally from the power of sin. Moreover, by the power of Christ crucified all evils are transformed. They are no longer to be feared but confidently embraced, even desired.

> How does this come to pass? Surely, it comes to pass when you hear that Jesus Christ, God's Son, has by his most holy touch consecrated and hallowed all sufferings, even death itself, has blessed the curse, and has glorified shame and enriched poverty so that death is now a door to life, the curse a fount of blessing, and shame the mother of glory. How, then, can you be so hardhearted and ungrateful as not to long for and love all manner of sufferings now that these have been touched and bathed by Christ's pure and holy flesh and blood and thus have become holy, harmless, wholesome, blessed, and full of joy for you? (142)

Mortal life might be said to undergo a process of transubstantiation in the believer, the accidents of existence remaining the same to outward view while the substance is profoundly changed. "In death we are like all other mortals: the outward mode of our dying is not unlike that of others, except the thing itself is different, since for us death is dead. In like manner, all our sufferings are like the sufferings of others, but only in appearance. In reality, our sufferings are the beginning of our freedom from suffering [*impassibilitatis initia*] as our death is the beginning of life" (142; translation emended).

The resurrection of Christ shows us that in the experience of pain, suffering, and death, nothing evil befell the Lord; he derived from it only good. To see this, to comprehend the eagerness with which Christ drained the cup of suffering so that we might not fear to drink after him, is to taste in the bitter myrrh he offers us the sweetness of the lily.

With this reflection on the passion of Christ, Luther completes the first panel of his altar screen and turns his attention to construction of the second, consisting of seven images of blessing parallel to the evils already delineated. In the initial section of this half of the treatise Luther retreats from his powerful understanding of the nature of suffering under the cross of Christ. At first he presents evil as the seasoning necessary to preserve the savor of blessing rather than as sweetness itself. "Is there anything that must not be tempered and sanctified with the relics of the cross to prevent decay, just as meat must be seasoned with salt lest it breed maggots? Why then do we not gladly accept this tempering sent by God, which, if he were not to send it, our own life, weakened by pleasures and blessings, would demand of itself?" (145-46).

The depth of the blessings within us, like that of our evils, is mercifully hidden from us since, according to Luther, this life could not sustain their revelation. However, they make their presence felt in the happy conscience that rejoices in trusting God and clinging to God's Word.

In the second image, that of the blessing before us, Luther again takes up the idea of death's transformation. It proves a blessing because it effects the permanent end to our earthly ills and to all our sins and vices. Knowing that our worst loss shall become our richest gain eclipses any pain endured in present evils. According to Luther, the curse of death, which entered the world as punishment for human sinfulness, was intended by God from the outset as a blessing for the believer.

> And that God appointed death to be the destroyer of sin can be gathered from the fact that he imposed death on Adam immediately after his sin as a cure for sin (Gen. 3:19). God did this before he drove him out of paradise to show us that death works us no evil but rather every good, since it was imposed in paradise as a penance and satisfaction. It is true that through the envy of the devil death entered into the world, but it is evidence of God's surpassing goodness that after death entered, it is not permitted to harm us, but is taken captive from the very beginning and appointed to be the punishment and death of sin. (151; translation emended)

Death is the agent of God's mercy among the elect and the execution of divine justice among the ungodly. Earlier Luther had exhorted his readers to feel compassion for the wicked and to pray for their enemies, who suffer harm from their evildoing greater than that endured by their victims. However, in considering the blessing beneath us, that is, the damned, he warns against misplaced mercy that degenerates into complicity with the sinfulness of the ungodly. Luther recognizes that God's battle on behalf of righteousness cuts through individuals. "What wonder, then, if by way of your present evil God punishes your enemy, that is, the sin in your body? You ought rather to rejoice in this work of God's supreme justice, which even without your prayer slays and destroys your fiercest foe, namely, the sin that is within you. But if you should feel pity for it, you will be found to be a friend of sin and an enemy of the justice at work in you" (157).

Yet ultimately the battle line is drawn between individuals as well, and to pity the condemned sinner is as inexcusable as to wish to protect one's own sin from God's wrath. The prospect of God's justice striking the damned offers a twofold comfort to Christians in Luther's view. They can be thankful that God in mercy will spare them such an extremity of suffering and thus face the present evil with a light heart. Moreover, they can rejoice in this revelation of God's righteousness that avenges the injuries inflicted upon the elect by their enemies. Indeed, in his preparation of the fifth image, Luther suggests that the evil one endures at the hands of the wicked works ultimately for one's good. It presents one with opportunities to exercise virtue, build strength, and acquit oneself meritoriously. This adversity keeps believers on the alert so that they might not succumb to the world's blandishments or be broken by its hostility. It trains them to cling solely to Christ. The worldly goods with which the ungodly frequently abound serve as a sign to Christians in their present sufferings of the far greater blessings, as yet invisible, that are theirs.

Luther also maintains that the bitterness of suffering is mitigated by the realization that we are not left to bear our evils alone. The blessing behind us is the experience of God's continuous care in the past, and blessing on our right is the fellowship of the church.

> Therefore, when we feel pain, when we suffer, when we die, let us turn to this, firmly believing and certain that it is not we alone, but Christ and the church who are in pain and are suffering and dying with us. Christ does not want us to be alone on the road of death, from which all mortals shrink. Indeed, we set out upon the road of suffering and death accompanied by the entire church. . . . All that remains for us now is to pray that our eyes, that is, the eyes of our faith, may be opened that we may see the church around us. (163; translation emended)

The final image Luther offers is that of the risen Christ. Here all evils have yielded to righteousness and life. The joy generated by contemplation of this vision is of a wholly different order from the grief caused by earthly evils. It virtually effaces them from our attention. The similarity of language used by Luther to describe the effect of the seventh image of evil and the seventh image of blessing is striking:

> If we have learned from the preceding images, those beneath and near us, to bear our evils with patience, then surely this last image, in which

> we are lifted above and outside ourselves, caught up into Christ and placed above all evils, should teach us that we ought not only to tolerate these evils, but love them, desire them, and seek them out. (144; translation emended)

> This, then, is the most sublime image, for in it we are lifted up not only above our evils, but even above our blessings, and we are set down in the midst of strange blessings gathered by the labors of another, whereas formerly we lay among evils that were also brought about by the sin of another and enlarged by our own. We are set down, I say, in Christ's righteousness. (165)

The Spirit works through the Word, writes Luther in the introduction to the *Fourteen Consolations*, so that whatever the earthly condition in which believers find themselves, it might be of indifference to them: "Therefore, the Spirit tries with great effort to draw one away from thinking about things and from being affected by them. When the Spirit has accomplished this, then all things, whatever they may be, are indifferent."[4] *Res indifferens*, a thing different, is considered neither good nor evil; it is neither sought nor avoided. "One's evils are only as great as one's knowledge and opinion of them; so it is with one's blessings" (146). Indeed, good and evil are subjectively determined; the validity of the judgment is a matter of proper perception. This whole treatise is concerned with what one sees. It presents fourteen images for contemplation, and their purpose is to renew our sight: "If we consider this rightly, we shall see how greatly we are favored by God."[5] "Oh, if we could only see the heart of Christ as he was suspended from the cross, anguishing to make death dead and contemptible. . . . If we could see this, then undoubtedly that precious myrrh dropping from Christ's lips and commended by his words would be sweet and appealing to us, even as the fragrance and beauty of the lilies."[6] "All that re-

4. WA 6:106.3, 1-32: "Ideo id omni studio conatur ut hominem a rerum opinione et affectua vocet. Quod ubi effecerit iam res quaelibet sunt indifferentes."

5. WA 6:114.4-5: "Quae omnia si digne videamus, simul videbimus, quanta benigniore dei dignatione."

6. WA 6:119.7-13: "O sicor liceat Christi intueri, quando in cruce pendens artabatur, ut mortem redderet mortuam et contemptibilem, . . . sine dubio fieret illa prima myrrha, stillantibus eius labiis et verbis Christi eam commendantibus, incundissima et dulcissima sicut odor et species liliorum."

mains for us now is to pray that our eyes, that is, the eyes of our faith, may be opened that we may see the church around us."[7] The consolation offered by the Word is a new vision, the power by faith to see suffering and death from the perspective of the crucified and risen Lord. It turns our common human view of these matters upside down,[8] lifting us, as Luther puts it, above our evils and our blessings, making of them *res indifferentes.*

This does not eradicate the pain or fear of our misery, but it robs it of its hopelessness. Luther does not at the heart of his consolation succumb to the temptation of denying the reality of suffering, either the Lord's or our

7. WA 6:132.20-22: "Hoc solum et nobis restat, ut oremus, quo nobis aperiantur oculi et videamus Ecclesiam in circuitu nostro, fidei inquam oculi."

8. Luther takes up this same idea in his Lenten sermon *Vom Blindgeborenen* (John 9:1-38) of 17 March 1518. He writes the following concerning the tempter's promise in Eden that the humans' eyes would be opened so that they would know good and evil like God (WA 1:270.4-10): "Also sind unser augen auffgethan, das ist, wir sind gantz blind worden, das wir den schein, wie itzt gesagt, auch gutachten, und armut, ungestalt etc. fuer boese halten. Das hat der teufel uns geleret, des augen sind es auch. Aber Christus ist darumb komen, das er diese augen lere zu thun, und die blindheit weg zu nemen, auf das wir nicht underscheid machen unter jung und alten, schoen und greulich etc." Of suffering and death Luther writes in this same sermon (WA 1:271.8-17, 21-25, 28-31; 272.3-9): "Wiewol der Heiligen bein sol man in silber fassen. Es ist auch gut und wol gethan. Man mag auch der Milchseugling wegen viel zulassen, als Bilde und dergleichen, die man einem andern verbieten mus. Darumb die da eines hohen grades sind, sollen die ding gering achten und die augen hoeher auff heben, denn Christus wird inen ein bessers fuer die thuer bringen, das sie in aller welt finden moegen. Denn er wird inen senden widerwertigkeit, truebsal, angst, sorge, betruebnis, armut, widerwillen etc., wird dir kranckheit zuschicken, und der teufel am ende deines lebens, an den letzten noeten, der wird dich on unterlas anfechten und dich erschrecken so hertiglich, das du genau verzagen must . . . Denn hab ein iglicher auffmerckung, was Gott wolgefalle, das er froehlich spreche: Ah mein Lieber Gott, ich gleub es gentzlich, du sendest mir das zu. Bis mir wilkomen, liebes Heilthum. Ich danck dir, mein fromer Gott, das du mich darzu wirdig schetzest, zu dem, das dir in deinem Leben das edelste gewesen. . . . Das ist das edelst Heilthum quod obviis ulnis et osculis debemus accipere, Das wir lieblich mit dancksagung empfahen sollen. Denn das heilthum hat Gott selbs mit seinem edelsten willen und wolgefallen seines Vaters geheiliget und gebenedeiet . . . So nu Gott uns das zuschickt, so lauffen wir zurueck und fliehen dafuer, Er wolt uns gerne geben so wollen wir nicht. Wir sind auch nicht alle wirdig. Es ist ein sonderlich anzeigung fromer kinder Gottes. Er gibt es offt, so wissen wir denn nicht, wo wirs lasen sollen. Denn dahin koempt es, das wir meinen, wir sehen wol, und sind gantz blind, das wir boese nennen, das Christus gut nennet."

own, a fault rightly found with numerous philosophical and religious approaches to the human condition.[9] He neither rejects the paradoxical concept of a God who smites us to make us whole nor betrays discomfort with confessing both God's absolute power and absolute love simultaneously. Luther never wholly drops from consideration the *Deus absconditus,* who does deliver creatures to temptation and evil and who is capable of damning the sinner, but he does not reflect upon this God apart from Christ, the *Deus revelatus.* That God does not remove suffering and immediately make straight the rough places of our lives isn't for Luther a negative reflection either on the extent of God's power or on the integrity of God's professed love for us. The absoluteness of that power is revealed in its extraordinary efficaciousness. God's power serves God's love, making itself susceptible to the suffering of creation so as to transform that suffering from within, and able always to bring life out of nothingness.

In his *Theology of the Lutheran Confessions,* Friedrich Mildenberger discusses the time and place of faith, emphasizing that belief is God's work, not our own. We are usually untroubled persons, people at ease, who imagine faith to be within our control, and who readily mistake our devotion to piety for experiencing the gospel. "The Reformers taught that we receive God's salvation in Christ only when we are past the point of being able to do anything. At this point, the point at which we are unable to do anything for ourselves, the Holy Spirit works faith. This kind of faith, therefore, comes only at a specific time and place. The time and place at which we experience spiritual temptation is the time and place at which God wills to create the faith which is God's own work in us."[10]

In the *Fourteen Consolations* Luther frequently employs the expedient of diminishing the seriousness of the experienced evil by obliging the sufferer to consider how much worse it could be for him and indeed is for many others. The sufferer who can successfully be exhorted to improve his attitude falls short of hearing the gospel. He is not yet at the point of utter helplessness; he is still able to do something, if only to look at others and generate guilt for his ingratitude, concluding that his misfortune is not so

9. I am indebted to Douglas John Hall, *God and Human Suffering: An Exercise in the Theology of the Cross* (Minneapolis: Augsburg, 1986), for sparking the reflections that follow.

10. Friedrich Mildenberger, *Theology of the Lutheran Confessions,* trans. Erwin Lueker (Philadelphia: Fortress, 1986), 41.

dreadful after all. This, one might say, is putting suffering in its proper perspective from a human point of view. The time and place for faith come, however, when suffering is left to stand undiminished by human reckoning and open to the working of the Holy Spirit. Then we regard it from that human point of view no longer. Luther once wrote to the citizenry of Miltenberg, which was being punished for its evangelical innovations: "[H]ell cannot be sad if God reigns there."[11] So it is with any cross laid upon us. The powerful theological and pastoral insight Luther offers in the *Fourteen Consolations* is the realization that what is perceived as evil can be transformed into a blessing, that sufferings of all kinds, and most especially death, become for believers signs of God's love and means of Christ's grace. This true consolation, like the righteousness of faith, is wholly God's gift.

11. LW 43:106.

PART V

The Pastor in the World

CHAPTER 16

Luther on Monasticism

Dorothea Wendebourg

"A Monastery is a hell, with the devil as both abbot and prior, and the monks and nuns the damned souls."[1] Thus wrote Martin Luther, the father of the Reformation, in 1533. "When you hear the word 'monk,' it is as if you heard the word apostate Christian, betrayer of the faith, a disciple of the devil."[2] These are harsh words, and a host of similar statements regarding monasticism is easily found, not just in Luther's writings, but in those of other reformers as well. It was, therefore, not without reason that monastic life very soon came to an end where the Reformation took hold. Protestant churches were, and to a large extent are, churches without monasteries.

There are good reasons to regard monasticism and Protestantism as mutually exclusive. And yet this is not the whole truth. This can be inferred from the simple fact that Martin Luther himself, and with him a number of fellow reformers especially of the Lutheran bent, had been friars or monks.

1. WA 38:148.30-32. "Ein Kloster ist ein Helle, darinn der Teuffel Abt und Prior ist, Munche und Nonnen die verdampten seelen."

2. WA 38:147.1-3: "wenn du das wort Munch horest, das es gleich so viel sey als hortesttu das wort Verleugneter Christ, Apostata vom glauben Christi, Ein bundgenos des Teuffels."

Translated by Alexandra Riebe, Berlin. It is a slightly changed text of a paper presented at a symposium entitled "Monasticism in East and West" in Dzaghatzer Monastery, Armenia, also edited in a collection of the papers presented there under the title *In Search of the Precious Pearl,* ed. Edward Farrougia (Rome: Pontifical Oriental Institute, 2005).

Among them were members of nearly all the great monastic families — Benedictines, Franciscans, Carthusians, Knights Templar, Dominicans, and, first and foremost, Augustinian Hermits. It is no accident that the first martyrs of the Reformation were monks as well, two young mendicants who were burned at the stake in Brussels in 1523. Such are the bare historical facts. But this is not all; to a large extent these men owed to monasticism the spiritual impulses that made them reformers. The vision of the Christian life and of the church with which they confronted the church of their time was inspired by ideals and insights that had been shaped in the course of their monastic lives. In short, "no Reformation without monasticism."[3] We need to ask, therefore, whether the spiritual legacy the reformers passed on to the Protestant churches is also not linked to the monastic tradition so closely as to render inadequate a simplistic opposition between monasticism and Reformation. Perhaps such a link between monasticism and Protestantism might serve as a new rationale for Protestant monastic life today. Those Protestant monastic communities that have come into existence lately, although few and far between, may be proof of this.

This brief introduction outlines the structure of my essay. I shall first deal with Martin Luther and his monastic roots; then I shall give a sketch of his critique of monasticism; next I shall describe the monastic features of the Reformation and especially Lutheran churches. Finally I shall look at how the complex relationship between monasticism and the Reformation might afford us a fresh rationale for monastic life within Protestantism today.

Luther the Monastic Reformer

Martin Luther, the first and most important of the reformers, was a monk, or more precisely, a friar. For nearly twenty years, between 1505 and 1524, he was an Augustinian Hermit, until 1511 in Erfurt in Thuringia, afterward in Wittenberg in Saxony. Luther, who lived to the age of sixty-three, wore the monk's habit between the age of twenty-two and forty-one, the most important years of his life and precisely the time that saw the beginning of the Reformation.

3. Johannes Schilling, *Gewesene Mönche. Lebensgeschichten in der Reformation,* lecture 26 in Schriften des Historischen Kollegs (Munich: Stiftung Historisches Kolleg, 1990), 33.

The significance of Luther's monastic roots for the Reformation becomes apparent when we look at other contemporary reform movements. None was as radical in the literal sense of the word; none went as deep, to the very roots of the church and the Christian life, as did Luther and the Lutheran Reformation. The fifteenth-century Hussites in Bohemia fought for better living conditions for the Czech people and for the restoration of the chalice to the laity. Huldrych Zwingli in Zürich aimed at an evangelical reformation of social and ecclesiastical life. Humanism was seeking remedies for grievances in education, church, and politics. All these elements were present in Luther's reformation, too. But they were not his first priority. What mattered most to him and the Reformation he began was the right relationship between God and humanity. In his view, the church no longer taught and preached according to the gospel; it thereby jeopardized salvation and made countless Christians fear for their souls. Such was his diagnosis. At this point he demanded that the church repent. It must preach and teach correctly about the relationship between God and humanity. It must preach and teach that God grants salvation in Christ alone through grace alone and that human beings receive this salvation through faith alone. This is the core of his call for reformation and the basis of his criticism of church structure, ethics, liturgy, and so on.

The radical, principled nature of Luther's diagnosis, criticism, and subsequent reform of the Christian life is directly linked to his monastic background. After all, for centuries the place for Christians who wanted to live a life "radically" in accordance with the gospel had been the monasteries. It was there that men and women strove to fulfill God's will in a special way by leading a life of humility and lifelong repentance, of incessant prayer and ascetic discipline. For this reason they endeavored to keep not just the Ten Commandments like all Christians; they also observed special "counsels" *(consilia)* like poverty, chastity, and obedience; this was the perfect "angelic" path, reserved for the few. The idea was to live a life in accordance with the words of the Sermon on the Mount, that great vision of the true Christian life described by Jesus himself, a life in perfect harmony with how God willed humanity to be.

It was this world that the young Martin Luther entered about five hundred years ago, in 1505. And he did so with great earnestness. In later years, after he had long since shed the monk's habit and after his acerbic criticism had swept away the monasteries, his adversaries would charge him with lax discipline as a monk and that for this reason he had decamped from the monastery. He was indignant at this charge and denied it emphatically: "The truth is, I was an observant and obedient monk. I kept the Rule so strictly that I dare say if ever a man entered heaven for being a monk, I would have entered it. All my fellow monks will confirm that this is the truth."[4] And indeed, several of his brethren affirmed, even after his death, that Luther had been a very conscientious monk who kept the Rule to the point of saintliness.[5] The monastic vows of poverty, chastity, and obedience were never a problem for him. He did his share of begging for alms, which was part of life in a mendicant order. With particular dedication he observed his liturgical duties: the Mass, the canonical hours, the rosary, because he considered them to be the most important aspect of monastic life. He showed great integrity, both human and spiritual; he was theologically competent and possessed leadership qualities, all of which very soon made him a figure of authority in his order. In 1509 he was made subprior in his monastery, then in 1515 he was put in charge of the convents of Thuringia and Meißen. In 1510-11 the monastery in Erfurt sent him to Rome for important negotiations with the master general. In modern parlance: he was regarded as having a great career ahead of him.

A career, however, had not been Luther's motivation when he became a monk at the age of twenty-two. When he broke off the studies of law that he had just begun, and knocked on the door of the Augustinian friars in Erfurt, he had only one motive in his mind: to become acceptable to God, the Lord of life and death. To fulfill God's will totally and thus please the eternal Judge, this was Luther's aim, as it was the aim of so many men and women before and around him who had chosen the monastic path, because like them he was convinced that this aim could best be reached in a monastery.

Fulfilling God's will totally for Luther meant doing more than just keeping the Ten Commandments, which was everybody's obligation. It also meant (and Luther accepted the classic medieval distinction)[6] observing those special "counsels" that governed the monastic life, namely, poverty, chastity, and obedience, as mentioned. They constitute the perfect

4. WA 38:143.25-28.

5. Otto Scheel, ed., *Dokumente zu Luthers Entwicklung,* 2nd ed. (Tübingen: Mohr, 1929), no. 534.

6. For example, WA 4:202.29-31; WA 2:168.6f.; LW 44:9. WA 56:62.29–63.19; LW 25:55.

(perfectus) path.[7] It is especially through them that a Christian is enabled to develop those virtues *(virtutes)* that prevail over human vices *(vitia)*. At the same time, they effect correction and improvement with respect to the three dimensions of human life: the individual's relationship to God, his neighbors, and himself.

> Humility; poverty; chastity against pride, the lust of the flesh, and the lust of the eyes. For as by humility man disposes himself toward God and becomes pleasing to him, by poverty he disposes himself toward his neighbor and becomes pleasing to him, and by chastity he disposes himself toward himself and becomes pleasing to himself, so by pride he stands against and resists God, by avarice against his neighbor, and by intemperance against himself.[8]

As this passage shows, poverty, chastity, and obedience are not simply external kinds of conduct. Rather, through monastic discipline an inner attitude is to become outwardly visible, while at the same time it is strengthened by that discipline. The demand for total obedience does not merely concern specific acts; it is directed at the person who acts, at his heart. This is what the Bible says, especially the Sermon on the Mount with its radical antitheses (Matt. 5:21-48), as the monastic tradition has always emphasized. For the monk Martin Luther it is a matter of course. Being obedient to God even in his innermost thought and will is what he strives for in his monastic life. In Jesus' words: "To love God with all his heart, with all his soul, and with all his mind." But it is at this point that he comes up against an insuperable limitation, an experience that throws him first into despair and then leads him to a complete reorientation. Perfect obedience and perfect love are what he cannot achieve. He remains a sinner, never quite in accord with the will of God. He is able to follow the monastic Rule, to keep monastic discipline; as far as his outward behavior is concerned, he is a model monk. But the more perfect his behavior, the more oppressive the experience that he is not master of his will. Time and again there are selfishness and defiance, there are pride and

7. WA 56:62.29.

8. WA 4:155.20-25: "humilitas, pautertas, castitas, contra superbiam vitae, concupiscentiam carnis et oculorum. Sicut enim per humilitatem ad deum, per paupertatem ad proximum, per castitatem ad seipsum disponitur et placet: ita per superbiam deo, per avaritiam proximo, per intemperantiam sibi dissentit et resistit."

lack of charity and thoughts that stray away from God. He seeks relief in the sacrament of penance and goes to confession as often as he can. His confessors tell him that he is creating problems where there are no problems; as long as he does not have to confess sins like murder, adultery, or theft, he need not worry; that what he is concerned about are *Puppensünden* ("a doll's sins"), sins that are small, childish, imaginary, and trifling.[9] Of course, this is not a satisfactory answer. Luther need not have become a monk had he only wanted to steer clear of murder and adultery. For him being a monk is about a perfection in which the stirrings of the heart are not a children's game but are of the utmost significance.

For years Luther felt anguished by his inability to attain the goal of monastic life. Never would he be so perfect as to be acceptable in the eyes of God. The redeeming solution revealed itself only after years of meditation on the Holy Scriptures. His dilemma was impossible to solve because his entire spiritual life so far had been based upon false premises, false with respect to God's relationship to him and to all human beings. God did not expect of him what Luther and his monastic and ecclesiastical environment thought: that he win God's approval through perfection, that he appease the eternal judge through obedience and thereby earn eternal life. God knows that sinners will never achieve perfection. And God himself presents the solution; he grants forgiveness, accepts and loves the sinner in spite of his sin, freely *(gratis)*. Or, more basically, God accepts the sinner for the sake of Jesus Christ, who died for sinners. He no longer looks upon the sinner as such, but regards him in conjunction with Christ, and Christ's perfection is taken as the sinner's in the eyes of God.[10] On this the Christian can rely and find peace of

9. WA TR 6, no. 6669.

10. Cf. WA 2:495.2-4 and 10-13; LW 27:227-28: "While he [sc. the believer] is being justified and healed, the sin that is left in his flesh is not imputed to him. This is because Christ, who is entirely without sin, has now become one with His Christian and intercedes for him with the Father. . . . Therefore all such statements praising the righteous are to be understood in the same way, namely, that the righteous are not wholly perfect in themselves, but God accounts them righteous and forgives them because of their faith in His Son Jesus Christ, who is our Propitiation." Cf. also the way Luther puts it later, e.g., WA 37:57.23-25: "Whatever we do in this life, God does not [want to] regard it as impure in itself, but everything is to be holy, precious and pleasing through this child [sc. His Son] who through His life makes the whole world holy." WA 46:44.34-38; LW 24:347: "This is a peculiar righteousness; it is strange indeed that we are to be called righteous or to possess a righteousness which is really no work, no thought, in short, nothing whatever in us

mind in his trust in Christ. Such trust, which only the Holy Spirit can give, is what we call faith *(fides)*. Thus faith in Christ replaces the struggle for perfection. In faith, and "only in faith" *(sola fide)*, humanity is what God wants it to be. For it is in faith that we realize and accept that we owe everything to Christ; it is in faith that we live "by grace alone" *(sola gratia)*.

The discovery that he was accepted by God on account of Christ alone through faith alone and that he had no need of that ever elusive perfection became for the monk Martin Luther the great liberating event of his life. And there was another aspect to this discovery. Paradoxically now, once he had entered into this new relationship with God, the desired obedience became attainable. Now it was possible to love God and his fellows wholeheartedly, without reservation or self-interest. Freed from the need to strive for perfection in order to gain something for himself, liberated from the pressure to score points with God, as it were, in order to become acceptable to him, Luther's will was now able to turn toward God and toward his neighbor for their own sake. Freed from the need to win God's love through his own love of God, his heart, which in Christ had received God's love as a free gift, was now free to return this love.[11] Perfect in the eyes of God through the perfection of Christ, he was able to show the corresponding signs of this perfection in his own life, at least up to a point. Of course, in this world he would never reach the state of being without sin like the angels. But the decisive change has occurred: his heart, the very center of his being and source of all his actions, has been changed. Rooted in faith, he has become a good tree that brings forth good fruit, the fruits of perfection that the Sermon on the Mount describes.[12]

The monk Martin Luther had arrived at his goal: no longer afflicted

---

but is entirely outside us in Christ and yet becomes truly ours by reason of His grace and gift, and becomes our very own, as though we ourselves had achieved and earned it."

11. WA 7:23.30-32; 24:9-15: "The commandments teach us and prescribe manifold good works, but this does not get them done. . . . Then comes the other word, the divine promise, and says . . . behold, believe in Christ in whom I declare you to have all grace, justice, peace, and freedom. If you believe, you have; if you do not believe, you have not. For what is impossible to you by all the works of the commandments, . . . you receive easily and at once by faith."

12. WA 7:32.13-27: "Just as the tree has to come before the fruit, and the fruit makes the tree neither good nor bad, but rather the tree makes the fruit, thus man first has to be good or bad in his person, before he does good works or bad. . . . But just as faith makes [sc. a person] good, in the same manner good works are made by faith."

by erroneous assumptions of perfection demanded of him, he embarked on a life of true perfection granted to him through faith in Jesus Christ. However, during his long years of meditation on the Scriptures Luther had gained yet another insight. These matters are not the concerns only of the monastics. Perfect obedience, perfect love of God and one's neighbor are the concerns of all Christians. It is not only from nuns and monks that God wants absolute love and devotion but equally from those who lead their lives in the world. Thus the traditional distinction between "commandments" and "counsels" can no longer be sustained. The ethic of the Sermon on the Mount is not just for the few. It is God's will that all Christians "do good and suffer ill, and that they are able and willing to do both heroically and to the utmost limits, like the martyrs."[13]

Therefore what the monk Martin Luther had discovered as the prerequisite for undivided love and devotion is valid not only for monks and nuns, but also for every Christian. Undivided love and devotion are the fruit of faith. And since it is through the sacrament of baptism that Christ's becoming one with humanity (which finds its realization in faith) comes about, undivided love and devotion are the fruit of baptism. Luther had recognized fairly early that the decisive step is not entering monastic life, but baptism. It is in baptism that we receive holiness;[14] holier we cannot become. Therefore it is baptism from which springs a holy life.[15] When he receives the sacrament of baptism, the Christian pledges to lead such a holy life: he promises "to slay sin and to become holy."[16] This is true of all Christians. "In baptism we all make one and the same vow: to slay sin and to become holy through the work and grace of God, to whom we yield and offer ourselves, as clay to the potter. In this no one is in a better position than another."[17] Hence the monk is not in a "better position" than he who leads a secular life; a Christian wife and mother pleases God no less than a monk, perhaps even more.[18]

13. WA 4:286.37f.: "bona facere et mala pati, utrunque heroico more et extremo et summo posse atque velle, ut in martyribus." Obviously these maxims echo the Sermon on the Mount, and Luther says (35) that these are *mandata,* i.e., commandments that are valid for all, not *consilia,* which represent the special ethics of those who choose a higher path.

14. WA 57:194.2-8.

15. WA 2:735.19-38; LW 35:40-41: Such a holy life is "the consequence of baptism."

16. WA 2:735.35f.

17. WA 2:34-37; LW 35:41.

18. WA 56:427.26–428.6; LW 25:419-20.

If it is true that the secular Christian is no less holy than the monk because both have received the same baptism; if in faith the one has the perfection of Christ no less than the other, and if this perfection disposes the one no less than the other to lead a holy life according to the Sermon on the Mount, then does it not follow that the monastic life loses all purpose? One might get the impression that it was Luther's intention to abolish monasticism. But that is not the case. None of his remarks quoted above are intended to call into question monasticism as such; rather, his intention was to give it its true place. Monasticism is one of a number of ways to "exercise" one's baptism.[19] For while it is true that "in baptism we all make one and the same vow . . . and no one is in a better position than another," it is no less true that "for a life in accordance with baptism, for the slaying of sin, there can be no one method and no one estate in life."[20] Christians must choose the way in which they want to lead their Christian lives, each according to his or her individual dispositions and circumstances, and one of the choices open to the baptized is monasticism. Monasticism is for those who believe that this is the best way for them to "complete their baptism," that is, live up to the consequences of their baptism.[21] It is "just as though two men went to the same city, and the one went by the footpath, the other by the highway, just as each thought best."[22] One person may lead a Christian life in the estate of matrimony with its joys and pains, another within the framework of monasticism. In other words, instead of a hierarchical structure, which places monasticism "above" secular life, there are now two equivalent Christian lifestyles. Yet Luther still sees one minor advantage to monasticism: because it involves more suffering than married life, it is better equipped to prepare for death, and therefore there is "more exercise" of baptism because in baptism we die to the world.[23] Whatever the choice, what matters (which unfortunately contemporary Christianity has forgot-

19. WA 2:736.12-18; LW 35:41. It is an "exercise" *(Übung)* of baptism.

20. WA 2:735.37–736.1; LW 35:41.

21. WA 2:736.3-7; LW 35:41. "It is true, then, that there is no vow higher, better or greater than the vow of baptism. . . . Over and above this vow, a person may indeed bind himself to an estate which will be suitable to him and helpful for the completion of his baptism."

22. WA 2:736.7f.; LW 35:41.

23. WA 2:736.12; LW 35:41. This is even more true, however, of those who hold ecclesiastical office because they also suffer on behalf of those for whom they are responsible (see also lines 18-22).

ten) is "our baptism and what it means, what vows we made there and how we are supposed to walk in its works and to attain its purpose." Therefore it is decisive for all estates within the church to know "how we are to act in them for the fulfilling of our baptism."[24]

Luther against Monasticism

While the monk Martin Luther was struggling for perfection, he had gradually come to realize that such perfection is different from, and achieved by other means than, what he had imagined when he first began life as a monk. Simultaneously he had come to realize that this perfection and the way to find it are the same for every Christian, for Christians "in the world" no less than for monks and nuns, even though they have chosen different lifestyles.

In the course of the years during which Luther developed these insights, he became more and more critical of monasticism and of those who lived the religious life. For a long time, however, his criticism was not intended to reject monasticism but to serve it. He wanted monastic life to be theologically and spiritually correct. Yet, around 1519-20, nearly fifteen years after entering the monastery, his criticism becomes sharper in tone and content, and in 1521 it culminates in his programmatic treatise *De votis monasticis iudicium (Judgment on the Monastic Vows),* and its verdict that it was legitimate, even necessary, to leave the monasteries.[25] The monastic institution was nothing but "a Babylon of error and ignorance, of disobedience and perfidy, sacrilege and blasphemy."[26] Or, in the words from 1533, which we cited at the beginning, a monastery is a hell.[27]

At the time, Luther was not the only one to criticize monks and monasteries. Many others were no less harsh in their attacks and equally drastic in their choice of words. This is true of critics within the religious orders, for example, in the controversy between observants and conventualists.

24. WA 2:736.25-29; LW 35:42.

25. WA 8:658.12f.; LW 44:383: "habes hic autoritate Christi, ut liceat, immo oporteat redire" [from the monastery back into the "world"].

26. WA 8:638.33-35; LW 44:351. "Babylonem quandam errorum, ignorantiarum, inoboedientiarum, perfidiarum, sacrilegiorum, blasphemiarum."

27. See above, n. 1.

And this is true of critics outside, like the humanists Erasmus of Rotterdam and Ulrich von Hutten, or of voices generally criticizing ecclesiastical abuses.[28] Yet again there is an essential difference. While the majority criticized the behavior of monks and nuns, their moral failures, the decline of discipline, the emptiness of the rituals (they attacked the unchaste monk, the rich monastery, the liturgically and spiritually lax convent), Luther had a different aim. We do find such criticisms in Luther, too, but only marginally. His central interest is, again, theological. What is the relationship between God and humanity that lies at the heart of monasticism?

His conclusion is devastating: the attitude toward God that was the prime motive of the majority of the religious in entering the monastery and formed the basis of their monastic lives directly contradicted the Christian faith. That is why Luther calls monasticism a Babylon and demands that people desert their monasteries.

Luther argues that hardly a monk or a nun has chosen the monastic life as a free response to the free gift of God's love in Jesus Christ. The majority do not understand their monastic lives to be the fruit of faith and the expression of the new relationship with God that they have received in Christ. They do not regard their religious life as a way to mirror the perfection of Jesus Christ, which they, like all Christians, have received in baptism and own in faith. Few, if any, see their monastic estate as just one possibility among others to do what all Christians are called upon to do, that is, live out the consequences of their baptism. Such an attitude toward monasticism is nowhere to be found among the monks and nuns of the day, as Luther knows only too well from his own experience, nor is it taught by the authorities of the orders and the church. What is supposed to be the objective and purpose of the monastic life, the motive that leads people to adopt it and the attitude that characterizes it, is actually quite different. Instead of being understood as the free response to God's free gift of love in Jesus Christ, monasticism is perceived as being instrumental in earning and intensifying his love. Instead of being the consequence of salvation,[29] it is

28. For example, the *Gravamina* movement.

29. Salvation *(salus)* must come before works, even monastic works (WA 8:605.21; LW 44:264). And this means, for example, in the case of chastity: "It is therefore Christ's intent that chastity should be a servant of the kingdom of heaven *(serva regni coelorum)*, and a willing servant, not something which earns the kingdom, for it already possesses the kingdom *(non quae illud mereatur, sed iam habet)*." (WA 8:585.24f.; LW 44:264).

considered to be the best way of earning it.[30] Monastic life was being chosen because it was believed to be especially conducive to or even indispensable for winning God's grace and becoming acceptable in his sight,[31] because it was believed to be singularly meritorious,[32] because it was expected it would reap unique rewards. "Show me, I beg you, a nun or a monk who is content with the penny common to us all."[33]

Thus, instead of being an expression of the freedom that humanity has received in Christ, monasticism leads straight into slavery. This is not to be understood in the superficial sense of submitting oneself to a specifically regulated life; any Christian is free to do so, and every Christian must submit to regulations, one way or another, in any case.[34] But it is true in the sense that monasticism, if conceived as a means of salvation, destroys the freedom that is intrinsic to the Christian faith, being free from the obligation to fulfill certain conditions in order to be accepted by God.[35] The paradigm of such renewed slavery is the perpetual vows. Even when they are taken in free response to God's unconditional love, the fact that they are a lifelong obligation changes their character and makes them a condition of salvation. "You cannot point out a single monk (apart from a miracle) who is not bound fast by this sacrilegious and blasphemous idea that he will be saved by keeping the rules of his order and actually damned if he does not."[36] Suddenly Chris-

30. WA 8:598.19-22; LW 44:285. WA 38:159.26f.

31. WA 8:596.7-9, 15f.; LW 44:281.

32. WA 8:611.3f.; LW 44:305.

33. WA 8:610.27f.; LW 44:305 (cf. Matt. 20:11f.)

34. WA 8:609.38f.; LW 44:303.

35. It is important not to misunderstand what Luther means by freedom. Freedom does not mean moral indifference or abolishing Christian ethics. What it does mean is freedom from all conditions in our relationship with God. See, e.g., WA 8:606.30-32; LW 44:298: "Christian or evangelical freedom, then, is a freedom of conscience which liberates the conscience from works. Not that no works be done, but no faith be put in them" [Est itaque libertas Christiana seu Evangelica libertas conscientiae, qua solvitur conscientia ab operibus, non ut nulla flant, sed ut in nulla confidat]. Good works are an integral part of the Christian life; since faith in Jesus Christ cannot be without fruit, "these can be no more omitted than can faith itself" [non possunt magis omitti quam ipsa fides], "nor are they less necessary than faith" [nec sunt minus necessaria quam fides], WA 8:608.31f.; LW 44:301.

36. WA 8:619.39–620.2; LW 44:320. See also WA 8:618.33-35; LW 44:319: a monk who has taken eternal vows is a prisoner to the idea that "you cannot be saved unless you keep the rules of your order, and you can only be saved if you do!"

tian freedom is no more, or, put differently, certainty is no longer established by the fact that it suffices to rely on Jesus Christ alone.[37]

Instead of being a way to "exercise one's baptism,"[38] monastic life was considered to be a higher state of grace, which is why the taking of the vows is referred to as a second baptism.[39] Consequently baptism is degraded: it is only through the monastic life that true holiness is achieved; the holiness received in baptism (which is Christ's holiness) is considered insufficient.[40] The result is a two-tiered system[41] within Christianity. Only those who choose the monastic path are considered perfect; the rest who live "in the world," notwithstanding that in baptism they have received Christ's perfection,[42] belong to a different and lower class of Christian.[43] "Who among the religious would allow himself to be put in the same class as a married man, a farmer, or a workman in the sight of God?"[44] This means, as a third consequence, that Christians "in the world" are exempt from living according to the perfection of Christ, which is already theirs in faith. They are only obligated to live according to ordinary civil standards of righteousness, that is, simply follow the commandments; not for them was the perfect obedience, which is only the "counsel" of the Lord.[45] In contradiction to the clear message of the gospel, this system ignores the fact that Christ enables and expects all who bear his name to live up to this perfection.[46]

37. WA 8:619.9-13; LW 44:319-20. Especially see line 13: the monk who believes that he can only be saved if he keeps his eternal vows relies on "works and merits over and above the works and merits of Christ."

38. See above, n. 19.

39. WA 38:158.7f.; see also WA 38:147.23-34; 151.26f.; 595.29-31; 618.10f.

40. WA 38:149.33–150.9.

41. WA 8:584.23f.; LW 44:262.

42. See above, n. 11.

43. WA 38:159.3-9.

44. WA 38:610.17f.

45. WA 38:610.11-18.

46. WA 8:581.19–582.36; LW 44:257-58. Luther notes with approval that Saint Francis of Assisi declared the gospel itself to be the Rule of his order (WA 8:579.26f.; LW 44:255). But that is exactly why he should not have made it a Rule only for one order, because thereby "he made the universal gospel intended for all the faithful into a special rule for the few. What Christ wanted to be universal and catholic, Francis made schismatic" (WA 8:579.40–580.1; LW 44:255). Besides, to select only the three monastic vows from the entire range of perfect obedience we find in the New Testament is nothing but arbitrary; as can be seen from the Sermon on the Mount, there are many more maxims that ought

Martin Luther's attacks on monasticism had an immense effect. Obviously he had hit a nerve among countless monks and nuns who recognized their own experiences in the words of the Augustinian Hermit from Wittenberg.[47] In large numbers they left their monasteries; before long, houses and convents had to be closed all across the country. "Monks and nuns are melting away and disappear like snow in the sun," Luther commented.[48] Of course, there were also some men and women religious in the regions now becoming Protestant who were not convinced by Luther's words; in some areas monastic life was interfered with and convents were closed by Protestant princes, sometimes with the use of force.[49] At any rate, in those parts where the Reformation took hold, monastic life soon came to an end.[50]

Luther for Monastic Ideals

The Reformation thus spelled the end of monasticism in the Protestant churches. But it was like the case of the kernel of wheat (John 12:24). In dying it brought forth new life. What was good and true about monasticism or could be obtained through it was destined to live on by ceasing to be monastic. Not an elite within the church but all Christians were to become in a sense monastic. As was explicitly stated in a sermon in 1618 by the Wittenberg theologian Balthasar Meisner, one of the leading representatives of Lutheran Orthodoxy of the seventeenth century: "The Church is like a

to be included in the "counsels" for those who seek perfection (WA 8:586.6-12; LW 44:265).

47. Cf. the reports of former monks and nuns in Schilling, *Gewesene Mönche.*

48. WA TR 2, no. 2359.

49. Such measures, "i.e. secularization, reorganization, even the closure of convents were nothing new or unheard of . . . they were actually quite common occurrences in line with late medieval church government and policy." See Werner Ziegler, *Reformation und Klosterauflösung in Reformbemühungen und Observanzbestrebungen im spätmittelalterlichen Ordenswesen,* ed. Kaspar Elm (Berlin: Duncker & Humblot, 1989), 585-614, especially 594. In the late Middle Ages both secular and ecclesiastical authorities resorted to these measures for various reasons. Mostly the motive was to lay their hands on the monastery's property. In his own time, Luther was sharply critical of this practice; see, e.g., WA TR 2, no. 1947.

50. For the few exceptions, see below.

monastery. . . . We are the monastic people inside it, we are all brothers and sisters in a house of God, in an order of Christians."[51] Or to quote a modern historian: "It could be argued that the Reformation understood itself as a new kind of monasticism, or at least could be understood as such."[52]

What is meant by this can be summarized in two double slogans. On the one hand, the Reformation brings about a delimitation and a universalization of monasticism; on the other hand, it brings about a radicalization and interiorization of the Christian life. In other words, monastic ideals are no longer limited to specific groups of people but are applied universally, and Christian life as such is to be lived radically and "from within." Both aspects are present in the first of the famous Ninety-five Theses, which initiated the Reformation before the eyes of the general public: "When our Lord and Master Jesus Christ said, 'Repent!' (Mt. 4:17), he willed the entire life of believers to be one of repentance."[53] Our entire life is to be a life of repentance, not simply single, isolated acts or deeds, because repentance includes both the attitude that governs a person inwardly and also the outward behavior that results from it. This is a classic monastic concept. Now it is to be applied universally; the life of every Christian is to be a life of such comprehensive repentance. In positive terms, delimitation and universalization mean that every Christian, young or old, man or woman, married or celibate, is called upon to fulfill God's will perfectly; no member of the church may assume he is exempt. Radicalization and interiorization, on the other hand, mean that to fulfill God's will, to which all Christians are called, is not simply a matter of keeping the commandments and living a socially acceptable life. Christianity is about surrendering one's entire life from within as Jesus himself exemplified and as he described it, especially in the Sermon on the Mount, when he specified how to deal with property, sexuality, and other people's lives.[54] The Christian is

51. "Die Kirche ist gleich als ein Kloster . . . Wir sind die Kloster-Leute darinnen/ wir allesampt sind Bruder und Schwestern in einem hause Gottes/in einem Christen-Orden," in *Geistreiche/Wolgegrundete Predigten Ußer das Edle tewre Buch der Augspurgischen/nunmehr vor Hundert Jahren ubergebenen Confession. Gehalten zu Wittenberg/in der Schlos-Kirchen/im 1618. und folgenden Jahren/Durch Balthasarem Meisnerum . . . Auffgesetzt/von M. Johanne Lucio,* pt. 1 (Wittenberg, 1630), 3.

52. Schilling, *Gewesene Mönche,* 28.

53. See Luther's sermons on Matt. 5–7 (WA 32:299ff.; LW 21:3).

54. See also WA 11:248.32–250.9; LW 45:87-89. WA 28:282.19-24; WA 39II:189.29f.; LW 34:306.

not only supposed to refrain from stealing; because of his love for his neighbor, he will go without and give to others. The Christian will not only refrain from killing his enemy; because of his love of his enemy, he will forgive him and not resort to revenge, and so on. "These words of Christ, though impossible to man's natural mind, are nevertheless necessary commandments which apply to all Christians."[55]

In short, Christianity is about following Christ in perfect love of God and of one's neighbor. Such perfect love is to determine the life of all Christians; it is the ethical principle guiding all who are baptized. They are called upon to live by it each in their own station, as father, mother, or celibate, in every profession and social class. "If you are a manual laborer, you will find that the Bible has been put into your workshop, into your hand, into your heart. It teaches and preaches how you should treat your neighbor. Just look at your tools — at your needle or thimble, your beer barrel, your goods, your scales or yardstick or measure — and you will read this statement inscribed on them."[56] Namely, every one of these ought to be used as a medium of love. Thus, filled with the love of God and of one's neighbor, all work becomes a religious service — another monastic principle that is being applied to all Christians and the way they conduct their lives. But the central truth that Luther had come to understand in the course of his life as a monk is also valid for all Christians: such love, which touches every aspect of one's life, including self-denial, suffering, and being disadvantaged, is only possible as a fruit of faith, faith that joins the Christians to Christ and grants them Christ's perfection. "Behold, from faith thus flow forth love and joy in the Lord, and from love a joyful, willing and free mind that serves one's neighbor willingly and takes no account of gratitude or ingratitude, of praise or blame, of gain or loss."[57] This quotation is from one of Luther's best-known works, *The Freedom of a Christian (De libertate Christiana),* which ends: "We conclude, therefore, that a Christian lives not in himself, but in Christ and in his neighbor. Otherwise he is not a Christian. He lives in Christ through faith, in his neigh-

55. WA 8:581.31f.; LW 44:258. Cf. WA 11:245.20-25; LW 45:81; WA 11:249.14-18; LW 45:87-88; WA 28:282.19; WA 32:299.28; LW 21:3; WA 39II:189.29f.; LW 34:306.

56. WA 32:495.29f.; LW 21:237.

57. WA 7:66.7-10 (and 36.3f.); LW 31:367: "Ecce sic fluit ex fide charitas et gaudium in domino et ex charitate hilaris, libens, liber animus ad sponte serviendum proximo, ita ut nullam habeat rationem gratitudinis, ingratitudinis, laudis ac vituperii, lucri aut damni."

bor through love. By faith he is caught up beyond himself into God. By love he descends beneath himself into his neighbor. Yet he always remains in God and in his love."[58]

However, this raises an objection that I do not want to ignore. Admittedly, neither where the Reformation took hold, nor anywhere else, was public life fully ordered and lived according to the principles of the Sermon on the Mount. As always there were, and of course still are, the police, the military, and the judicial system, by which citizens are to be protected from violence, instead of simply suffering it. There are economic structures that are designed, at best, to ensure a measure of justice, not loving renunciation of all worldly goods. All this is quite obvious. So is the reason why: these structures serve to preserve the world in view of its present condition of sin. For a Christian is "a rare bird"; people with the new heart of faith are "not very common."[59] This means not only that in absolute terms Christians are a minority. It also means that of all the baptized, only a minority actually "use" their baptism. And even those who "earnestly desire to be Christians"[60] are no angels and are not yet free from sin. Given this state of things, all social order would collapse were it not for those who are called upon to fight against evil, if need be by the use of force. Otherwise, not only would faithful Christians suffer (for whom suffering might be regarded as part of their life as Christians), but violence and murder, unchecked exploitation, and the law of the jungle would also destroy society in general. For this reason there is a need, as long as the world exists, for structures and actions designed to ensure safety and juridical as well as social justice. God the Creator himself requires them in order to preserve his creation until he will bring about the new heaven and the new earth.[61]

But does this not lead back to a double standard, to two different moral codes for Christians, in other words, to exactly the concept that Luther had rejected in his critique of monasticism? Indeed, he does speak of

58. WA 7:69.12-16 (and 38.6-10); LW 31:371: "Concludimus itaque, Christianum hominem non vivere in seipso, sed in Christo et proximo suo, aut Christianum non esse, in Christo per fidem, in proximo per charitatem: per fidem sursum rapitur supra se in deum, rursum per charitatem labitur infra se in proximum, manens tamen semper in deo et charitate eius."

59. WA 18:310.16, 15, and 15.13f.; LW 46:29.

60. WA 19:75.5; LW 53:63.

61. WA 11:251.22–253.18; LW 45:91-93. WA 15:302.14-29; LW 45:258. WA 15:306.28-36; LW 45:263. WA 17I:333.17-29.

two different ethical codes.[62] But they are not meant to be applied to two groups of Christians, a more demanding standard for the more radical, and a more moderate standard for ordinary Christians. Rather, all Christians participate in both, the "monastic" and the civil ethical codes. With regard to their own lives, they are bound by the principles of love, suffering, and self-denial, which Jesus taught in the Sermon on the Mount. But when Christians find themselves in positions of responsibility, be it in politics or in their professions, they must contribute to ensuring safety and justice for all by way of social and civil order, thereby, as it were, leaving their specific ethical sphere for that of the world.[63] Participation in these two codes of ethics is a constant balancing act. Which path to choose, which principle to apply, which code to follow in a given situation is always a matter of decision, and no Christian can take this decision on behalf of another or allow another one to do so for him. Each new situation demands a fresh decision, which, like any other in a Christian's life, must be made in one's heart, before God.[64]

This is a highly ambitious spiritual concept. There is no denying the fact that in reality Protestant Christianity more often than not settled simply for a bourgeois and middle-class code of ethics. We may compare this phenomenon to those symptoms of decline, which we see time and again in the life of religious orders. And just as in the history of the religious orders there have always been protest movements, reforms, and revivals having the true Christian life as their goal, so such reforms have occurred in the history of the Protestant churches, for example, Pietism or various revival movements. But these revivals were, generally speaking,[65] aimed not

62. These are the two ethical codes of the two realms, the two ways in which God rules the world *(Zwei-Regimenten-Lehre)*. On the one hand there is God's government of the world by means of those structures and mandates that God has given to all mankind in order to preserve the world. On the other hand there is God's government by the Holy Spirit in faith, whose standards apply only to Christians. Luther obviously is inspired by Augustine's concept of the two *civitates*, but in contrast to the North African theologian, he insists that the realm of the world, too, has to be characterized primarily as governed by God.

63. WA 11:253.19-35; LW 45:93-94.

64. WA Br 3, no. 861, 484.5–485.1 and 22-24.

65. In the case of Pietism the matter is more complex. After Lutheran Orthodoxy had upheld the ideal of the "general reformation of the church," Philipp Jakob Spener, the father of Pietism, propagated the idea of concentrating on the spiritual edification of

at the reform of individual groups of Christians, but at leading the whole church back to Christian integrity. The universalization of monasticism, which the Reformation had brought about, also characterized the Protestant reform movements that were to follow.

To conclude this section I would like to point out that the universalization of monasticism brought about by the Reformation was not restricted to the principles of ecclesiology and ethics.[66] It also found its way into spiritual practice. Two examples may illustrate this: the importance of the Psalter and the Lutheran form of morning and evening prayer.

The Psalter, of course, has always been the prayer book in monastic tradition. When Luther was a monk and also later, nothing was dearer to his heart than the Psalter; no other book of the Bible was as often the sub-

---

those members of the parishes "willing" to be edified, in order to improve the spiritual condition of the whole church in this way (see the preface to his influential program *Pia desideria* from 1675). August Hermann Francke aimed directly at the improvement of the church's condition by way of fostering a spiritual elite, namely, spiritually mature pastors. Nikolaus Ludwig Graf von Zinzendorf again propagated the edification of "the pious ones" as a means of reforming the church from within. But there were also radical pietistic groups who had given up the ideal of reforming the whole church and chose the way of a separate life for the perfect Christians.

66. Even on the principle level, there are a number of other examples. For example, the idea of the church as a spiritual community instead of a hierarchic structure, an idea dear to the Reformation, has monastic roots. See Reinhard Schwarz, "Luthers unveräußerliche Erbschaft an der monastischen Theologie," in *Kloster Amelungsborn 1135-1985*, ed. Gerhard Ruhbach and Kurt Schmidt-Clausen (Hannover: Kloster Amelungsborn, 1985), 209-31, especially 217-20; "Luther's Unalienable Inheritance of Monastic Theology," *American Benedictine Review* 39 (1988): 430-50, especially 443-46. Karl Holl points out that Luther's idea resembles that of Saint Basil the Great, except that Basil believed that his ideal of the Christian community could be realized only in a monastic framework, while Luther applied it to the whole church. See Karl Holl, "Die Entstehung von Luthers Kirchenbegriff," in *Gesammelte Aufsätze zur Kirchengeschichte*, vol. 1, *Luther*, 6th ed. (Tübingen: Mohr, 1932), 288-325, especially 300f. The same is true for the high regard for the Christian's work "in the world" as a true "calling" *(Beruf);* before Luther the only "calling" of value was that to monastic life. Cf. Karl Holl, "Die Geschichte des Wortes Beruf," in *Gesammelte Aufsätze zur Kirchengeschichte*, vol. 3, *Der Westen* (Tübingen: Mohr, 1928), 189-219, especially 214-19. We could also mention Luther's existential, experience-related understanding of theology that puts him much closer to the monastic than to the scholastic tradition. Cf. Ulrich Köpf, "Monastische Traditionen bei Luther," in *Luther — zwischen den Zeiten. Eine Jenaer Ringvorlesung*, ed. Christoph Markschies and Michael Trowitzsch (Tübingen: Mohr Siebeck, 1999), 17-35, especially 30f.

ject of his exegesis. This passion became his legacy to that part of Christendom that came under his influence. The Psalter came to be regarded as the "layman's Bible." A host of small, separate editions were printed for the use of those members of the congregation who were able to read. Every Christian, not just nuns and monks, was supposed to meditate on the psalms regularly and to learn as many of them by heart as possible. Another way of increasing the popularity of the Psalter was to compose hymns in the vernacular based on psalms. Luther had invented this new genre,[67] and many poets and composers in the churches adopted it. These hymns were free renderings of the psalms set to music, to be sung by the congregation. Thus the Latin Psalter, which had formed the core of the monastic hours, was replaced with a Psalter in the vernacular, which became part of the liturgy of all Christians.

In the Small Catechism, the most important handbook of Christian instruction of the Lutheran tradition and a basic element in the official teaching of the Lutheran church, we find a short order for morning and evening prayer, the "blessing for the morning" *(Morgensegen)* and the "blessing for the evening" *(Abendsegen)*. These prayers are designed to mark the spiritual beginning and end of each day for the whole family. They are combined with the Lord's Prayer, the creed, and a hymn: a small breviary for the Christian household. The idea behind this practice is undeniably monastic, and of monastic origin are especially those parts that form the center of the short liturgy: the blessings for morning and evening. The former had been a traditional monastic morning blessing, now used by Luther, with only slight alterations, as the standard morning prayer for "the world," with a parallel version made up for the evening.[68] For centu-

67. The most famous example being, of course, the hymn "A Mighty Fortress Is Our God," based on Ps. 46.

68. The original prayer came from a Latin collection of late-medieval texts and spiritual instructions by the Dutchman Johannes Mauburnus (d. 1501-2). Here, too, it was to be combined with other liturgical elements, of which Luther kept only the first, an invocation of the Trinity together with the sign of the cross (in Mauburnus the invocation was christological, followed by the above-mentioned prayer, a petition to the Blessed Virgin Mary asking her blessing, a psalm of praise, and a hymn to the Virgin that referred to her as the source of our salvation and our praise). In Luther's version the prayer is in German, therefore shorter and stylistically simpler than the original, but in other respects more specific. E.g., Luther gives thanks for "protection during the night from all perils and dangers" (where Mauburnus has only a general thanksgiving for protection at night),

ries and up to the present day, Lutheran families have thus started and ended each day with a prayer that originally had its place in the monastery.

Lutherans and Monasticism

Martin Luther's critique of monasticism evoked an enormous response from monks and nuns in Germany and beyond. Where the Reformation was taking hold, monastic life more or less came to an end. However, we must not overlook Luther's positive comments about individual monks and the religious life, even amid his sharpest criticisms. Time and again he refers positively to some of the great monks of the past, for example, the fathers of the Egyptian desert especially Saint Anthony,[69] Saint Francis of Assisi,[70] and most of all the one monk who influenced his spiritual development more than any other, Saint Bernard of Clairvaux.[71] He exempted them from his criticism because in his eyes these fathers had been different from the monasticism he attacked, and even where they had participated in its more problematic features, they had been able, amid structures that were wrong, to live a life that was spiritually right.[72]

Luther's admission that in the past there had been monks who were different from the mainstream he was now attacking so sharply is mirrored in the positive picture of monasticism also to be found in *De votis monasticis.* Side by side with his sharp rejection of lifelong vows we find

---

he asks for protection from "all sin and evil, that my entire life and work may please thee" (where Mauburnus asks that "my service [*servitus*] may be pleasing to thee"). Luther also added a formula of commitment, which entrusts one's whole life to God, and a plea for protection by God's guardian angel. See WA 30I:394.3-5. Cf. Mauburnus, *Rosetum . . .* (Basel, 1504f.), VIII^{r-v} (to be found in parts in E. Sander, "Miszellen zum frühen und späten Luther als Ergänzungen und Berichtigungen zur Weimarer Ausgabe," *Zeitschrift für Kirchengeschichte* 56 (1937): 593-604, especially 599.

69. WA 8:578.16; LW 44:253. See also WA 8:646.11; LW 44:363, where Luther refers to "the old monks and hermits," and WA 8:612.8; LW 44:308, his reference to the *Vita Patrum.*

70. WA 8:587.32–588.2; LW 44:268. In Luther's eyes, Saint Francis's good impulses were corrupted by those who came after him. Cf. also above, n. 46.

71. WA 8:601.18; LW 44:290. WA 8:612.27; LW 44:308. WA 8:617.9; LW 44:316. WA 8:622.28; LW 44:325. WA 8:628.25; LW 44:334.

72. WA 8:617.9-13; LW 44:316. WA 8:658.15-20; LW 44:383.

suggestions for alternative vows that would be legitimate because they would not contradict the gospel: "Look, O God, I vow to thee this kind of life, not because I think this is a way to attain righteousness and salvation or to make satisfaction for my sins. . . . [But] I take this way of life upon myself for the sake of disciplining my body, of serving my neighbor, and of meditating upon thy word. I do this just as another man may take up farming or a trade — everybody for his own exercise *(exercitium)* — without any thought of merit or justification, which exists before all this in faith."[73] The monastic path is not a "higher path" of special value in God's eyes and does not bring man any closer to him than he is already in Christ. It is one of several choices of how to live the consequences of one's faith, choices that have equal value in the eyes of God and differ in form only, according to each Christian's individual gifts and inclinations. The insight that the difference between the monastic and the nonmonastic path is a difference between two lifestyles on the same level and that the difference does not imply superiority of the one over the other (the insight the young monk Martin Luther had gained before he ever contemplated leaving the monastery) also runs like a thread through his positive comments long after he had ceased to be a monk. If you become a monk "because either your situation has brought you to embrace this kind of life, or it appeared to be the best way of life for you, without your thinking thereby that you are better than he who takes a wife or takes up farming, in that case you are neither wrong to take vows nor wrong to live this way."[74] Phrases like "because either your situation brought you to embrace this kind of life" or "it appeared to be the best way of life for you" imply that a Christian has found in himself a particular gift and decides to live accordingly. For everyone must serve God "with the gift he has."[75]

This is done by the monk who lives in accordance with the gospel "freely" *(gratis)*,[76] without any claim to gain "an advantage . . . in [his] relationship with God,"[77] that is, without expecting to get any closer to God or to gain a greater share of salvation through monastic life. The decision in favor of the monastic life is taken "without any thought . . . [of] justifica-

73. WA 8:604.10-22; LW 44:294.
74. WA 8:610.7-10; LW 44:304.
75. WA 8:612.4f.; LW 44:308.
76. WA 8:612.4; LW 44:308.
77. WA 8:610.6f.; LW 44:304.

tion," that is, of being thereby accepted by God.[78] Those who choose this way of life have received salvation and justification already, through faith in Christ; justification "exists before all this."[79] Thus their monastic life is a lifestyle that their faith "uses"; it is an "exercise" of their faith,[80] as Luther puts it in a slight modification of the phrase "exercise of baptism" that we quoted earlier. Like all other ways of exercising one's faith, this way is free before God; no one must be coerced or feel bound to remain within the monastic estate, as if otherwise there were the risk of falling into sin or from God's grace. Permanent vows therefore are not compatible with legitimate monasticism. The decision in favor of this particular way, "if godly, must include the freedom to retract the vow."[81] Should circumstances change, whether external or personal, anyone who has chosen the monastic path must be free to renounce it, with no fear of God and no reproaches from others. The only principle that must never be violated is every Christian's commitment to love.[82]

78. See above, n. 74.

79. Cf. WA 8:604.22; LW 44:294.

80. WA 8:604.33; LW 44:295: "usus et exercitium."

81. WA 8:614.11f.; LW 44:311. Heinz-Meinolf Stamm, *Luthers Stellung zum Ordensleben* (Wiesbaden: Steiner, 1980), 161, who looks at Luther's critique from a Roman Catholic point of view, emphasizes its positive aspects, and claims that Luther did not in fact reject perpetual vows but only a specific understanding of them. But Stamm misses the point; Luther says quite clearly that "the monastic vow is by its very nature *(ex natura sua)* contrary to the word of God, the gospel, faith, Christian freedom and the commandments of God." See WA 8:640.25f.; LW 44:354, and WA 8:612.34; LW 44:309. Quite another matter is the *res votorum*, that is, the way of life to which monks and nuns commit themselves, which is not to be rejected. See WA 8:161.36f.; LW 44:316. But committing oneself to it by lifelong vows is in contradiction to the gospel, to faith, and to freedom, because the monk will believe that his standing in the eyes of God depends on keeping the vows, that his salvation would be in jeopardy if he revoked them, and because he would abide by his choice not "for the joy it brings" (cf. below, n. 82) but because he has vowed to do so; otherwise there would be no need of their irrevocability. Besides, the actual practice of dispensations showed that irrevocability was not always insisted upon, with significant inconsistencies in granting exceptions to the rule. See WA 8:633.36–639.24; LW 44:343-52. In view of this distressing practice, the appropriate and legitimate form of taking the vows, e.g., regarding celibacy, could only be something along the following lines: "I vow to thee chastity as long as I can; but when I find I cannot keep this vow that I be allowed to marry." WA 8:633.1f.; LW 44:341-42.

82. WA 8:664.22f.; LW 44:393. There may even be cases in which love actually demands that the monastic life be given up. WA 8:610.10f.; LW 44:304.

If these are its governing principles, then monasticism is a good thing. Then monks and nuns pursue this path simply "because by virtue of this Spirit of freedom it brings them joy,"[83] because the Holy Spirit moves them to live in this and no other way.[84] If monasticism were practiced like this, there would be no reason to abolish it. If it had been like this, Luther says in a letter to the aged Benedictine abbot Heino Gottschalk of Oldenstadt, he would have remained in the monastery.[85] He goes on to defend and to encourage monks, nuns, and convents that have reorganized their monastic life according to the principles of the Reformation, like Heino and his fellow monks have done. Because Heino was distressed by the antimonastic measures taken by his duke, Luther writes to him. A monk who, like Heino Gottschalk, leads his life in accordance with the gospel may "with great benefit remain in the monastery," and indeed should do so "in the freedom of the Spirit."[86] In several other cases Luther makes similar statements.[87] The best known is his defense of the Brethren of the Common Life of Herford. They, too, had changed their monastic life according to the principles of the Reformation. Yet they were attacked by Protestant pastors, and the local council threatened to close their house. Asked for his support, Luther wrote to the council: "such communities are extraordinarily pleasing to me,"[88] and observed that at Herford the old monastic habit and Christian freedom were joined in a happy union.[89] To the Brethren themselves he wrote in a similar vein: "Your way of life, since you teach and live according to the Gospel, pleases me no end." If only "there had been, and today there were more convents like yours! . . . Abide by your way of life and use it to spread the Gospel (as you do)!"[90]

Some convents and monasteries of this kind were indeed able to live

83. WA 8:655.3; LW 44:377.

84. WA 8:654.37f.; LW 44:377.

85. WA Br 4, no. 1228, 391.37f.

86. WA Br 4, no. 1228, 391.18 and 32f. Abbot Heino in fact remained a Protestant monk to the end of his life. Significantly, he had no objection to the duke seizing the monastery's property; at last, so he said, he was free from all concerns of money and possessions. See Stamm, *Luthers Stellung zum Ordensleben,* 151f.

87. For example, in the case of abbess Elisabeth of Gernrode, also a Benedictine. See WA Br 5, no. 1425, 84.73.

88. WA Br 6, no. 1900, 255.16f.

89. WA Br 7, no. 2144, 113.7f.

90. WA Br 6, no. 1901, 255.8–256.1 and 14f.

on.[91] These communities followed strict rules in the tradition of the old orders,[92] which included obedience toward the abbot/abbess or prior/prioress, celibacy, monastic hours, and a monastic habit. There were no vows. Any supposed superiority of the religious life over life in the world was rejected.[93] Here Luther's ideas of a legitimate religious life were indeed realized, but these convents were few and far between.[94] Practically none of them have survived, or, if they have, they have changed almost beyond recognition.

But for several decades now there has been a change. We observe a *mouvement de communautés* in the churches of the Reformation, a movement to rediscover life in religious communities.[95] There are a number of contributing factors. On the one hand, there is a new development within the Protestant churches themselves. Quite a few Protestant Christians feel that something is missing in the church if there are no monastic communities, no possibilities of realizing this particular way of life. On the other hand, there is the modern ecumenical movement that has brought many Protestants into contact with male and female religious (monastics) from other denominations, in particular, Roman Catholicism. The spiritual attitude shown by many of them, especially after Vatican II, has little in common with the monasticism Luther criticized. Many Roman Catholic monks and nuns will readily concede that the religious life is not superior to other ways of being a Christian, but one particular way of living the

91. The majority were transformed into institutions that showed at least some monastic features: some monasteries were joined with schools and became responsible for their liturgical life, others were simply transformed into schools in which pupils and teachers lived together along monastic lines. Cf. Johannes Halkenhäuser, *Kirche und Kommunität. Ein Beitrag zur Geschichte und zum Auftrag der kommunitären Bewegung in den Kirchen der Reformation* (Paderborn: Verlag Bonifacius-Druckerei, 1978), 68f., especially 90, 102. That many monasteries closed completely need not be delineated here; geographically the picture varies considerably.

92. They adapted the rules of the Augustinians, Cistercians, and, generally, the Benedictines. See Halkenhäuser, *Kirche und Kommunität,* 90-103.

93. Halkenhäuser, *Kirche und Kommunität,* 91-95 and 99-102.

94. There were a small number of convents in northern Germany, mostly for women, which survived because they continued the medieval tradition of offering a way of life to unmarried female members of the aristocracy. See Halkenhäuser, *Kirche und Kommunität,* 82-105.

95. See, for example, Giovanni Miegge, "Monachesimo protestante," *La Luce* 35 (1945): n. 49, 3, and Halkenhäuser, *Kirche und Kommunität.*

faith common to all.[96] Thus it is much easier today for Protestants to see the positive side of this way of life and to ask whether their own church might not, in this respect, find something to learn.[97] Both factors have directed attention to Luther's more positive comments on monasticism, which at other times had been overlooked in favor of his more critical judgments.[98]

After the nineteenth century had already seen a massive revival of a kind of Protestant monastic life, namely, the flourishing houses of deaconesses *(Diakonissenanstalten)*,[99] a host of new religious communities have come into existence in the Protestant churches since World War II. They call themselves "communities" *(communautés)*, thus indicating that they have a regulated communal life without being simply Protestant copies of

96. The official Roman Catholic position according to Vatican II is not quite as unproblematic. Although some documents (*Lumen Gentium,* 44) make an attempt to concede that it is a mark of every Christian's life to follow Christ, others speak of "perfection" (e.g., the decree *Perfectae Caritatis,* which deals with the religious orders) in close connection with the three Counsels *(Perfectae Caritatis 1)*, and refer to those who live in a monastic setting as living "wholly for God" and in renunciation of the world *(Perfectae Caritatis 5)*. On the other hand, the same document says that the religious life is only of a symbolic nature (Art. 5, quoted below in n. 102; see the edition in *Lexikon für Theologie und Kirche* and its critical comment on the apparent ambivalence). Another problem for Protestants is the fact that the same word, "consecration" *(consecratio)*, is used for both baptism and the taking of vows, even though the second is conceived as rooted in the first. And finally there remains the special difficulty of the permanent vows.

97. The new Roman Catholic view of monasticism has in turn led to a new understanding of Luther's critique among Roman Catholic theologians. Thus, e.g., Otto Hermann Pesch: "The exciting thing about Luther's critique of monasticism is that we read it today with realistic hope for a religious life of the future, in view of which all his criticism would be not only unjust, but totally unfounded." See his "Luthers Kritik am Mönchtum in katholischer Sicht in Strukturen christlicher Existenz," in *Beiträge zur Erneuerung des geistlichen Lebens,* ed. Heinrich Schlier et al. (Würzburg: Echter-Verlag, 1968), 81-96 and 371-74, especially 96. Cf. also René H. Esnault, *Luther et le monachisme aujourd'hui. Lecture actuelle du* De votis monasticis iudicium (Geneva and Paris: Labor et Fides, 1964). In this context also belongs Stamm's *Luthers Stellung zum Ordensleben,* cited above (n. 81).

98. For example, Luther's letter to the Brethren of Herford "is frequently cited in protestant convents." See Halkenhäuser, *Kirche und Kommunität,* 65 with n. 91.

99. I can make only a passing reference to earlier developments, for example, the occasional spiritual communities of eighteenth-century Pietism (the pilgrims' hut of G. Tersteegen and his followers, the monastery of Ephrata in Pennsylvania).

the traditional orders.[100] The best known are those of Reformed provenance, like Taizé or Grand-champs. But there are quite a few Lutheran communities, too. The latest report of the Evangelische Kirche in Deutschland lists no fewer than twenty-seven religious communities, mainly Lutheran, some of which have several branches and subdivisions.[101] Similar developments can be observed elsewhere, such as in Scandinavia or in the United States.

This is a most welcome development. It provides Protestant churches with a type of Christian lifestyle that, although it obviously had to be sacrificed in the sixteenth century for the sake of the integrity of the faith, in our time can greatly contribute to their spiritual health. This is true in several ways; here I mention only two. First, the existence of a monastic beside a nonmonastic lifestyle takes into account the individual variety among Christians, the multiplicity of spiritual inclinations and capacities, the diversity of charisms within the church. This aspect had been stressed in Martin Luther's reflections on monasticism referred to above. But it was largely forgotten in the history of the Lutheran as well as in that of the other Protestant churches. To rediscover it today is all the more important as modern society tends toward ever greater diversity of life. Monasticism can give spiritual depth to this phenomenon while, at the same time, keeping it from leading to destructive fragmentation.

Second, the rediscovery of monastic life in Protestantism today concerns not only individual Christians, but also the church as a whole. Monastic life, if lived and understood in the right way, can be a symbolic realization of the essence of Christian existence precisely as the Reformation

100. Cf. E. Müller-Gangloff, "Korrespondenz über 'Kommunität,'" 20 September 1955-56: 158: "'community' is an excellent term, because, on the one hand, it is richer than the term 'brotherhood,' on the other hand, it is more modest and less pretentious than 'order.' . . . Community means more than brotherhood, less than monastery, and characterizes more accurately than order what these new Protestant monastic groups are about." One should not put too much emphasis on terminology, however; after all, there is some variation as to how Protestant communities refer to themselves. Some actually use terms like "ordo," "brotherhood," "sisterhood," etc.

101. Ulrich Wilckens, "Die evangelischen Kommunitäten," in *Bericht des Beauftragten des Rates der Evangelischen Kirche in Deutschland für den Kontakt zu den evangelischen Kommunitäten,* Text 62 (Hannover: Kirchenamt der Evangelischen Kirche in Deutschland, 1997), 36-38. There are also about thirty communities whose members do not live together permanently and which in some cases include couples and families.

had rediscovered it, and can thus help all believers to realize this essence in their own lives. In concrete terms, monasticism is a specific way of living out that which characterizes Christian life as such: perfection in Christ, a perfection that is substantially that of the incarnate Son of God, but is made ours in faith and lived out in a life of unreserved love. Members of monastic communities do not have more of this perfection, which would be a contradiction in terms. But they realize it in their own way, in a symbolic one-sidedness, a conscious reduction of complexity. By limiting their participation in common social life, they renounce the fullness of the human dimension that is given to all people for living out their lives, and given to Christians as the arena in which to live their faith and to express their love. Yet they concentrate on lending visible expression to the completeness of trust in Christ, which is at the heart of the Christian faith, and to the freedom of letting go and giving away that is at the heart of Christian love.[102] Such one-sidedness is at the same time easier and more difficult than the "ordinary" Christian life. It is easier because monastic life with its limited range of involvements and responsibilities requires less of that arduous task of deciding on the right code of behavior in given contexts and situations, and involves perhaps less of that danger of falling back into a complacent middle-of-the-road Christianity mentioned above. It is more difficult because renouncing vital dimensions of life is, of course, not congenial to human nature. At the end of the day, however, it is a matter of spiritual inclination and spiritual choice. Those choosing the conscious one-sidedness of monastic existence are living symbols of that radical belonging to God that is the core of every Christian's life. Thus they are a constant reminder to their fellow Christians of the spiritual center that keeps them focused in the middle of their own manifold lives: Jesus Christ.

102. This understanding converges with the decree *Perfectae Caritatis* 5 of Vatican II insofar as here, too, monastic life is referred to as an "expression," namely, of baptism. But with regard to the qualification of this "expression," it states the exact opposite. According to *Perfectae Caritatis,* monasticism is a "fuller expression" *(plenius exprimit)* of baptism, not a lifestyle of conscious one-sidedness as presented here.

CHAPTER 17

Luther on the Role of Secular Authority in the Reformation

James M. Estes

With the publication of the *Address to the Christian Nobility of the German Nation* in August 1520, Martin Luther became the first of the reformers to appeal directly to the German princes to take decisive action in support of an ecclesiastical reformation that would have to be effected in defiance of Rome.[1] In so doing, he was continuing the already centuries-old propensity of German ecclesiastical reformers to seek from secular rulers the reforms that the clerical hierarchy either would not or could not provide.[2] But the traditional appeal to secular authority did not come easily to Luther.[3] Indeed, because of his persistent refusal, unique among the Lutheran

1. The following abbreviation is used in the notes: "Trüdinger" refers to Karl Trüdinger, *Luthers Briefe und Gutachten an weltliche Obrigkeiten zur Durchführung der Reformation,* Reformationsgeschichtliche Studien und Texte 111 (Münster Westfalen: Aschendorff, 1975). When quoting the LW text, I have sometimes made slight adjustments. Most of these were inspired by my conviction that the proper translation of *weltlich* is usually "secular" or "worldly" and not "temporal."

2. On the late-medieval development of princely responsibility for religious reform and the emergence of *Landeskirchen* (territorial churches), see Manfred Schulze, *Fürsten und Reformation: Geistliche Reformpolitik weltlicher Fürsten vor der Reformation* (Tübingen: Mohr [Siebeck], 1991).

3. Although the topic of Luther's views on church and state is a very old one, literature on the subject that takes account of all the available evidence is rare. There was long a tendency to concentrate narrowly on Luther's thought in the 1520s and to leave out of account important evidence from 1530 and later. A prime example of this was the "classic"

reformers, to attribute to secular authority *as such* any responsibility for the establishment and maintenance of true religion,[4] his arguments justifying governmental action in support of religious reformation had a complexity and an inner tension unmatched in the simpler (and more easily summarized) thought of Philip Melanchthon and others.[5]

In the beginning — during the more than two years between the posting of the Ninety-five Theses and the publication of the *Address* — Luther directed his appeals for reform not to princes but to pope and bishops, to whom he attributed the pastoral responsibility for nourishing the people with the word of God and removing all threats to their eternal salvation. Although he quickly came to the conclusion that bishops and prel-

essay, "Luther und das landesherrliche Kirchenregiment" (1911), in which Karl Holl provided much shrewd analysis of the writings of the 1520s but had nothing to say about the copious evidence that in the 1530s Luther's views had changed. See Holl's *Gesammelte Aufsätze zur Kirchengeschichte* I, 7th ed. (Tübingen: Mohr [Siebeck], 1948), 326-80. The closest thing to a comprehensive work in English is W. D. J. Cargill Thompson, *The Political Thought of Martin Luther,* ed. Philip Broadhead (Brighton, Sussex: Harvester Press, 1984), especially chapters 3, 4, 8, and 9. Unfortunately, Professor Cargill Thompson did not live to revise his manuscript or supply it with notes. Moreover, though he was aware of Luther's later thought, he had not yet managed to do full justice to it. This, plus numerous errors in the transcribed text that distort or defeat meaning, has resulted in a work that must be used with caution and is not as useful to nonexperts as the author clearly intended it to be. My own recently published thoughts on the subject are cited in the notes that follow, as are the most useful works by German scholars.

4. Luther's stubborn refusal to accept the then common belief that the political commonwealth and secular authority have an intrinsically religious purpose is difficult to explain. Suffice it to say here that it probably derived initially from his training as a scholastic theologian in the school of Ockham (rather than as a humanist in the school of Erasmus), and that it was reinforced by (1) his conviction that authority in the church belonged to all Christians equally, and (2) his unhappy experiences with the princes of his day. See James M. Estes, "Luther's First Appeal to Secular Authorities for Help with Church Reform, 1520," in *Continuity and Change: The Harvest of Late Medieval and Reformation History,* essays presented to Heiko A. Oberman on his 70th Birthday, ed. Robert J. Bast and Andrew C. Gow (Leiden: Brill, 2000), 48-76; here 72-73 with footnotes 72 and 73.

5. See James M. Estes, "The Role of Godly Magistrates in the Church: Melanchthon as Luther's Interpreter and Collaborator," *Church History* 67 (1998): 463-83. For more on the historical origins of the majority view represented by Melanchthon, see Estes, "Erasmus, Melanchthon, and the Office of Christian Magistrate," *Erasmus of Rotterdam Society Yearbook Eighteen* (1998), 21-39, and "*Officium principis christiani:* Erasmus and the Origins of the Protestant State Church," *Archiv für Reformationsgeschichte* 83 (1992): 49-72.

ates could not claim special authority to rule the church *de jure divino,* he still thought that the responsibility to do so was unquestionably theirs *de jure humano.* They were among the "powers that be" that Christians should obey.[6] Only in the spring of 1520 did Luther, having concluded that Rome was the seat of Antichrist, abandon hope that bishops and prelates would initiate reform and decide to call upon secular princes to intervene in the attempt to rescue Christendom. The earliest indication of this intention is found in two works published in rapid succession in June 1520: *Treatise on Good Works*[7] and *On the Papacy in Rome.*[8] The relevant content of the two treatises can be summarized briefly as follows.[9] Secular authority is a divine institution to which all Christians owe obedience except when it commands something contrary to Scripture. But its office is the purely secular one of providing for the temporal welfare of its subjects and punishing violations of the second table of the Decalogue (murder, theft, adultery, public drunkenness, and so forth). It "has nothing to do with the preaching of the gospel, or with faith, or with the first three commandments" (that is, the first table).[10] In other words, secular authority as such includes no routine responsibility for the establishment and maintenance of true religion.

There are, nonetheless, two good reasons for appealing to the secular authorities to lend a hand with the reformation of the church. The first is that the clergy, "the spiritual authorities," have, like parents gone mad, forfeited their right to be obeyed. They do not preach the gospel, faith is being destroyed, and Christendom is going to wrack and ruin. In this emergency,

6. Scott Hendrix, *Luther and the Papacy: Stages in a Reformation Conflict* (Philadelphia: Fortress, 1981), 1-32.

7. LW 44:21-114; WA 6:202-76. The *Treatise* is a discussion of Christian ethics in the traditional form of a commentary on the Ten Commandments, which Luther (again following tradition) divides into the first table (commandments 1-3) and the second table (commandments 4-10), making the fourth commandment the occasion for his discussion of the obedience owed to the secular and spiritual authorities.

8. The pamphlet was written in response to one by the Leipzig Franciscan, Augustine Alveld, in defense of the divine right of the pope to govern the church. The full title was *On the Papacy in Rome, against the Most Celebrated Romanist in Leipzig:* LW 39:55-104; WA 6:285-324.

9. For a more detailed and fully annotated summary, see Estes, "First Appeal," 52-59.

10. LW 44:92; WA 6:259.

"anyone who is able to do so" should help in whatever way he can. But "it would be best — indeed it is the only way left to us — if kings, princes, nobles, cities, and communities would take the first step in this matter, so that bishops and clergy (who are now afraid [of Rome]) would have reason to follow."[11] In other words, in an emergency that the clergy either cannot or will not deal with, secular rulers should do what is necessary to restore the proper functioning of the spiritual authorities.

The second reason for calling on the secular authorities is that many ecclesiastical abuses are in fact secular crimes committed by "spiritual" persons. In their obsession with wealth and power, "the Romanists" shamelessly abuse their ecclesiastical authority to raise money, thus making themselves guilty of robbery, theft, extortion, and other violations of the second table. Therefore, out of concern for the temporal welfare of their subjects as well as for the honor of Christ, princes and nobles must exercise their God-given authority against the "blasphemous knavery" that the pope refuses to correct.

A related consideration was Luther's observation that, in contrast to the true, inward, spiritual church that is governed by Christ alone and has no physical or temporal attributes, the earthly, physical church has laws, ceremonies, usages, and other external trappings that are man-made and thus not essential elements of the spiritual church. Though the two churches are inseparable, for no external church exists without at least some people who are true Christians, they must be carefully distinguished from one another, lest spiritual status be attributed to worldly things. Initially aimed at dissolving the presumed identity of the Roman Church with the true church, this line of reasoning also posed questions about who should control the external, man-made trappings of any earthly church.

The *Address to the Christian Nobility* (1520)

While *On the Papacy in Rome* was still in press, Luther announced to friends his intention "to issue a broadside to [Emperor] Charles and the nobility of Germany against the tyranny and baseness of the Roman curia." By mid-August the "broadside" had grown into the *Address to the*

11. LW 44:91; WA 6:258.

Christian Nobility.[12] In the preface, Luther wrote: "[I have] put together a few points on the matter of the reform of the Christian estate, to be laid before the Christian nobility of the German nation, in the hope that God may help his church through the laity, since the clergy, to whom this task more properly belongs, have grown quite indifferent." In the first of the treatise's three parts, Luther calls upon emperor and imperial nobility to summon a church council and provides a theological justification of their right to do so. The second and third sections contain a catalogue of ecclesiastical abuses with Luther's proposals for reform.[13]

In the first part of the treatise, Luther pictures the "Romanists" as having built three defensive walls to protect themselves from reform. The first wall is the claim that spiritual authority is above secular authority and that, consequently, the secular authorities have no jurisdiction over the spiritual authorities. This is the wall that protects the Romanists from action by the secular authorities against those ecclesiastical abuses that are in reality secular crimes. The second wall, the claim that only the pope may interpret Scripture, and the third, the claim that only the pope can summon a council and confirm its decrees, together make it impossible for Christian rulers to summon a council that will judge the pope on the basis of Scripture and enact needed reforms. Luther's weapon against these walls "of straw and paper" is the doctrine of the priesthood of all believers, which he here fully elaborates for the first time. With respect to the first wall, Luther rejects the traditional notion that Christians are divided into "the spiritual estate" (pope, bishops, priests, and monks) and "the secular estate" (princes, lords, artisans, and all other laypeople). On the contrary, all Christians are, by virtue of baptism and faith, equally members of the spiritual estate and, consequently, priests. Those who officiate as priests are simply those designated by the call of the community to exercise, on behalf of all, the priestly authority that is common to all. Thus the only difference between clergymen and laypeople is their office in the community. Clergymen are no more Christian or "spiritual" than anyone else.

But the priesthood of all believers also means that Christian secular

12. *To the Christian Nobility of the German Nation on the Reform of the Christian Estate:* LW 44:123-217; WA 6:404-69. Cf. the much longer discussion in Estes, "First Appeal," 58-70.

13. For the reasons that Luther may have had for believing that the authorities might respond positively to his appeal, see Estes, "First Appeal," 61-62.

rulers are no less Christian than anyone else. Indeed, since they have the same baptism, the same faith, and the same gospel as do other Christians, it must be conceded that they too are "priests and bishops" and that "their office [of government] . . . has a proper and useful place in the Christian community." Significantly, however, Luther here reasserts the equality of all Christians. "Because we are all priests of equal standing, no one must push himself forward and take it upon himself, without our consent and election, to do that for which we all have authority. For no one dare take upon himself what is common to all without the authority and consent of the community." In other words, Christian secular rulers have exactly the same authority in the church as other Christians, no less authority but also no more.

What this means with respect to the first wall of the Romanists is that there is no ground for the old and long-disputed clerical claim to be "above" secular authority and consequently exempt from the jurisdiction of the civil courts for violations of civil law. Quite the contrary. Because the office of secular authority is the divinely mandated one of punishing the wicked and protecting the good (Rom. 13:3-4), it follows that popes, prelates, and all other clergymen are answerable to that authority for their secular crimes. So if the pope and his "mob" are guilty of robbing and defrauding Christians by collecting annates, selling bishops' *pallia*, peddling indulgences, and so on, secular authorities are free to exercise their office against them just as they would against laypeople. In his catalogue of the "robbery, thievery, and skullduggery" inflicted on Germany by the pope and the Romanists, Luther repeatedly insists that both the emperor in particular and the princes in general have, by virtue of their secular authority alone, the right and duty to protect their subjects against such criminal behavior.

With respect to the second wall, Luther asserts that the claim that the pope alone may interpret Scripture and that he is infallible in matters of faith is an outrageous invention of the Romanists. The point is not simply that the pope is subject to Scripture (rather than vice versa) but also that the whole Christian community has the right and duty to judge the pope in the light of Scripture and, if necessary, to side with Scripture against the pope and call the Romanists to account for their transgressions against Scripture. To do this, however, they must have resort to a council, something against which the Romanists have erected their third wall.

For Luther, the provision of church law that the pope alone can summon a council and confirm its decisions is a human regulation and thus valid only "as long as it is not harmful to Christendom or contrary to the laws of God." Since, however, the pope clearly deserves punishment at the hands of a council, the regulation giving him the sole right to summon one is no longer valid. Although Luther points out that many church councils have been convoked by emperors (e.g., Constantine and the Council of Nicea), his crucial point here is that all Christians have the priestly right to summon a council if one is needed and the pope refuses to call one. "[W]hen necessity demands it, and the pope is an offense to Christendom, the first man who is able should, as a true member of the whole body, do what he can to bring about a truly free council." It is clear, however, that Christians are not all equal in their ability to do this effectively. Those participants in the priesthood of all believers who are best able to summon a council and compel participation in it are the secular authorities, who alone possess a divinely established authority over everyone in the community. In this emergency "in the spiritual city of Christ," they thus have a special obligation to intervene and call the Christian people together in a church council.

Luther's argument here is nothing if not complicated. It involves a cumbersome distinction among (1) the routine authority that the prince exercises as political sovereign; (2) the routine authority that the prince as baptized Christian shares equally with all other Christians; and (3) the special authority that the prince as baptized Christian has in an emergency because he happens to be a prince. Having declared that the routine authority of the prince *as prince* pertains only to the second table of the Law and has nothing to do with the gospel, faith, or the commandments of the first table, Luther cannot, even in an emergency, call upon the secular rulers *as secular rulers* to exercise an authority in the church that they do not possess. So, while he can ask them as secular rulers to deal with secular crimes committed by the clergy, he cannot ask them as secular rulers to summon a church council. For that purpose he has to address them as individual Christians and participants in the priesthood of all believers and ask them to do what all Christians have the right to do. In so doing, however, he invokes their status as secular rulers to establish their *special* responsibility to use their princely authority on behalf of their fellow Christians in an emergency. If they take this "first step," bishops and clergy will once again be free to do a proper job of exercising their spiritual office.

In the *Address,* certain other matters of importance are left unclear. Luther is clear that "in spiritual offices such as preaching and giving absolution" the clergy have independent jurisdiction but that "in other matters" they are subject to secular authority. As we have already seen, he is also clear that those "other matters" include secular crimes committed by clergymen. But what about those external, worldly aspects of clerical life that are not, in Luther's view, part of the inward and spiritual church? Luther here inclines toward the view that all matters of property and goods are the proper concern of the secular authorities, who might concede to church officials a degree of control over the properties from which clergymen derive their incomes. But he has nothing to say about those externals, like ceremonies and vestments, that are closely connected with the spiritual office without being an integral part of the spiritual church. He would soon prove reluctant to give control of such things to the secular authorities.

Instead of calling a council, as Luther had proposed, the Christian nobility of the German nation, in diet assembled, gave their approval to Emperor Charles's Edict of Worms (May 1521), which gave effect to Luther's excommunication (January 1521) by imposing imperial outlawry on him. In due course the constituent territories of the empire (principalities and imperial cities), rather than the empire as a whole, would become the focus of effective reform. But this was by no means clear in the immediate aftermath of the Edict of Worms. For one thing, there were still no "Lutheran" princes. Though he protected Luther, Frederick the Wise of Saxony never saw fit to defy the emperor by becoming an avowed partisan of the evangelical movement; he concentrated on keeping peace and order rather than actively promoting religious change. The first truly evangelical elector would be Frederick's brother, John the Steadfast, who succeeded him in 1525. In Hessen, meanwhile, the other homeland of the German Reformation, Landgrave Philip did not adhere to the evangelical cause until 1524. Most German governments, though resentful of Rome and reluctant to enforce the Edict of Worms, were either indifferent to Luther or still undecided about him and worried about the possible political and social cost of supporting his movement. But a few princes, like Duke George of Albertine Saxony, were openly hostile and joined the Habsburgs in punishing any who manifested support for Luther. All in all, it is not surprising that Luther now took the view that princes "are generally the biggest fools or the worst scoundrels on earth, [from whom] one must constantly expect the worst . . . and look for little good, especially in divine matters which concern the salvation of souls."[14]

The Treatise *On Secular Authority* (1523)

Meanwhile, the years 1521-26 were the classic period of the German Reformation as a spontaneous popular movement. Under the leadership of gifted preachers and pamphleteers, evangelical reform took root in one town after another and spilled over into the countryside as well. In 1522 Luther himself, impressed with what the Word alone had already accomplished without force,[15] reached the exuberantly optimistic conclusion that the faithful dissemination of the Word alone would destroy "the swarming vermin of the papal regime" in only two years.[16] Given this optimism about the irresistible spread of reform, and given also his perception that wise and upright princes were in critically short supply, Luther had little reason in the immediate aftermath of the Diet of Worms to make reform a princely responsibility. His principal concerns were, rather, (a) to encourage Christian communities to reform themselves and (b) to denounce as illegitimate the efforts of hostile princes to intervene in matters of faith.[17]

With respect to the first aim, the immediate question was what local communities or congregations should do if bishops, abbots, or other prel-

14. LW 45:113; WA 11:267.30–268.3.

15. LW 51:77-78; WA 10:18-19 (the "Invocavit Sermons" cited below in n. 31): "[F]aith must come freely, without compulsion. Take myself as an example. I opposed indulgences and all the papists, but never with force. I simply taught, preached, and wrote God's Word; otherwise I did nothing. And while I slept, or drank Wittenberg beer with my friends Philip [Melanchthon] and [Nicholas von] Amsdorf, the Word so greatly weakened the papacy that no prince or emperor ever inflicted such losses upon it. I did nothing; the Word did everything. . . . [The Word] is almighty and takes captive the hearts, and when the hearts are captured, the [devil's] work will fall of itself."

16. LW 45:67-69; WA 8:682-83 (*A Sincere Admonition to All Christians to Guard against Insurrection and Rebellion*, March 1522).

17. *That a Christian Assembly or Congregation Has the Right and Power to Judge All Teaching and to Call, Appoint, and Dismiss Teachers, Established and Proven by Scripture*, published in May 1523: LW 39:305-14; WA 11:408-16. See also the treatise *Concerning the Ministry* (1523): LW 40:7-44; WA 12:169-96.

ates refused to provide them with suitable pastors. In 1523, asked for his advice by officials in the small Saxon town of Leisnig, Luther argued that, by virtue of the priesthood of all believers, all Christians have the right and duty to judge doctrine in the light of Scripture and to reject what is contrary to it. If, therefore, bishops and other prelates teach and rule contrary to the gospel and refuse to appoint Christian pastors, a Christian community in possession of the gospel has the right and duty "to avoid, to flee, to depose, and to withdraw from the authority" of such corrupt bishops and choose its own pastor. If there were good bishops willing to serve the gospel by appointing good pastors, one could allow them to do so. But even good bishops should not have the power to appoint good pastors without the will, the election, and the call of the congregation. Luther also upheld the right of local communities or congregations freely to choose suitable forms of worship to replace the Mass and other Catholic ceremonies inconsistent with evangelical doctrine.[18]

With respect to the second aim, denouncing princely interference in matters of faith, Luther made the prohibition of his translation of the New Testament (published in September 1522) by Catholic princes in Albertine Saxony, Bavaria, Brandenburg, and Austria the occasion for publishing the treatise *On Secular Authority: To What Extent It Should Be Obeyed.*[19] The work opens with Luther's sour observation that, having tried unsuccessfully in the *Address to the Christian Nobility* to teach the German princes "their Christian office and functions," he now finds it necessary to switch tactics and explain "what they should omit and not do." For in their mad folly, princes believe that their subjects are bound to obey them in everything, and they issue proclamations requiring their subjects to believe and worship as they prescribe. Claiming to be doing their duty as Christian princes, they are in fact scoundrels who suppress the faith, deny the divine word, and blaspheme God. They must be resisted, "at least with words." Luther's verbal resistance took the form of what is commonly called his *Zwei-Reiche-Lehre,* the doctrine of the two kingdoms.[20]

18. LW 53:19-40; WA 12:205-20 (*An Order of Mass and Communion for the Church at Wittenberg,* 1523).

19. LW 45:77-129, where it is given the title *On Temporal Authority;* WA 11:245-80. An elaboration of ideas first worked out in sermons of October 1522 (WA 10III:371-85), the treatise had been completed by Christmas 1522 but did not appear in print until the following year, probably in early March.

20. As presented for the first time in *On Secular Authority,* the doctrine of the two

The entire human race, says Luther, is divided into two classes, those who belong to the kingdom of God and those who belong to the kingdom of the world.[21] Those who belong to the kingdom of God are the true believers in Christ. In the kingdom of God, Christ alone rules by his Holy Spirit, without force. If all the people in the world were true Christians, there would be no need for temporal law or the sword, for Christians would voluntarily do far more than the law demands. Thus they would have no need for laws, courts, litigation, judges, and the other trappings of secular authority. Unfortunately, however, "there are few true believers, and still fewer who live a Christian life." Christians are a minority of sheep lost in a majority of wolves and lions who pay no heed to the gospel and are not ruled by it. If the wicked majority were not restrained by external force, the world would be reduced to chaos and "no one could support wife and child, feed himself, and serve God."[22] For this reason God has established the temporal sword outside the kingdom of God and given it authority to restrain evil deeds and maintain order. That is why Saint Paul says (1 Tim. 1:9) that "the law was not made for the righteous but for the lawless and the disobedient" and calls secular authority (Rom. 13:4) "God's servant" for the rewarding of good and the punishment of evil.

---

kingdoms seems simple and straightforward, and for present purposes it can be treated as such. In fact, however, the *Zwei-Reiche-Lehre,* as Luther developed it over the years, was a complex set of doctrines whose inherent difficulty was compounded by his imprecise use of terms that have several possible meanings: *Reich, regnum, Welt, weltlich,* and more. No other aspect of Luther's social and ethical teaching has produced so much discussion or controversy. W. D. J. Cargill Thompson has done a particularly good job of sorting out the difficulties and bringing clarity to the subject. See his "The 'Two Kingdoms' and the 'Two Regiments': Some Problems of Luther's *Zwei-Reiche-Lehre,*" *Journal of Theological Studies,* n.s., 20 (1969): 164-85; reprinted in Cargill Thompson, *Studies in the Reformation: Luther to Hooker,* ed. C. W. Dugmore (London: Athlone, 1980). Cargill Thompson's first note provides a list of the most important books and articles on the topic available at the time.

21. LW 45:88-104; WA 11:249-61.

22. Two years earlier (13 July 1521), Luther had made this point even more forcefully in a letter to Melanchthon. Referring to the use of the sword by secular government as "a necessity of life," Luther observed that if people obeyed the gospel, the sword of government would not be necessary. "If the sword were abolished, however, how long would the church of God exist in this world, since, of necessity, the wicked are in the majority. Owing to the lawlessness of the wicked, no one could be safe from bodily harm or the destruction of his property." LW 48:259; WA Br 2:357.44-47.

Both kingdoms are thus ordinances of God and both are necessary, "the one to produce righteousness, the other to bring about external peace. Neither one is sufficient in the world without the other." Secular government cannot make anyone righteous in the eyes of God, and spiritual government cannot maintain external peace and order in human affairs. Therefore, although Christians do not need the secular sword for themselves, they understand that it is "most beneficial and necessary for the whole world." So they willingly submit to it, pay their taxes, and honor those in authority. If called upon to do so, moreover, they willingly serve others by bearing the temporal sword and helping to preserve peace and order. Indeed, "it would even be a fine and fitting thing if all princes were good, true Christians," for, as a service of God, "the sword and authority . . . belong more appropriately to Christians than to any other men on earth."

This distinction having been made, "the main part of the treatise" follows.[23] It is essential, Luther says, to consider carefully how far the arm of secular government extends, "lest it extend too far and encroach upon God's kingdom and government," with "intolerable and terrible injury" as the result. For the authority of secular government extends "no further than to life and property and external things on earth," to things that it can "see, know, judge, condemn, change, and modify." Since God alone knows the hearts and minds of human beings and only he can awaken faith in them through his Word, he does not permit anyone other than himself to rule over the soul. "Over what is on earth and belongs to the temporal, earthly kingdom, man has authority from God; but whatever belongs to heaven and to the eternal kingdom is exclusively under the Lord of heaven." Thus it is the height of folly when princes command their subjects to believe what popes, fathers, and councils have decreed contrary to the word of God. They are assuming a power over souls that belongs solely to God. What one believes is a matter for each individual conscience, "and since this takes nothing away from secular government, the latter should be content to attend to its own affairs and let men believe this or that as they are able and willing, and constrain no one by force." So if Christians are commanded by their government to surrender their copies of Luther's New Testament, they should refuse to do so and accept passively whatever punishment may follow this refusal. To the objection that by issuing such commands secular power does not force people to believe anything but is

23. LW 45:104-18; WA 11:261-71.

simply ruling externally in such a way as to prevent them from being deceived by false doctrine, Luther responds that this is the job of bishops and not of princes. Heresy is a spiritual matter that cannot be restrained by force; only God's word can defeat it. Like true faith, moreover, false faith thrives under persecution, which is thus a worse than useless weapon for combating it.[24]

It should be emphasized here that Luther's distinction between the spiritual realm and the secular realm is not the same as his distinction between church and state. His "spiritual kingdom" is indeed the same thing as the "true, inward, spiritual church" that is ruled by Christ alone. But his "earthly, physical church" has a foot in both realms. If its man-made externals are not an essential part of the spiritual kingdom, do they not fall by definition into the category of the "external things on earth" that secular government can "see, know, judge, and modify" as it sees fit? The list of Lutheran theologians who would answer yes to that question is long,[25] but in *On Secular Authority,* Luther has not yet joined it. Indeed, he poses the question of the authority to regulate such externals in a way that precludes any role for secular government and addresses only the role of bishops. How, he asks, shall the church be governed outwardly, seeing that Christians have no secular sword of their own? He responds with a brief elucidation of the implications of the priesthood of all believers. Since all Christians are equally priests and have "the same right, power, possession, and honor," it follows that priests and bishops are "neither higher nor better than other Christians." Their ministry or office is simply that of preaching the Word. With respect to the external ordering of the church, they have no more authority or power than other Christians, and they must "impose no law or decree on others without their will and consent." Luther does not here address the question of how this "will and consent" of the community is to be determined or enforced.[26]

24. Similarly, in 1524, in his *Letter to the Princes of Saxony concerning the Rebellious Spirit* (the "rebellious spirit" in question being Thomas Müntzer in Allstedt), Luther argued that since only the word of God can destroy heresy, secular rulers should take no action against sects that "fight with the word" and do not engage in actual rebellion: LW 40:49-59; WA 15:210-21. As we shall see, however, he soon changed his mind about this.

25. Melanchthon had already done so in his *Themata ad sextam feriam discutienda,* written at the same time that Luther was working on his *On Secular Authority.* See Estes, "Erasmus, Melanchthon," 30-31.

26. The treatise concludes (LW 45:118-29; WA 11:271-80) with a section of advice to

The problem with Luther's sharply drawn distinction between secular authority and spiritual authority was that it applied not only to "papist scoundrels" like Duke George but, once they had appeared on the scene, to princely supporters of the evangelical cause as well. As a result, the arguments in the treatise would, for many years to come, find their way into the works of those who demanded for themselves and others the right peacefully to believe and worship as they pleased and who denied the right of secular governments to require their adherence to any prescribed orthodoxy of faith and practice.[27] A distinguished list of Lutheran theologians would thus be constrained to demonstrate that the *cura religionis* of Christian magistrates was in fact perfectly compatible with the distinction between the two kingdoms and their appropriate governments.[28] In the meantime, it took Luther himself a few years to sort out his thinking on the subject.

The Problem of Order and the Saxon Territorial Visitation (1523-28)

He quickly found that it was scarcely possible for communities to deal with the practical problems of reform without the cooperation and assistance of the secular authorities. Local congregations often sought the aid of the authorities, who might have rights of patronage, in their search for a suit-

---

the "very few" princes who would like to be genuinely Christian rulers on how they should use their authority. It is an entirely conventional "mirror of princes" in which the prince is admonished to pray to God for wisdom, to enforce the laws without undue severity, to devote himself with Christian selflessness to the welfare of his subjects, to beware of flatterers among his courtiers, to deal justly with evildoers, and so forth. There is not one word to indicate that responsibility for the establishment and maintenance of true religion is any part of the job of a Christian prince.

27. For an early example of this, see the so-called Anonymous Memorandum of 17 March 1530 in James M. Estes, trans. and ed., *Whether Secular Government Has the Right to Wield the Sword in Matters of Faith: A Controversy in Nürnberg in 1530 over Freedom of Worship and the Authority of Secular Government in Spiritual Matters* (Toronto: Centre for Reformation and Renaissance Studies, 1994), 41-54. (Authorship of the memorandum has since been attributed to Georg Fröhlich, a *Kanzleischreiber* in Nuremberg.)

28. For three early examples, see the memoranda by Johannes Brenz and two Nuremberg theologians in Estes, *Whether Secular Government*, 55-118.

able pastor. Moreover, the control of church property and income was such a jumble of legal entitlements in the hands of individuals and institutions (including town councils and territorial princes) that governmental intervention was usually needed to achieve order and stability. So already in 1522-23, while maintaining the independence of the local Christian community in these matters, Luther issued numerous appeals to both local authorities and the elector to provide assistance, arguing that it was in their interest both as Christian brothers and as secular rulers to do so.[29] In the circumstances, it was not easy (and evidently not urgent) to distinguish clearly between the role of the prince or magistrate as Christian brother and that as secular ruler, and Luther employed language that did not do so.[30]

Another difficulty in the path of reformation was the tendency of conflicts between the advocates of reform and their opponents to produce public disorder. From the beginning, Luther was adamant that genuine reform had to be free of the taint of disorder or revolution. In the wake of the so-called Wittenberg disorders that occurred during his "exile" in the Wartburg (May 1521–February 1522), Luther reproved his colleagues Gabriel Zwilling and Andreas Karlstadt for having introduced reforms (e.g., communion in both kinds) at too rapid a pace, to the accompaniment of violence against opponents and in defiance of the will of Elector Frederick. Reforms, he said, were to be undertaken only after preaching had adequately prepared the people to understand and accept them, lest the "weaker brethren" be alienated from the gospel, and only with the knowl-

29. On the problem of finding pastors, see Trüdinger, 54-57; on the difficult matter of church property and income and the payment of pastors, see 57-62.

30. In May 1522, for example, he wrote to Georg Spalatin, urging that the elector should admonish the town council in Eilenburg to appoint a new pastor: "Nam et principis vt Christiani fratris etiam principis nomine interest lupis [false preachers] aduersari et pro sui populi salute sollicitum esse." WA Br 2:515. In their introduction to the LW translation of *On Secular Authority* (LW 45:78), the editors cite this letter as evidence that Luther made princes responsible for promoting the "salvation" of their subjects. In so doing, they read far too much into the word *salute* (the ablative of *salus*) and make Luther say something he was at pains to deny in the treatise being introduced. Like the German word *Heil*, the Latin *salus* can mean "salvation" in the theological sense, but the root meaning is simply "health, welfare, safety." So all Luther is saying here is that it is in the elector's interest, both as Christian brother and as prince, to be concerned for the *welfare* of his people, without troubling himself to elaborate further.

edge and approval of the authorities, lest "reform" become synonymous with "rebellion."[31]

As the 1520s wore on and the Reformation continued to spread in Saxony, Luther became increasingly impatient with the obstacles to reform and, abandoning his optimism about what the Word alone could achieve, called on secular authorities to remove the obstacles in question. In so doing, he remained faithful to his distinction between secular and spiritual authority by enlarging the scope of what secular rulers as guardians of peace and order could do to regulate ecclesiastical matters. In Wittenberg, for example, the Catholic canons in the chapter of the All Saints Collegiate Church *(Allerheiligenstift)* continued to celebrate endowed Roman Masses after the rest of the community had come to accept that the sacrament was to be distributed in both kinds to a gathered congregation in accordance with its scriptural institution. They were, in other words, not "weaker brethren" with whom one had to be patient but rather hard-necked adherents of error whose offenses had to be curbed. In 1522-23, Luther tried unsuccessfully to get Elector Frederick, who was patron of the chapter, to put an end to the "abomination" of the Mass. Toward the end of 1524 he returned to the attack, now decrying the Mass not simply as an abomination but also as "idolatry" and "blasphemy." Since "blasphemy of the name of God" was, along with perjury and slander, a crime in secular law, Luther could summon "princes and governors, burgomasters, councilors, and judges" to extirpate it, lest the terrible wrath of God come upon them as well as the idolatrous priests. This inspired the local authorities in Wittenberg to apply pressure and thus secure the agreement of the remaining canons to suspend the celebration of Mass. The elector tacitly accepted this development.[32]

31. See the *Eight Sermons at Wittenberg, 1522* (the so-called Invocavit Sermons): LW 51:7-100; WA 10III:1-64. See also Ulrich Bubenheimer, "Luthers Stellung zum Aufruhr in Wittenberg 1520-1522 und die frühreformatorischen Wurzeln des landesherrlichen Kirchenregiments," *Zeitschrift der Savigny-Stiftung für Rechtsgeschichte,* Kanonistische Abteilung, 71 (1985): 147-214. Although Bubenheimer is, in my opinion, too eager to see Luther already far advanced on the road to *das landesherrliche Kirchenregiment* in 1522, this is nonetheless an important and illuminating study.

32. In addition to the sources cited in Trüdinger, 45-47, see *The Abomination of the Secret Mass* (LW 36:311-28; WA 18:22-36), which Luther wrote in the wake of the controversy in Wittenberg and published in 1525. In the present connection, see particularly the concluding paragraphs of the treatise.

In the following year, there was a similar controversy with the canons of the collegiate chapter in Altenburg, which was also under the patronage of the elector. When the new elector, John the Steadfast, acting on Luther's advice, ordered the abolition of Mass and other "unchristian" ceremonies in the chapter, the Catholic canons objected that, according to Luther's own teaching, the elector could not force anyone to faith. Luther responded with a variation of the argument that he had rejected in *On Secular Authority*, namely, that the prince was not forcing anyone to faith or the gospel, but merely forbidding public blasphemy, that is, the celebration of Mass. In so doing, he was exercising his routine jurisdiction over public crimes, leaving the canons unmolested in the possession of whatever faith they might wish to practice in private. In a memorandum for the elector written early in 1526, Luther added the argument, borrowed from the reformers in Nuremberg, that secular rulers cannot allow their subjects to be led into disunity and division by discordant preaching, lest tumult and faction be the result. In the interest of public peace and order, only one doctrine can be preached in any community.[33]

In this campaign for the abolition of Mass in Wittenberg and Altenburg, Luther had thus availed himself of two ideas that were already very old and that would live on for some time yet as working assumptions of both Roman Catholic and Protestant political thought. One was that a community divided in religion is ungovernable. The other was that the wrath of God is not just the distant fate of private individuals in eternity but rather the impending historical experience of the land and people whose ruler tolerates idolatry and blasphemy. In both cases it is thus the concern of the prince as prince, not just as Christian brother, to intervene in the interests of secular peace and order. At the same time, Luther was also giving expression to the idea (strange to modern ears but taken seriously by Lutheran princes, magistrates, and theologians in this period) that personal freedom of faith does not include freedom of public worship. It should be noted, however, that while Luther had at this stage concluded that secular government has the obligation to abolish false religion on the

33. Trüdinger, 48-50. As Trüdinger notes on p. 50, Luther subsequently upheld this principle even when it worked to the disadvantage of the reform movement and evangelical preachers had to leave a political jurisdiction in which they were not welcome. On the other hand, for instances in which Luther advised against enforcing the same principle against Catholics, see n. 52 below.

ground that it is a threat to peace and order, he still resisted the logical corollary (long since adopted by his fellow reformers) that secular government as such has the duty to establish and maintain true religion on the ground that it promotes public peace and order.

In the meantime, two developments had brought Luther to the verge of calling on the elector to impose a common church order in Saxony. The first was the accumulation of evidence that the progress of reform, which had now spread virtually everywhere in the elector's domains, had produced problems so serious and widespread that, as Luther had put it in 1520, there was no hope save with the secular authorities. The second was the death of Frederick the Wise in May 1525 and the succession of the openly evangelical John the Steadfast, something that opened new prospects for fruitful princely action in support of reform.[34] By the end of September 1525, Luther had decided that the elector should inaugurate a territorial visitation, and his letters over the following fourteen months with the electoral court and others about this reveal much about the conditions that needed to be dealt with.[35]

To begin with, church finances were in a state of disorder. Much of the wealth of the abandoned monasteries was being appropriated by nobles and others for their own use rather than being applied, as Luther had recommended, to the religious, educational, and charitable purposes intended by the founders.[36] Moreover, many of the congregations that had been happy to exercise their right to call an evangelical pastor were either unable or unwilling to pay him a decent salary, with the result that material want was undermining the effective performance of the church's ministry. Public worship, too, was in a state of confusion and disorder. In addition to the continued celebration of the Roman Mass in certain monastic and collegiate churches, the unrestricted exercise of congregational freedom in externals had produced in the churches where Roman rites had been abol-

34. This can be viewed as an early example of Luther's tendency to moderate his wariness of princely intervention in proportion to his trust in the good intentions of the prince in question. The tendency reached its peak in the 1530s in the works to be discussed below.

35. Trüdinger, 68-71. Only one of the letters dealt with by Trüdinger (Luther to Elector John, 31 October 1525) has been translated: LW 49:133-33. Evidence in addition to that provided by Trüdinger is cited in the notes that follow.

36. See LW 45:169-76; WA 12:11-15 (Luther's preface to the *Ordinance of a Common Chest*, 1523).

ished such a bewildering variety of ceremonies that ordinary people were "confused and offended," again to the detriment of effective ministry.[37] All this drove Luther to the conclusion that, the rights of local congregations and their pastors notwithstanding, a common order in the elector's territories was urgently needed. As if these problems were not enough, it was also clear that many pastors were incompetent and that some were *Schwärmer.*

Once again, Luther distinguished between those things within the routine jurisdiction of secular authority and those that were the province of spiritual authority. He advised the elector that all the abandoned monasteries and foundations had automatically fallen under his authority as prince and that he thus had the duty to inspect them, put their affairs in order, and see to it that their resources were used to support those churches and schools not otherwise adequately endowed with income. Moreover, he attributed to the elector, as "supreme guardian of the younger generation," the power to compel communities that had the wherewithal to do so "to support schools, preacherships, and parishes" just as one would compel them "to contribute to . . . the building of bridges and roads, or any other of the country's needs." Otherwise "the land will be filled with wild, loose-living people."

The achievement of uniform ceremonies, on the other hand, was a more complicated problem. While Luther, as already noted, regarded the suppression of "external abominations" and doctrinal divisions as something within the jurisdiction of secular authority, he continued to believe the things he had said about the rights of congregations and the power of the church freely to choose its own ceremonies. So when, in the summer of 1525, he began to urge that a common order of worship should be observed in every principality, he argued that such a common order should be the result of the voluntary cooperation of the pastors, who would consider the edification of the laity more important than their own freedom to alter ceremonies at will.[38] He continued to defend this voluntaristic approach even after he had begun to agitate for the imposition of a common order by means of a visitation.

37. LW 53:46-48, 61; WA 18:417-18; 19:72 (cf. following note).

38. See LW 53:45-50; WA 18:417-21 (*A Christian Exhortation to the Livonians concerning Public Worship and Concord,* 1525). See also LW 53:61-62; WA 19:72-73 (Luther's preface to *The German Mass and Order of Service,* 1526); and WA Br 4:157-58 (Luther to Philip of Hessen, 7 January 1527).

When, after many delays, the visitation commission was finally established in February 1527 and given its *Instruktion* by the elector in June, it included, as Luther had recommended, experts on property and finance as well as on doctrine and personnel. In early July the difficult and time-consuming process of visitation began, and the visitors were soon supplied with a set of instructions (a compendium of the doctrines and practices to which the pastors had to adhere) written by Melanchthon.[39]

With the benefit of hindsight, it is clear that the visitation that commenced in 1527 was the beginning of *das landesherrliche Kirchenregiment* (church government by the territorial prince) in Saxony.[40] At the time, however, Luther still refused to see it that way. When Melanchthon's instructions for the visitors were published in 1528, they included a preface by Luther in which he attempted to square the visitation with the view of secular authority to which he had adhered ever since 1520.[41] The original and primary function of bishops, he wrote, was to visit pastors and congregations. But the bishops have neglected this duty for so long that the church has become "grievously confused, scattered, and torn." In this emergency, the Wittenberg theologians wished to have "the true episcopal office and practice of visitation re-established." But, lacking either a call from God or a "definite command" from the Saxon congregations to do so themselves, they have appealed to the elector, "that out of Christian love (since he is not obligated to do so as a temporal sovereign)" he might use his princely authority to "call and ordain" competent persons to perform this episcopal office for the welfare of "the wretched Christians in his territory." Although these visitors will have no authority to "issue any strict commands," as though they were exercising a new form of papal authority, good and devout pastors will "willingly, without any compulsion" accept the common order prescribed to them "until God the Holy Spirit brings to

39. Trüdinger, 71-74. At Luther's insistence, Melanchthon was elected to the visitation commission by the theology faculty of the University of Wittenberg.

40. There has been scholarly controversy on this point: see Trüdinger, 72, with n. 23. See also *Archiv für Reformationsgeschichte* 61 (1970): 144-47 (review by Irmgard Höss of Hans-Walter Krumwiede, *Zur Entstehung des landesherrlichen Kirchenregiments in Kursachsen und Braunschweig-Wolfenbüttel* [1967]).

41. *Instructions for the Visitors of Parish Pastors in Electoral Saxony:* LW 40:269-320; WA 26:195-240. Luther's preface is on pp. 269-73 in LW and pp. 195-201 in WA. The published text of the *Instructions* bore the name of no author, only the personal seals of both Luther and Melanchthon on the title page.

pass something that is better." If any obstinately and perversely refuse to accept the common order, the elector will be asked to take action against them. For while the elector "is not obligated to teach and rule in spiritual affairs, he is obligated as temporal sovereign to prevent strife, rioting, and rebellion" among his subjects, just as the emperor Constantine, refusing to tolerate the dissensions in the empire caused by Arius, "summoned the bishops to Nicaea and . . . constrained them to preserve unity in teaching and faith."

This justification of the territorial visitation makes clear that Luther's desire for a church that was free to govern itself by voluntary cooperation was now hopelessly at odds with the demonstrated inability of the reformed congregations to achieve order and stability without help in the form of something more substantial than occasional princely intervention in emergencies. The effort to uphold the distinction between the prince as prince and the prince as Christian brother, when in practice he had to be both at once, was approaching the point of absurdity. To say that it exceeded the authority of the prince as prince to establish a visitation and thereby assume responsibility for the establishment of true doctrine and worship, but that it was well within the ordinary authority of that same prince to abolish false or schismatic doctrine or worship, was to strain the limits of common sense. Moreover, to call upon pastors to conform "willingly [and] without compulsion" to the new order while threatening them with secular penalties if they failed to do so was, to paraphrase Cargill Thompson,[42] to bring the authority of the prince into the church by the back door. Luther himself was fairly quick to perceive that he could not go on arguing his case in this way. The first surviving evidence that he had seriously rethought his position dates from 1530.

The Commentaries on Psalms 82 (1530) and 101 (1534-35)

By 1530 the Reformation was becoming, in an ever-longer list of principalities and cities, a movement concerned with the establishment and protection of an organized territorial church with an increasingly well-defined and government-imposed orthodoxy of faith and practice. Luther was well aware that his own doctrine of the two kingdoms was being used by those

42. Cargill Thompson, *Political Thought,* 146.

who opposed this development and who wanted to prove that Christian governments had to tolerate all peaceful religious groups in their territories.[43] Long convinced that public blasphemy was a crime and that religious divisions threatened the peace and stability of a community, Luther now saw as well the need of governmental protection for the legitimately called and regularly appointed pastors of the struggling new churches in Saxony and elsewhere against Anabaptist "corner preachers" *(Winkelprediger)* and other troublemakers.[44]

Addressing this situation in his commentary on Psalm 82 (1530),[45] Luther made the psalm's description of secular rulers as "gods" and as "sons of the Most High" who should show partiality to the godly (vv. 1-2, 6) the basis for an unqualified assertion that the first and highest duty of princes and lords was "to honor God's Word above all things and . . . to further the teaching of it" by supporting pastors and securing their freedom to preach as well as by warding off sects and false teachers. By serving God in this way, a prince not only preserves peace and unity but also increases God's kingdom and helps many to salvation.[46] Gone here is the old distinction between the prince as prince and the prince as Christian brother. Gone too is the limitation of princely intervention to emergencies. Luther appears to have been the first of the reformers to read this psalm text in this way.[47] Melanchthon praised Luther's commentary highly and immediately added Psalm 82:6 to his arsenal of texts proving that the secular office includes not just the obligation to keep peace but especially the duty to provide for true doctrine and worship.[48] Luther, however, would persist in his refusal to locate princely responsibility in the secular office itself, with characteristically difficult and complicated results.

43. He had, for example, received a report of the arguments of the "anonymous memorandist" in Nuremberg (see n. 27 above): WA 31I:183-84.

44. See LW 13:64-67; WA 31I:211-13 (the psalm commentary cited in the following note). See also the treatise *On Infiltrating and Clandestine Preachers:* LW 40:383-94; WA 30III:518-27. "Clandestine preachers" is the LW rendering of *Winkelprediger.*

45. *[Commentary on] Psalm 82:* LW 13:41-72; WA 31I:189-218.

46. LW 13:51-67; WA 31I:198-213.

47. At least his is the earliest such use that I have so far been able to identify.

48. The reference occurs for the first time in a letter to Archbishop Albrecht of Mainz, 3 June 1530 (*Melanchthons Werke,* ed. Robert Stupperich et al., vol. 7/2 [Gütersloh: Gerd Mohn, 1975], 164) but is a regular feature of Melanchthon's writings on the subject thereafter (e.g., the Apology of the Augsburg Confession and all future editions of the *Loci*).

Luther's last extended treatment of the role of princes in the church is found in the commentary on Psalm 101 that he wrote in 1534 and published in 1535.[49] His comments on verses 2-5 constituted a *Fürstenspiegel* (mirror of princes) for his own prince,[50] Elector John Frederick of Saxony, who had succeeded his father in 1532 and whose piety and good intentions Luther knew and trusted. The personal connection was crucial because Luther, whose opinion of princes in general had not improved much (if at all), attached more importance to the actual qualities of specific princes than to abstract models of what a good prince should be,[51] a predisposition amply evident in this commentary. Where his aim in *On Secular Authority* had been to keep the Duke Georges of this world from frustrating the spread of reform, his aim now was to get the John Fredericks of this world to nurture and protect what the reformers had so far accomplished.

Accepting the common attribution of the authorship of Psalm 101 to King David, Luther treats it as a self-portrait of David in his capacity as a ruler in both spiritual and temporal matters. Unlike the general run of kings and princes, who are the natural enemies of God, David is steadfast in the faith, establishes and maintains true doctrine and worship among his subjects, abolishes heresy and idolatry, and so on. This kind of behavior is so exceptional, such a rare and precious gift of God, that it cannot be taken as a model for all princes. Those kings and princes who, like Elector John Frederick, are equal to the task should follow David's example. The most that can be asked of ordinary princes is that they should avoid joining forces with those of their fellow princes who are the enemies of God and Christ.

Having elaborated on this theme at considerable length, Luther then launches into a vehement reassertion of the necessary distinction between the secular and spiritual realms. Even where it exists among the godless, secular government is God's "ordinance and creation," which means that "the secular kingdom . . . can have its own existence without God's kingdom." It is a realm governed by human reason, and the works of the heathen writers concerning it (especially Aristotle, Plato, and Cicero) are

49. *[Commentary on] Psalm 101:* LW 13:145-224; WA 51:200-64.

50. LW 13:166-201; WA 51:216-45.

51. See Wolfgang Sommer, *Gottesfurcht und Fürstenherrschaft: Studien zum Obrigkeitsverständnis Johann Arndts und lutherischer Hofprediger zur Zeit der altprotestantischen Orthodoxie* (Göttingen: Vandenhoek & Ruprecht, 1988), 26. See n. 34 above.

better than those of the Christians. For this reason, God sharply separates his kingdom from that of the world. It is the devil who tries to "cook and brew these two kingdoms into each other" by tempting secular rulers into trying "to be Christ's masters and teach him how He should run His church and spiritual government."

Luther, however, knows that "proponents of logic" will object that in this psalm David "mixes the spheres of spiritual and secular authority together and wants to have both." He responds by drawing a distinction between commanding and obeying, ruling and serving. God is the one supreme authority over all creation, and all without exception owe obedience to him. It follows that, if David or some other godly prince, having heard from the preachers that everyone (princes included) must fear God and keep his commandments, orders his subjects to fear God and heed his word, he is simply doing his duty as a faithful and obedient servant and not meddling in spiritual government at all. For, with respect to the service of God, there is no distinction between spiritual and secular. "All should be identical in their obedience and should even be mixed together like one cake, everyone . . . helping the other to be obedient." To be sure, princes have no authority to change the Word of God or to dictate what shall be taught. But princes who are God-fearing Christians can and should serve God by supporting true preaching and abolishing what is contrary to it, and those who object to this with whining quibbles about the confusion of spiritual and secular authority are talking nonsense.[52] The spiritual and secular realms are, in other words, separate but not opposed, each in its own way serving the will of God in cooperation with the other.[53]

52. An important qualification not expressed here but made clear in other contexts is that secular government could undertake ecclesiastical reformation only where there was no clear legal impediment to its doing so. In particular, Luther and the other Wittenberg theologians took the view that the rights of Catholic patrons who would not cooperate with governmental reform efforts could not simply be set aside. With respect to specific disputes in Bremen, Frankfurt am Main, and Augsburg in 1533-36, they argued that respect for the legal rights of important Catholic patrons was more important to the cause of peace in the empire than observance of the principle that two competing confessions could not be tolerated in one territorial jurisdiction. See Trüdinger, 50-54.

53. This argument is so similar to one of those used by two of Luther's colleagues during the controversy in Nuremberg in 1530 (see Estes, *Whether Secular Government*, 73-118), one of whom was probably Luther's personal friend Wenceslaus Linck, that one suspects this to be another case of influence from that quarter.

With the commentary on Psalm 101 Luther had thus arrived, in his own good time and by his own tortuous route, at a somewhat long-winded and convoluted affirmation of the *cura religionis* of secular magistrates that later generations of Lutheran court preachers and theologians would perceive to be essentially the same as that in Philip Melanchthon's contemporary second edition of the *Loci communes.*[54] Although he still refused to say (with Melanchthon and many others) that *all princes* have been commanded to establish and maintain true religion, he allowed that *all princes who happen to be genuinely pious Christians* and who can be trusted to act for the good of the church have been called to do so. Though Luther did not spell it out, the clear implication of this was that the office of Christian prince extends to the first table of the Decalogue as well as to the second table and that princely intervention is not limited to ecclesiastical emergencies or to circumstances in which public peace is threatened. Where Luther's language and logic coincided most closely with those of Melanchthon was in his emphasis on the prince's role as *servant* of the church rather than its master. Both viewed the Christian prince as someone burdened with obligations to the church rather than endowed with power over it, and as someone subject to the Word of God as interpreted by the theologians rather than free to impose his own version of the truth. Above all, the rights of the pastors in the exercise of their ministry were not to be trampled by princes and their officials.[55]

As his writings from 1530 onward demonstrate, Luther's reservations

54. See Sommer, *Gottesfurcht und Fürstenherrschaft,* 82-104 and passim. On the likelihood that Luther took account of Melanchthon's views in rethinking his own position, see Estes, "Role of Godly Magistrates," especially 474-83.

55. Particularly in the period of institutional consolidation that followed the Religious Peace of Augsburg in 1555, the organizers of the Lutheran territorial churches sought to guarantee this clerical independence by placing supervision of the pastors in the hands of a hierarchy of professional churchmen that was responsible directly to the prince as governor of the church rather than to his secular administration. The earliest and best example of this known to the author was the system of church governance established by Johannes Brenz in Württemberg in 1551-59 and much imitated elsewhere. See James Estes, "Johannes Brenz and the German Reformation," *Lutheran Quarterly* 16 (2002): 373-414. However much the clergy may in fact have proved subservient to the interests of the state, especially in the period after the Peace of Westphalia, this system of ecclesiastical self-administration lasted until the reforms of the Napoleonic period formally turned the German churches into the useful instruments of the state that the Enlightenment believed they should be.

concerning the princely class and his old fears that princely authority was likely to be extended further than was appropriate persisted to the end of his life. He still sometimes spoke of the prince as prince and the prince as Christian as though they were different people.[56] And it was only in later years (1539-42) that he referred to secular rulers as "emergency bishops" *(Notbischöfe)*, "bishop" being his normal designation for the ecclesiastical visitors and superintendents, whom he wanted to operate with as little governmental interference as possible.[57] Interference by city hall or the princely court in the free exercise of the pastoral ministry invariably aroused his ire.[58] Nevertheless, he did not retreat from the position that he had taken in the commentaries on Psalms 82 and 101. Quite the contrary. On at least two occasions (in 1536 and 1543) he gave his unqualified endorsement to Melanchthon's view of the *cura religionis* of Christian secular rulers.[59] In 1545, moreover, for a new edition of Melanchthon's visitation instructions, he revised the preface that he had written in 1528, eliminating the passages about the elector's not being obligated as temporal sovereign to rule in spiritual matters, and adding a passage praising those German rulers who, "driven by the dire need of the church," had undertaken the reformation of their lands.[60] That was his last word on the subject.

56. WA 32:440 (sermon on Matt. 5–7, 1532): "A prince can indeed be a Christian, but it is not as a Christian that he must rule; and in so far as he rules, he is not called a Christian but rather a prince. The person is a Christian, but the office or principality has nothing to do with his Christianity" (my translation).

57. Trüdinger, 78-79, with n. 69.

58. See, for example, the letter to Daniel Greiser, 22 October 1543 (WA Br 10:436), in which he objects sharply to the new excommunication ordinance of Duke Maurice of Albertine Saxony, according to which secular officials were to control the imposition and enforcement of excommunication. See also the letters to Gabriel Zwilling, 30 September 1535 (WA Br 7:280-81); to Sebastian Steude, 24 August 1541 (WA Br 9:501-2); and to the mayor and city council of Creutzberg, 27 January 1543 (WA Br 10:255-58).

59. *Melanchthons Briefwechsel: Kritische und Kommentierte Gesamtausgabe. Regesten,* ed. Heinz Scheible, vol. 2 (Stuttgart-Bad Cannstatt: Frommann-Holzboog, 1998), no. 1739, 2-3 (Luther's signature to a memorandum of 23 May 1536 in which Melanchthon summarized his view of the Christian magistrate as custodian of both tables of the law); and WA 54:14-15 (Luther's enthusiastically laudatory preface for the published texts of declamations by Elector John Frederick's two sons, written for them by Melanchthon and summarizing his view of the office of a godly prince).

60. WA 26:197-98.